JUDAIC PERSPECTIVES ON ANCIENT ISRAEL

EDITED BY JACOB NEUSNER,
BARUCH A. LEVINE, AND
ERNEST S. FRERICHS

Literary Editor: Caroline McCracken-Flesher

FORTRESS PRESS PHILADELPHIA

Library of Congress Cataloging-in-Publication Data

Judaic perspectives on ancient Israel.

1. Bible. O.T.—Criticism, interpretation, etc.
2. Bible. O.T.—Criticism, interpretation etc.,
Jewish—History—20th century. I. Neusner, Jacob,
1932–. II. Levine, Baruch A. III. Frerichs,
Ernest S. IV. McCracken-Flesher, Caroline.
BS1192.J83 1987 221.6 86-45908
ISBN 0-8006-0832-1

2662A87 Printed in the United States of America 1-832

For

HAROLD LOUIS GINSBERG

Preeminent Jewish scholar
of the Hebrew Bible
in the twentieth century

Teacher, inspiration, model
by whose words we live

CONTENTS

Part Two. Religion and History

Part Three. Literature

Part Four. Traditions of Scholarship

Part Five. Theology

PREFACE

Judaic perspectives on ancient Israel convey the vision formed by contemporary Jewish scholars of the Hebrew Scriptures, the literature, religion, history, exegesis, and theology of the written Torah. These perspectives come to us from many countries. The present volume includes work by Jewish scholars of the Hebrew Bible who teach in the state of Israel, Canada, and the United States, as well as elsewhere.

The fact that today a cadre of Jewish biblical scholars flourishes hardly is to be taken for granted. As recently as the end of the Second World War one could count less than a score of full-time, professional scholars in the field of biblical studies. There was a mere handful scattered among the Hebrew University of Jerusalem (then the only Jewish university in what would become the state of Israel), Dropsie College, some of the Hebrew teachers' colleges, as well as in the Jewish seminaries of the United States, particularly Hebrew Union College, the Jewish Institute of Religion, and the Jewish Theological Seminary of America. In all the world not many more than twenty scholars held full-time positions as professors in the field of biblical studies. A Jew teaching the Hebrew Scriptures in a secular, and, consequently, a Gentile university was unknown. True, some pulpit rabbis tried their hand at this and that. But none of them made a memorable impression in biblical studies, though many tried.

So here we mark the end of that first large generation of professional scholars of Jewish origin and Judaic conviction in this field of scholarship. That is to say, we look back, over the past forty years, on the growth of a sizable cadre of Jewish biblical scholars and today seek perspective on what they have accomplished in the framing of a Judaic perspective on ancient Israel. Ideally, we should review papers by no fewer than five or six times the number of people actually represented in these pages. We do present an ample selection of the work of important scholars, younger and older. We recognize that several times their number today flourish in universities both in the state of Israel and in the United States and Canada, as well as in Western Europe, South Africa, Australia, and other parts of the French-, English-, Italian-, and Spanish-speaking worlds. (That German no longer serves as a language of Jewish biblical scholarship requires notice, but no comment.) This book, then, through the sample at hand, illustrates and celebrates the coming of age of a whole generation of learning.

Let us make explicit what we celebrate and what we merely take for granted. Jews have worked on the theological and philological exegesis of the Hebrew Scriptures from their formation onward. So there is nothing to treat as remarkable in the work of lower criticism and philology, though much good work goes on. No age, including ours, has lacked substantial figures following the received approach to learning. But clearly, prior to our own day, it was rare for Jews to participate in the common and critical enterprises of biblical studies. Their work was not read by Gentiles, and they rarely paid much attention to what Gentiles accomplished. However, by dismissing as "higher anti-Semitism" the brilliant achievements of the most substantial critical minds of the age, and in failing to confront them, they prevented Jewish participation in the nascent school of critical historical study—no less decisively than the suppression of Catholic modernism in the same age obliterated for an entire generation the Roman Catholic hope to join in the common enterprise. To be sure, much scholarship on ancient Israel exhibited premises about the Jews lifted straight from the philosophical anti-Semitism of the age, but Jews rarely learned what the critical school had to teach—and not all of the lessons, by any means, rested upon bigoted premises.

True, such lonely but towering figures as Yehezkel Kaufmann, M. Z. Segal, Umberto Cassuto, and I.L. Seligmann took seriously the important theses of critical scholarship. But Segal and Cassuto contributed mainly to exegesis, and Kaufmann, for his part, exercised limited influence, mainly among Israelis and a few United States Jewish scholars who treated him as a kind of cult figure. Overseas, in the exile, such protean figures as H. L. Ginsberg stood pretty much alone.

Today, by contrast, Jewish biblical scholars teach in a broad variety of universities, diverse types of which are represented in this book. They hold positions in Protestant and Roman Catholic theological faculties. Israeli scholarship in biblical studies attains a paramount role not only in archaeological and lower critical studies, where it has long taken pride of place, but in important areas of historical inquiry as well. Both Israeli and Diaspora biblical scholars of the senior ranks exercise substantial influence in all areas of biblical learning, lower and higher critical alike. For Jews, therefore, the field is now wide open.

A mark of Jewish scholarship's maturity derives from the following simple fact: Jews in biblical studies, such as those represented here, feel free to write articles that, lacking the author's identification, no one will have known came from a Jew. At the same time these same scholars publish articles expressing distinctively Judaic issues and questions. In this book we have deeply Judaic writings by scholars perfectly able to address issues of a neutral character and to do so in a language of thought that everyone in the world may share. Jewish biblical scholars therefore find the freedom to work as Jews out of the Judaic tradition and also to explore the common and shared methods and issues of the scholarly world overall. That kind of unselfconscious freedom to do what they want and to be what they want proves that the field of biblical studies today affords ample space for the people of Israel, both in the land of Israel and throughout the exile. It is time to say so, to celebrate that freedom scarcely dreamt of by the generations before our own. That astonishing freedom represents only one of the intellectual gifts presented by secular and humanistic universities to the people of Israel throughout the world.

Yet it remains to ask what exactly we editors claim it is that marks scholarship in the biblical area as Jewish, and how we classify the work at hand. We do not claim there is a "Jewish school of biblical studies." We do, however, maintain that Jewish scholars in biblical areas exhibit traits that mark them in common and distinguish them from others.

There is no "Jewish school," in a narrow sense. Scholars of Jewish origin follow accepted methods and procedures. But they also bring to bear a very distinctive viewpoint. So we recognize, first, that we cannot claim Jewish Bible scholars differ from Gentile scholars in the essential conduct of their research. This fact surprises, because a hundred years ago Jewish biblical scholars performed utterly distinctive work—indeed, they lived behind a curtain of their own language and in a ghetto walled in by their own minds. Yet, second, in this book we claim to demonstrate through example and illustration that there is a distinctively Jewish stake in modern biblical studies. Jewish scholars approach the subject in some ways that differ from non-Jews. This comes as a surprise since the Gentile and neutral world of the academic humanities finds itself able to understand the language and thought-world of these Jewish scholars.

So Jewish biblical scholarship in some aspects follows a definitively Judaic program, and yet it gains a hearing in the world at large. The two facts of the day (first, that there are biblical scholars who are Jews; second, that there is a Jewish approach to biblical scholarship) become important for this single reason: the Jewish presence finds an ample and open place in the larger world of biblical learning. So the academic world listens to Jews speaking as Jews about ancient Israel, and it also listens to Jews speaking as part of a common discourse. Jewish scholars no longer speak a private language mainly to one another on the one side, nor do they give up all marks of a distinctively Jewish approach on the other. There is a middle range, a realm of free choice.

But the question remains, in what ways do Jewish biblical scholars form an identifiable group? The answer is, they share three major characteristics. First, they take up texts neglected by others, or treated by others in a quite different framework. In our book the interest in Leviticus and Numbers is one example of that fact. Second, they draw upon a corpus of exegetical traditions that has been neglected up to now. In our book the exegetical papers consistently appeal to the received Jewish exegetical tradition on the one side, and display a deep mastery of the Hebrew language on the other. The editors would claim that the two go together. Without denigrating non-Jewish biblical scholars in their mastery of Hebrew(!), we do claim that among Jewish scholars (both Israeli and Western), the world rightly takes for granted knowledge of Hebrew that does not consistently characterize non-Jews. All Jewish biblical scholars read modern Hebrew and take with utmost seriousness the work of colleagues in the state of Israel. Nearly all of them read both historical and other writings in all the European languages, so they do not do their work behind a language curtain, as do colleagues in continental Europe, particularly. And third, at some very specific points, Judaic perspectives on ancient Israel lead to a distinctively and particularly Judaic inquiry into a biblical text or problem. That is self-evident in the theological papers presented here. Clearly, then, Jewish biblical scholars can be defined as a distinct group.

In all, we think this book serves as a landmark in the unfolding of Judaic studies because together and in the aggregate the authors show what is distinctively Jewish and what is of a common and universal character in the work of biblical scholars who are Jewish. Without the names attached to the papers, as we said, in many instances we should know beyond doubt that the author is Jewish. Surely this provides a fair criterion for proving that there is such a thing as "Jewish biblical scholarship." But the Jewish presence in biblical studies would be misrepresented if we published a book in which all the papers exhibited distinctively and identifiably Jewish traits. So the mix here is ideal. Many of the papers themselves comprise small monographs. Indeed, as we review the collection, we are amazed at the quality our colleagues have attained as a group.

We intend that this book serve as an important piece of evidence for the history of the Jews and of Judaism in modern times because it shows the interesting ways in which Jewish Bible scholars are both Jewish and modern, in varying ways and proportions, at one and the same time. We also hope it will present an uncommonly rich account of the history of ancient Israel's life and religion, and hence on a second count may deserve note.

J.N. [For the editors]

Program in Judaic Studies
Brown University
Providence, Rhode Island

ABBREVIATIONS

AB	Anchor Bible
ACJD	Abhandlungen zum christliche judischen Dialog
ADAJ	*Annual of the Department of Antiquities of Jordan*
AfO	*Archiv für Orientforschung*
AHw	Wolfram von Soden, *Akkadisches Handwörterbuch*
AnBib	Analecta biblica
ANET	J. B. Pritchard, ed., *Ancient Near Eastern Texts.* 3d ed. Princeton: Princeton Univ. Press, 1969.
AOAT	Alter Orient und Altes Testament
APOT	R. H. Charles, *Apocrypha and Pseudepigrapha of the Old Testament.* 2 vols. Oxford: Clarendon Press, 1913.
ARM	Archives royales de Mari. Textes cunéiformes.
ASOR	American Schools of Oriental Research
BA	*Biblical Archaeologist*
BAR	*Biblical Archaeologist Reader*
BASOR	*Bulletin of the American Schools of Oriental Research*
BASORSup	*Bulletin of the American Schools of Oriental Research.* Supplementary Studies.
B.C.E.	before the Common Era
BDB	F. Brown, S. R. Driver, and C. A. Briggs, eds., *Hebrew and English Lexicon of the Old Testament.* Oxford: Clarendon Press, 1953.
BeO	*Bibbio et oriente*
BETL	Bibliotheca ephemeridum theologicarum lovaniensium
Bib	*Biblica*
BibOr	*Biblica et orientalia*

BN	*Biblische Notizen*
BW	*Biblical World*
BWANT	Beiträge zur Wissenschaft von Alten und Neuen Testament
BZAW	Beihefte zur *Zeitschrift für die alttestamentliche Wissenschaft*
ca.	circa
CAD	*The Assyrian Dictionary of the Oriental Institute of the University of Chicago*
CB	Cambridge Bible
CBOTS	Coniectanea biblica. Old Testament Series
CBQ	*Catholic Biblical Quarterly*
BCSC	Cambridge Bible for Schools and Colleges
CD	Cairo (Genizah text of the) Damascus (Document)
C.E.	the Common Era
cf.	compare
chap(s).	chapter(s)
CIS	*Corpus inscriptionum Semiticarium*
CRB	Cahiers de la Revue biblique
CTA	A. Herdner, *Corpus des tablettes en cunéiformes alphabétiques decouvertes à Ras-Shamra 1929 à 1939.* Paris, 1963.
DLZ	*Deutsche Literaturzeitung*
ed(s).	editor(s), edited by, edition(s)
EM	*Encyclopedia Maqra'it*
EncJud	*Encyclopaedia Judaica*
esp.	especially
ET	English translation
EtB	Etudes bibliques
EThL	*Ephemerides theologicae lovanienses*
EvTh	*Evangelische Theologie*
fig(s).	figures(s)
FRLANT	Forschungen zur Religion und Literatur des Alten und Neuen Testaments
HAR	*Hebrew Annual Review*
HAT	Handbuch zum Alten Testament
Hermeneia	Hermeneia—A Critical and Historical Commentary on the Bible
HibJ	*Hibbert Journal*
HSM	Harvard Semitic Monographs
HSS	Harvard Semitic Series
HTR	*Harvard Theological Review*
HUCA	*Hebrew Union College Annual*
IB	*The Interpreter's Bible*
ICC	International Critical Commentary
IDB	*Interpreter's Dictionary of the Bible*

IDBSup.	*Interpreter's Dictionary of the Bible, Supplement*
IEJ	*Israel Exploration Journal*
JA	*Journal asiatique*
JANES	*Journal of the Ancient Near Eastern Society*
JAOS	*Journal of the American Oriental Society*
JBL	*Journal of Biblical Literature*
JESHO	*Journal of the Economic and Social History of the Orient*
JHS	*Journal of Hellenic Studies*
JJS	*Journal of Jewish Studies*
JNES	*Journal of Near Eastern Studies*
JPOS	*Journal of the Palestine Oriental Society*
JPS	Jewish Publication Society
JQR	*Jewish Quarterly Review*
JR	*Journal of Religion*
JSOT	*Journal for the Study of the Old Testament*
JSOTSup.	*Journal for the Study of the Old Testament*. Supplement Series.
JSS	*Journal of Semitic Studies*
KAI	H. Donner and W. Röllig, *Kanaanäische une aramäische Inschriften*
KAT	E. Sellin, ed., Kommentar zum Alten Testament
KEHAT	Kurzgefasstes exegetisches Handbuch zum Alten Testament
LCL	Loeb Classical Library
l(l).	line(s)
LXX	Septuagint
MDAI.K	Mitteilungen des deutschen archäologischen Instituts. Abteilung Kairo.
MRS	Mission de Ras Shamra
MT	Masoretic Text
NCBC	New Century Bible Commentary
NEB	New English Bible
n.f.	neue folge (new series)
NICOT	New International Commentary on the Old Testament
NJPS	New Jewish Version
n(n).	note(s)
n.s.	new series
OIP	Oriental Institute Publications
Or.	*Orientalia* (Rome)
OrSuec	*Orientalia Suecana*
OTL	Old Testament Library
PAAJR	*Proceedings of the American Academy of Jewish Research*
para(s).	paragraph(s)
PEQ	*Palestine Exploration Quarterly*
pl(s).	plate(s)

1QH	*Thanksgiving Hymns* from Qumran Cave 1
1QIsa^{a}	First copy of Isaiah from Qumran Cave 1
1QM	*War Scroll* from Qumran Cave 1
1QS	*Rule of the Community, Manual of Discipline,* from Qumran Cave 1
4QSam^{a}	First copy of Samuel from Qumran Cave 1
RB	*Revue biblique*
RivBib	*Rivista biblica*
RLA	*Reallexicon der Assyriologie*
SBB	Stuttgarter biblische Beiträge
SBL	Society of Biblical Literature
SBLDS	Society of Biblical Literature Dissertation Series
SBS	Stuttgarter Bibelstudien
SBT	Studies in Biblical Theology
ScrHie	*Scripta Hierosolymitana*
SIDA	Scripta intituta Donneriani Aboensis
SJLA	Studies in Judaism in Late Antiquity
ST	*Studia theologica*
StBiFranc	*Studi francescani. Biblioteca*
STDJ	Studies on the Texts of the Desert of Judah
StudOr	Studia orientalia
s.v(v).	under the word(s)
THAT	*Theologisches Handwörterbuch zum Alten Testament*
ThWAT	G. J. Botterweck and H. Ringgren, eds., *Theologisches Wörterbuch zum Alten Testament*
ThZ	*Theologische Zeitschrift*
TOTC	Tyndale Old Testament Commentaries
trans.	translator, translated by
TRu	*Theologische Rundschau*
TSJTSA	Texts and Studies of the Jewish Theological Seminary of America
TynB	*Tyndale Bulletin*
UT	C. H. Gordon, *Ugaritic Textbook*
UUÅ	Uppsala universitetsårsskrift
VNAW	Verhandlingen der Koninklijke Akademie ven Watenschappen te Amsterdam. Afdeeling Letterkunde nieuwe reeks.
VT	*Vetus Testamentum*
VTSup	*Vetus Testamentum,* Supplements
v(v).	verse(s)
WC	Westminster Commentaries
WMANT	Wissenschaftliche Monographien zum Alten und Neuen Testament
WZ(H).GS	*Wissenschaftliche Zeitschrift der Martin-Luther-Universität*

	Halle-Wittenberg. Gesellschaft- und sprachwissenschaftliche Reihe.
WZKM	*Wiener Zeitschrift für die Kunde des Morgenlandes*
ZAW	*Zeitschrift für die alttestamentliche Wissenschaft*
ZDMG	*Zeitschrift der deutschen morgenlandischen Gesellschaft*
ZDPV	*Zeitschrift des deutschen Palästine-Vereins*

CONTRIBUTORS

Robert Alter
University of California
Berkeley, California

Ernest S. Frerichs
Brown University
Providence, Rhode Island

Richard Elliott Friedman
University of California
San Diego, California

Stephen A. Geller
Dropsie College
Philadelphia, Pennsylvania

Frederick E. Greenspahn
University of Denver
Denver, Colorado

Edward L. Greenstein
The Jewish Theological Seminary of America
New York City, New York

Mayer I. Gruber
Ben Gurion University of the Negev
Beersheva, Israel

Baruch Halpern
Vanier College, York University
Toronto, Ontario, Canada

Stephen A. Kaufman
Hebrew Union College–Jewish Institute of Religion
Cincinnati, Ohio

Jon D. Levenson
The Divinity School, The University of Chicago
Chicago, Illinois

Baruch A. Levine
New York University
New York City, New York
(Ben Gurion University of the Negev)

Jacob Milgrom
University of California
Berkeley, California

Alexander Rofé
The Hebrew University
Jerusalem, Israel

Lou H. Silberman
University of Arizona
Tucson, Arizona

H. Yavin

ERNEST S. FRERICHS

INTRODUCTION: THE JEWISH SCHOOL OF BIBLICAL STUDIES

The "Jewish school of biblical studies" is a term difficult to define for earlier ages and controversial in contemporary application. It can only be understood as a school without an exclusive urban center (as in the American examples of the Baltimore or Chicago schools), without a designated master, and without a national limit. Insofar as the contributors to this volume reflect several national communities, not only with respect to citizenship, but also in terms of their personal educational histories, they exemplify the truly international character of the Jewish school of biblical studies.

The commonalities which inform the contributors to this work do not stem from disciplinary uniformity, nor from the conduct of scholarship in the same kinds of educational settings. The essays come from those who are known variously as historians, philologists, literary specialists, or theologians. Their scholarly craft is exercised in a variety of institutional settings—private secular and public secular universities, rabbinical seminaries and research centers.

The analytical methods used by the contributors are easily accessible to other scholars who share their disciplinary fields. No claim is made that the methods of analysis could not be grasped by another scholar in the same field. The public character of such scholarship exposes it to the criticism of others who share their disciplinary perspective; it also ensures that the scholarship can be enriched by the critiques of others who may not share the concern for the focus of research. No argument is made here that the perspectives of the contributors are private to the author or only to the others in the "school."

What constitutes, then, a Jewish school of biblical studies? Is there a definition and a cohesion beyond that imposed by the covers of this book? The question has been addressed before in related, if not identical, terms. It is confronted directly by some contributors to this volume. Among recent discussions of the nature of "Modern Jewish Bible Research" was the symposium by that title at the Eighth World Congress of Jewish Studies in 1981.

The discussions at that time were clear in pointing up certain characteristics of Jewish biblical scholarship. Among these is certainly an unqualified command of Hebrew, and of Hebrew in all of its phases from the Bible to its contemporary form. Negatively, Jewish biblical scholarship is understandably conducted without christological assumptions. Indeed, the publications of Jewish biblical scholarship often highlight the christological character of research on the Hebrew Bible as conducted by the Gentile world of biblical scholarship. A further characteristic of Jewish biblical scholarship can be noted in the commentaries produced by that scholarship. These commentaries rely heavily on the traditions of previous Jewish scholarship and the names of major figures like Rashi are frequently cited. Beyond this is the recognition that the methods of Jewish biblical research often rest on a heavy use of philological analysis. The philological analysis accompanies the emphasis on the importance of Hebrew-language learning in the resources of a Jewish biblical scholar.

All of these characteristics, and more, are present in this collection of essays. The approaches stem from many disciplinary backgrounds and the topics of discussion are broader than the exegesis of particular biblical texts. It is our contention that a common environment of learning is conveyed, whatever the topic. On occasion the issues are strictly historical, dealing with the history of pre-monarchic Israel, or the narrative of David and Goliath, or the development of monotheism in Israel. At other points the approach to Bible is conducted by literary norms reflecting contemporary and ancient patterns of literary analysis. Several essays speak to the history of Jewish biblical scholarship, seeking to explain the present situation or to correct mistaken views of the past. The organizational categories are not watertight and several of these essays could be placed equally well in another category. If changed, however, they would lose nothing of their character as examples of Jewish biblical scholarship.

The rise of a modern school of Jewish biblical studies represents a response to a void. Moshe Goshen-Gottstein argued in the Eighth World Congress of Jewish Studies that there was an early positive interaction between Jewish and Christian biblical research in the sixteenth century and that the isolation of Jewish biblical scholarship is a relatively modern event, occurring in the late nineteenth century. In the internal aspects of Jewish Bible research this isolation was exacerbated by the absence of biblical study from the programmatic statements of the *Wissenschaft des Judentums.*

A further case for separation was the fact that biblical study in the nineteenth century was not only in the hands of Christian scholars, but in the hands of Christian scholars who were theologians. The theological understanding of biblical studies was dominant. Even in critical circles little interest was expressed in the traditional forms of Jewish biblical scholarship. A school of Jewish biblical studies in the nineteenth century would have been a strange current in the mainstream of Judaic studies and an adversarial expression, at best, in the Christian expression of biblical scholarship.

The nineteenth-century separation was highlighted by the overwhelming influence of the Wellhausen program in the late nineteenth- and early twentieth-century biblical scholarship. For Christian scholarship Wellhausenism turned critical attention away from traditional theological concerns and directed scholarly energies toward certain kinds of literary-historical analysis, so-called source analysis. The typical consequence for Christian scholarship was to solidify for decades the questions that would be addressed to the Bible, but also to broaden the circle of biblical scholars to include a growing number of scholars in nontheological faculties.

For Jewish biblical scholarship, the rise of the Wellhausen approach was to call into question central assertions of the Jewish tradition about the origins of the Bible as Scripture, a concern of conservative Christian scholars as well. The conclusion of Jewish biblical scholarship in this period was either to reject outright the claims of the Wellhausen approach on the origins of the Pentateuch or to demonstrate the limitations of such a perspective as defensible definitions of literary analysis. A related concern for Jewish scholarship was to reject the adequacy of Wellhausen-based explanations for the history of Israel, early and late. Typical of scholars who devoted their skills to demonstrating the untenable character of conclusions derived from approaches based on the Wellhausen program were figures like Umberto Cassuto and Yehezkel Kaufmann.

The least acceptable element in the Wellhausen program for Jewish biblical scholars was the denigration of Jewish history, the elevation of the preexilic period to a prime status and the corresponding reading of the postexilic period as one of darkness and decline. Issues of nomenclature were very much in evidence and continue to be so. The tragic dimensions of terms like "late Judaism" were not easily resolved by resorting to terms such as "postbiblical Judaism." Similar problems plague the Christian-oriented term "intertestamental Judaism" and are still unresolved in the more current term "early Judaism."

Change in these matters comes slowly. Habits of mind are formed, traditions established, and scholarly tracks are followed in the definitions of scholarly appointments, in the categories of scholarly publications, and in the encouraged interactions between Jewish and Christian biblical scholars. The openness of professional societies is a requirement of modern Western societies as a consequence of pluralism; the changes in approaches to scholarship are achieved less quickly.

Reflective of both inertia and change in such matters are the volumes issued across the last forty years to chronicle the state of biblical studies. It is inevitable that the term "biblical studies" in such a context will mean the Christian Bible of two testaments. On occasion the delineation will be for the Old Testament and, more recently, for the Hebrew Bible.

These publications are intended to survey the current "state of the question" and often to note future research areas. Sometimes these are independent volumes, often they are periodic publications of the professional societies devoted to biblical studies. The Society for Old Testament Studies in England has sponsored such a series beginning with the 1925 publication of *The People and the Book,* edited by Arthur S. Peake. This series has continued with a recent example in George W. Anderson's editing of *Tradition and Interpretation.* The University of Chicago published in 1947 *The Study of the Bible Today and Tomorrow,* edited by Harold R. Willoughby. In 1968, as one of a series of eight Chicago volumes, J. Coert Rylaarsdam edited *Transitions in Biblical Scholarship.* The Society of Biblical Literature celebrated its 100th meeting in 1964 with a volume of essays on *The Bible in Modern Scholarship.* Marking the 1980 Centennial of the SBL, Douglas A. Knight and Gene M. Tucker edited a volume on *The Hebrew Bible and Its Modern Interpreters,* published in 1985.

Recognizing the restraints rising from the different auspices of these volumes and an approximate span of forty years, certain observations can still be made. Jewish biblical research is frequently viewed as a separate category of scholarship, often accompanied by an independent treatment of Catholic biblical scholarship. Biblical scholarship without further modifiers must be understood in these surveys as reflecting Christian and Protestant definitions. The latest publication in this grouping, the 1985 SBL volume, shows some sensitivity in this question with its use of the term "Hebrew Bible." More controversial in this regard was the 100th SBL meeting volume which preserved a category called "The First Christian Century" in which a Christian scholar discussed that century as Christian history while a Jewish scholar discussed it as Jewish history.

Certain fields of Jewish biblical research are regularly noted and evaluated with respect to their scholarly merits and their contribution to the particular subaspect of biblical studies. This would be true with respect to the ongoing recognition of the importance for textual studies of the Hebrew University Bible Project. Likewise the sponsorship by the Jewish Publication Society of an English translation of the Hebrew Bible has been regularly reviewed and compared with other modern English translations of the Bible. In such surveys, especially in the more recent ones, appropriate recognition is given to the central role of Jewish biblical scholars in research centered on the investigation of Israelite cult, ritual, and sacrifice.

Indicative of the deeply entrenched Christian character of biblical scholarship is the division of the field into "subdisciplines." As these come to be viewed as "traditional," any other organizational pattern for biblical study becomes difficult.

The distance from some earlier pattern of organization is clear. In 1909, for example, Henry B. Swete could edit a volume of *Essays on Some Biblical Question of the Day* and include an essay by the then Regius Professor of Hebrew, R. H. Kennett, on the "History of the Jewish Church from Nebuchadnezzar to Alexander the Great." The editor also invited Israel Abrahams to contribute an essay on "Rabbinic Aids to Exegesis," a title and a topic which appears quite frequently in such volumes. The "subdivisions" of biblical research may now see the subject of Professor Kennett's essay as "the Persian Period," but there will still be presumptions that Jewish biblical scholarship will focus on the temple and the synagogue, on questions of cult, ritual, and sacrifice. The integration of Jewish biblical studies into the wider agenda of biblical studies generally is still very much in process.

That such integration is possible requires a recognition of certain changes which have occurred, most especially in the United States. For one thing, a school of Jewish biblical studies requires a setting beyond that secured through the settings of institutions devoted to rabbinical education. What was needed, and what has occurred, is a certain secularization and a certain humanization of scholarship. As that has occurred, there has been a desirable crossing of approaches between those scholars whose scholarship is worked out in the settings of professional school faculties and those who work in arts and sciences faculties. This volume contains essays from scholars who come from both settings and their ability to speak in common ways to each other and to the world is presumed.

For such a setting for Jewish biblical studies to arise, however, it was necessary for the modern secular university to develop in the United States. This development would break the assumption that biblical scholarship was the sole domain of theological faculties. Even when that break occurred, it required at least a further generation to free the patterns of departmental organization which used the template of a Christian theological faculty to define the appointment fields. The rise of Judaic studies within such universities has given further opportunity to review how the organization of scholars and scholarship shall be defined. Jewish biblical scholarship during that transition has often been divided into other sectors—Near Eastern studies, Semitic languages. The positive side of such changes for Jewish biblical scholarship has been the expansion of Hebrew literary studies into other disciplinary avenues, especially comparative literature.

The outcome of such changes, especially in the United States, has been to provide a setting in which a school of Jewish biblical studies can exist and even prosper. By the emphases which inform its scholarship and by the quality of its contribution to learning, such a school offers significant opportunity for the reintegration of Jewish biblical scholarship into international scholarship in this field. The atmosphere of our day, in both religious and secular settings, demands that scholarship be public and accountable. The recognition of a school of Jewish biblical studies is, in fact, a contribution to such openness by ensuring that the character of Jewish scholarship will be properly defined, expressed, and recognized.

Part One

EXEGESIS

1 BARUCH A. LEVINE

THE EPILOGUE TO THE HOLINESS CODE: A PRIESTLY STATEMENT ON THE DESTINY OF ISRAEL

The Epilogue to the Holiness Code, preserved in Lev. 26:3–45, is the only composition within the Book of Leviticus that is not either legal or ritual. Even narrative appears only rarely in Leviticus, serving primarily to position the priestly *tôrôt* and the rites that initiate the Israelite cult within the period of the Sinai migrations, thereby linking them directly to Moses and the Sinaitic theophany. In contrast, the Epilogue is an intricate literary composition written in what some might classify as "heightened prose" and showing a marked incidence of parallelism.

Ultimately, the Epilogue is patterned after biblical and other ancient Near Eastern blessings and curses, though it reveals significant variations on these conventional models. But it follows directly upon a collection of laws known as the Holiness Code (Lev. 17:1—26:2). Indeed, all three of the Torah's law codes conclude with epilogues. The Deuteronomic law codes end with an epilogue per se, preserved in chapter 28, yet even the curses of chapter 27 qualify as such. And the Book of the Covenant (Exodus 21—23) provides a brief epilogue in Exod. 23:20–33. In all three compositions, the verb *šāmaʿ*, "to heed," is pivotal.

This all accords with ancient Near Eastern conventions. The Code of Hammurabi likewise concludes with an epilogue, while curses follow the specifications of treaties, the delineations of boundary stones, and the legacies of royal inscriptions.[1] Indeed, the Egyptian execration texts are so called because of the detailed curses they invoke.[2]

In all of these sources, the epilogue's position is the key to its function; one is not to be punished unless first admonished. Well-being, peace, and prosperity—in short, all the blessings individuals and nations seek from divine powers—are made contingent on obedience to codes of law, treaties, oaths, and royal decrees, while divine wrath is the misfortune of the disobedient. (One cannot fail to note that much more space is normally allotted to elaborating horrendous punishments than is devoted to spelling out rewards, testifying to the sad truth that fear of punishment is more real even than the prospect of success!)

Our Epilogue presents us with particular, priestly notions on the meaning of the covenantal relationship between Israel and God. To those who might violate the covenant, the most awful threat is exile, bringing with it the danger of collective extinction in hostile lands. Still, as we have it, the Epilogue reveals internal development, through successive responses to crises, and it ends with the assurance of at least a partial restoration.

To demonstrate how different stages in the internal development of the Epilogue relate to historical events, I will first present an original translation with notes. After this, I will discuss the nature of the text's diction, since diction is the key to historical provenance.

Lev. 26:3–45

3. If you follow my statutes, observe my commands and carry them out—
4. I shall bring your rains in their season,
So that the earth yields its crop,
And the tree of the field bears its fruit.
5. Your season of threshing will overtake the vintage,
And vintage will overtake sowing.
You will eat your bread in abundance;
You will dwell securely in your land.
6. I shall institute peace in the land;
you will lie down with none to disturb.
I shall rid the land of wild beasts;
No sword will traverse your land!
7. You will repulse your enemies;
They will fall before you at the sword.
8. Five of you will drive off a hundred;
A hundred of you will drive off a myriad!
9. I shall turn toward you;
I shall make you fertile,
And I shall increase your numbers.
I shall maintain my covenant with you.
10. You will eat stored grain;
You will remove stored grain before the new.
11. I shall place my residence among you;
My feelings will not spurn you.
12. I shall walk about among you.
I shall be your God;
You will be my people.
13. I am YHWH, your God, who freed you from the land of the Egyptians, from being slaves to them.
I broke the bars of your yoke,
I enabled you to walk at full stature.

14. But if you do not heed me, and fail to observe all of these commands—
15. If you reject my statutes, and your feelings spurn my commands, thus abrogating my covenant—
16. I, in turn, shall do the following to you:
    I shall subject you to convulsions,
    Consumption and fever;
    That exhaust the eyes,
    And cause the body to suffer pain.
    You will sow your seed for naught;
    Your enemies will consume it.
17. I shall set my face against you.
    You will be battered before your enemies;
    Your foes will tyrannize you.
    You will flee though none pursues!
18. If, after these, you fail to heed me,
    I shall punish you sevenfold
    For your offenses!
19. I shall wreck your powerful glory!
    I shall make your skies as iron;
    Your soil as bronze!
20. Your strength will be spent for naught;
    Your land will not yield its crop;
    The tree of the field will not bear its fruit!
21. If you relate to me with coldness,
    And do not willingly heed me,
    I shall afflict you increasingly;
    Sevenfold for your offenses!
22. I shall drive the beasts of the field among you.
    They will bereave you of your children;
    They will destroy your livestock;
    They will diminish your numbers;
    Your roads will be desolate!
23. If, after these, you are not chastened by me,
    And you relate to me with coldness–
24. I, too, shall relate to you with coldness!
    I shall afflict you sevenfold,
    For your offenses!
25. I shall brandish a sword over you,
    Enforcing the threats of the covenant.
    You will huddle in your towns,
    But I shall spread pestilence among you.
    You will be given over into the power of the enemy.
26. When I break your "support of bread,"
    Ten women will bake your bread—
    In a single oven!
    They will dispense your bread by weight;
    You will partake, but not be sated!
27. If, after this, you do not heed me,
    And you relate to me with coldness—
28. I, too, shall relate to you with furious coldness!
    I shall punish you sevenfold,

For your offenses!
29. You will eat the flesh of your sons;
The flesh of your daughters will you eat!
30. I shall ruin your cult-platforms;
I shall cut down your Hammon-altars;
I shall heap your corpses
Atop your cadaverous fetishes!
My feelings will spurn you!
31. I shall leave your towns in ruins;
I shall devastate your sanctuaries;
I shall not inhale
Your sweet-smelling offerings.
32. I, myself, shall devastate your land!
Your enemies, who occupy it,
Will be devastated at the sight of it!
33. And as for you—
I shall scatter you among the nations!
I shall come after you with an unsheathed sword!
||Your land will be desolate;
||Your towns will be in ruins!
34. ||Only then will the land atone for its sabbaths,
||The whole time of its desolation,
||When you are in the land of your enemies.
||Then the land will cease producing;
||Thus will it atone for its sabbaths.
35. ||The whole time of its desolation
||It will, indeed, cease producing;
||As it did not cease producing
||On your sabbaths, when you lived in it.
36. ||Those of you who survive—
||I shall implant "softness" in their heart,
||In the lands of their enemies.
||The sound of a driven leaf
||Will put them to flight!
||They will flee the flight of the sword;
||They shall fall, though none pursues!
37. ||They will stumble over each other,
||As if by the sword,
||When no pursuer is there!
You will lack the strength to stand up
Before your enemies.
38. You will perish among the nations;
The land of your enemies will devour you!
39. |Those of you who survive—
|Will be heartsick over their sins,
|In the land of their enemies.
|Even more—they will be heartsick
|Over the sins of their forebears,
|That are still with them.
40. |They will confess their sins,
|And those of their forebears;

|When they broke faith with me.
||Even more—that they related to me with coldness.
41. ||I, too, shall relate to them with coldness!
||I shall allow them to perish in the land of their enemies!
||Surely then their thickened heart will submit;
||And then—they shall atone for their sins!
42. ||I shall remember my covenant with Abraham,
||And my covenant with Isaac!
||And my covenant with Jacob shall I remember.
||And—the land I shall remember!
43. ||The land will be abandoned without them;
||It will atone for its sabbaths.
||While it lies desolate of them—
||Just as they will atone for their sins.
||All because they rejected my laws,
||And their feelings spurned my statutes!
44. |So even when they are in the land of their enemies
|I have not rejected them,
|Nor have I spurned them—
|To destroy them altogether,
|So abrogating my covenant with them.
|For I am YHWH, their God!
45. |I shall remember in their favor
|The covenant with the ancients,
|Whom I liberated from the land of Egypt
|In the sight of the nations,
|Thereby becoming their God.
|I am YHWH![3]

These notes are limited to salient points of textual criticism and philology. Matters of interpretation and nuances evident in the translation will be treated later.

v. 5

The Hebrew noun *dâiš*, "season of threshing," is unique to this passage, although Deut. 25.5 comes quite close: "You shall not muzzle an ox *while it is threshing (b'dîšô)*." Our verse adds to the inventory of agricultural seasons a term such as those we find, for instance, in the ancient Gezer calendar.[4]

The form *dâiš* reflects a diphthong and derives from a hollow root, *d-w-š* (or *d-y-š*). A possible analogue is *qâiṣ*, "season of fruit-cutting; summer fruit" (Isa. 28:4; Micah 7:1).

v. 9

Where context so indicates, the verb *hēqîm* may connote the inception of a covenant (cf. Gen. 6:18). In our verse, *hēqîm* means "to maintain in force; in effect"; the opposite of *hēp̱ēr*, "to nullify, abrogate." These terms are contrasted in Ezek. 16:59–62, and in our text through vv. 9 and 15. Such balanced usage manifests a legal matrix appropriate to a covenant.

There are many similar instances. For example, in Numbers 30 we read that vows pronounced by a woman "remain in force" (the Qal stem, *qûm*) under certain conditions. It is up to the father or, later, the husband of such a woman either to "confirm" (the Hiphil, *hēqîm*) or to "nullify" (*hēpēr*) them. Likewise, also in a legal context, the field purchased by Abraham "became (his) legally" (*wayyāqom*), according to Gen. 23:17. According to the law of Lev. 25:30 and 27:19, under specific conditions an urban dwelling could become "the legal property" (*w'qām*) of its purchaser.

All of the above citations are attributable to the priestly source (P).[5]

v. 10

"Stored grain" is a functional rendering of *vāšān nôšān,* "very old." Cf. the new JPS translation, and see also Lev. 25:19–22.

v. 11

The verb *gā'al* is quite rare in Scripture. It warrants special comment because it is crucial to the Epilogue, as will become evident. It means "to abhor, spurn, treat with disgust," and is a synonym of *mā'as,* "to despise, reject," as in vv. 43–44 below. Usually, it is linked to *nepeš,* that thoroughly ambiguous term which, in our context, has been rendered "feelings." Cf. Jer. 14:19; Ezek. 16:5, 45.

For both verbs, the primary image seems to be physical spoilage or filth. *mā'as* appears in Lam. 3:45, "You have made us as *filth and refuse* [*s'ḥî ûmā'ôs*]," and functions in a mixed simile in Jer. 6:29–30:

> The bellows puff
> The lead is consumed by fire.
> The smelter smelts for naught;
> The dross is not separated.
> They are called 'dreggish silver' (*kesep nim'ās*),
> Because YHWH has discarded them (*mā'as . . . bāhem*).

As for *gā'al,* in 2 Sam. 1:21 we read:

> For there, the shield of warriors was corroded (*nig'al*);
> The shield of Saul—unpolished with oil.

And Job 21:10 states:

> His bull impregnates, and does not spoil (*w'lo'yag'îll*)
> His cow calves, and does not miscarry.

In our Epilogue, both verbs connote rejection and unacceptability in the covenantal context.

v. 13

The "bars" (*môṭôt*) of the "yoke" (*'ôl*) were tied to the neck of the work animal with "thongs" (*môsērôt*). Cf. Jer. 5:5 and 27:2, and see also Jer. 28:10–13, where we read that the bars of Jeremiah's yoke were broken, setting him free. Clearly, that the bars of the yoke are broken expresses liberation.

Gustav Dalmann has described the yoke, which is still used in many parts of the Middle East today; it has not changed very much since antiquity.[6] The person who is "subjugated" is quite literally bent over. Once the bars of the yoke are broken, he can stand "at full stature." This particular shift in the erstwhile prisoner's position is conveyed by the unique Hebrew word *qômᵃ-miyyût* (adverbial).

v. 16

While the two medical terms occur only here and in Deut. 28:22, they may nonetheless be explained. Hebrew *qadaḥat* derives from the verb *qādaḥ* "to burn, flare" (said of fire, and especially of fuming rage [Deut. 32:22; Jer. 15:14; etc.]), hence, "fever." Hebrew *šaḥep̱et* is rendered "consumption" on the basis of the Arabic cognate *saḥafa,* "to remove the fat; flay" (in reference to animals).[7] I translate *behālāh* "convulsions," in context.[8]

Hebrew *m'dîḇôt nep̱eš* requires comment. First, the form *m'dîḇôt* reflects syncope of radical Aleph; *mad'îḇôt* becomes *m'dîḇôt.* As for *nep̱eš,* cf. *daᵃḇôn nep̱eš* in Deut. 28:65. Hebrew *nep̱eš* is rendered "body" in the new JPS translation because the symptoms are best taken as somatic, having to do with disease.

v. 21

Hebrew *qerî,* and the idiom *hālak 'imm . . . [b] qerî* (literally, "to walk with . . . with coldness"), are unique to the Epilogue. *Targum Onkelos* renders them by Aramaic *b'qašyû,* "with hardness, obduracy." The derivation of Hebrew *qerî* is uncertain. The Sifra' derives it most obviously from the verb *q-r-h* "to happen by chance," explaining that this implies an attitude toward God's laws which regards them as impermanent. More likely, *qerî* derives from *qārar,* "to be cold," as D. Z. Hoffmann suggests.[9] If so, the morphology reflects a degree of drift between geminate and third-weak verbs. Cf. the nominal form *qārāh,* "cold wave," in Nahum 3:17, etc., and *m'qērāh,* "cool chamber," in Judges 3:24.

v. 22

The verb *s-k-l,* and related forms, always refer to the loss of offspring, human or animal. The parallel word, both in Hebrew and in Ugaritic, is *'ulmān,* "widowhood" (Isa. 47:8–9). In the Ugaritic epics we read of the moribund divinity, Mot-wa-Shar, *bdh ḫ ṯkl / bdh ḫṭ ulmn,* "In his one hand is the rod of bereavement / In his other hand—the rod of widowhood."[10]

v. 25

The unique clause *ḥereb nôqement n'qam b'rît* is rendered, "a sword enforcing the threats of the covenant." It has usually been translated " . . . that avenges the covenant," or the like, the sense being that the sword avenges violations of the covenant. My translation was prompted by a comment of the Sifra' on this verse. The Sifra' speaks of "*nāqām* that is in the covenant, and *nāqām* that is not in the covenant," thus, *nāqām* is synonymous with the oaths and adjurations (Hebrew *'ālôt habb'rît;* cf. Deut. 29:20). This suggested to me that the sword enforces the threats, bringing upon violators the punishments concerning which they had been admonished.[11]

v. 30

This single verse contains several archaeological terms of interest. Hebrew *bāmāh* is a term designating various cult installations. Etymologically, *bāmāh* means "back, shoulder," as we now know from Ugaritic, where we find *bmt pḫl*, "the back of a mare," on which goods are loaded, etc.[12] Hebrew *bāmāh* has the following two connotations: (1) it functions topographically, alluding to the high shoulders or peaks of mountains (Amos 4:13; Deut. 32:13; etc.); (2) it operates architecturally, connoting a raised structure, as is its sense here. (This is the sense of *bāmôt* in the Book of Kings, etc.) Both options express a semantic transaction whereby the physiognomy of humans and animals is transferred—in the first case, to the natural world, and in the second, to architecture.[13]

The term *ḥammānîm* has been translated "incense altars" (e.g., in the new JPS translation), a meaning proposed by H. Ingholt in "Le Sens du Mot *Ḥammān.*[14] Ingholt notes that an Aramaic inscription written on a Palmyrene *Palmyra* altar (*CIS* II, 3978), speaks of *ḥmn'dnh w'lt'dh,* "this *ḥammān* and this altar." On the reverse side of the altar there is a relief depicting two standing men, who are named in the inscription. There is an incense stand or altar between the men. To Ingholt, this means that the *ḥammān was* the incense altar. This same sense appears in another Palmyrene inscription (*CIS* II, 3917). There we read *ḥmn' klh hw w'trh w'p ṭll 'drwn' klh.* Someone had dedicated "the complete *ḥmn;* it and its emplacement, and even covered the entire chamber with a roof."

The etymology of *ḥmn* may have been confused by this evidence. By interpreting it to signify an incense altar, one suggests that the term derives from the verb *ḥ-m-m,* "to be hot." This is an inappropriate interpretation, for *ḫmn,* written with a loop, *Ḫeṭ,* is now attested in Ugaritic. There, the root meaning is "to be hot," the other *Ḫeṭ!* Therefore, in turn, the word *ḥammāh,* "sun," is not relevant. The conjecture that *ḥammānîm* were "sun disks" or the like must be discarded. This is not to say that a *ḥammān* could not be dedicated to Shamash or to other gods, of course, just that this is not implied by the term itself.

Further, in the Ugaritic ritual texts we read of offerings brought "at the *hmn*" (*hmnh*). *ḫmn* (Akkadian: *ḫa-ma-nu*) appears also as an element in personal names. In the Ugaritic rituals, the *ḫmn* occurs in the context of temples and altars and appears to designate an artifact or even a chamber in a temple.

Finally, it is quite possible, though not certain from the Ugaritic evidence available at the present time, that the divine name *Ḥammôn*, as in *Baal-Ḥammôn,* is embedded in this term. *Baal-Ḥammôn* is first recorded in a Phoenician inscription from Zinjirli usually dated to the ninth century B.C.E. (*ANET,* p. 500). He was very prominent at Carthage, and his cult continued long after.

The biblical evidence correlates well with the evidence from Ugarit and Palmyra. The *ḥammān* is said to be installed "above" altars and cult platforms (*bāmôt,* cf. 2 Chron. 14:4; 34:3ff.). Whether the *ḥammān* was always used as an incense altar is not certain (cf. Isa. 27:8–9). I chose in the end to leave the term *ḥammān* untranslated, rendering it "*Ḥammôn*-altar," with the strong implication that the name of the deity, *Ḥammôn,* is integral to it.[15]

Hebrew *gillûlîm* (always in the plural) is a derisive term, probably derived from the verb *g-l-l,* "to roll" (a stone). From this we have *gal,* "a pile, mound of stones," an unflattering way of characterizing pagan statues, artifacts, and the like. Our verse paraphrases Ezek. 6:4b, "I shall cast your slain before your fetishes (*lip̱neî gillûlêik̲em*)." Here we read *w'nāṯattî pigrêik̲em 'al pigrêi gillûlêik̲em,* literally, "I shall heap your corpses atop the corpses of your fetishes." The problem is that elsewhere, *peger* refers to the corpse of an animate being, and would not apply to a statue or cult object.

Moshe Greenberg called my attention to the analogue in Jer. 16:18, "Because they have defiled my land with the *carcasses* of their abominations (*b'nib̲lat šiqqûṣeîhem*)." Just as Hebrew *n'b̲ēlāh,* which elsewhere designates the carcass of a living being, may be applied in derision to a zoomorphis or anthropomorphic cult object, so may *peger*! (cf. Pss. 115:15ff.; 135:16ff.).

v. 36

Hebrew *môrek,* "softness," derives from *r-k-k,* "to be soft." It is unique to this passage. According to Deut. 20:8, the "soft of heart" are cowardly and unfit for military service.

v. 39

For Hebrew *yimmaqû,* literally, "they will waste away, melt," (compare nominal *maq,* "rot," in Isa. 3:24 and 5:24, and note that one's eyes may "melt" in their sockets [Zech. 14:12]).

v. 40

Hebrew *hiṯwaddāh,* "to confess," actually means "expose or reveal" (one's self). It conveys the opposite of concealment. Consider Ps. 32:5: "My offenses I inform you, and my wrongdoing I have not concealed. I said: 'I shall confess (*'ôdeh 'alêi*) my transgressions.'" Consider also Prov. 28:13: "One who conceals his transgressions shall not prosper, but one who confesses (*môdeh*) and abandons will be shown kindness." The process is actually quite simple; once exposed, sins, like demons, can be trapped and eliminated.[16]

v. 41

The translation here is based on the Septuagint's *kai 'apolô 'autous,* "I shall destroy them." This in turn reflects a Hebrew text which reads *w'ha'abadtî 'ôṯām* instead of Masoretic *w'hēḇē'tî 'ôṯām,* "I shall bring them." The latter would be a strange way of characterizing exile, and the attempt of the new JPS translation to rescue the MT by translating: "—shall have removed them" in my opinion is forced. Most likely, the Hebrew text was altered because of the implications inherent in saying that God would destroy his people in exile! Aside from the theological problem involved there is also the fact that in v. 44 God states he did not destroy the people in exile. On the other hand, v. 38 states that they were to perish in exile, and uses the same verb, *'āḇad,* in the Qal-stative.

As we will later observe, v. 41 is a later interpolation, and the fact that in the Epilogue as we have it it seems to contradict v. 44 is not as much of a problem as it seems. For the same compositional reasons, v. 38 does not really contradict v. 44. Rather, it is typical of interpolations that they mitigate or redefine what will happen. Thus v. 39, which is part of an addition to the primary Epilogue, speaks of survivors immediately after v. 38 speaks of perishing. I might add that the verb *'āḇad,* surely in its stative form, here may be used to convey a process that is not yet complete.

The puzzling and unique combination, *'o 'āz,* literally "or then," requires comment. I compare it with *kî 'āz,* "for then, surely then," in Josh. 1:8: "For then (*kî 'āz*) you will prosper, and then (*o' 'az*) you will succeed." The same sequence occurs here: "Surely then their thickened heart will submit, and then they will atone for their sins."

The image of the "uncircumcised" heart, which we translate "thickened heart," of course is known from Deut. 10:6 and Jer. 9:25 (see also Ezek. 44:7). It seems that whenever the image of the foreskin is employed, the physical condition original to the image peers through simile and metaphor. Thus, thickness of heart prevents one from feeling the proper emotions or thinking proper thoughts. Similarly, one whose earlobe is too thick cannot hear God's words (Jer. 6:10). In Exod. 6:12 we read of thickened lips that make articulate speech difficult. Even trees and vines classified as *'arēlîm* are untrimmed, according to the law of Lev. 19:23.

COMPOSITION AND LITERARY STRUCTURE

In our text the Epilogue is composed of the following two principal parts: (1) a promise of reward (vv. 3–13); (2) an admonition (vv. 14–45). We should bear in mind that the Epilogue is a mosaic of themes and diction, drawing on diverse literary traditions. It presents a polychrome appearance. Since this is the case, we must take care in matters of internal stratification. The Epilogue coheres rather loosely, and we should not be troubled by its minor instances of abruptness.

Fortunately for us, H. L. Ginsberg has done some recent work on parts of the Epilogue. Following his principles, we can analyze the Epilogue's composition as follows:

1. vv. 3–33a, 37b–38 form the primary Epilogue;
2. vv. 39–40b, 44–45 make up the first "post-catastrophe" addition, in Ginsberg's terminology;
3. vv. 33b–37a, which comprise the theme of desolation, Israel's submission, the atonement of land and people, and the patriarchal covenant, are both later interpolations.[17]

One justification for this scheme is founded partly in the Epilogue's diction, and partly in its themes. These will be examined in depth as we proceed. For now, it is enough to note certain structural evidence for the proposed breakdown. First, the primary Epilogue ends in v. 33a with the scattering of the people in hostile lands. This is after the destruction of the land has already been projected. Verse 37b continues with the prediction that the people will be crushed by exile and will perish in the lands of their enemies (v. 38). On the other hand, v. 33b returns to the theme of desolation. Still, in v. 36, for example, it refers to survivors before anything has been said about large-scale losses of life. Similarly, vv. 39–40a end with the remorse and confession of the people who survive the "perishing" of v. 38, whereas v. 40b quite abruptly speaks of more anger on God's part and more coldness on Israel's. It is better, then, to link v. 40a with vv. 44–45 so that following upon confession, God remembers his covenant of the exodus and does not allow the people to become entirely extinct in exile. Verses 40b–43 are in themselves probably composite, but for our purposes it is sufficient to note that they link with vv. 33bff. in using the image of the land's barrenness. This is expressed as involuntary Sabbaths imposed on it. The patriarchal covenant seems to be a separate theme.

In summary, as far as content is concerned, the breakdown implies the following conclusions. The primary Epilogue ends in doom, as is to be expected in this sort of curse. This result is mitigated by the first additions, which project the remorse and confession of the people who survive in exile. These induce God to reaffirm his covenant of the exodus. In practical terms, this means that at least part of the people will be restored to the land. The later interpolations introduce the theme of atonement, for land and people describe the terror of exile, speak of submission, and introduce a second covenant, one with the patriarchs.

As for the relative chronology of the Epilogue and its additions, that will be discussed when we turn to diction and provenance. There, we will clearly see why we must analyze the Epilogue's scheme in this way. The breakdown is not merely a matter of logical continuity, textual coherence, or literary structure, as might seem at this point. Rather, it is based on the history of biblical ideas.

To return to our scheme, the structure of the primary Epilogue (vv. 3–33a) reveals a symmetry of contrasts (e.g., between the promise of reward and the threat of punishment). In the promise, the land will be fertile (vv. 4–5, 10), and in the admonition it will be unproductive (vv. 16, 19–20, 26). This theme is expressed in the same language. In the promise, YHWH will turn with favor toward his people (v. 9), and in the admonition, he will set his face against them (v. 17). Verse 9 of the promise states that Israel will be able to repulse enemies, and in vv. 17 and 25 of the admonition we read that they will be battered by enemies. Returning to the promise, v. 6, we read that the land will be rid of wild beasts, and in v. 25 of the admonition, that wild beasts will devour the people. Verse 6 further states that no sword will traverse the land, whereas v. 25 of the admonition speaks of a sword bringing destruction. And the opposite of secure settlement in the land, promised in v. 5 for an obedient Israel, is the exile threatened in v. 33a.

It occurs to me that *t'qûmāh,* the ability to "stand up" in v. 37b, may be a play on *qôm^{a}miyyût,* "at full stature," which appears in v. 13 of the promise. Instead of being free as the people were when they left Egypt, when the bars of their yoke were broken so that they stood tall, they will soon be bent over as captives in exile. In fact, Deut. 28:48, the last verse of the primary Deuteronomic curse, also speaks of subjugation in exile.[18]

Clearly, the primary Epilogue is composed in an escalating scale. If one set of punishments fails to secure Israel's obedience, more and worse punishments will accumulate. This escalation is emphasized by periodic refrains which may be charted as follows:

v. 18: Israel's failure to heed results in sevenfold punishments.

v. 21: Israel's coldness and their failure to heed result in sevenfold punishments.

vv. 23–24: Israel's failure to be chastised and their coldness result in YHWH's coldness and the sevenfold punishments.

vv. 27–28: Israel's failure to heed and their coldness result in YHWH's coldness and sevenfold punishments.

The effect of this escalation is both disheartening and, in a curious way, encouraging. God will not relent, and will steadily increase punishment, finally exiling the people. On the other hand, the conditional formulation of the admonition leaves a way open for Israel at any of several stages. One is reminded of ten plagues in the Book of Exodus. (I am indebted to Moshe Greenberg for calling my attention to it.) Amos 4:6–11 is likewise an oracle composed on an escalating scale. I present it here in edited form to highlight its relevance to the structure of our Epilogue.

> I, on my part, have given you
> Cleanness of teeth in all your towns . . .
> Yet you did not turn back to me
> —declares the Lord.
>
> I therefore withheld the rain from you
> Three months before the harvest time . . .
> Yet you did not turn back to me
> —declares the Lord.
>
> I scourged you with blight and mildew,
> Repeatedly, your gardens and vineyards . . .
> Yet you did not turn back to me
> —declares the Lord.
>
> I sent against you pestilence
> Repeatedly, in the manner of Egypt . . .
> Yet you did not turn back to me
> —declares the Lord.
>
> I have wrought destruction upon you
> As when God destroyed Sodom and Gomorrah . . .
> Yet you have not turned back to me
> —declares the Lord.

Amos notes situations that have already occurred but whose portents went unheeded by Israel. Our Epilogue, by contrast, is predictive. Nonetheless, by comparing the two we can observe broad affinities between prophecies of doom and admonitions. These affinities will link our Epilogue to the prophecies of Jeremiah and, even more dramatically, to those of Ezekiel.

The predictive orientation of our Epilogue justifies my translation of its verbs as indicatives rather than modals. God does not exhort Israel explicitly; though tradition, represented by the Sifra', construes the conditional formulation of the Epilogue to this effect. In fact, the Epilogue is bland and cruel precisely because it lacks such exhortations as we find in Deut. 11:13–28. There, God warns the people to beware of temptation to stray, and urges upon them life-giving obedience. Here, the binary alternatives of following and disobeying are presented in a matter-of-fact tone.

As far as its literary composition is concerned, our Epilogue resembles Deut. 28:1–48. (As regards diction, however, the two compositions have little in common, as we shall see.) Our Epilogue's additions share the same sort of mitigations or redemptive opportunities as occur in Deuteronomy.[19] Thus, Deut. 30:1–10, occurring within the later conclusion to the Book of Deuteronomy (Deut. 28:49—30:20), states that Israel will be restored to their land if they turn back to YHWH sincerely. This same thought is expressed in Deut. 4:25–31. There, should Israel anger YHWH and consequently be exiled, the chance of restoration will still exist if the people seek God from the lands of exile. Ginsberg's point is that in both Deuteronomy and Leviticus, the classic admonition which typically ends in doom is amended to allow for survival and restoration.

Both Deut. 28:1–48 and our Epilogue resemble in this shared composition the Epilogue to the Code of Hammurabi. At the conclusion of the laws, Hammurabi adjures his successor on the throne to uphold his laws, honor his name, etc. He poses the same, binary alternatives as we find in the Pentateuchal epilogues:

> If that man (the king who shall be raised up in the land) has heeded (the verb *šemû*) my words, which I have inscribed on my monument, has not made light of my commandments . . . may Shamash enlarge that man's empire like mine, the just king, and may he lead his people with justice.
>
> If that man has not heeded my words which I have inscribed on my monument . . . may the great god, Anum, the father of the gods, deprive that man . . . of royal splendor, break his scepter, curse his destiny, etc.[20]

There are, of course, basic differences in the relationships projected in the Epilogue to the Code of Hammurabi, but the affinities in the terms used for the statements are instructive.

DICTION AND PROVENANCE

Diction is often the key to historical provenance, and this is especially true of our Epilogue. By studying the choice of words and idioms, and by analyzing just how ideas are expressed, we may be able to suggest a historical setting for the Epilogue, in its several strata.

But before engaging the particular problems of diction raised by the Epilogue (especially the relation of the Epilogue to Ezekiel), a word should be said about the more obvious links of diction with ancient Near Eastern blessings and curses, biblical and extrabiblical. The most obvious parallel is Deut. 28:1–48, whose diction differs noticeably from that of our Epilogue. Deuteronomy 28 (chap. 27 also) speaks of blessing and curse, as is true of other Deuteronomic statements of a similar sort, such as Deut. 11:15–28. These terms of reference are entirely absent from our Epilogue. In contrast, our Epilogue emphasizes *b'rît*, "covenant," a term which never occurs in Deut. 28:1–48 or in the rest of the chapter. (The postscript in 28:69 is clearly a priestly insertion.) To be sure, our Epilogue and Deuteronomy 28 share several clichés. For instance, both mention *qadaḥat* and *šaḥep̱et* (Lev. 26:16; Deut. 28:22); both refer to skies of iron and soil of bronze (Lev. 26:19; Deut. 28:33); both talk of eating the flesh of children (Lev. 26:29; Deut. 28:53ff.); both admonitions speak of being battered (the verb *niqqap*) by enemies (Lev. 26:17; Deut. 28:7, 25); both refer to exhausted eyes and languishing bodies (Lev. 26:16; Deut. 28:65); both contain reference to rains in their season (Lev. 26:3; Deut. 28:12). And finally, the term *miṣwāh*, "command," first introduced by the Deuteronomist, was appropriated by the priestly writers and thus occurs in both epilogues.[21] For the rest, each epilogue draws on its own literary traditions.[22]

What is common to the two epilogues is generally conventional for this genre. Eating the flesh of one's dead children is depicted in several biblical passages. In fact, we find the same depictions in the vassal treaty of Esarhaddon—just as we find there references to iron soil and bronze heavens as a way of depicting drought.[23]

But recent discoveries have provided even more parallels, showing just how intimately biblical and other ancient Near Eastern curses are related in their diction. The most recent discovery is the bilingual statuary inscription in Aramaic and Akkadian from Tell-Fekherye, in Northeast Syria, near Tell-Halaf (Gozah). It probably dates from the ninth century B.C.E. Like all such royal inscriptions, the text includes a section of curses. In line 22 of the Aramaic version we read *wm'h nšwn l'pn btnwr lḥm w'l yml'nh*, "May one-hundred women bake bread in an oven, but let them not fill it!" The Akkadian version is slightly different, but also of interest. It reads, *l mē āpiāte lā u[šam] lâ tinûra*, "May one hundred baking-women not even fill an oven!" It has been duly noted that these statements recall Lev. 26:26: "Ten women will bake your bread in a single oven; they will dispense your bread by weight." In the vassal treaty of Esarhaddon we find the similar image, "May your finger-tips not dip in the dough; may the dough be lacking from your kneading-troughs."[24] And if we carry the comparisons a step further, this treaty curse recalls Deut. 28:5 and 17, where the kneading-troughs of the blessed contain much dough!

Depicting exile as the "scattering" of a nation is also common diction. It links v. 33a of our Epilogue not only to Deuteronomy and to the prophecies of Jeremiah and Ezekiel, but also to the curses in the Epilogue to the Code of Hammurabi, for instance. The Hebrew verb *zērāh*, "to scatter," is paralleled by the statement *na-ás-pu-úḫ ni-ši-šu*, "the *scattering* of his people."[25] Also, the characterization of defeat as not being able "to stand up" before enemies, conveyed in our Epilogue by the original locution *t'qûmāh* (v. 37b), finds a parallel in the vassal treaty of Esarhaddon. There, the following statement appears: *(at)-tú-(nu ina* IGI) LÚ.KÚR *la ta-za-za-a-ni*, "May you not *stand* before your enemy!"[26]

A thorough investigation would undoubtedly turn up many more analogues. Our purpose is only to suggest that diction may often be a conventional phenomenon. While it may broaden our vistas, it may also focus our attention narrowly on specific literary sources.

H. L. Ginsberg has provided us with a reliable point of departure for discussing diction as the key to historical provenance in our Epilogue. He observes that the first "post-catastrophe" addition to the primary Epilogue (vv. 39–40a and 44–45) reflects the theme of Ezekiel 20.[27] In the year 591 B.C.E., after the first deportations from Judah and Jerusalem by the Babylonians, the prophet Ezekiel reviews Israel's covenantal relationship with God. He perceives its history as a chain of disloyalty on Israel's part. At several critical junctures, YHWH has been all but ready to nullify the covenant made at the exodus because Israel has violated its terms in failing to observe his laws. Each time, however, YHWH stopped short out of concern for his reputation. He had sworn to Israel "in the sight of the nations" (*l' 'êinêi haggôyîm*), so to nullify the covenant would invite desecration of his "name" (Ezek. 20:8b–9, 17, 21b–23). At last, however, YHWH went through with his threats, exiled his people, and let their land be destroyed. Still, all was not lost, for God would again restore at least part of his people.

Now, as Ginsberg notes, the phrase *l' 'êinêi haggôyîm* is exclusive to our Epilogue (v. 45), to Ezekiel, who employs it in several oracles, and to Isaiah (52:10), in an oracle of restoration. There we find *l' 'êinêi kol haggôyîm,* "in the sight of all the nations." Clearly, the prophet who gave us the beautiful restoration oracle of Isa. 52:7–10, which announces the end of the exile and the return to Zion, echoed Ezekiel 20, and also Ezekiel 36:15–21. Ginsberg also calls attention to Ezekiel's use of the verb *m-q-q,* "to melt, waste away." In v. 39 of the "post-catastrophe" addition to our Epilogue, we read, "Those of who survive will be *heartsick over their sins,*" (*yimmaqqû ba'a wônām*), and so on. (This is Ginsberg's rendering of *yimmaqqû,* which aptly conveys the functional sense that the people will experience remorse over their sins.) Only our Epilogue and Ezekiel know of the combination *māqaq* + *b'awôn* (see Ezek. 4:17; 24:33; and also 33:10).[28]

If the first additions to our Epilogue contain specific ideas taken by our author from Ezekiel, as Ginsberg correctly concludes, then we must be well into the sixth century, at the earliest. Therefore, the interpolations in vv. 33b–37a and 40b–43 must be regarded as subsequent. We are fortunate in having evidence to support this claim. If we look at vv. 34–35 and v. 43, we find a usage attested elsewhere only in Isa. 40:2. I refer to the idiom *rāṣāh 'awôn,* "to atone, expiate a sin." We read in Isa. 40:1–2:

> Comfort, oh comfort my people,
> Says your God.
> Speak kindly to Jerusalem,
> Proclaim to her
> That she has completed her service;
> That her sin has been expiated (*ki nirṣāh 'awônāh*).

According to v. 43 of our Epilogue, both the land and the people atone for their sins. The people atone through submission to God after the prolonged sufferings of exile; the land atones by "making up" for its neglected sabbath years. The sabbatical theme, so prominent in the Holiness Code (Lev. 23:15ff.; 25:1–22; etc.), here is applied with cruel irony; because the land did not lie fallow every seventh year while the Israelites lived on it, as had been commanded, it will now lie desolate, bereft of its people. This complex of diction must surely lead us to Deutero-Isaiah, late in the exilic period.

Ginsberg also helps us in clarifying the literary-historical analysis of the Epilogue's later interpolations. Verse 42 speaks of the covenant with the patriarchs. Ginsberg argues persuasively that this concept of a covenant is an exilic creation, for preexilic sources know only of the conditional covenant of the exodus. In our case, this theme was quite possibly borrowed from Exod. 6:2–9, a priestly passage. That text mentions too all three patriarchs, but in their proper order, not reversed as we receive them in v. 42. It follows, therefore, that the dominant themes of the later interpolations are both exilic at the earliest.[29]

So we may refer to three stages in the Epilogue's composition. First comes the primary Epilogue, then the first "post-catastrophe" addition, which brings us well into the sixth century, then the later interpolations. These take us virtually to the end of the exile.

We must now direct our attention to the primary Epilogue itself. In my opinion, the same criteria which endorse an exilic provenance for the first additions allow us to propose an exilic date for the primary Epilogue, for it, too, contains diction and themes taken from Ezekiel.

Of course, here we enter into a larger debate concerning the relation of the priestly source to Ezekiel in literary-historical terms. This subject has been discussed from various points of view. Recently, Avi Hurvitz has devoted a monograph to linguistic evidence bearing on the relationship. In it, he argues that the priestly source generally antedates Ezekiel. Since his method emphasizes matters of diction, and since he devotes considerable attention to several locutions which occur in our Epilogue, we must evaluate his evidence.[30]

Hurvitz deals primarily with the process of replacement. This involves considering where later usages replace earlier ones. Obviously, later usages indicate the relative lateness of the sources in which they occur. In a less systematic way, Hurvitz also draws linguistic conclusions from the absence of what he considers to be early locutions in similar statements. Thus, if our Epilogue uses one of these allegedly early locutions and, in a close paraphrase, Ezekiel does not, this is seen as indicating that Ezekiel is later than the Epilogue. Involved in this method are assumptions about just how "primitive" certain words are, and the implication that biblical diction shows a progressive tendency to distance God from direct references of a primitive or irreverential sort. Of course, there are elements of late language in Ezekiel. But while these may be original, they could also result from later editing. In any event, one of the two instances of replacement presented by Hurvitz is probably invalid.[31]

More germane to our discussion is Hurvitz's treatment of the verb *gāʿal,* "to spurn, abhor." Hurvitz examines in *gāʿal* an attempt to demonstrate that three passages in our Epilogue are earlier than three passages in Ezekiel which closely paraphrase them. This verb is one of those he regards as primitive and offensive—witness the fact that in the Hebrew Bible one never "spurns" God, as the direct object, but only indirectly "spurns" his laws, statutes, etc. Hurvitz also shows that Ezekiel, unlike our Epilogue, never mentions God as the subject of this verb (Lev. 26:11, 30, 44). Therefore, Hurvitz concludes, our Epilogue predates Ezekiel, by whose time it was already improper to speak of God as having such coarse emotions!

Let me state at the outset that there is a flaw in Hurvitz's argument. The verb *gāʿal,* which is infrequent in the Hebrew Bible, when it appears, is usually linked with *nep̲eš.* Thus, one's "feelings" spurn, abhor! Now this idiom may have been first introduced through Jeremiah (14:19). There we read "Have you indeed rejected Judah?" (*h^amā'ōs mā'astāh*), "Have your feelings spurned Zion?" (*gāʿ^alāh nap̲šek̲ā*). Since the subject is God, to agree with Hurvitz we would have to assume that a coarse idiom first introduced by Jeremiah was already unacceptable to Ezekiel! Even if we assume, for purposes of argument, that Jeremiah uses an old idiom, we would have to suppose that between Jeremiah and Ezekiel this idiom had become unacceptable. This is highly unlikely. But let us examine actual examples from Hurvitz. First, he contrasts "All because they rejected my laws, And their feelings *spurned* my statutes," and "They refused to obey my laws, And for my statutes—*they did not follow them*" (Lev. 26:43; Ezek. 5:6). According to Hurvitz, here Ezekiel mitigates the coarseness of Leviticus, refraining from using *gāʿal,* and substituting another way of expressing disobedience.

Hurvitz considers, second, Lev. 26:30 and Ezek. 6:3–5a:

> I shall ruin your cult-platforms;
> I shall cut down your Ḥammon-altars;
> I shall heap your corpses
> Atop your cadaverous fetishes.
> *My feelings will spurn you!*
> (Lev. 26:30)
>
> I shall destroy your cult-platforms;
> Your altars will be desolate;
> Your Ḥammon-altars will be broken;
> I shall cast your slain before your fetishes!
> I shall dump the corpses of the Israelite people
> Before their fetishes. . . .
> (Ezek. 6:3–5a)

Again, Hurvitz contends that the verb *gāʿal* does not occur in the corresponding sequence of Ezekiel because it was considered too primitive, and thus had to be excised.

Third, for our purposes, Hurvitz contrasts Lev. 26:11–12 and Ezek. 37:26b–27:

> I shall place my residence (*miškānî*) among you.
> My feelings will not spurn you.
> I shall walk about among you (*w'hiṯhallaḵtî*)
> I shall be your God;
> You will be my people.
>
> (Lev. 26:11–12)
>
> I shall place my sanctuary (*miqdāšî*) among them forever.
> My presence will rest over them.
> I shall be their God;
> They will be my people.
>
> (Ezek. 37:26b–27)

Here we can clearly see what I consider a problem in Hurvitz's method. If we are to accept his analysis, the following must be the case: (1) Ezekiel omitted the verb *gā'al* because it was unrefined; (2) Ezekiel also omitted using the form *hiṯhallēk,* since it was too anthropomorphic; (3) Leviticus is too early to speak of "residing over" (*šāḵan* + *'al*), so it uses instead *šāḵan* + *b, b'ṯôk,* "to reside among." Although all three items are directly relevant to the same source, Hurvitz discusses each of them separately, and under different headings. Hurvitz thus fails to focus on the literary unit and, in my opinion, presents an imprecise picture of the problem of diction.

To me, there are alternative explanations for the paraphrastic relationship between these Levitical passages and their parallels in Ezekiel. It might appear, for instance, that Ezek. 5:6 adapts Lev. 26:43. But there are two reasons for doubting this. First, the idiom *b'ḥuqqîm/b'ḥuqqôt* + *hālak,* "in statutes + walk" (in contrast to *hālak* + *b'ḥuqqîm/b'ḥuqqôt*), is one of Ezekiel's favorites (see 11:12, 20; 18:9, 17; 20:13, 18–19, 21; 33:15). One could say that he used it here for that very reason. Second, the oracle of Ezekiel does not end in v. 6, as one might infer from Hurvitz's edited citation of it. In fact, it continues through Ezek. 5:9. Further, throughout, its terms of reference are *ḥuqqîm* and *mišpāṭîm,* "statutes and judgments." This, indeed, is the point of Ezekiel's oracle: Israel was even more wicked than neighboring nations in violating God's laws, therefore, God will exact "judgment" from them. So one could say that it is Leviticus that departs from Ezekiel's diction! (It should also be noted that v. 43 of our Epilogue was analyzed earlier as part of a later interpolation on grounds of literary composition and diction.)

As for Lev. 26:30 and Ezek. 6:3–5a, in our Epilogue, the clause "My feelings will not spurn you" concludes v. 30, whereas in Ezek. 6:3ff. the description of the destruction of cult-places continues until v. 7. If we were to accept Hurvitz's analysis, we would have to assume that this clause ought to have appeared between Ezek. 6:5a and 6:5b. But those flow quite well as they are. Further, since the author of our Epilogue adds a thought missing in Ezekiel's repeated depictions of the cult-places (the notion that the fetishes are lifeless), I suggest that our author adapted Ezekiel's statement in speaking of *pigrêi gillûlêiḵem,* literally, "the corpses of your fetishes."

Finally, as I noted above, Lev. 26:11–12 is discussed by Hurvitz under three separate headings. To illustrate that it could well have been our author who utilized Ezek. 37:26b–27 and not vice versa, as Hurvitz maintains, I have indented two clauses appearing in the Leviticus passage. Our author may have used Ezekiel's statements as an *inclusio,* introducing the following two thoughts: one, God will be present among his people; he will "walk about" among them (the verb *hiṯhallēḵ*). This is older diction to be sure (see Gen. 3:8), and utilized in Deuteronomistic literature (Deut. 23:15; 2 Sam. 7:6). Two, God will not "spurn" Israel. Further, our author may have condensed two of Ezekiel's statements into one. I have indicated this possibility by bracketing Ezek. 37:26b. I wonder whether one may properly compare "I shall place my residence among you" (Leviticus), where *miškān* means "residence," with "My Presence will rest over you" (Ezekiel), where *miškān* does not designate a residence but seems to anticipate the later term *š'ḵînāh,* "divine presence," in its connotation. Since Ezekiel uses *miškān* in this verse, it might serve as his replacement for *kāḇôd* (see Exod. 34:16 and Isa. 4:5–6). I also note that the idiom *šāḵan + b/b'ṯôk,* which Hurvitz regards as earlier diction, is used by First Zechariah (2:14–15 and 8:3) and in the last eight chapters of Ezekiel (43:9).

For our discussion, however, the key is *gāʿal.* Why Ezekiel eschews its use, when God is its subject, is not certain. Still, it is clear that he does so not because he writes much later than Jeremiah. In other words, the difference cannot demonstrate that Lev. 26:3–45 antedates Ezekiel. In my scheme, the author of our Epilogue appropriated the idiom *gāʿal + nep̱eš* ("feelings/spurn") from Jeremiah. In the Epilogue, it marks critical junctures in the dynamic of relationships between God and Israel. This process begins in v. 11b, where we are told that God's feelings will not spurn Israel. At that point, the promises of well-being are reaching their climax. In vv. 14–15 the first punishments are introduced. God begins to punish Israel at the point when Israel "spurns" his laws and statutes. The punishments then escalate through waves until, in v. 30, we read that God "spurns" Israel. At that point, no further opportunities are given for averting exile, the final disaster. Indeed, the primary Epilogue actually breaks off in v. 33a, after vv. 31–33a project destruction and dispersion.

The author of the "post-catastrophe" addition adopted the same code-word: Here, redemption becomes possible because God has not ever "spurned" Israel in this author's view. Such "spurning" would have brought about Israel's utter extinction in exile. Further, it would have damaged God's reputation in the sight of the nations (vv. 44–45). So after Israel confessed, showing remorse, God reaffirmed the covenant of the exodus. Thus, the mitigation of doom formulated by the author of the first addition to the primary Epilogue revolves around the verb *gāʿal*. And even the author(s) of the later interpolations knew the same code. For example, the exile was prolonged and expiation delayed because Israel had persisted in "spurning" God's laws and statutes.

Thus, my reasons for assuming that the author of the primary Epilogue drew on Jeremiah are not limited to Jeremiah's knowledge of the idiom *gāʿal* + *nep̱eš*. I count also its operation. For Jeremiah too, "spurning" may have served to mark the critical juncture at which God determines there is no return and that matters have gone too far to avert destruction and exile. Let us examine Jer. 14:19ff.

> Have you indeed rejected Judah? (*hamā'ôs mā'astāh*)
> Have your feelings spurned Zion? (*gāʿalāh nap̱šeḵā*)
> Why have you smitten us
> Allowing us no healing?
> To hope for wholeness
> When there is no wellbeing?
> For a time of healing—
> And behold—terror?
> We realize, YHWH, our guilt,
> The sins of our forebears,
> For we have offended against you.
> Do not reject us utterly, (*tin'aṣ*)
> For your name's sake.
> Do not desecrate your glorious throne!
> Remember! Do not annul your covenant with us!

In Jeremiah, this is a last appeal, for as we continue in chap. 15 we read of God's refusal to reconsider, and the sentence of exile.

Why should our author use the verb *gāʿal?* Like Jeremiah, he found it a way to signal the point where God lost patience with a recalcitrant Israel and exile became inevitable. Our author effectively answers Jeremiah's question in the affirmative. Finally, God has spurned Zion!

The hypothesis that our author drew on Ezekiel's diction is supported when one considers that the primary Epilogue is replete with Ezekiel's distinctive language. Naturally, some of this diction is shared by Jeremiah. Note the following examples: one, the verb *zērāh*, "to scatter," characterizes dispersal or exile in v. 33a. This usage probably originated in Jeremiah (15:7, the Qal; the Piel, Jer. 31:10; 49:32; 51:2). Ezekiel elaborates upon it in 5:10; 6:5, 8; 12:14–15; 20:2, 23; 22:15; 29:12; 30:26. Two, in v. 19, our author speaks of "your powerful glory" (*g''ôn uzḵem*). It is his way of referring to the land, most likely, for he goes on to speak of drought, and the failure of the soil to yield its produce. This locution is known elsewhere only in Ezek. 30:6 (a reference to the temple of Jerusalem), and in Ezek. 7:24; 30:18; 33:28). Three, in speaking of swords, only Ezekiel and our author use the precise idiom *hērîq ḥereḇ 'aḥareî*, literally, "to unsheath the sword after" (see Lev. 26:33a; Ezek. 5:2;

12:14). Further, only Lev. 26:6 and Ezek. 14:17 know of the combination *ḥereb* + *ʿāḇar,* "a sword-traverses," and only Lev. 26:25 and Ezekiel (in 5:11; 6:3; 11:8; 14:17; 29:8; 33:2) know the idiom *hēḇîʾ ḥereb ʿal,* "to brandish a sword over." Four, to refer to sustenance, both our Epilogue (v. 26) and Ezekiel (4:16; 5:16; 14:13) use the idiom *maṭṭēh leḥem,* "support of bread." Elsewhere it is found only in Ps. 105:16, which is clearly a late text. We can contrast with these *mišʿan leḥem,* "support of bread," in Isa. 3:1. And last, many scholars have observed that most of the promise (Lev. 26:3–13) bears remarkable similarity to Ezek. 34:25–28. This the reader can note in further detail.[32]

When we encounter a situation like the one outlined here, we are warranted in attributing literary provenance. Thus, we can say our primary Epilogue emerged from the same literary circles as Ezekiel, and was, at the very least, contemporaneous with Ezekiel. But more likely, it echoes Ezekiel's prophecies. We see on every side that our Epilogue condenses or encapsulates diction that is virtually pervasive in Ezekiel. We are not dealing simply with individual parallels or single attestations, but with major themes expressed in identical diction. Consequently, we may propose the following historical progression through the three essential layers of our Epilogue. First comes the primary Epilogue, which is exilic, at the earliest. It serves to explain the exile as the final outcome of a long series of confrontations between Israel and God. Next, the "post-catastrophe" addition explains how restoration becomes possible from exile, when all hope seems lost. The later interpolations serve to explain why the exile lasted so long, and they are a product either of the last years of exile, or of the period of the first return.

First, Zechariah, who began to prophesy in the second year of Darius, 520 B.C.E., speaks of the same themes that pervade our Epilogue. The ancestors, he says, failed to heed prophetic admonitions:

> Your ancestors—where are they?
> And the prophets—will they live forever?
> But my words and my statutes,
> With which I charged my servants, the prophets,
> Did they not overtake your fathers?
> They finally acknowledged:
> "What YHWH of Hosts had in mind to do to us,
> Because of our ways and our deeds,
> He actually did to us!"
>
> (Zech. 1:5–6)

The words *d'ḇārai w'ḥuqqaî,* "my words and my statutes," may be an allusion to the requirement that Israel obey God's laws and statutes, a notion prominent in our Epilogue. Failure to heed them was the cause of the exile. While prophets are not always around to admonish the people, the laws and statutes, once promulgated, endure. Obedience to them in effect replaces heeding the voice of the Lord, so that our Epilogue may speak of "heeding" laws and statutes, just as the Deuteronomistic statements do, and as we find in certain prophecies.

In Zech. 2:3ff. we note a reference to the "scattering" of Israel, through the verb *zērāh.* In a cryptic oracle, the prophet envisions the "scattering" of the "scatterers," so to speak, that is, the expulsion of the conquerors who had exiled Israel. Still further, in Zech. 2:10ff., we read words reminiscent of our Epilogue and of priestly diction:

> Shout for joy, daughter of Zion!
> For here I come!
> I shall dwell in your midst (*w'šākantî b'tôkēk*), declares YHWH.
> On that day, many peoples will attach themselves to YHWH.
> They will become my people.
> I shall dwell in your midst!

Our prophet adopts the idea that non-Israelites will attach themselves (the verb *nilwāh*) to the restored community of returning exiles, a theme expressed in Isa. 56:3 and Jer. 50:5 (cf. Isa. 14:11). He thereby extends the parameter of the covenant. However, he also echoes the emphasis on God's immanence; God will reside among the people, a theme reiterated in Zech. 8:3, 8.

Finally, we find in Zech. 7:11ff. a way of defining the enigmatic word *qerî,* "coldness," which recurs in the Epilogue:

> They refused to pay heed!
> They presented a balky back and turned a deaf ear!
> They hardened their heart like adamant . . .
> Even as He called and they would not listen,
> "So," said YHWH of Hosts, "Let them call—
> And I will not listen!"[33]

So the final version of the Epilogue may well have been addressed to the Judeans of the first return. It was to serve as a warning to them not to replicate the errors of their ancestors. In a restored Judea, with the temple at its core, it became all-important to obey God's laws, commands, and statutes, especially his statutes (*ḥuqqîm/ḥuqqôt*), terms which often refer particularly to religious law.

EPILOGUE TO THE EPILOGUE

I could not possibly have chosen a text for study that more clearly illustrates the relevance of my being a Jew to my scholarship. My methods of study hardly differ from those of my colleagues who are not Jewish, and I certainly do not claim that my insights surpass theirs! What may be different is my response to the poignant message of the Epilogue, with its startling alternatives of survival and extinction. Of course, the sufferings projected in the

Epilogue pale before the actual record of the Holocaust. But the theme of restoration leaves room for great hope. The modern Jews who "survive," with all that survival connotes, are not terror-stricken, as v. 37 of the Epilogue states. We do not flee at the sound of a driven leaf, either individually (Job 13:25), or collectively. The modern restoration to the land of Israel is more impressive, in significant respects, than was the Second Commonwealth. The time has come to cease adulating our ancestors, and to begin to perceive the opportunities and the challenges of the future, always mindful of what covenant imposes on us. The historical "brinkmanship" of which the Epilogue speaks has too often endangered us, and we must stop testing the limits of historical possibility.

Jewish tradition frequently breathes new life into the unique diction of a single, biblical verse. The beautiful word *qôm^{a}miyyût,* in v. 11 of our Epilogue, served as the stimulus for a fervent hope, expressed in the Grace after Meals:

> May the Merciful-One break off our yoke from our neck, and may He enable us to walk at full stature to our land![34]

NOTES

1. See G. R. Driver and J. C. Miles, *The Babylonian Laws* (London: Oxford Univ. Press, 1955), 2:95–107, for the Epilogue to the Code of Hammurabi. Along with blessings, the Epilogue contains lengthy curses.

2. See the sources cited in nn. 18–19, and note the following: L. W. King, ed., *Babylonian Boundary Stones and Memorial Tablets* (London: Oxford Univ. Press, 1912). The *kudurru,* "boundary stone," called down curses upon any and all who would alter established boundaries (cf. Deut. 27:17). For a translation of the Aramaic treaty from Sefire, see *ANET,* 3:659ff. (F. Rosenthal). For Akkadian treaties see *ANET,* 3:531ff. (E. Reiner). For Hittite treaties, see *ANET,* 3:199ff. (A. Goetze). Some Egyptian execration texts are translated by J. A. Wilson in *ANET,* 3:326ff. Some Phoenician and early Aramaic building inscriptions, also containing blessings and curses, are translated by F. Rosenthal in *ANET,* 3:653–55.

3. In the format of the translation, one vertical line (|) marks off the first "post-catastrophe" addition to the primary Epilogue, and two vertical lines (||) mark off the later interpolations. Part of v. 41 is underlined to indicate that the translation is not based on the Masoretic text. See the notes to v. 41.

4. The text of the Gezer calendar may be found in J. C. Gibson, *Textbook of Syrian Semitic Inscriptions* (London: Oxford Univ. Press, 1971; reprinted 1976), 1:2ff.

5. See the discussion in B. A. Levine, "Late Language in the Priestly Source: Some Literary and Historical Observations," *Proceedings, Eighth World Congress of Jewish Studies (Jerusalem, 1981), Panel Sessions: Bible Studies and Hebrew Language* (Jerusalem: World Union of Jewish Studies, 1983), 69–82.

6. Gustav Dalmann, *Arbeit und Sitte im Palästina* (Gütersloh: Bertelsmann, 1932), 2:99–105, and pls. 18–21b, 29–42.

7. On the verb *šaḥap* in Late Hebrew, see "*š-ḥ-p* (verb)," in *Aruch Completum* (Vienna: A. Kohut), 5:54.

8. The verb *bāhal* always connotes rapid motion. For possibly somatic usages, cf. Jer. 15:8 and Ps. 6:3–4.

9. See D. Z. Hoffmann, "Lev. 26:21," in *Leviticus* (Jerusalem: Mossad Harav Kook, 5713–5714 [1954]), 351.

10. See O. Loretz et al., *Keilalphabetischen Texte aus Ugarit,* AOAT 24, no. 1 (Neukirchen-Vluyn: Neukirchener Verlag, 1976), 23:8 (the birth of the gods).

11. Perhaps the Sifra''s comment was prompted by a statement in the Epilogue to the Deuteronomic laws, Deut. 28:61: "plagues which are not mentioned in this Book of Teaching."

12. See Loretz, *Keilalphabetischen Texte aus Ugarit,* 19.2.59–60 (the Aqhat epic), and 4.4.14–15 (the Baal-Anat cycle).

13. See B. A. Levine, "Cult Places, Israelite," *EncJud* 5:1162ff.

14. H. Ingholt, "Le Sens du Mot *Hammān,*" *Melanges Syriens offerts à R. Dussaud* (Paris: Geuthner, 1939), 2:795–802, and pls.

15. H. W. Haussig et al., *Götter und Mythen im Vorderen Orient* (Stuttgart: E. Klett, 1965), 271ff.: see "Baal-Ḥammôn," and literature cited.

16. See B. A. Levine, *In the Presence of the Lord,* SJLA 5 (Leiden: E. J. Brill, 1974), 82, and n. 73.

17. See H. L. Ginsberg, *The Israelian Heritage of Judaism* (New York: Ktav, 1982), 79ff., 100ff. In this one particular I differ from Ginsberg's breakdown: in v. 40, the words *b'ma'alām 'ašer mā'alû bî,* "When they broke faith with me," could just as well be part of the first addition, since they paraphrase Ezek. 39:26, and convey the same sense.

18. Cf. Deut. 28:48, "He will place an iron yoke on your neck until he destroys you."

19. See Ginsberg, *Israelian Heritage.*

20. See Driver and Miles, *Babylonian Laws,* 98–99, ll. 2ff., with deletions.

21. See B. A. Levine, "Miswah," in *ThWAT* 4 (1984): 1086ff.

22. One notes, for instance, the correspondence between v. 8 of our Epilogue and Deut. 32:30: "How could one have routed a thousand / Or two put ten thousand to flight . . ."

23. On cannibalism, see *CAD,* A, I, 250, under *akālu,* "to eat," l. b. See esp. D. J. Wiseman, "The Vassal Treaties of Esarhaddon," *Iraq* 20 (1958): 60–61, ll. 448ff., and 71–72, ll. 570ff. Also, cf. Jer. 19:9; Ezek. 5:19; Lam. 2:20; 4:10. On skies of bronze and soil of iron, see Wiseman, "Vassal Treaties of Esarhaddon," 69–70, ll. 528ff.

24. Now see J. C. Greenfield and A. Shaffer, "Notes on the Curse Formulae of the Tell Fekherye Inscription," *RB* 92 (1985): 47–59, and literature cited. See Wiseman, "Vassal Treaties of Esarhaddon," 61–62, ll. 447–48.

25. See Driver and Miles, *Babylonian Laws,* 100–101, l. 74.

26. See Wiseman, "Vassal Treaties of Esarhaddon," 69–70, ll. 534–35.

27. See Ginsberg, *Israelian Heritage,* 105ff.

28. See ibid., 80 n. 96.

29. Ibid., 107, and n. 136.

30. See A. Hurvitz, *A Linguistic Study of the Relationship between the Priestly Source and the Book of Ezekiel,* CRB 20 (1982), 32ff., 92ff., 102–7.

31. Ibid., 94ff., discuss Ezek. 17:13–14. Following Walther Zimmerli, he finds the later verb *'āmad,* "to stand," as a replacement for *qûm,* "to stand," with reference to a covenant. More likely, this rendering by the new JPS translation is correct: "He took one of the seed royal and made a covenant with him . . . and carried away the nobles of the land . . . so that it might be a humble kingdom (*mamlāḵāh*) and not exalt itself, but keep his covenant *and so endure* (*lišmôr b'rîṯô l' 'omdāh*)." The antecedent of *l' 'omdāh,*

literally, "for its standing," is thus *mamlākāh,* "kingdom," not *b'rît,* "covenant," as Hurvitz believes. As for the Piel form, *qiyyēm,* "to fulfill," which is indeed a later form than *hēqîm,* the Hiphil, the single example in Ezek. 13:6 cited by Hurvitz is valid, though not the best example to prove his point.

32. There are many additional instances of Ezekiel's diction in the Epilogue. They are too numerous to cite in detail. One telling example is the adverbial *ya'an ubiya'an,* "all because of," in v. 43. This occurs elsewhere only in Ezek. 13:10 and 36:3.

33. For the hardness of adamant, cf. Ezek. 3:8–9.

34. This study grew out of my work on the commentary to Leviticus which will be published in the Bible Commentary of the JPS under the editorship of Nahum H. Sarna.

2 MAYER I. GRUBER

WOMEN IN THE CULT ACCORDING TO THE PRIESTLY CODE*

Contemporary biblical scholarship comprises two main approaches to the issue of women's participation in the Israelite cult as it is reflected in the Hebrew Scriptures. The first of these approaches, which is exemplified by Clarence J. Vos, Susan T. Foh, and I. J. Peritz, treats the Hebrew Bible as monolithic.[1] The aim of these scholars' common approach is twofold. First, it seeks to catalogue the various biblical texts which can be shown to encourage women's participation in the cult. Second, it seeks to argue that those texts which limit the participation of women in the cult are meant not to discriminate against women but rather to benefit women or to protect the family. The scholars who adopt this approach assume as a matter of course that during the post–Old Testament period, until Christianity came to their rescue, Jewish women suffered a precipitous decline as regards their position in religious life.[2]

The second main approach to the issue of women's participation in the Israelite cult also assumes that the position of women declined in Judaism as it is exemplified by Rabbinic literature. The second approach, which differs from the first approach primarily in its acceptance and utilization of the documentary theory of the Pentateuch, seeks to trace the history of the decline in women's cultic status in the Israelite and Persian periods also. According to this critical approach, the Priestly Code and other postexilic biblical texts severely limited the participation of women in the cult which, it was held, was significantly greater in the period of the Judges and the early monarchy.[3]

This approach should lead us to expect that the law codes of J and E suggest

---

*This article is expanded from a paper presented at the Eleventh Congress of the International Organization for the Study of the Old Testament in Salamanca, Spain, August 1983.

much more extensive participation of women in the cult than is reflected in P. Moreover, if, as the exponents of the critical approach would have us believe, the history of women's participation in the Israelite cult is one of steady decline from the period of Judges and the monarchy to the period of the Talmuds, we should expect that on the issue of women's participation in the cult Deuteronomy should embody a position midway between that of JE and that of P. This is precisely the impression one receives from the standard article, "Women in the Old Testament," in *IDBSup*. There we read as follows: "In Deut. 16:16 only males were designated to observe religious festivals."[4] Wittingly or unwittingly, this standard article does not mention that Deut. 16:16 simply quotes an old law found in JE at Exod. 23:17 and at Exod. 34:23.[5] When Deuteronomy speaks in its own right on the subject of women in the cult, however, it has this to say:

> And Moses instructed them as follows: Every seventh year, the year set for remission, at the Feast of Booths, when *all Israel* comes to appear before the LORD your God in the place which he will choose, you shall read this Teaching aloud in the presence of *all Israel.* Gather the people—men, women, little children,[6] and the strangers in your communities—that they may hear and so learn to revere the LORD your God and to observe faithfully every word of this Teaching. (Deut. 31:10–12)

The article cited remarks concerning this passage and Deut. 12:12, both of which explicitly call for the participation of women in cultic observances,[7] "While not excluded altogether from cultic observances, women were inferior participants obeying rules formulated by men."[8] Since this remark does not appear accurately to describe women's position according to Deut. 31:10–12 and Deut. 12:12, the question arises of whether the critical presentation of P's position vis-à-vis womankind accurately reflects the laws commonly assigned to P.

In P's description of the building of the tabernacle in Exod. 38:8 we read of "the serving women who served at the entrance of the Tent of Meeting." Understandably, Exod. 38:8 is one verse which many of those who insist on the postexilic dating of P are happy to see as a preexilic element in P.[9] Otherwise they would have to reckon with the distinct possibility that postexilic P is the only source of the Pentateuch that specifically mentions women functionaries in the official Israelite cult.[10] That Exod. 38:8 may actually speak of women functionaries in the cult whose activity was similar to that of the Levites of the Book of Numbers finds support in the use of the same verbal root *ṣb'* to describe the service of the Levites in Num. 4:23 and Num. 8:24.[11]

However, in commenting on the other biblical reference to "women serving at the entrance of the tabernacle" at 1 Sam. 2:22,[12] David Qimḥi suggests that the term may designate simply the women who came to the sanctuary to present offerings specifically required of them such as the burnt offering and the sin offering which, according to Lev. 12:6, had to be presented by the mother after childbirth.

> On the completion of her period of purification, for either son or daughter, she shall bring to the priest, at the entrance of the Tent of Meeting, a lamb in its first year for a burnt offering, and a pigeon or a turtledove for a sin offering.[13]

It should be emphasized that this reference to a sacrifice presented specifically by a woman is found in P. Mention should also be made of Lev. 15:29, also P, which speaks of the sin offering and the burnt offering to be presented by a woman who had recovered from an abnormal vaginal discharge.[14]

It should not be surprising that Lev. 12:6 and 15:29 are featured prominently in the writings of scholars who have adopted what I have called the monolithic approach, while they are passed over in silence by those who seek to argue that P has worked to exclude women from cultic observance.[15]

If, as Qimḥi suggests, the women performing an act of divine service at 1 Sam. 2:22 may have been women who came to present sacrifices incumbent upon women, it is equally plausible to suggest that these women, who suffered abuse at the hands of the sons of Eli, may have come to present any of the various kinds of obligatory or free-will offerings which could be presented by men and women on an equal basis (see below). It has already been suggested that the ritual of purification for the recovered leper, described in Leviticus 14, must apply to both men and women since Lev. 13:29 explicitly speaks of "a man or a woman [who] has an infection on the head or in the beard."[16] It ought also to be mentioned that Num. 6:22—again P—explicitly states that a Nazirite vow, which requires an individual to assume for a limited period the purity rules normally observed by an officiating high priest, may be undertaken by a man or a woman.

Caroline M. Breyfogle, however, comments on Num. 6:22 in these words:

> . . . P cannot be accused of any special leaning toward woman. He excludes the women of the priestly families from sharing the meal of the most holy offerings (Lev. 6:18, 29; 7:1, 6; Num. 18:9, 10), and places a lower estimation upon woman in general (Lev. 27:2f.). In consideration of this exaltation of the cult and this growing depreciation of woman, there is every probability that the inclusion of "woman" (Num. 6:1) is due to the fact that she actually did take upon herself the vow of the Nazirite in the early period of the Old Testament.[17]

In view of the widely held belief that the Mishnah elaborates P's anti-feminist tendency,[18] it ought to be pointed out that not only does P alone among biblical sources refer unequivocally to a woman Nazirite, but also that the Mishnah in Nazir 3:6 reports how, partially under the supervision of the School of Hillel, Queen Helene of Adiabene observed a Nazirite vow of many years' duration.[19]

There is no escape from the fact that P singles out women for subordination to men when it endows the father with the authority to annul the vows of his daughter "while in her father's house, *binĕ 'urêāh*, 'in her youth'" (Num. 30:4) and when it endows the husband with the authority to annul the vows of his bride at the time of her marriage (Num. 30:9) and of his wife throughout the duration of the marriage (Num. 30:11–14).[20] Clearly, P does not likewise endow the wife with such authority over her husband's vows nor the mother with such authority over her son's vows.[21] On the other hand, P does reaffirm the independence of the adult single woman to make vows as it reaffirms also her responsibility to fulfill them: "As for the vows of a widow or of a divorcee, whatever she has imposed upon herself shall be incumbent upon her (to fulfill)" (Num. 30:10).[22] Moreover, even the daughter "in her father's house in her youth," the bride, and the married woman are obligated to fulfill all vows they may have imposed upon themselves which father, bridegroom, and husband, respectively, have not annulled, *bĕyôm šomĕ'ô*, "at the time of his hearing" (Num. 30:6, 9, 13).[23]

It should be noted that in the Hebrew Bible vows generally constitute a commitment to present a cultic offering.[24] Hence Numbers 30 makes explicit the role of women in presenting voluntary offerings. Voluntary offerings are discussed in P without explicit reference to women donors at Lev. 7:16–17; Lev. 27; Num. 15:1–10; 29:39; and in H at Lev. 22.[25] The only other explicit references to women's vows in the Hebrew Bible are at Exod. 35:22 (also P), 1 Sam. 1:11 (Hannah's pledging her as-yet-unconceived son to the service of the LORD at Shiloh), Deut. 23:19 (a prostitute's being forbidden to present her *'etnan* "fee for services rendered" "in payment of any vow"), Prov. 7:14 (The strange woman tells the foolish young man that she is free to arrange a liaison with him because "With respect to the peace offerings that were incumbent upon me, today I fulfilled my vows"),[26] and Prov. 31:2 where Lemuel tells us that his mother called him *bar-nĕdārāy,* "son of my vows."[27]

Contrary to the accepted wisdom of modern biblical scholarship, Rabbinic *halakah*—far from seeking to strengthen the apparently misogynic tendency of Numbers 30—seeks to limit the authority of the father and the husband to annul the vows of daughter and wife.[28] Rabbinic *halakah* limits the authority of the father to annul his daughter's vow by interpreting *binĕ'rêāh* "in her youth" at Num. 30:4 to mean that the father's authority to annul his daughter's vows applies only while the daughter is a *na'ărāh.*[29] In Rabbinic Hebrew the latter term designates "a girl between the age of twelve years and a day and twelve years and a half plus one day."[30]

Rabbinic *halakah* limits the authority of the husband to annul his wife's vows to those vows which involve either self-denial or matters of mutual concern to the husband and wife.[31] In other words, Rabbinic *halakah* does not see Numbers 30 as granting the husband any authority to interfere with the wife's ability to commit herself to present voluntary cultic offerings.

Vos notes that "Lev. 4:27 refers to *nepeš 'ahat mē'am hā-āreṣ* ['one soul from among the people of the land'], from which although it is an unusual expression, there is no reason to exclude the feminine sex."[32] I would go further. I would argue that one of the characteristic features of the cultic legislation of P is the use of the neutral, nonsexist expression *nepeš* and *'ādām,* both meaning "person," in referring to cultic acts which can or should be performed by either men or women or to cultic offenses committed by either men or women.[33] Typical of this usage is Lev. 2:1: *wĕnepeš kî-taqrîb qorban minḥāh,* "As for a person, when she shall present a meal offering."[34] Other examples include Lev. 4:2, 27; 5:1, 17 and 21.

If there is any doubt as to whether or not *nepeš* or *'ādām* in Lev. 1:5 is, in fact, neutral language, consideration of Num. 5:5–7 should put it to rest. There we read as follows:

> The LORD spoke to Moses, saying: Speak to the Israelites: When a man or woman commits any wrong toward an *'ādām,* thus breaking faith with the LORD, and that *nepeš* feels guilt, they shall confess their wrong-doing, which they have done, and he shall make restitution in the principal amount, and he shall add one fifth to it, and he shall give it to him whom he has wronged.[35]

If, as we have seen, *'ādām,* like *nepeš,* designates "person," whether male or female, and if, as we have seen, the neutral noun *nepeš* may be followed by an impersonal verb in the third person (*wĕnēšîb,* "he or she shall give"), we can appreciate as brilliantly correct the Rabbinic exegesis of Lev. 1:5 found in Sifra' and reflected in Mishnah Zebaḥim 3:1 and Mishnah Ḥullin 1:1.[36] According to this exegesis, the impersonal verb *wĕšāḥaṭ,* "he or she shall slaughter," is proof that the slaughter of animals both for sacrifice and for purely human consumption is not a priestly function and that it should be performed by women as well as by men.[37] A preexilic precedent for the Rabbinic position on this point is found in 1 Sam. 1:25 where it is said *wayyišḥăṭû,* "They [i.e., Hannah and Elkanah] slaughtered the bull, and they brought the boy [i.e., Samuel] to Eli."[38]

Conceivably, the realization that P's cultic legislation contains nonsexist neutral language may encourage many more scholars to assign passages in P containing *'ādām* and *nepeš* to a preexilic stratum in P.[39] We should note, therefore, that statements in the scholarly literature notwithstanding, the contemplation of women's participation in the cult in postexilic literature is not confined to P. The postexilic Chronicler in 1 Chron. 25:5 speaks of both the fourteen sons and the three daughters of Heman as having played in the temple orchestra in the days of David, while Ezra 2:65 and Neh. 7:67 tell us that both men and women sang apparently at the same time in the temple choir in the Persian period. We should also note the presence of both men and women at the cultic gathering at the water gate described in Nehemiah 8.

It goes without saying that according to all the available sources, including P, men and women were less than equal participants in the cult in ancient

Israel. It is equally clear, however, that P has many more positive possibilities to suggest to us about the place of women in biblical thought than we could possibly learn from the repetition of the standard cliché that P with its laws of purity led to the virtual exclusion of women from the cult.[40] Moreover, P's awkward sentences beginning with *nepeš* and ending with a verb in the impersonal third person should provide encouragement for moderns who struggle to construct nonsexist language.[41] In fact, the use of such language in P confirms the Qoheleth's adage "There is nothing new under the sun" (Qoh. 1:9), as well as that of the Rabbinic sage Ben Bag Bag, who said of the Pentateuch, "Turn it, turn it again . . . it is all in there" (*Mishnah 'Abot* 5:22).

NOTES

1. Clarence J. Vos, *Women in Old Testament Worship* (Delft: Judels & Brinkman, 1968); Susan T. Foh, *Women and the Word of God* (1970; reprinted, Grand Rapids: Baker Book House, 1980); I. J. Peritz, "Woman in the Ancient Hebrew Cult," *JBL* 17 (1898): 111–48. It should not be surprising that studies of women's role in the Hebrew Scriptures stem primarily from two periods, the three decades beginning in 1890, and the period beginning in the mid-1960s. Clearly, the role of women in ancient Israel has been a subject of great concern to scholars, theologians, and believers, especially during those periods when the struggle for women's rights has been a major sociopolitical issue.

2. See Vos, *Women in Old Testament Worship,* 50; Peritz, "Women in the Ancient Hebrew Cult," 114. Foh (*Women and the Word of God*, 90) states, "There is no doubt that Jesus' treatment of women was a radical break with the status quo." Contrast Bernadette J. Brooten, *Women Leaders in the Ancient Synagogue,* Brown Judaic Studies 36 (Chico, Calif.: Scholars Press, 1982), 150: "The inscriptional evidence for Jewish women [synagogue] leaders [in Italy, Asia Minor, Egypt, and Palestine in the period 27 B.C.E.–6th cent. C.E.; there, p.1] means that one cannot declare it to be a departure from Judaism that early Christian women held leadership positions."

3. Friedrich Heiler, *Die Frau in den Religionen der Menschheit* (Berlin: Walter de Gruyter, 1977), 73; Caroline M. Breyfogle, "The Religious Status of Women in the Old Testament," *BW* 35 (1910): 419; Carol M. Meyers, "The Roots of Restriction: Women in Early Israel," *BA* 41 (1978): 91–103; 42 (1979): 6–7; P. A. H. de Boer, *Fatherhood and Motherhood in Israelite and Judean Piety* (Leiden: E. J. Brill, 1974); Leonard Swidler, *Biblical Affirmations of Woman* (Philadelphia: Westminster Press, 1979), 158–59.

4. Phyllis Trible, "Women in the Old Testament," *IDBSup.*, 964; see also Swidler, *Biblical Affirmations of Woman,* 146; Phyllis Bird, "Images of Women in the Old Testament," in *Religion and Sexism,* ed. Rosemary Radford Reuther (New York: Simon & Schuster, 1974), 54.

5. S. R. Driver, *A Critical and Exegetical Commentary on Deuteronomy,* ICC, 3d ed. (Edinburgh: T. & T. Clark, 1902), 198; G. Ernest Wright, "The Book of Deuteronomy," *IB,* 12 vols. (New York & Nashville: Abingdon Press, 1953) 2:435. George Adam Smith (*The Book of Deuteronomy,* CBSC [Cambridge: Cambridge Univ. Press, 1918], 214) argues "That only *males* are mentioned here, while vv. 11, 14 include among the worshippers *daughters, bondwomen* and *widows,* is no proof that this summary [v. 16] is from another hand than the three preceding laws (Steuern.). It is the same author but he is quoting the older law. In contrast with its confinement of the law

to *males* D's inclusion of women is characteristic; see on v. 21." Similarly, Gerhard von Rad, *Deuteronomy,* trans. Dorothea Barton, OTL (Philadelphia: Westminster Press, 1966), 113. See also John H. Otwell, *And Sarah Laughed* (Philadelphia: Westminster Press, 1977), 154–55. Peter C. Craigie, in *The Book of Deuteronomy,* NICOT (London: Hodder & Stoughton, 1976), 246, notes "All your males—these words seem to indicate the minimum requirement of the law, though it is clear from the preceding verses (particularly vv. 11, 14) that others could also attend the three annual feasts at the sanctuary of the Lord." Moshe Weinfeld, *Deuteronomy and the Deuteronomic School* (Oxford: Clarendon Press, 1972), explains that "according to the BC [= Book of the Covenant] law [i.e., Exod. 23:17] only males are obliged to make the pilgrimage to 'behold' the face of the Lord, whereas the author of Deuteronomy, who is familiar with this law and even cites it on one occasion (16:16), has extended its application to all members of the Israelite household, male and female alike (16:11 and 12)" (pp. 291–92). First Sam. 1:21–22 suggests that Elkanah was surprised by Hannah's decision to absent herself from the periodic festival and that Hannah found it necessary to justify her absence. Note that her rationale for absenting herself is not the dispensability of women in the cult but her contention that nursing her baby must take precedence over her participation in the cultic celebration. Martin Noth suggested that the laws of the Covenant Code emanate from the very period represented by the narrative contained in 1 Samuel 1. See Martin Noth, *The History of Israel,* trans. Stanley Godman (London: A. & C. Black, 1958), 103–4. It is conceivable, therefore, that the Covenant Code's restriction to males of the obligation (but not the right) to appear three times a year at the shrine may reflect the canonization of the legal precedent established by Hannah and approved by Elkanah at 1 Sam. 1:21–23. It is reasonable to assume that this provision may have been misconstrued as a law excluding women from the cult (so, for example, E. B. Cross, *The Hebrew Family* [Chicago: Univ. of Chicago Press, 1927], 49). Deuteronomy seems to have found a way to ensure that men could not deny women the best of both their worlds—nursing their babies and participating in the cult. By insisting in Deut. 31:12 that "men, women, and little children" assemble for the septennial reading of the Torah, D obviates the very real danger that a woman will be prevented from attending because she is in some hidden place nursing her baby. No man need ask "Why does she bring her noisy baby to the Temple?" D's Torah has already informed him that she brings the nursing baby because God commands the baby herself to be present. That later generations were perplexed as to why the baby is so commanded is reflected in Rashi's comment ad loc.: "'The little children'. Why should [the little children] come? [The answer is that they should come] in order to [give God a pretext to] reward those who bring them [the little children]"; cf. *Devarim Rabbah* ad loc. Menahem Haran, *Temples and Temple-Service in Ancient Israel* (Oxford: Clarendon Press, 1978), 304–7, argues that the pilgrimages of Exod. 23:17 = Exod. 34:23 = Deut. 16:16 are not to be compared with those of 1 Samuel 1. The former are obligatory, public, and thrice yearly. The latter are voluntary, private, and annual. On the other hand, Haran contends the absence in P of "the ancient rule that the obligation to appear before Yahweh is incumbent only on males," reflects P's taking it "for granted that the entire family participates in the feast-pilgrimage" (p. 293). Moreover, he argues that "even J and E admit indirectly that whole families take part in the *ḥaggîm*" (p. 294; see also pp. 293, 300, 302). In fact, at Exod. 10:8–11, J intimates that the cultic dispensability of women is a characteristically Gentile attitude!

6. Heb. *wĕhaṭṭap.* Note that Num. 16:27; 2 Chron. 20:13 and 31:18 all distinguish between *bĕnêhem,* "their children," and *ṭappām,* "their babies." (See dictionaries.)

7. See also Deut. 12:18; 16:11 and 14; 29:10 and 17; see Weinfeld, *Deuteronomy and the Deuteronomic School,* 291.

8. Trible, "Women in the Old Testament," 964.

9. Peritz, "Women in the Ancient Hebrew Cult," 146; Bird, "Images of Women in the Old Testament," 68; de Boer, *Fatherhood and Motherhood,* 29. Contrast Paul Heinisch, *Das Buch Exodus,* HAT (Bonn: Hanstein, 1934), 254: "Ein Glossator dachte nun, wie in späterer Zeit, so hätten schon am mosaischen Heiligtum Frauen sich durch Ubernahme entsprechendes Arbeiten nutzlich gemacht, durch Putzen, Waschen der Priesterkleidung, Ausbessern der verschiedenen Gewebe, sie hatten vielleicht auch beim Gottesdienst gesungen. . . ." On the other hand, Brevard S. Childs (*The Book of Exodus* [Philadelphia: Westminster Press, 1974], 636) states, "There is insufficient evidence to decide whether older historical material is involved or later midrashic exegesis. The literary form would favor the first alternative." In *Exodus* (NCBC [rev. ed.; Grand Rapids: Wm. B. Eerdmans, 1980], 330) J. P. Hyatt does not even consider the possibility that the cultic functionaries in question existed prior to the period of the Second Temple. He surmises that if indeed such women existed in the Second Temple, their function may have been "prostitution as 1 Sam. 2:22 seems to imply, and the mention of the mirrors [Exod. 38:8] may suggest." In fact, the only basis for Hyatt's surmise that the women in question were prostitutes is the allegation in 1 Sam. 2:22 that having intercourse with them was one of the crimes of the sons of Eli which caused the priesthood to be taken away from their family. Hyatt's reasoning is similar to that of the male chauvinist judge and jury who assume that every rape victim is a whore. If 1 Sam. 2:22 proves that the cultic functionaries in question were prostitutes, then 1 Sam. 2:11–17 must prove that a characteristic obligation of the priesthood was to commit sacrilege. In fact, just as 1 Sam. 2:11–17 alleges that sacrilege was one of the crimes of the sons of Eli, so does 1 Sam. 2:22–23 allege that sexual harassment of women in the workplace was another of their offenses.

10. In his "La femme dans l'ancien Israel" (*Histoire mondiale de la femme: pré-histoire et antiquité,* ed. Peter Grimal [Paris: Nouvelle Librairie de France, 1965], 247) Jean Bottero mentions only the prophetess and the necromancer (Exod. 15:2; Judges 4:4; Isa. 8:3). That the latter cannot be called a functionary of the official Israelite cult is demonstrated, *inter alia,* by Lev. 19:31; Deut. 18:11; 1 Sam. 28:3; and 1 Chron. 10:13. On the possibility that the prophetess may have been a cultic functionary, see Gerhard von Rad, *The Message of the Prophets* (New York: Harper & Row, 1965), 32. He notes ". . . that women are quite naturally spoken of as prophets (Exod. 15.20; II Kings 22.14; Neh. 6.14), whereas the idea of women priests was quite inconceivable, rather militates against the thesis of cultic prophets." Against the idea that the *gĕdēšāh,* the prostitute, is a cultic functionary, see my "The *gādēš* in the Book of Kings and in Other Sources," *Tarbiz* 52 (1983): 173–76 (in Hebrew); contrast Baruch A. Levine, "Priests," *IDBSup.,* 688.

11. S. R. Driver, *The Book of Exodus,* CBSC (Cambridge: Cambridge Univ. Press, 1911), 391. In *Das Buch Exodus* ([Graz and Vienna: Styria, 1911], 342) Johann Weiss follows Ernst Friedrich Karl Rosenmüller, Karl Friedrich Keil, and George Rawlinson in surmising that the expression refers to "weibliche Handarbeiten (Waschen, Nähen, Weben, Scheuern, etc.)."

12. P. Kyle McCarter (*1 Samuel,* AB, 8 [Garden City, N.Y.: Doubleday & Co., 1980]) argues from the absence of this clause in both 4QSam[a] and Codex Vaticanus of LXX (but not from the Lucianic Recension of LXX) that the clause "and that they were having intercourse with the women serving at the entrance of the tabernacle" is an interpolation in MT (p. 81). Moreover, he notes that the alleged interpolation "is couched in the technical terminology of the priestly legislation of the Tetrateuch," and he suggests that it "may have arisen from an annotation by a postexilic scholar." So already Henry Preserved Smith following Wellhausen, August Klostermann, Driver,

and K. Budde in *A Critical and Exegetical Commentary on the Books of Samuel,* ICC (Edinburgh: T. & T. Clark, 1899), 20.

13. In his *Leviticus* (trans. J. E. Anderson, OTL [Philadelphia: Westminster Press, 1965]) Martin Noth remarks, "It is part and parcel of the subject-matter, but all the same remarkable, that in this case the woman herself, and not her husband, appears with an offering" (p. 98). Noth's sense of radical amazement seems not to be shared by the allegedly misogynic Hebrew exegetical tradition. Noth states unequivocally (p. 95) that "the cultic inferiority of the female sex is expressed in giving the female birth a double 'uncleanness' effect" (see v. 5). As noted already in *m. Yadayim* 4:6 and *t. Yadayim* 2:19, greater defilement is not necessarily an indication of lesser social worth. Hence, a corpse defiles more than a dead pig, the latter more than a dead frog. David I. Macht points out ("A Scientific Appreciation of Leviticus 12:1–5," JBL 52 [1933]: 254–55) that a distinction in the length of the period of impurity of the mother after the birth of a girl or a boy respectively is attested in many places in the ancient and modern world. In some cultures, he points out, it is the birth of a boy which is followed by the relatively longer period of impurity. An up-to-date, objective, crosscultural study of this issue is clearly in order.

14. The identical offering—two turtledoves or two pigeons—is to be presented also by a male who recovers from an abnormal genital discharge. So Lev. 15:14.

15. Foh, *Women and the Word of God,* 83; Vos, *Women in Old Testament Worship,* 77–79; so also Otwell, *And Sarah Laughed,* 167; cf. S. Terrien, "The Omphalos Myth and Hebrew Religion," *VT* 20 (1970): 337; Trible, "Women in the Old Testament," 964 (she ignores Lev. 15:29, while she refers to Lev. 12:16 as follows: "At the end of her purification, the mother herself sought atonement through the male priest of the local sanctuary").

16. So NJPS. Vos (*Women in Old Testament Worship,* 77–79) applies the ritual to men and women; David Marcus ("The Term 'Chin' in the Semitic Languages," *BASOR* 226 [1977]: 54–55) argues that the term *zāqān* here means "beard" rather than "chin" because (1) Biblical Hebrew has no term for "chin"; (2) the entire section—Lev. 13:29–37—deals with the recognition of leprous afflictions of the hair, Heb. *neteq;* and (3) the ancient Versions render *zāqān* here by words meaning "beard." As pointed out by Marcus and by S. E. Loewenstamm ("Did the Goddess Anath wear a beard and side-whiskers?" *Israel Oriental Studies* 4 [1974]: 1–3), the Ugaritic cognate *dqn* does indeed denote "chin" as well as "beard." The key passage for the former meaning is *CTA,* 6 I:3, *thdy lḥm w dqn*, "She (Anath) lacerates (her) two cheeks and chin."

17. Breyfogle, "Religious Status of Women," 411; an example would be the mother of Samson; so L. Elliott Binns, *The Book of Numbers,* WC (London: Methuen & Co., 1927), 37; contrast Robert G. Boling, *Judges,* AB 6A (Garden City, N.Y.: Doubleday & Co., 1975), 219 n. 4.

18. Breyfogle, "Religious Status of Women," 419; Foh, *Women and the Word of God,* 90–91.

19. On the text and its parallels in Josephus and elsewhere, see Lawrence H. Schiffman, "Proselytism in the Writings of Josephus: Izates of Adiabene in Light of the Halakha," in *Josephus Flavius: Historian of Eretz-Israel in the Hellenistic-Roman Period,* ed. Uriel Rappaport (Jerusalem: Yad Izhak Ben Zvi, 1982), 253–54 (in Hebrew). It has been suggested that Berenice's vow referred to in Josephus *War* II. 15:1 was one of Naziriteship; see George Buchanan Gray, *Numbers,* ICC (Edinburgh: T. & T. Clark, 1903), 61; Binns, *Book of Numbers,* 37.

20. As for the assumption that Rabbinic *halakah* continues the alleged misogynic tendency of P, see, with reference to the relationship of Mishnah Nedarim to Num. 30:1–6, Jacob Neusner's *A History of the Mishnaic Law of Women, pt. 3: Nedarim,*

Nazir: Translation and Explanation, SJLA 33 (Leiden: E. J. Brill, 1980), 7–8: "From Scripture's perspective, we need hardly wonder why Nedarim is located where it is, since the important aspect of the topic—the father's or husband's right to abrogate or confirm the vows of a daughter or a wife—absolutely requires placing a tractate on vows in the context of women's law. Indeed, what we now appreciate is an amazing shift in the treatment of the topic. For Mishnah, while conceding that there is a special aspect of vows relevant to women, reconsiders the law in a neutral, non-sexual framework: vows taken by man or woman, and what we must know about them."

21. M. Haran ("Neder," *EM* 5:788 [in Hebrew]) surmises that the father could also annul the vows of his son. Moreover, assuming that "his vow" in 1 Sam. 1:21 is identical with the vow of Hannah (v. 11), Haran explains that Hannah's vow is called "his," i.e., Elkanah's, vow because Elkanah assented to it. Haran appears to suggest that Elkanah had the authority either to assent or to annul Hannah's vow. If so, Numbers 30's apparently misogynic tendency is not an innovation of P but simply the reaffirmation of an old law from the pre-monarchic period. Note, however, that in general Haran insists on an early date for materials found in P. See Haran, *Temples and Temple-Service,* 3–12, 146–48, and passim.

22. *M. Nedarim* 11:10 enumerates nine additional categories of women whose vows can be annulled neither by their fathers nor by their husbands. As explained in *Tg. J.* ad loc., the Mishnah's nine categories can be summarized as follows: (1) adult single woman; (2) a *naʿărāh* whose father has died; and (3) a *naʿărāh* who was married and then widowed or divorced. Cf. *b. Nedarim* 89b.

23. *M. Nedarim* 10:8 defines *bĕyôm šomĕʿô* "on the day of his hearing" to mean a full calendar day from nightfall to nightfall rather than any period of twenty-four hours' duration. So Maimonides, *Mishneh Torah, Laws of Vows* 12:15, and Joseph Qaro, *Shulḥan ʿAruk, Yoreh deʿah* 234:21. For other views see *b. Nedarim* 76b–77a.

24. See G. Henton Davies, "Vows," *IDB* 4:792–93.

25. Voluntary offerings are discussed in D at Deut. 12:6, 11, 26, and 23:22. There is no discussion of the voluntary offering in the law codes of J and E, hence there is no basis for comparing P's treatment of women in Numbers 30 with their treatment in JE.

26. In his *In the Presence of the Lord* (SJLA 6 [Leiden: E. J. Brill, 1974], 18–45) Baruch A. Levine has shown that *šĕlāmîm,* traditionally rendered "peace offerings," should properly be rendered "gifts of greeting." Cf. pp. 42–43.

27. R. B. Y. Scott explains in *Proverbs-Ecclesiastes* (AB 18 [Garden City, N.Y.: Doubleday & Co., 1965], 184), "a son in anticipation of whose birth the mother had made vows; cf. I Sam i 11, 27." Note the Aramaism *bar-nĕdārāy* rather than classical Hebrew's *ben-nĕdārāy.* The Aramaism, a sign of late Hebrew, suggests that the pervasive influence of P in the postexilic period did not inhibit the king's mother from undertaking the vow. On the provenance of Prov. 31:1–9 see N. H. Tur-Sinai, *Mišlê Šĕlomoh* (Tel Aviv: Yavne, 1947), 3–4; Charles T. Fritsch, "The Book of Proverbs," *IB,* 4:775. As noted by Haran, "Neder," 790, late Heb. *bar-nĕdārāy* is an echo of Ugar. *bn ndr* in *UT* 144:4. Still later we read in *t. ʿArakin* 3:1: "The mother of Rimaṭyah, whose daughter was sick, said, 'If my daughter recover from her illness, I shall give [to the Temple] her weight in gold'. She [the daughter] recovered from her illness. She [the mother] went up to Jerusalem, and she weighed her in gold." As we see from *m. ʿArakin* 5:1, the final clause means that indeed the mother weighed out a quantity of gold equal to her daughter's weight, and this the mother presented to the Temple.

28. See above, nn. 18 and 19.

29. Maimonides, *Mishneh Torah, Laws of Vows,* 11:6–7; Joseph Qaro, *Shulḥan ʿAruk, Yoreh Deʿah* 234:1.

30. H. Freedman, *Nedarim Translated into English with Notes, Glossary, and Indices,*

The Babylonian Talmud, ed. I. Epstein (London: Soncino Press, 1936), 289.

31. Self-denial: *t. Nedarim* 7:1. According to *Siphre d'Be Rab* (ed. H. S. Horovitz [Leipzig: Gustav Fock, 1907] 206, ll. 7–9), this qualification is inspired by Num. 30:14, "Every vow and every sworn obligation of self-denial may be upheld by her husband or annulled by her husband." The rendering of the verse is taken from NJV. Mutual concern: *t. Nedarim* 7:1. According to *Siphre d'Be Rab* (p. 206, ll. 10–11), this qualification is inspired by Num. 30:17: "Those are the laws that the LORD enjoined upon Moses as between a man and his wife. . . ." The rendering of the verse is taken from NJV.

32. Vos, *Women in Old Testament Worship,* 79. Otwell (*And Sarah Laughed,* 206) attributes to Vos the view that *'ādām* and *nepeš* in Leviticus 1—11 "have a generic force and mean mankind." Otwell himself remarks, "Even without accepting this, we have ample evidence that women regularly brought sacrifices."

33. See Charles A. Briggs, "The Use of *nepeš* in the Old Testament," *JBL* 16 (1897): 24. He notes that the noun *nepeš* is attested in the meaning "person, anyone" twice in Deuteronomy (Deut. 24:7; 27:25), four times in Ezekiel (Ezek. 18:4 [three times]; 33:6), once in Proverbs (Prov. 28:17), and elsewhere only in H (seven times: Lev. 17:10, 12, 15; 20:6 [twice]; 22:6–11) and in P (twenty-nine times: Lev. 2:1; 4:2, 27; 5:1, 2, 4, 15, 17, 21; 7:18, 20, 21, 25, 27; 23:29, 30 [twice]; Num. 5:6; 15:27, 30; 19:22; 31:19, 28; 35:11, 15, 30 [twice]; Josh. 20:3–9). Briggs lists separately the occurrences of the expression "that person shall be cut off from her people," which is used only in P (Gen. 17:14; Exod. 12:15, 19; 31:14; Lev. 20:21, 27; Num. 9:13; 15:30–31; 19:13, 20) and in H (Lev. 19:8; 22:8). Briggs points out that the use of *nepeš* to mean "person" "is especially characteristic of H, P, and writers related to them." See now also C. Westermann, "*naefaeš* Seele," *THAT* 2 (1976): 90.

If proof be needed that P employs *'ādām* to mean "human being of either sex," such proof is available in the very first chapter of the Hebrew Bible in Gen. 1:27: "God created the human being . . . He created them male and female." From this verse, Janice Nunnally-Cox has drawn the conclusion that it is P's account of the creation of man and woman which is nonsexist (*Foremothers: Women of the Bible* [New York: Seabury Press, 1981], xiv. This inescapable conclusion, which flies in the face of the conventional wisdom concerning the role of postexilic P in promoting misogyny (see Trible, "Women in the Old Testament," 966), led Norman K. Gottwald to suggest that Gen. 1:1—2:3 may be "a foreign element in the P tradition" (*The Tribes of Yahweh* [Maryknoll, N.Y.: Orbis Books, 1979], 796–97). On Gen. 1:27, see Phyllis A. Bird, "'Male and Female He Created Them': Gen. 1:27b in the context of the Priestly Account of Creation," *HTR* 74 (1981): 129–51. Note that Bird's interpretation of *bĕṣelem 'ĕlōhîm* (pp. 137–45) has recently been confirmed by Jeffrey H. Tigay, "The Image of God and the Flood," in *Studies in Jewish Education and Judaism,* ed. Alexander M. Shapiro and Burton I. Cohen (New York: Ktav, 1983), 169–82. On *'ādām* as a generic term referring to human beings of both sexes, see Bird, "Images of Women in the Old Testament," 49, 72–73.

34. R. K. Harrison, in *Leviticus* (TOTC [Leicester: Inter-Varsity Press, 1980]), remarks, "The feminine gender of the noun here is purely coincidental, and in no way conflicts with or contradicts subsequent masculine terminology in the verse" (p. 49).

35. For the rendering "feels guilt" see Jacob Milgrom, *Cult and Conscience: The Asham and the Priestly Doctrine of Repentance,* SJLA 18 (Leiden: E. J. Brill, 1976), 10.

36. P's employment of both *nepeš* and *'ādām* in the sense "person" forces us to reject the following suggestion made by Edward L. Greenstein in his stimulating "Theories of Modern Bible Translation," *Prooftexts* 3 (1983): 14: "The concept of 'person', devoid of connotations of gender, may not have been part of ancient Israel's mindset. . . ." We

must likewise reject his contention that the language of the Hebrew Bible is male-oriented. The demonstration that biblical Heb. *bānîm* and *'ābôt* can mean "children" and "parents" (sons and/or daughters and fathers and/or mothers), respectively (Harry M. Orlinsky, "Male-Oriented Language in the New Bible Translations," SBL Annual Meeting, New Orleans, November 1978), is confirmed also for Mishnaic Hebrew at *m. Qiddushin* 1:7 with respect to *bēn,* "child," and *'ab,* "parent," at *b. Qiddushin* 29a and 30b. Greenstein rejects it out of hand.

37. Harrison renders, "The bull is then slaughtered (Heb. *šāhaṭ*), a common technical term . . ." (p. 45). He does not say by whom it is then slaughtered.

B. Zebaḥim 32a explains that the intent of *m. Zebaḥim* 3:1 is not to permit sacrifices slaughtered by women only after the fact but to declare it fully in order that women should slaughter animals for sacrifice. Tosafot to *b. Ḥullin* 2a point out that since women should slaughter animals for sacrifice according to *m. Zebaḥim* 3:1, *a fortiori* women are included in the generalization "All should slaughter" with respect to nonsacrificial slaughtering at *m. Ḥullin* 1:1. The view of Tosafot is reconfirmed by Jacob ben Asher (d. 1340 C.E.) in Ṭur, Yoreh De'ah 1, and by Joseph Qaro (1488–1575 C.E.) in his commentary, Beth Joseph. Qaro argues against the assertion of Jacob Landau (fifteenth century C.E.) in his *Sepher ha-Agur* that slaughtering of animals by women is forbidden "because I have never seen it." Clearly, what bothered Jacob Landau was that in his native Germany he had never seen women slaughtering animals. Hence, he reacted negatively to the fact that in Italy women did serve as ritual slaughterers. Qaro argued that "I have never seen it" is not a valid argument against anything. For extensive bibliography on women serving as ritual slaughterers among the Jews of Renaissance Italy see Cecil Roth, *The Jews in the Renaissance* (Philadelphia: Jewish Publication Society, 1969), 344. Alexander Rofé has pointed out to me that women continued to practice ritual slaughter among the Jews of Italy into the twentieth century. In *The Woman in the Perspective of Judaism* (Tel Aviv: Jezreel, 1953), 134 (in Hebrew), Shlomo Ashkenazi presents extensive documentation concerning Jewish women performing ritual slaughter in various parts of Europe in the sixteenth and seventeenth centuries.

For a preexilic precedent at least for secular slaughter, if not for sacral slaughter by a woman, see 1 Sam. 28:24: *wattĕmaher wattizbāḥēhû,* "She hurried to slaughter it." In view of 1 Sam. 1:25 and 28:24, as well as the materials discussed in n. 40, Vos's suggestion that women did not function as priestesses in ancient Israel because "it would be difficult to conceive of a woman's . . . slaughtering . . . sizeable animals" is to be rejected on two counts: (1) Slaughtering was not a priestly function; (2) Israelite and Jewish women, and many other women throughout the world, have been known to slaughter all kinds of animals (*Women in Old Testament Worship,* 193). Vos's line of reasoning was anticipated by Elizabeth Mary MacDonald in *The Position of Women as Reflected in Semitic Codes of Law* (Toronto: Univ. of Toronto Press, 1931): "Even if woman's ritual uncleanness had not excluded her from the office, she was by nature excluded from the sacrificing priesthood. The slaughtering of animals is contrary to her nature, and in the period when sacrifice was less formal and offered at a family altar, the act was performed by the man" (p. 268). See also O. J. Baab, "Woman," *IDB* 4:865. Ilse Seibert demonstrates the fallaciousness of this line of reasoning by the numerous pictorial illustrations of women engaging in sacrifice from all over the ancient Near East which she includes in her book *Women in the Ancient Near East* (trans. Marianne Herzfeld [Leipzig: Edition Leipzig, 1947]). For discussion of textual references to women slaughtering sacrifices in ARM 10, see Bernard Frank Botto, *Studies on Women at Mari* (Baltimore and London: Johns Hopkins Press, 1974), 128–29.

38. Otwell, ignoring the syntax, which requires that those who "brought the boy"

were also those who "slaughtered the bull," remarks, "Presumably the personnel of the shrine killed the bull" (*And Sarah Laughed,* 167). Contrast Rashi's comment ad loc.: "He [Samuel] rendered them a legal decision that the slaughtering of animals for sacrifice may be performed by non-priests. . . ." The latter comment is based on a midrash attributed to R. Eliezer [b. Pedath] at *b. Berakot* 31b. Contrast Bird, "Images of Women in the Old Testament," 81 n. 34.

39. See n. 33 para. 2.

40. Terrien, "Omphalos Myths," 337; Trible, "Women in the Old Testament," 964–66. Moshe Weinfeld, "Pentateuch," *EncJud* 13:240, argues that "increasing information about the cult of the peoples of the Ancient Near East corroborate" Yehezkel Kaufmann's contention "that it is impossible to explain the development of P against the background of the Second Temple period." In support of this contention Weinfeld (p. 241) notes that "there are allusions to laws of purity and impurity in the literature of the Monarchy (I Sam. 21:6; II Sam. 11:4; II Kings 7:3; Hos. 9:9). In addition, it is known that these laws were carefully observed by all the peoples of the Ancient Near East." Weinfeld refers to a Hittite text from the thirteenth century B.C.E. and an Assyrian text dated to the period 1324–1074 B.C.E. Seibert cites these same texts (*Women in the Ancient Near East,* 40). The relevant passage from the Hittite text, *KUB* 13, 4, is rendered as follows by A. Goetze in "Instructions for Temple Officials," in *ANET,* 209, ll 74–83: "Whoever sleeps with a woman, if his superior (or) his chief constrains (him), he shall say so. If he himself does not dare tell him, he shall tell his fellow servant and shall bathe anyway. But if he knowingly postpones it and without having bathed approaches the gods' sacrificial loaves (and) libation bowl in an unclean condition, or (if) his fellow servant knows about him—namely that he placed himself first—but nevertheless conceals it, (if) afterward it becomes known, they are liable to the capital penalty; both of them shall be killed." The Assyrian text is found in Ernst Weidner's "Hof- and Harems-Erlasse assyrischer Könige aus dem 2. Jahrtausend v. Chr," *AfO* 17 (1954–56): 276, ll 46–47: *sinniltu ša ekallim ša lā qarabšani ana pān šarri lā terrab,* "As for a woman of thc harem for whom intercourse is forbidden (because she is menstruating), she may not come into the presence of the King"; cf. *CAD* Q, 233b. Like Weinfeld, Bird does not assign the origin of the cultic impurity of the menstruating woman to P ("Images of Women in the Old Testament," 54). Indeed, like Weinfeld, she sees this as a common characteristic of "Israelite religion, following widespread ancient practice." Tikva Frymer-Kensky ("Pollution, Purification, and Purgation in Biblical Israel" in *the Word of the Lord Shall Go Forth: Essays in Honor of David Noel Freedman,* ed. Carol L. Meyers and M. O'Connor [Winona Lake, Ind.: ASOR and Eisenbrauns, 1983], 399–414) likewise takes it for granted that "the ideas of pollution, purity, and purification [reflected in the legislation of P and H] were fundamental concepts of biblical Israel." Bird ("Images of Women in the Old Testament") surmises that "the frequent and regular recurrence of this cultically proscribed state in women of childbearing age must have seriously affected their ability to function in the cult" (p. 54). Judith Ochshorn argues a similar case in *The Female Experience and the Nature of the Divine* (Bloomington: Indiana Univ. Press, 1981), 229–30. It has been pointed out by Robin Marantz Henig, however, that "Menstruation as we know it today is largely a product of contraception and of an increase in the number of childbearing years. Until this century, most women spent the years between their first menses around the age of 14 and their menopause at age 35 or 40 either pregnant or breastfeeding. Today, improved nutrition and health care have pushed the onset of first menses earlier, to about age 12, and delayed menopause until about age 50. Over the course of her life, the average healthy woman now spends a total of nearly seven years menstruating" ("Dispelling Menstrual Myths," *New York Times Magazine,* 7 March

1982, 65). It has been scientifically demonstrated that if a mother nurses her baby and does not provide supplementary bottles or solid food, the return of the menses may be delayed for a period of time ranging from ten to fourteen months following her giving birth. See Derrick B. Jelliffe and E. F. Patrice Jelliffe, *Human Milk in the Modern World* (Oxford: Clarendon Press, 1978), 117–24. R. V. Short ("Breast Feeding," *Scientific American* 250, no. 4, April 1984, 23–29) reports that in contemporary Bangladesh, mean lactational amenorrhea (i.e., suppression of the menses as a consequence of nursing) is eighteen and one-half months. Evidence that prolonged nursing (by modern American or Israeli standards) was taken for granted in ancient Israel is supplied by Isa. 28:9–10, according to which ancient Israelites nursed their children until the latter were ready to learn the alphabet. See Aaron Demsky, "A Proto-Canaanite Abecedary," *Tel Aviv* 4 (1977): 16. Additional evidence for prolonged nursing is contained in Isa. 7:15 (see commentaries), 1 Sam. 1:22–24 (so C. U. Woolf, "Nurse," *IDB* 3:572), and for a later period, 2 Macc. 7:27: "My son, have pity on me. I carried you nine months in my womb, and nursed you for three years. . . ." The rendering of the last citation is taken from RSV.

41. A most lucid survey of this subject with extensive bibliography is provided by Mary Ritchie Key, *Male/Female Language* (Metuchen, N.J.: Scarecrow Press, 1975).

3 JACOB MILGROM

THE STRUCTURES OF NUMBERS: CHAPTERS 11—12 AND 13—14 AND THEIR REDACTION. PRELIMINARY GROPINGS

In Honor of Robert Gordis

Structural analysis is a new discipline in literary criticism pioneered primarily in France, and it has been applied with measurable success to biblical narrative.[1] Yet even though there is a group of structuralists who read papers at every annual meeting of the Society of Biblical Literature, they have a small constituency only, and their influence is slight. Biblical scholarship in Israel also registers an impulse toward structural analysis. This is generated in particular through Meir Weiss and his students.[2] But here again one can hardly detect any impact on other colleagues.[3] As for Germany and England, the two other major centers of biblical scholarship, there structural analysis is virtually ignored. It is my intention to demonstrate that this new discipline is indispensable to a proper understanding of biblical narrative. To support my thesis I have chosen to look closely at the narratives of Numbers, chapters 11—14.

The question asked by this paper would not have sounded alien to the medieval Jewish exegetes. To be sure, their theological presuppositions would not have allowed them to think in terms of redactional history; however, their very assumption that the received text was an organic unity forced them to be on the lookout for connective and associative links both between pericopes and within them. Thus, even though the principle of redaction was non-existent for them, the medieval exegetes were alert to the problem of structure. So their findings, though rudimentary, are invaluable.

THE STRUCTURE OF CHAPTERS 11—12

These two chapters comprise three units of complaints. First, at Taberah, Israel complains about the forced march (11:1–3).[4] Second, Israel then complains at Kibroth-hattaavah about meat. This complaint is intertwined with Moses' worries concerning his burden of leadership (11:4–34). Finally, backed by Aaron, Miriam complains at Hazeroth about Moses' monopoly of the leadership (12:1–15). The stylistic and thematic interrelation of these complaints reveals their structural unity. This can be demonstrated by the common pattern of topical progression (a–f) undergirding the first and last complaints, which frame the two chapters as an inclusion.

Complaint I. Taberah (11:1–3)		*Complaint III. Hazeroth (12:1–15)*	
a.	People complain 1a	a′.	Miriam and Aaron complain 1–2a
b.	God hears, fumes, punishes 1b	b′.	God hears, fumes, punishes 2b, 4–5, 9–10
c.	People appeal to Moses 2a	c′.	Aaron appeals to Moses 11–12
d.	Moses intercedes 2bα	d′.	Moses intercedes 13
e.	Appeal answered 2bβ	e′.	Appeal answered 14
f.	March delayed —	f′.	March delayed 15

The last component, the nature of the punishment, requires a word of explanation. Not only are the guilty punished (Miriam in 12:9–10 and the camp's edge [or leaders?] in 11:1), but the entire people suffer the consequence by having their journey delayed (seven days in the case of Miriam, as the text makes explicit [12:15], and an unspecified period at Taberah). The very fact that there is no travel notice between Taberah and Kibroth-hattaavah, as would normally be expected at the end of 11:3, means that for the redactor the two sites are identical. This is confirmed by the list of stations in chapter 33. There, Kibroth-hattaavah is listed, but Taberah is omitted (33:16). (Deuteronomy 9:22 represents a different tradition.) Also, the brief aside on Moses' uniqueness in chapter 12 comprises an editorial comment and a poetic insert (12:3 and 12:6–8).

The middle unit, Complaint II, is itself a conflation of two complaints. Israel complains about meat and Moses about leadership (11:4–35). The two complaints may originally have been discrete, but they have been intertwined to create the impression that the grumbling of the people triggered an equivalent response from Moses (e.g., vv. 11–15). Instead of interceding for the people and attempting to stay God's wrath, he actually adds his complaint to theirs. In the long list of instances where Moses acts as Israel's defender before the Lord, this pericope stands out as the lone exception. Elsewhere Moses' intercessions are of the following two types: whenever God announces a punishment beforehand, Moses tries to abort it;[5] however, when God punishes without warning (only, it should be noted, in those incidents where the people defy God directly), Moses can only try to mitigate the punishment.[6]

There are three ostensible anomalies. First, God punishes Miriam and Aaron without first notifying Moses, and all Moses can do is to ask for mitigation (chap. 12; see Moses' second type of intercession, above). Yet the sinners have attacked not God but Moses. Here, the reason for God's punitive actions is patently clear. Miriam and Aaron contest Moses' leadership and God punishes them to vindicate Moses. Indeed, that Moses does not intercede in his own behalf leads the redactor to comment, "Moses was a very humble man" (12:3). The second anomaly involves the rebellion of Dathan and Abiram (in distinction to the rebellion of Korah [Numbers 16]). Moses does not intercede to avert or mitigate their punishment. On the contrary, he not only requests punishment but even specifies its form (16:28–30). Yet here too the punishment serves as Moses' vindication. Furthermore, it authenticates his leadership by springing from his own initiative.

However, the third anomaly, the Kibroth-hattaavah episode (11:4–34), truly is an exception. Here God's wrath against Israel (10) is not followed by Moses' intercession but by his personal complaint (11–15) climaxed by his doubts concerning God's powers (21–22). Indeed, it is Moses' failure to "stand in the breach" (cf. Ezek. 22:30; Ps. 106:23) that explains why the story of the elders is interwoven with the story of the quails—Moses must be punished. As is clear from the Deuteronomic parallels (Deut. 1:12), Moses had requested human help to ease his leadership burden. But in this pericope, his plea for assistance (11–13) is inserted into the people's demand for meat (4–9, 13), thus showing that he expected his assistance to come from God. Evidently, the fusion of these two stories is an attempt to demonstrate that Moses was punished by the diminution of his spiritual powers (the story of the elders) for failing to intercede for the Israelites when they craved meat (the story of the quail) and for failing to believe that God could provide it. The pericope's literary structure bears out my contention that this purpose underlies the coalescence of the two stories.

Complaint II. Kibroth-hattaavah (11:4–34)

A. *People's Complaint: Meat 4–10a, bα*	
Riffraff instigate people	4–6
God fumes	10bα
B. *Moses' Complaint: Assistance 10bβ–15*	
Moses is upset with God	10bβ
Moses indulges in self-pity	11–15
Give me assistance or death	11–12, 14–15
I cannot supply meat	13
C. *God's Answer to Both Complaints 16–24a*	
God instructs Moses to:	
Choose elders: God will authorize them	16–17
Ready people: *He* will provide meat	18–20
Moses: Where will you get meat	21–22
God: Wait and see	23
Moses tells people to get ready	24a

B′.	*God Authorizes Elders: Diminishes Moses 24b–30*	
	Moses chooses and assembles elders	24b–30
	God distributes Moses’ spirit	25
	Eldad and Medad prophesy	26–27
	Joshua protests	28
	Moses acquiesces	29
	Moses and elders return to camp	30
A′.	*God Supplies Meat: Punishes Complainers 31–34*	
	Meat brings death	31–33
	Dead are buried giving name to site	34

Unit II contains five sections. The complaints are expressed in A and B, and C, the middle section, both comprises God’s answer to A B and anticipates the fulfillment of B′ A′. The fulfillment occurs in reverse order; the structure, so to speak, turns back on itself, employing a literary technique called chiasmus or introversion. This pattern can only be appreciated when the opposite parts are compared.

A and A′ both deal with the people’s complaint. They exhibit the same language in *wayyiḥar-’ap YHWH, wĕ’cp YHWH ḥāra* (10:33), *ha ’sapup, wayya ’aspu . . . ’ā sap* (4:32) and *hit’awwû, ta’awâ; hatta’awâ . . . hammit’awwîm* (4:34). The language also highlights contrasts. For instance, they sit and weep (4), and only rise (32) to gather quail; they recall the free food spread about on Egyptian soil (5), and now the free quail is spread about in the camp (31–32); in the desert they have seen no food but manna (6), and now they see only quail (31). Finally, their punishment fits the crime; their parched gullets (6) are now stuffed with the quail of death (33).

B and B′ both deal with Moses’ private complaint. The complaint itself drips with self-pity, Moses begins and ends with the accusations that God has wronged him (root *r‘h* 10b, 15) and that if the Lord really loved him (*māṣā ḥēn be‘ênê* 11–15), he would let him die rather than let him lead this people. The people’s complaint for meat (A) is echoed in Moses’ complaint (13) because, again in his self-pity, he imagines it his responsibility to supply the meat (21–22). So Moses’ collapse deserves not just an answer but a rebuke and that rebuke is already intimated in God’s answer (C). God will ordain assistants, but only by drawing from Moses’ power (17); Moses’ assistants may not be his equals, but he cannot but be diminished. However, in the fulfillment section (B′), something unanticipated happens. Eldad and Medad receive the prophetic gift directly from God and not from Moses (26). Moreover, they continue to prophesy. Their gift, then, is permanent, not transient like that of the elders (25). Joshua astutely recognizes the implication; Moses has rivals. Moses’ powers are not just diminished, he is also faced with qualified competitors. This unanticipated event, which alarms Joshua (28), comprises Moses’ punishment—it may even have given Miriam and Aaron sufficient grounds for their rebellion against Moses’ authority (12:2). Moses, however, greets the verdict with neither resistance nor resignation, but with joy. It demonstrates his humility and his greatness, and for these he is rewarded by being elevated as the prophet par excellence (12:6–8).

The complaints (A, B) and their solution (B′, A′) exhibit inner linkage. The two complaints have in common the term *bĕqereb* (4, 20, 21), referring to each of the dramatis personae of this story. The *'ăsapsup* "in the midst of" Israel (4) initiates a lust which displaces the Lord who hitherto had been in Israel's "midst" (20) and initiates Moses' complaint about his role in Israel's "midst" (2).[7] Moreover, the passages share the word *'ākal,* "eat." It appears seven times, at 1, 4, 13, 18 (twice), 19, and 21. The idea that the redactor may have purposely chosen the number seven for the occurrences of *'ākal* is supported by the verb's absence in the account of the eating of the quail, where it might have been expected (31–33, A′). The two solutions (B′ A′) are tied together by the word *rûaḥ,* meaning both spirit and wind; God's *rûaḥ* invests the elders, Eldad and Medad (25, 26, 29), and it brings the quail (31).

Section C is pivotal. There, God answers the complaints A B and anticipates the results B′ A′. Thus, God reminds the people of their lament (4, 18) and quotes verbatim their demand for meat (4b, 19a), while also indicating that he has seen through the complaint to the rebellion which motivates it (20b). Similarly, God responds to Moses that God will lighten his administrative load (*nāśā'* occurs three times in 7; cf. 11, 12, 14). C's anticipatory nature is manifest in the case of Moses' complaint, where the solution is completely spelled out in advance. Moses shall gather seventy elders of the people (16, 24), and God will come down to speak with him, draw from his spirit, and put it on the elders (17, 25). The answer to the people's complaint is not revealed even to Moses since it comprises their punishment, yet it is subtly intimated by the precise fulfillment of Moses' skeptical challenge about where God will get animals (meat) for the people to gather and slaughter (22, 32). The structure of chapters 11—12 can be represented diagrammatically as follows:

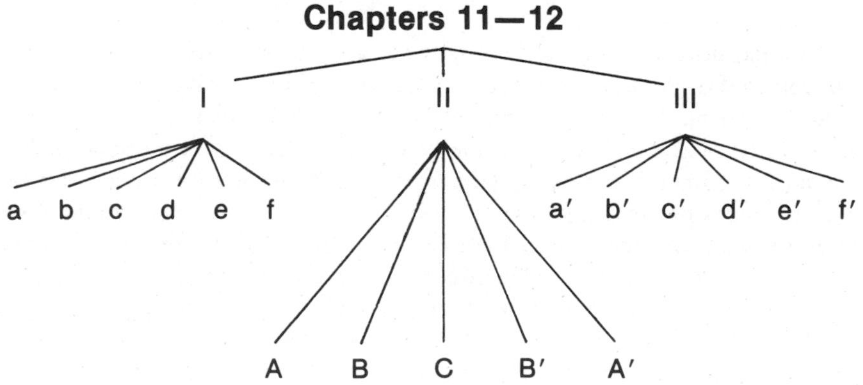

The three complaint units are themselves sequentially and thematically linked. Units I and II are bound by the key word *ra'*. The very first verse labels the complaint *ra'*, "evil" (11:1). Indeed, the people's complaint has totally reversed the divine promise of *ṭôb* ("good") emphasized in the previous section (10:29 and 32), for they now refer to Egypt as *ṭôb* (11:18; cf. 14:3). As we noted, Moses himself is so demoralized by the people's complaints that he too attributes *ra'* to God (11:10, 11, 15). Also, fire "eats" the camp edge (*'ăsapsup?* I), and the people who eat the quail spread at the camp's edge (11:18 [twice], 19, 21, 32–33, II) in answer to their request for food (11:4, 13, 18, II).[8] The alien elements (II) initiate Israel's grumbling about the food; the latter, in turn, incite Moses' grumbling about his leadership burden (II). Thus, Moses provides a base on which Miriam and Aaron may grumble about Moses' monopoly of leadership (III). When they also complain about Moses' alien wife, the circle of complaints which was begun by aliens is now closed. Finally, units II and III are linked by the similar images and vocabulary which picture the fate of those who lust and that almost experienced by Miriam. Miriam's half-eaten *bāśār* (12:12) is reminiscent of the half-eaten "*bāśār* still between their teeth, not yet chewed" (11:33).[9]

The figure of Moses unites all the incidents, and his manifestations form a symmetric pattern. At the beginning and end he relays appeals to God, that is, he performs his prophetic function (I, III; i.e., 11:1 and 12:13). In the interim, encouraged by the people, Moses himself complains (11:11–15, II). He is rebuked by challenges to his leadership (11:25–29, II; 12:2–3, III). Moses meets these tests, demonstrating his humility and his sincere desire to share his power (12:3, III; and 11:29, II), and thereupon, God declares him the unique prophetic leader (12:6–8, III). Another common motif is the apparent concession God makes to the rebels and that ultimately proves to be a deception.[10] God provides meat that is death-dealing (11:4, I; 19–20, 31–34, II), provides Moses with assistants who temporarily diminish him (11:11–12, 14–15, 24–29, II), and he summons Aaron and Miriam together with Moses before he separates them from Moses in order to punish Miriam (12:4–5, 9–10, III).

Another, final unifying element is the inherent topographic code.[11] Israel has departed from impure Egypt and is headed for the holy land, Canaan. The wilderness lying in between is ambiguous terrain, and hence the camp must be kept sacred. The inside and outside of the camp are discrete domains. For instance, the manna of blessing falls inside, the quail of punishment outside, and the edges of the camp burnt by God's wrath (11:1) may be synonymous with the *'ăsapsup*, "the gathered ones" (11:4), the alien edge of society. God's grace toward Israel is marked by movement toward Canaan (11:35; 12:16), his punishment by delays (at least two days for gathering the quail and burying the dead [11:32, 34]—it could have lasted a whole month [11:20–21]—and seven days for Miriam [12:15]). Corresponding to this horizontal plane is a vertical one on which up-down stands for Canaan-Egypt. The manna is heavenly food, but the fish-meat and vegetables come from below. The quail ostensibly falls from the air, but this is a deception, for according to the text, it arises from the sea (11:31).

Itinerary notices (11:35; 12:16) link the units (the omission of a link between I and II is deliberate). They are the last stage in the redaction.

THE STRUCTURE OF CHAPTERS 13—14

The overall structure of Numbers 13—14 can be outlined as follows:

A. *The Scouts' Expedition 13:1–24*	
1. God decides on reconnaissance (and conquest)	1–2
2. Moses chooses and instructs scouts	3–20
3. Expedition fulfilled	21–24
[a. All of Canaan	21]
b. The Hebron area	22–24
B. *The Scouts' Report 13:25–33*	
1. Majority report: objective	25–29
2. Caleb's counterreport	30
3. Majority report: subjective	31–33
C. *The People's Response 14:1–10a*	
1. Majority response: abandon project	1–5
2. Joshua and Caleb's counterresponse	6–9
3. Majority response: stone opposition	10
B′. *God's Response 14:10b–38*	
1. Destroy Israel, save Moses	11–12
2. Moses intercedes	13–19
3. God mitigates decree	20–35
a. Adults die, save Caleb	20–25
[b. Adults die, save Joshua and Caleb	26–35
—anticipation of fulfillment (death of spies)	36–38]
A′. *The People's Expedition 14:39–45*	
1. People decide on conquest	39–40
2. Moses protests	41–43
3. Expedition aborted	44–45

Except for the first, each of the five sections contains destruction planned, intercession attempted, destruction fulfilled. Only in the first is there a harmonious progression from God to people to fulfillment (A). In the other four sections, the first component points to destruction (whether initiated by scouts, God, or people), the second attempts to avert the destruction, and the third shows that the attempt fails (except for partial success in B′). The introverted structure of these two chapters becomes apparent when we compare the parallel sections. A and A′ frame the structure in an inclusion, the people's attempt to retrace the steps of the scouts for the purposes of conquest. The people act in defiance of God, however, so their expedition is aborted. The goal is the same, *'ālâ hāhār*, "go up to the hill country" (13:17; 14:40, 44), however, the second expedition meets with frustration, as indicated by the opposite results: "by the Lord's command" is opposed to "transgress the Lord's command" (13:3; 14:41), "they went up via the Negeb" is set against "the Amalakites . . . came down" (13:22; 14:45) and land of fertility is counterpointed by land of destruction (13:23; 14:45).

It is only in B B′ that we find the word *yākōl,* "can (conquer)" (13:30, 31; 14:16). The scouts conclude that Israel cannot conquer the land; Caleb avers that it can, but the nations conclude that it is God who cannot. Therefore when the scouts say that Israel cannot, they really mean that God cannot (cf. also 14:3, 4, 43). Israel believes its scouts who only see giants (13:28, 32, 33). But those who have been privileged to see God's wonders (14:22) and even his presence (14:10, 14) in contrast to other nations who only have heard (14:13, 14, 15). Therefore, those whose vision is distorted will not view the promised land (14:23).

The middle section (C) is the pivot around which the entire story turns. As indicated by the repetition of the following key idioms, it follows logically from the preceding section. Caleb and Joshua confirm that the land indeed is "flowing with milk and honey" (13:27; 14:8) and is "an exceedingly good land" (13:19; 14:7), and as for "the people of the country" (13:28; 14:9), Israel will devour them and not be devoured (13:32; 14:9). Section C is even more tightly linked with the sections that follow, for it is the people's reaction to the scouts' report that determines the nature and form of their punishment. The murmuring against Moses is exposed as murmuring against God (14:2, 27), and it is tantamount to rebellion (14:9, 11, 23, 35). Those who would rather die in the desert are destined to do so (14:2, 28–29, 32); those who made Moses and Aaron fall in fear will fall in death (14:5, 29, 32), and their children, whom they were certain would be taken captive, are destined to enter the land (14:3, 31). In the meantime, the leader whom they wished to depose will be saved (14:4, 12), while those who wanted to return to Egypt will now have their wish, but only to die on the way (14:4, 35), those who feared to die by the sword have their fears realized (14:3, 43), those who did not believe that "God is with us" now discover that he is not (14:9, 42–43), and those who would have killed the faithful scouts are killed by the enemy (14:10, 45).[12]

Literary criticism has dissected these two chapters into two main sources. In addition, glosses, redundancies, and inconsistencies have been detected.[13] These trouble spots are arguable, but two inconsistencies are irrefutable. First, the country reconnoitered by the spies comprises on the one hand the entire land of Canaan (13:2, 17), from its southern to its northern extremity (13:21), but on the other hand, it includes only the area around Hebron in the south (13:22–24). Second, although Caleb appears as both the lone dissenter to the spies' report (13:30) and the lone exemption from the punishment (13:30; 14:24), he is joined by Joshua in both these roles (14:6–7, 38).

The literary structure of these chapters supports this two-source theory.

Section B′, which is particularly large (28 verses), shows signs of duplication and accretion in its content. For instance, vv. 36–38 comprise a redactional interpolation anticipating the long-range result of God's decision. More importantly, there are two passages describing the mitigation of the divine decree (14:20–25, 26–35) which not only show signs of duplication (cf. 21 and 28) but also include contradictions. The first passage posits that, of the adults, only Caleb (and Moses) will survive the trek (14:20–25, esp. 24), but the second includes Joshua (and presumably Aaron; 14:26–35, esp. 26 and 30). Section A (24 verses) is top-heavy also, since it includes both the scout list (13:4–16) and the two traditions concerning the territory reconnoitered by the scouts. (It tells of the Negeb up to Hebron and the entire length of the promised land [see, for example, 13:22–24, 21].) These two interpolations are credited to the Priestly source (13:21; 14:26–28). However, even the main, hypothetically original story contains Priestly material. For example, 14:1–10 is replete with Priestly vocabulary. Thus, the Priestly interpolations represent a recension, and the Priestly material in the original story may indicate the same. Diagrammatically, the subdivisions of chapters 13—14 appear as follows:

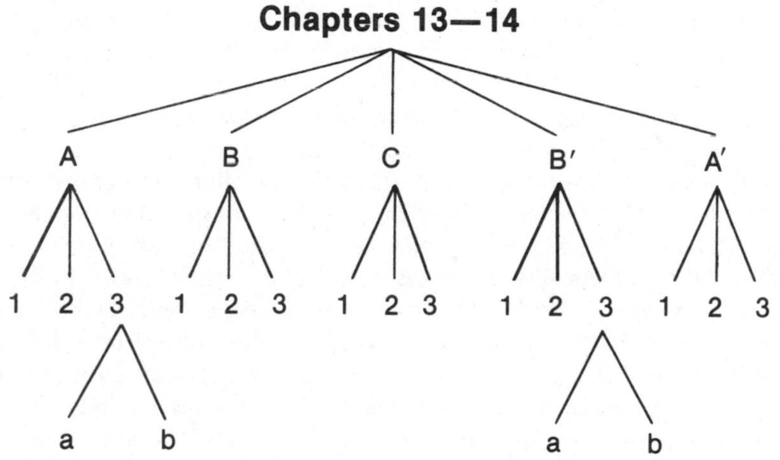

The existence of two separate traditions is confirmed by the Deuteronomic account and its reflex in Joshua which assume that the scouts only got as far as the Hebron area and that Joshua was not among them (Deut. 1:19–46; Josh. 4:6–15; Deut. 1:24; cf. Num. 32:9). This latter point is underscored in Deuteronomy, where another reason altogether is cited as Joshua's qualification to enter the land, his appointment as Moses' successor (Deut. 1:37–38). This can also be deduced from Caleb's remark to Joshua which by implication denies that Joshua was a member of the expedition. Caleb says "Moses sent me [not 'us'] . . . and I [not 'we'] gave him a forthright report. While my [not 'our']

companions who went up with me [not 'us'] took the heart out of the people, I [not 'we'] remained loyal to the lord my [not 'our'] God" (Josh. 14:7–8). Moreover, the Deuteronomic account attributes the reconnaissance to the initiative of the people rather than to God (Deut. 1:22; Num. 13:1–3).

As shown by the composite structure, the two traditions have been artfully woven together. However, in one instance in particular, God's response (B′), there is an extra large bulge. The doublet, 14:20–25, 26–35, throws the structure out of balance. But each part contains vital information, and this made it impossible for the redactor to keep one and omit the other. The first includes the promise of Hebron to Caleb (14:25), the second includes Joshua among the survivors (14:30). Moreover, the two doublets in the structure, A3 and B′3, stand in chiastic relationship to one another, the Joshua tradition precedes in the first doublet (A3a), whereas the Caleb tradition precedes in the second (B′3a). Most critics would also claim that the first tradition is predicated on the fact that only Caleb and his descendants will inherit the land, that is, the rest of the Israelites, including their children, will die in the desert. This is unlikely, however, for it would imply that the only concession Moses won from God was that Caleb would enter the land instead of himself (14:20 and 14:12)! Rather, we must assume that both traditions assume the punishment does not include the children. This is confirmed by Deut. 1:35, which explains that the term "not one of these men" means "this evil generation" (cf. Num. 14:22).

Despite Deuteronomy's dependence upon the first tradition (Caleb-Hebron), it is clear that at least in its final form, Deuteronomy held before it both traditions. As shown by the following considerations, the entire text of Numbers 13—14 is reflected in Deut. 1:19–46. First, the judgment against the adults in Deut. 1:35 implies the exemption of the children. The explicit mention of this in Deut. 1:39 is the same style and idiom of Num. 14:31, 33, the second tradition.[14] Second, Deut. 2:14 is also dependent on the second tradition through 14:33: Third, the expedition consists of one member from each tribe (Deut. 1:23), and is thus based on 13:2, which critics assign to the second tradition. Since the Deuteronomic account gives no indication of having been edited later to harmonize with Numbers 13—14, it must be concluded that the present, composite text of Numbers is old and, more importantly, that both traditions preceded the writing of Deuteronomy.

THE REDACTION

How do the issues of this structural analysis illumine the problem of redaction? The answer must be postponed until we bring into the picture the narrative of Korah's rebellion (Numbers 16). Its very proximity to our chapters raises the possibility that it underwent the same redactional process. The complex redactional history of this chapter discloses two basic recensions, analyzed elsewhere,[15] which can be summarized by the following tables.

I. *Penultimate Recension*
Introduction: Korah, Dathan and Abiram, chieftains versus Moses and Aaron, 1–4 (earlier version)
- *A. Dathan and Abiram versus Moses,* 12–15
  - B. *Korah and chieftains versus Aaron,* 16–18 (*'ădātĕkā* means "chieftains")
    - C. *Korah and 'ēdâ versus Moses and Aaron,* 19–22
      - 1. At the tabernacle, 19
      - 2. God threatens *'ēdâ,* 20–21
      - 3. Moses and Aaron intercede, 22
    - C′. *'ēdâ* spared at the tabernacle, 23–24, 26a*a*, 27a (miškan YHWH*)
  - B′. Korah and the chieftains incinerated at the Tabernacle, 35 (plus Korah, *wattēṣē' 'ēš**)
- *A′. Dathan and Abiram swallowed,* 25, 26 (-*'ēdâ*), 27b–34 (-Korah, *lāhem**)

II. *Ultimate Recension (MT)*
Introduction: Korah, Dathan and Abiram, chieftains versus Moses and Aaron, 1–4 [Korah and Levites versus Aaron, 5–7, 8–11 (*'ădātĕkā* means "Levites")]
- A. Dathan and Abiram versus Moses, 12–15
  - B. Korah and chieftains versus Aaron, 16–18
    - C. Korah and *'ēdâ* versus Moses and Aaron, 19–22
    - C′. *'ēdâ* spared at dwellings of Korah and Dathan and Abiram, 23–27a
      - 1. God orders removal of *'ēdâ,* 23–24
      - 2. Moses removes *'ēdâ,* 25–27a
- A′ + B′ (part). Korah and Dathan and Abiram swallowed, 27b–34
  - B′ (part). Chieftains incinerated, 35

A comparison between the two recensions reveals important differences that can be summarized as follows: the penultimate recension bears a clear, introverted structure, A B C C′ B′ A′. Three rebellions have been artfully woven together. The scope of each rebellion increases, for they are led respectively by individuals (Dathan and Abiram), 250 chieftains (*nĕśî'îm*), and the entire community (*'ēdâ*). The targets of the rebellions also increase from Moses through Aaron to Moses and Aaron. In the ultimate recension, which corresponds to the MT, these three changes have taken place: (1) Korah's death has been transferred from the fire to the earthquake so that he becomes associated with the deaths of Dathan and Abiram; (2) the Levite passage constituting the fourth rebellion against Korah has been inserted (vv. 5–11) and breaks the structural movement toward crescendo. Now, a group precedes individuals (Levites, vv. 5–11, and Dathan and Abiram, vv. 12–15). This constitutes a second revolt against Aaron, and thus unbalances the ascending order of Moses, Aaron, Moses and Aaron. (3) The chieftains' incineration has been transferred to the end of the fused account so that it can introduce the new account of the dedication of the censers (17:1–5). The purpose of all these changes in the ultimate recension is that all four received traditions concerning rebellions in the wilderness against Moses and/or Aaron should be attributed to the machinations of Korah.[16]

The significance of this analysis of the Korah narrative becomes manifest once it is recognized that its source attribution is undisputed in the scholarly community: Nadab and Abihu are attributed to the Epic tradition, the rest of the chapter to P. It is striking, then, that all the changes and additions in the ultimate recension are the work of P, and that there is, moreover, a good deal of P material embedded in the penultimate recension (16:12, 3–4, 16–24, 26a*a*, 27a, 35).[17] Thus, two strands of P have to be posited, the earlier one (P_1) contained in the structure, the late one (P_2) supplementing and altering the structure.[18]

How does this dissection of chapter 16 compare with those of 11—12 and 13—14 in regard to P material? First, let it be noted that chapters 11—12 betray no bulges in their structure. Indeed, in view of our findings in the Korah narrative, none should be expected; all agree that chapters 11—12 contain no trace whatever of P! On the other hand, 13—14 exhibit significant bulges and again, unsurprisingly, they belong to P (13:21; 14:26–38). Moreover, not all of P is accounted for by these bulges; P is also embedded in the reconnaissance story itself (13:1–16; 14:1a, 2, 5–7, 10).[19] Thus the redactional process turns out to be exactly the same for both the Korah narrative (chap. 16) and the reconnaissance narrative (chaps. 13—14); Priestly matter (P_1) is integrated into the penultimate structure which is intruded upon by subsequent Priestly additions (P_2). Now, there can be no doubt concerning the nature of P_2. It is clearly the work of a redactor. And not only is this redactor inserting new elements, thereby changing and distorting the finished structure before him, but as shown by the Korah analysis, he is also being forced into making textual alterations to effect his purpose.

What, however, of P_2? Is it a redaction or a source? Is its insertion the work of its author, who then must be identified as the redactor of the structure, or is it the work of some other redactor who used P as one of his sources? There is no clear-cut evidence on which we can base a decision. Since the redactional activity of P is present throughout the Pentateuch, however, the chances are that P_1 is none other than the redactor who created the finely wrought penultimate structures of chapters 13—14 and 16. In other words, at least in these chapters, P_1 and P_2 are not sources but redactions.[20] Their authors integrated Priestly materials with preexisting ones, and thus were responsible, in the main, for the received text of the Tetrateuch.[21] It remains for us to discover whether this picture holds true for the other wilderness narratives.

NOTES

1. See A. J. Greimas's seminal works *Sémantique structurale* (Paris: Larousse, 1966) and *Du Sens: Essais Sémiotiques* (Paris: Seuil, 1970). See also J. Calloud, *L'Analyse Structurale due Récit* (Lyon: Profac, 1977), English translation by D. Patte, *Structural*

Analysis of Narrative (Philadelphia: Fortress Press, 1976). For a lucid introduction and illustration of the discipline, see R. M. Polzin, *Biblical Structuralism* (Philadelphia: Fortress Press, 1977).

2. Meir Weiss's pioneering work is *The Bible and Modern Literary Theory* (Jerusalem: Bialik, 1962) (in Hebrew). His most prominent student is Y. Zakovitch (*For Three... And for Four* [Jerusalem, 1979] [in Hebrew]).

3. A notable exception is M. Greenberg, *Ezekiel, 1—20* (Garden City, N.Y.: Doubleday & Co., 1983).

4. Cf. Num. 10:33 and *m. Agada* and *Ramban* on Num. 11:1.

5. For example, the golden calf (Exod. 32:9–14, 30–34; 33:12–19; 34:5–9), the spies (Num. 14:11–20), Korah (Num. 16:20–22; 17:9–11).

6. For example, Taberah, "in the ears of the Lord" (Num. 11:1); the serpents, "the people spoke against God" (Num. 20:5).

7. Oral observation by Jeremy Judah Milgrom.

8. Ibid.

9. Ibid.

10. See D. Jobling, *The Sense of Biblical Narrative,* JSOTSup. 7 (1978), 21–62.

11. In *The Narrative Style of the Priestly Writer* ([Rome: Biblical Institute, 1971], 114) S. E. McEvenue also detects a five-part introverted structure in Numbers 13—14, but he limits it to the speeches.

12. For example, G. B. Gray, *Numbers,* ICC (New York: Charles Scribner's Sons, 1903).

13. I am indebted to I. J. Ball for this insight.

14. The dependency of Deuteronomy on Numbers in these passages was convincingly demonstrated by S. E. McEvenue, "A Source-Critical Problem in Num. 14, 26–38," *Bib* 50 (1969): 453–65.

15. See J. Milgrom, "Korah's Rebellion: A Study in Redaction," in *De La Torah au Messie, Mélanges Henri Cazelles,* ed. J. Doré et al. (Paris: Desclée, 1981), 135–46.

16. For the textual changes and other details, see ibid, 139–42.

17. Following Gray, *Numbers,* 188.

18. Earlier scholars also spoke of two P strata, cf. G. von Rad, *Die Priesterschrift im Hexateuch,* BWANT 4, no. 13 (Leipzig-Stuttgart, 1934), and his predecessors cited there.

19. Following the most recent source analysis of J. de Vaulx, *Les Nombres* (Paris: Gabalda, 1972), 174.

20. This position approaches that of F. M. Cross, *Canaanite Myth and Hebrew Epic* (Cambridge: Harvard Univ. Press, 1973), 293–325. Cross also regards the Priestly work as a recension and not as an independent source. Earlier, I. Engnell came to a similar conclusion, holding that exilic P assembled older P material into the Tetrateuch (see *A Rigid Scrutiny,* ed. J. T. Willis [Nashville: Vanderbilt Univ. Press, 1969], 58, translated from *Svenkst Bibliskt Uppslagsverk* [Stockholm: Norsted, 1962]). However, neither Engnell nor Cross maintains that P comprises two recensions.

21. It is very likely that H also participated in the redactional process. This subject requires separate investigation. As for D, the bulk of it is clearly later than P_1 (see provisionally J. Milgrom, "Profane Slaughter and a Formulaic Key to the Composition of Deuteronomy," *HUCA* 47 [1976]: 1–17, and n. 12 above).

4 STEPHEN A. KAUFMAN

RHETORIC, REDACTION, AND MESSAGE IN JEREMIAH

What constitutes a "Judaic" perspective on Ancient Israel? What kind of article would be suitable for such a volume? At a recent World Congress of Jewish Studies several sessions were devoted to the subject of "Modern Jewish Bible Research."[1] Of course, little agreement was reached on either just what it is that distinguishes biblical research done by Jewish scholars from that of their Gentile colleagues, or on what should be distinctive about their work. A few participants argued that Jewish scholarship at its best should be indistinguishable from Gentile scholarship at its best. But most thought otherwise.[2] Perhaps somewhat more surprising, however, the discussions centered around superficials, like use or misuse of medieval Jewish commentaries, mastery of Hebrew, absence of christological presuppositions, and thus implied that in all other respects, Jewish scholarship defies characterization.

I would argue otherwise, both as regards what Jewish biblical scholarship has been and what Judaic perspectives on Ancient Israel should try to be. With a few noteworthy exceptions, Jewish Bible scholarship in our generation, in Israel and in the Diaspora, has concentrated on the Torah. Practically the entire list of major scholars is closely associated with one or more of the first five books of the Bible. Such names as Greenberg, Weinfeld, Haran, Sarna, Paul, Speiser, Milgrom, B. Levine, Brichto, Rofé, and Fishbane, among others, easily come to mind. I myself plead guilty to the affliction—almost all of my previous meager efforts have been devoted to this corner of the field. Some of the younger scholars are concentrating elsewhere, to be sure, but few have or will ever show the breadth of H. L. Ginsberg's interest and mastery. The reverse is also true; those major scholars who concentrate on Pentateuch constitute an almost exclusively Jewish fellowship.

The other major characteristic of the current generation's scholarship is its passion for antiquity. (Again, the recent work of H. L. Ginsberg is the notable exception to the rule that regularly finds Jewish scholars—the theological liberals as well as the traditionalists—trying to prove that biblical material stems from the oldest possible strata and that things are as close to Moses as they possibly could be.)[3] Only the ancient, it seems, is significant. We must justify our existence, you see, and the more ancient the fundamental Jewish insights, the more authentic our claim. If such attitudes are no longer couched in the blatant fundamentalist formulations of Segal or Cassuto, they appear nonetheless in the crypto-fundamentalist guise of Yehezkel Kaufmann's positions.[4]

For me, an authentic Jewish perspective on Ancient Israel must constantly keep in mind one thing, and attempt to do two things. It must keep in mind that the Ancient Israelites were not Jews—that the Bible, while it is a Jewish book, by and large is not a Jewish creation. We can mine that book for what it can tell us about the origin and development of the institutions that later were to constitute Judaism, but the mine will only yield its ore if we approach it without presuppositions. When we begin by assuming that Moses was a true monotheist and that he celebrated the Sabbath because "the Bible tells us so," then we are never able to trace the development of monotheism or of the Sabbath in our sources. If we refuse to consider the possibility that the religious institutions of Israel evolved during the biblical period—because that is what Wellhausen thought, and Wellhausen was an anti-Semite—then we may be guilty of scholarship as prejudiced as his.

Just as an eye focused on the origin of the social and religious institutions of Judaism must be fundamental to a Judaic perspective, so, too, must be a sensitivity for possible biblical origins for many of the literary institutions of later Judaism. But in these respects, and in general, much of recent Jewish Bible scholarship has tended to concentrate on the trees while ignoring the forest.

Herein I attempt a corrective approach to several of these characteristics of Jewish scholarship. I hope I see the forest without ignoring or misunderstanding the trees. I know I am dealing with נ״ך and not with תורה (although Deuteronomy remains a theme in my work that I cannot avoid), and I think I can show that "Jewish" ways of reflecting on the biblical text are already intrinsic to the text itself. In the end it is the Bible that constitutes the first "Judaic" perspective on Ancient Israel!

The first chapters of Jeremiah have long been grist for the critical mill. Their apparent aptness for such analysis stems not only from internal considerations but also from the implicit challenge presented by the story of Jeremiah's book—the challenge to discover the original book of oracles (the so-called *Urrolle*) dictated by Jeremiah himself.[5] As in most endeavors in the area of biblical criticism, however, the results of such enquiries cannot be said to have produced many widely accepted conclusions. Even S. Mowinckel's long-followed tripartite division of the Jeremianic material into A (authentic poetic oracles), B (biographic prose), and C (prose Deuteronomic redaction) no longer seems to offer a very productive perspective on the material.[6] Although, following Mowinckel, most students of the matter have tended to assume that the poetic (A) material represents the original oracles of the prophet while the prose sermons are "Deuteronomistic" retellings of those oracles, the Jeremianic origin of some if not most of the prose material has also been regularly supported.[7]

Not surprisingly then, recent research has tried to develop new ways to analyze this material, and, also not surprisingly in light of current interests, the new approaches have primarily been in the area of structural and rhetorical analysis.[8]

Chapter 3 of Jeremiah has proven to be an especially challenging area of investigation for such studies due to its combination of what appears to be a carefully constructed poetic oracle interrupted by a prose *pesher,*[9] plus its explicit reference to the divorce regulation of Deut. 24:1–4. My intent here is to essay yet another such analysis of Jeremiah chapter 3, demonstrating that the proper key to understanding the history of its redaction may well lie in recognizing that the techniques of reading "Scripture," indeed of "playing" with Scripture, normally associated only with much later times, are already to be found within the biblical text itself.

And when the sound of the text itself is somewhat muted, there is a place to turn for guidance: the paracanonical Hebrew literature of the postbiblical period. The master manipulators of biblical texts who produced the Temple Scroll, the pesharim of Qumran, the targumim and midrashim, and the pseudepigraphic literature of late Second Temple and Rabbinic times (and, of course, Christian Scripture) did not invent their techniques out of whole cloth, nor were they dependent solely (perhaps not even primarily) on Hellenistic literary practices. Much of what they did was already frequently done in such early periods that it is already in the Bible.

I have previously argued that much of current literary-critical and redaction-historical research is wasted effort.[10] I have heretofore found little of value in so-called canonical criticism. Why then do I venture into such treacherous territory? Because I believe that the biblical text obviously does have a history and that some of that history can be recovered, but that to recover it we must let the text speak on its own terms, not impose on it our own sensibilities of style and form.[11]

Three relatively recent works by W. Rudolph, David Jobling, and William L. Holladay deal with Jer. 3:1—4:4 extensively.[12] All three attempt to uncover the original Jeremianic poem in this material, rejecting out of hand any serious consideration of the chapter's prose material. Now I agree that recovering the original words of Jeremiah, although probably hopeless, remains a legitimate scholarly endeavor. I would argue, however, that by ignoring the prose, these works throw out the baby with the bath water. Whatever the origin of the prose, after all, its author had before him a poetic text to all intents and purposes identical with the one the critics are attempting to uncover. Why not make use of the clues that he offers us! Indeed, only by considering the message and function of the prose insertions can one ever hope to achieve an understanding of the structure of the redacted text itself. And it is, after all, the profundity of the redacted text in its current shape that attracts our interest in the first place.

According to Rudolph, our text is a single bipartite poem, each part consisting of four four-line strophes:[13]

3:1	3:21–22
3:2–3a	3:23–25 (with glosses)
3:3b–5	4:1–2
3:19–20	4:3–4

Jobling proposes the following scheme:

	Part I		Part II
IA	3:1	IIA	3:12b–13
IB	3:2–3a	IIB	3:21–22
IC	3:3b–5	IIC	3:23–25
ID	3:19–20	IID	4:1–2

For Holladay, this section is only the second half of a "Harlotry Cycle" whose first half is 2:5–37. It is divided into four sections:

3:1–5 (A-B-A′ structure with chiasm).
3:12b–14a (A-B-A′ structure, possibly with inclusio).
3:19–20 (no structure of its own! but echoes vv. 1–5).
3:21–25 (echoes all three earlier sections).[14]

Jobling's approach is commendable. It seeks to find in the poetry of Jeremiah a patterned symmetry that delights our senses. I, too, would be delighted with such regularity and tight structure. But would Jeremiah?

Let us begin at the beginning:

3:1:

לאמר
הן ישלח איש את־אשתו והלכה מאתו והיתה לאיש־אחר
הישוב אליה עוד
הלוא חנוף תחנף הארץ ההיא
ואת זנית רעים רבים ושוב אלי נאם־ה׳:

> Saying:
> If a man divorces his wife and she leaves him and marries another, may he return unto her? Is not that land utterly defiled? But you have whored with many "friends" and would return to me?[15]

Commentators are nearly unanimous in taking this verse to be a part of Jeremiah's original poetic oracle.[16] Why? Is it poetry? Not unless you believe that everything set as poetry by Rudolph in the various editions of *Biblica Hebraica* is by definition poetry. Where is the parallelism or the balanced structure of stichoi and cola? But I would go even further. Could it possibly be part of the original oracle? Is its concept of return the same as that in the rest of the poem? Is its concept of "defiled land" the same? I think not, and hope to show it. I believe that it has normally been accepted as part of the poem precisely because of its relationship to Deuteronomy. Everyone looks for the influence of Deuteronomy in Jeremiah, after all. But is there no other evidence from the text itself that would help us determine the status of this verse?

According to W. Thiel, "Das 3 6–18 eine Grösse eigener Art darstellt, die mit dem Kontext ursprünglich nicht zusammengehangen haben kann, ist seit langem erkannt."[17] But by the time he concludes his discussion of the passages themselves, Thiel as much as admits that they really do belong in their context. That is to say, in spite of what earlier scholarship might have claimed, although the prose intrusion in Jeremiah 3 may not be as old as the poetry surrounding it, it stems from no context other than that wherein it currently resides. It is, as indicated above, a prose *pesher,* as it were, on the poetic oracle. This much has been noted before, but neither the methodology of the *pesher* nor its implications have been explored. For we have here, after all, the comments of an author writing not long after the oracle was delivered. Let us ask him what the oracle looked like!

> 3:6: So the Lord said to me in the days of King Josiah, "Have you seen what faithless Israel has done? She has gone[18] up to every high hill and under every green tree and whored there. 7: But I thought that after she had done all these things she would return to me, but she did not. Then her treacherous sister Judah saw more 8: that[19] I had divorced faithless Israel and presented her with her severance papers, but treacherous Judah her sister did not fear, but went and whored herself. 9: (And it shall be that from the sound of her whoring) she defiled herself with the land and committed adultery with the stones and the trees. 10: But even after all this her treacherous sister Judah returned to me only falsely, not with all her heart."

This passage is obviously far from problem-free in and of itself, and several of its problems impinge on our own inquiries. The repetition of the key thematic terms of the poetic oracle ("harlotry," "treachery," "defilement," and, of course, "return") make it crystal clear that this is no prose passage extracted from another source, but an original reinterpretation of the oracle. Verse 10, however, makes no sense where it now stands, for our writer has just finished saying that Judah went and whored as well, not that she gave any sign of repentance. A correct understanding of the compositional principles displayed by this prose "oracle" leads us not only to a solution to its original structure but also serves as the key to understanding the redactional history of the entire pericope in which it stands.

Using an "exegetical" approach not unlike that of the *pesharim* from Qumran and the latest levels of the Palestinian Targum, vv. 6–10 constitute an idea-by-idea commentary on an original poetic oracle—a commentary wherein key words and ideas are repeated in their original order, but often completely reinterpreted.

2. שאי עיניך על שפים וראי איפה לא שגלת
על דרכים ישבת להם כערבי במדבר
ותחניפי ארץ בזנותיך וברעתך 3. (ו) ימנעו רבבים
(ומלקוש לוא היה)[20]
ומצח אשה זונה היה לך מאנת הכלם
. . .
19. ואנכי אמרתי איך אשיתך בבנים
ואתן לך ארץ חמדה נחלת צבות גוים
ואמר אבי תקראו לי ומאחרי לא תשובו
20. אכן בגדה אשה מרעה כן בגדתם בי בית ישראל נאם־ה׳
21. קול על שפיים נשמע. . . .
23. אכן לשקר מגבעות המון הרים . . .

6. ויאמר ה׳ אלי בימי יאשיהו המלך
הראית אשר עשתה משבה ישראל
הלכה היא על־כל־הר גבה ואל־תחת כל־עץ רענן ותזני שם
9. והיה מקל זנותה ויחנף את־הארץ ותנאף את־האבן ואת־העץ
7. ואמר אחרי עשותה את־כל־אלה אלי תשוב ולא שבה
ותראה בגודה אחותה יהודה
8. כי על־כל־אדות אשר נאפה משבה ישראל
שלחתיה ואתן את־ספר כריתותיה אליה
(ולא יראה בגדה יהודה אחותה ותלך ותזן גם היא)
10. וגם־בכל־זאת לא־שבה אלי בגודה אחותה יהודה בכל־לבה
כי אם־בשקר נאם־ה׳

With v. 9 moved up like this, vv. 6–10 are seen to repeat the sequence of the poem's themes and words quite precisely. Note especially the following verbal and conceptual correspondences:

vv.	6b	‹	2a
	6c	‹	2b
	9	‹	2c

7a	⟨	19
7b	⟨	20
10	⟨	23

And now v. 10 makes sense in its proper context—immediately following versa 8a. (So too does 8b stand clearly now as a doublet to 7b.) To be sure, common sense might have enabled us to suggest that v. 9 should be placed right after v. 6, but common sense, while it may be all we need to propose emendations and analyze glosses and dittographies, should never be enough to allow us to move verses around at will! We rely instead on internal evidence—the evidence of the *pesher*-like structure of our text.

We may be accused of more than a tad of circular reasoning here; move v. 9 because the *pesher* structure demands it, yet move v. 9 and behold—a *pesher!* But bear with us; when the whole picture is revealed the likelihood of circular reasoning should seem small.

On the basis of this same internal evidence we can now ratify our idea that v. 1 is not a part of the poetic oracle beginning in v. 2. The prose of vv. 6–10 gives no indication of knowing such a verse at the beginning of the oracle. On the contrary. Verse 1 seems to be motivated by the mention of Deuteronomic ספר כריתותיה in the prose text (v. 8)! The divorce law of Deuteronomy 24 decrees that a remarried divorcée may not be retaken in marriage by her first husband—so v. 1 reminds us. But that is hardly the message of the poetry of the early Jeremianic oracle. The oracle, after all, is clearly a call to return. (Indeed the need to harmonize this dichotomous view of "return" has produced a substantial corpus of exegetical text-wrestling from earliest times.) The phrase ותחניפי ארץ in the oracle means "you defiled the land"—making it sterile (as in Num. 35:33). In the prose, ותחנף את הארץ has been reinterpreted to mean "she polluted herself *with* the land," just as the gloss explains: "She committed adultery with stones and trees."[21] But in v. 1 this has been reinterpreted yet again. There, חנף means "to become godless," as in the late Rabbinic and Syriac usage, "pagan, apostate."[22]

Thus, v. 1 is an introductory addition, but an addition that like vv. 6–10 has no other original locus but this. For not only do its themes rework those of the chapter—both prose and poetry—its very words are a play on the words in the beginning of the oracle:

1. הן ישלח איש את־אשתו והלכה מאתו והיתה לאיש־אחר
הישוב אליה עוד
הלוא חנוף תחנף הארץ ההיא
ואת זנית רעים רבים ושוב אלי נאם־ה׳:
2. שאי עיניך על שפים וראי איפה לא שגלת
על דרכים ישבת להם כערבי במדבר
ותחניפי ארץ בזנותיך וברעתך 3. וימנעו רבבים

Note the following parallel sequences in these two verses:

Verse 1	Verse 2
הלכה	דרכים
הישוב	ישבת
אליה	להם
עוד	כערבי
תחנף הארץ	ותחנו יפי ארץ
זנית	בזנותיך
רעים	וברעתך
רבים	רבבים

Should we be surprised to find such a playful attitude toward a prophetic text within Scripture itself? No more so, perhaps, than we should be surprised to find a *pesher* within Jeremiah or midrashic kinds of thought permeating the composition of Deuteronomy.[23] If vv. 6–10 constitute an early example of *pesher,* then perhaps v. 1 resembles nothing so much as the poems of the earliest haggadic midrashim! We need to examine the biblical text for other such introductory verses.

If v. 1 cannot be included in the original poem, neither, then, can the concluding lines of our large compositional unit, 4:1–2. These two sets of verses constitute the outermost *inclusio* of the large chiastic structure of our unit:

A Introduction 3:1
B Poetic oracle part 1 3:2–5
C Prose expansion 3:6–11
D Core climactic message 3:12–13
C′ Prose expansion 3:14–18
B′ Poetic oracle part 2 3:19–25
A′ Conclusion 4:1–2

Now I am the first to admit that making pretty geometric designs out of biblical texts is an exercise that has recently been carried to ludicrous extremes.[24] But no serious scholar can ignore the massive evidence that has been accumulated over the past thirty and more years indicating the importance of *inclusio* and chiasm (nested *inclusio*) in biblical literature. And of all the books of the Bible, Jeremiah may well show the greatest frequency of these rhetorical structures, especially in its first twenty chapters—even more so than noted by Jack R. Lundbom in his ground-breaking work.[25] In our particular passage, chiasm governs not only the larger structure as a whole, but obtains within each set of matching "paragraphs" as well.

In paragraph sets C and B, the relationships are relatively large-scale and conceptual, with some verbal repetitions and echoes:

C: a 6. ויאמר הי אלי בימי יאשיהו המלך . . .
הלכה היא על־כל־הר גבה . . .

	b	8. שלחתיה ואתן את־ספר כריתותיה אליה
	c	10. וגם־בכל־זאת לא־שבה אלי בגודה אחותה יהודה בכל־לבה
	c′	14. שובו בנים שובבים
	b′	כי אנכי בעלתי בכם
		. . .
	a′	18. בימים ההמה ילכו בית־יהודה על־בית ישראל
B:	a	2. שאי עיניך על שפים וראי
	b	איפה לא שגלת
		על דרכים יובת להם כערבי במדבר
		ותחניפי ארץ בזנותיך וברעתך 3. וימנעו רבבים
	c	ומצח אשה זונה היה לך מאנת הכלם
	d	4. הלוא מעתה קראתי לי אבי
		. . .
	d′	19. ואנכי אמרתי איך אשיתך בבנים
	c′	24. והבשת אכלה את יגיע אבותינו מנעורינו
	b′	25. נשכבה בבשתנו ותכסנו כלמתנו
		כי לה׳ אלהינו חטאנו
	a′	ולא שמענו בקול ה׳ אלהינו

In the framework verses (paragraph set A), however, the chiastic relationship is evident at the level of each individual line!

3:1	a	הן ישלח איש את־אשתו והלכה מאתו והיתה לאיש־אחר
	b	הישוב אליה עוד
	c	הלוא חנוף תחנף הארץ ההיא
	d	ואת זנית רעים רבים ושוב אלי נאם־ה׳
4:1	d′	אם־תשוב ישראל נאם־ה׳ אלי תשוב
	c′	ואם־תסיר שקוציך מפני ולא תנוד
	b′	ונשבעת חי־ה׳ באמת במשפט ובצדקה
	a′	והתברכו בו גוים ובו יתהללו

The verbal repetitions between line pairs a–a′ and d–d′ are striking. (It is most surprising that Lundbom missed it!) The other line sets are connected only conceptually (law, abomination).

From the beginning of the composition to its end we have been turned 180 degrees! Indeed, our lines constitute only one example of a key feature of chiasm in Jeremiah, a feature I term "antithetic chiasm." As in 3:1, which proscribes repentance, and 4:1–2 which prescribe it, the outermost *inclusio* of the larger compositional units in Jeremiah frequently demonstrate rhetorical reversal, as I hope to illustrate at length in another study.[26] But sometimes rhetorical reversal is operative throughout a composition as well. Such is the case with our passage, where each paragraph reverses the message of its earlier counterpart. What could possibly be more appropriate in a composition devoted to "turning around"!

Yet a final example of chiasm in our composition remains to be discussed. It is found in the apparently unmatched lines within large unit B′ vv. 20–23, which, like the framework passages, form their own line-by-line chiastic pattern as follows:

a	20	אכן בגדה אשה מרעה כו בגדתם בי בית ישראל נאם־ה׳
b	21	קול על־שפיים נשמע בכי תחנוני בני ישראל
c		כי העוו את־דרכם שכחו את־ה׳ אלהיהם
d	22	שובו בנים שובבים ארפה משובתיכם
c′		הננו אתנו לך כי אתה ה׳ אלהינו
b′	23	אכן לשקר מגבעות המון הרים
a′		אכן בה׳ אלהינו תשועת ישראל

By now it should not surprise us to discover that the core of this chiasm, too, is the plea שובו! Indeed, these are probably the core verses of the original poetic oracle.

What we have attempted here, with a few backward glances, is a rhetorical analysis of Jeremiah's current shape. Having begun at the end, one might be tempted to move further back in time and to delineate the prophet's original poetic oracle, determining as well the precise history of the redactional process it has undergone. But however noble the intention, to go much beyond what we have already done is, as I have tried to demonstrate elsewhere, to attempt the impossible.[27] Nevertheless, it is clear that the several levels of our composition stem from the various periods of Jeremiah's career (and perhaps that of early post-Jeremianic disciples) in terms of their historical-theological perspective. The basic oracle is a call to repentance, while the main prose additions (and v. 1 as well) reflect a later period when divine judgment was certain. The composition as a whole reflects a desire for consolation and physical return (e.g., 3:12–13—the core; and 4:1–2—the conclusion), but there may also be additions dreaming of a truly miraculous restoration.

Moses and Abraham may have been the founders of Yahwism, but Jeremiah and Deutero-Isaiah were the true prophetic founders of Judaism. Here I have tried to show that, in a very real sense, the Book of Jeremiah itself constitutes the Judaic reflections of Jeremiah and his disciples on Jeremiah's own Yahwistic-Israelite prophecies.

NOTES

1. The formal papers of these sessions were published in *Proceedings of the Eighth World Congress of Jewish Studies: Jerusalem, August 16–21, 1981, Panel Sessions: Bible Studies and Hebrew Language* (Jerusalem: World Union of Jewish Studies, 1983).

2. Moshe Goshen-Gottstein's presentation "Modern Jewish Bible Research: Aspects

of Integration" (pp. 1–18 in the previously mentioned volume) is noteworthy in this regard. Goshen-Gottstein's call for a serious Jewish approach to biblical thought was eagerly received, but four years ago I was less willing to accept his claim that Jewish scholars only delude themselves if they think they are accepted as full members of the scholarly community by even the most sympathetic of their Christian fellows. Lamentably, he is undoubtedly correct.

3. L. H. Ginsberg's rejection of the theories of Y. Kaufmann is nowhere more evident than in his *Israelian Heritage of Judaism,* TSJTSA 24 (New York: Ktav, 1982).

4. I readily acknowledge that most of my colleagues of the Kaufmannian persuasion have worked honestly, long, and hard to demonstrate their positions, using the best of modern methodologies. What I am reacting to is not their work, but rather the motivation that appears to drive that work. There remains, however, one area of the argument wherein reason has succumbed to prejudice. The arguments of Wellhausen are rejected by many Jews simply because of their presumed anti-Semitic motivation. Obviously, arguments can be sound in spite of their motivation, but when it comes to Wellhausen and company this is forgotten because, unlike anti-Semitic Assyriologists or Egyptologists, Wellhausen dealt with (and defamed) Judaism directly.

5. Cf. Claus Rietzschel, *Das Problem der Urrolle* (Gütersloh: Mohn, 1966); A. Baumann, "Urrolle und Fasttag: Zur Rekonstruktion der Urrolle des Jeremiabuches nach den Angaben in Jer. 36," *ZAW* 80 (1968): 350–73.

6. Sigmund Mowinckel, *Zur Komposition des Buches Jeremiah* (Kristiania, 1914). Mowinckel's thesis was actually only a slightly modified version of that suggested by B. Duhm in 1901. Cf. John Bright, *Jeremiah,* AB 21 (New York: Doubleday & Co., 1965), lx.

7. Cf. esp. the B. Child's bibliographical summary in *Introduction to the Old Testament as Scripture* (Philadelphia: Fortress Press, 1979), 342ff.

8. Significant works in this area are: William L. Holladay, *The Architecture of Jeremiah 1—20* (Lewisburg, Pa.: Bucknell Univ. Press, 1976), and Jack R. Lundbom, *Jeremiah: A Study in Ancient Hebrew Rhetoric,* SBLDS 18 (Missoula, Mont.: Scholars Press, 1975). Lundbom's elucidation of the widespread use of *inclusio* and chiasm in Jeremiah will remain a valuable contribution for a long time. Holladay uses a rather ad hoc approach to structural analysis, totally ignoring the importance of strophic structure in biblical poetry. On the other hand, he is to be applauded for insisting on the importance of analyzing the continuity of the text as it stands, unlike Bright who, in his widely read commentary (*Jeremiah*), falls victim to the limitations of form criticism and completely rearranges the text of Jeremiah as he would like to see it.

9. The designation *pesher* is used rather cavalierly by Holladay (*Architecture of Jeremiah,* 47–48) to describe the prose material, but other than pointing out that the prose material uses "several phrases from the poetry in the vicinity," he neglects it and its implications altogether.

10. Stephen A. Kaufman, "The Temple Scroll and Higher Criticism," *HUCA* 53 (1982): 29–44; "Deuteronomy XV and Recent Research on the Dating of P," in *Das deuteronomium,* ed. N. Lohfink, BETL 68 (Leuven: Leuven Univ. Press, 1985), 273–76.

11. Because when we do the latter, we do not even do it right! Witness the story of *inclusio* and chiasm. For centuries they have been staples in the canons of musical and literary form. Yet how many paid attention to their ubiquity in the Bible? Only now that our attention has been drawn to these features do we realize that they constitute one of the major compositional principles of biblical Hebrew literature, probably second only to parallelism itself. Nevertheless, and somewhat incredibly, they merit only the briefest concern in the two "latest words" on biblical Hebrew poetry, M. O'Connor,

Hebrew Verse Structure (Winona Lake, Ind.: Eisenbrauns, 1980), and J. Kugel, *The Ideal of Biblical Poetry* (New Haven: Yale Univ. Press, 1981).

12. W. Rudolph, *Jeremia,* 3d ed. (Tübingen: Mohr, 1968); David Jobling, "Jeremiah's Poem in III 1–IV 2," *VT* 28 (197): 45–55, and Holladay, *Architecture of Jeremiah,* 46ff.

13. In fact this is Jobling's elaboration (interpretation?) of a relatively minor observation of Rudolph's already found in the 1947 edition of the latter's commentary (*Jeremia,* 25). It does not seem to me that Rudolph is at all concerned with the kind of issues with which Jobling struggles.

14. This analysis is typical of Holladay's approach throughout the book. It requires no further discussion.

15. The lonely, introductory לאמר is missing in the versions, yet most commentators assume that an original ויהי דבר ה' אלי has been omitted in the MT. I assume, rather, that it is an addition.

Neither of the other major Septuagintal divergences are acceptable a priori, the first ("she" return to "him") because the action of returning is clearly associated with the husband in Deuteronomy 24 on which our passage is based, the second ("that woman" instead of "that land") because of the importance of the notion of defiled land in the subsequent text. This is a fine example of how, frequently, text criticism cannot be successfully accomplished without an awareness of literary-critical considerations.

16. Even Lundbom (*Jeremiah,* 37 n. 8) has fallen into the trap, relying on the similarity of הן in 3:1 and הנה in 3:5 to establish an *inclusio* and finding "many nice balances." (Note that he thinks 3:1–5 constitutes an original unit all by itself.)

17. W. Thiel, *Die deuteronomische Redaktion von Jeremia 1—25* (Neukirchen: Neukirchener Verlag, 1973), 83f.

18. Revocalizing as a perfect, of course.

19. Deleting ואדא as a doublet gloss (with V). The text is quite nonsensical otherwise.

20. I omit this from the poem as an obvious doublet of the next four words.

21. Note that the context supports the Masoretic vocalization of ותחנף as a *qal* against all the versions!

22. Is this semantic development dependent on the usage גוי חנף in Isa. 10:6?

23. Cf. my "The Structure of the Deuteronomic Law," *MAARAV* 1 (1979): 105–58.

24. Perhaps the most grotesque attempt is that of Jacob Bazak, *Structures and Contents in the Psalms: Geometric Structural Patterns in the Seven Alphabetic Psalms* (Jerusalem–Tel Aviv: Dvir, 1984) (in Hebrew).

25. See nn. 8 and 11 above.

26. Some other examples of "antithetic chiasm" in Jeremiah are the "great *inclusio*" of 1:5—20:18 and the major *inclusio* 5:15—10:25.

27. See n. 10.

Part Two

RELIGION AND HISTORY

5 BARUCH HALPERN

"BRISKER PIPES THAN POETRY": THE DEVELOPMENT OF ISRAELITE MONOTHEISM*

In any academic discipline there are issues that are noticeably central and others that are noticeably peripheral for the mainstream of active scholars. In biblical studies the center of interest is and has always been the history of Israelite religion. Histories of Israel in the nineteenth century amounted most frequently to discussions of cultic and theological development, and we should elicit no substantial remonstration by observing that the single most influential work in modern biblical criticism has been Julius Wellhausen's *Prolegomena to the History of Israel* (1878), a work dedicated to the history of the cult. Today, a glance at the professional journals or at classroom textbooks will establish that the history of Israelite religion remains the central node of scholarly and lay interest.

Among the questions relating to Israel's religious odyssey, that of the origin of monotheism is intellectually and theologically primary. It is, however, a complex matter. To date, the most comprehensive and convincing attempt to deal with it remains that of Yehezkel Kaufmann. Still, Kaufmann's work, formulated in conscious response to that of Wellhausen, has not enjoyed widespread acceptance. Clearly, any reevaluation of the entire question must inevitably involve the coordination of intellectual with political and social history. Only in the context of an analysis of international and domestic discussions can the whole course of the crystallization of monotheistic theologies be understood. Kaufmann's work, while cognizant of these complica-

*This study was supported by the Institute for Advanced Studies at the Hebrew University, the National Endowment for the Humanities, and the Albright Institute of Archaeological Research in Jerusalem (a branch of the American Schools of Oriental Research).

tions, concentrated primarily in intellectual history. It is the point of this present study, as a prolegomenon to a full-dress history of the idea, to address and reassess Kaufmann's and his contemporaries' notions of the development of monotheism in Israel. Our emphasis here falls on the history of ideas; the sociopolitical provenience, dissemination, and socialization of the ideas that were developed remain to be treated. I hope to undertake that task in a subsequent work.

I

Pitched to a group of undergraduates, the question "What is monotheism?" almost invariably elicits the answer "belief in one God," or "the belief that only one God exists." Christians, Jews, Muslims—the respondent will testify that since these embrace the Bible they are the identifiable monotheists. The Bible is the root of Western culture, and the Bible admits of no equivocation on this point; there is only one God.

Westerners, it need hardly be said, pride themselves on their monotheism. They cherish derogatory but quaint ideas about polytheists (who worship idols and other fetishes; practice sympathetic magic; see gods, almost paranoiacally, in every tree and under every bed; and sacrifice virgins to volcanoes). Under the circumstances, it is not surprising that the student who first furnished the definition of monotheism squirms skeptically on learning that Psalm 82 depicts YHWH judging the gods in their assembly, that Psalm 29 enjoins the gods to praise YHWH, and that according to Deuteronomy 32 and much other biblical thought, each people had been allotted its own god as Israel had been allotted YHWH (32:8–9;[1] cf., for example, Micah 4:5). The Israelites, insists the student, could not be polytheists—they had received the revelation at Sinai! Even hearing that Israel considered YHWH the chief god does not mitigate this first flush of indignation. After all, the pagan Greeks and Romans had chiefs of the gods. Could it not be that those notorious Israelites had simply backslid into paganism? Or—and here is the inspiration—are not those other gods really angels? A sigh of comfort regained; once more the ancient Israelite has been rescued from the heresy of not being us.

But let us press this hypothetical student of ours further, employing that petty, sadistic process of embarrassment that is called the Socratic method. "How do we, now, differ from pagans?" "We only have one God." "Do Catholics believe in saints, Jews and Muslims in angels, Protestants in devils?" "That is different," comes the response! "Do angels not live forever, enjoy supernatural powers, exist in a dimension different from that inhabited by mortals?" "Still different"! And should we press the point that angels and devils, being divine, may be called gods, that the difference between monotheism and polytheism in the student's mind is the difference between God and god—between two ways of spelling the same word—we shall meet with the no longer smug but nevertheless obstinate assurance that modern Christianity or Judaism or Islam is somehow being kicked unfairly in the knee. There is only one God; no other gods need apply.

This fictitious interchange has of course less to do with Israelite monotheism than with the definition of monotheism and with the peculiar semantic restriction the word "god" has undergone in Western parlance. Still, it does illustrate the obstacles that intrude into investigations of biblical religion. Concepts aside, the terms themselves are loaded, and without being altogether clear. To be monotheist is good; but is one a monotheist if one believes, as scholars have long recognized Israel did, that the gods meet in a heavenly council which is counterpart to the pantheons of contiguous non-monotheistic cultures?[2] Does calling the old gods "angels" alter affairs? Can the monotheist direct prayer or sacrifice to other gods or angels and still remain a monotheist?

More than has been supposed, these definitional questions have affected the course of scholarly discussion. Israel produced monotheism, it is universally agreed, no later than the time of Deutero-Isaiah (ca. 540–520 B.C.E.), who exudes it. But as to earlier Israel, opinions vary widely. The most common view has been that early Israel was henotheistic or occasionally even monolatrous, but not monotheistic. In its extreme and most common manifestation, this position is buttressed by citations of biblical texts recognizing the activity of gods other than YHWH (as Judges 11:24). Thus, T. H. Robinson could write in his commentary to Amos "Amos approached near to monotheism, but did not actually reach it, for in his eyes there are, apart from YHWH, other gods, standing, it is true, on an inferior level to him (5, 26)."[3] However, more moderate scholars have understood that the rigid boundary erected by Robinson is too stark, that while the religion of prophets such as Amos may not quite turn on denying the existence even of the subsidiary deities, it was not for this reason to be classified as polytheistic.[4] Indeed even scholars such as J. Wellhausen, a staunch proponent of the view that early Israel was merely henotheistic, if that, exhibit a telling terminological flexibility.[5] Wellhausen writes the following: "Moab, Ammon, and Edom, Israel's nearest kinsfolk and neighbours, were monotheists in precisely the same sense in which Israel itself was."[6] That is to say, these neighboring peoples devoted themselves primarily to the worship of a single "high god."

The issue of the relationship of Israel's religion to her neighbors' religions has proved generally valuable in clarifying this school of thought's views. As early as 1913, J. Hehn differentiated three types of monotheism to be found in ancient Mesopotamia.[7] Hehn's work formed the basis for considerable historical theological discussion which culminated in G. Widengren's 1936 treatment of Israel's religion as a sort of "affective monotheism," the most pronounced of the varieties of quasi monotheism (the others were "solar" and "national," the latter being the variety to which Wellhausen had consigned Israel and her neighbors.[8] Affective monotheism consisted of preferring a single god, but not through dogma, rather as an expression of devotion. Other gods could simultaneously be recognized, but sole supremacy was ascribed to the god who was the object of adulation. Widengren singled out Nabonidus as an example (though he was certainly exceptional, and in any event contemporary with Deutero-Isaiah). However, like Hehn and his predecessor B. Baentsch, he also noted a tendency for the chief god to absorb the powers of lesser colleagues—a tendency marked already in the Babylonian epic of creation, the *Enuma Elish,* which dates from the second millennium B.C.E.[9] In the Babylonian epic, Marduk is awarded the names and powers that make him the equivalent of the pantheon incarnate (note 7.140; 4.4, 6; 6.122ff.).

Widengren construed this as evidence that Babylonian religion had "strong monotheistic tendencies" despite its unconvincing, flattering nature. And the prestige of Asshur in Assyrian culture seems, if anything, to have been even greater than that of Marduk at Babylon.[10] Thus, in Mesopotamia, the high god attracts to him- or herself the power of the pantheon as a whole. To this phenomenon, V. Nikiprowetzky has compared the use of *theos* in Greece as a means of expressing the outcome of the combined interventions and deliberations of the several gods, and thus as a sort of monotheism-by-default.[11] But this more impersonal concept is more profitably compared to the still less personal Chinese T'ien. Furthermore, Hehn noted that the trend toward a greater central god in Mesopotamia had not there issued in the full-scale elimination of the other gods.[12]

All the scholars so far enumerated thus concur that early Israel was somehow not quite monotheistic, despite its concentration on YHWH as the special deity of the people and the supreme causal force in the cosmos. On the other hand, Israel's neighbors were not fully polytheistic, for their cults centered about particular high gods. Monotheism developed only late in Israel during the exile (586–538 B.C.E.), and even then these scholars maintain, isolated groups continued to worship gods other than YHWH. Indeed, they suggest that the Jewish colony at Elephantine still patronized divinities called *ʿnt*-Bethel and *ʾšm*-Bethel at the end of the fifth century.[13] Monotheism, then, developed only late, and was generalized later still.

There is a second school of thought on the subject of Israel's monotheism. It is portrayed as the "Mosaic revolution" school, for its proponents maintain that Israel was from the outset fundamentally monotheistic.[14] This school's ablest advocate has been Yehezkel Kaufmann. Kaufmann observed that it is possible for monotheists to believe in the puissance of more than a single god. Indeed, he said:

> Even the worship of other supernatural beings . . . cannot be considered in necessary contradiction to monotheism. . . . The One is not necessarily "jealous" in a cultic sense. There is room in monotheism for the worship of lower divine beings—with the understanding that they belong to the suite of the One. Thus Christianity knows the worship of saints and intercessors, as does Islam. . . .

> Israelite monotheism tended toward cultic exclusivism and was crystallized in this form in the Bible. But during the pre-exilic period Israel was still moving from the basic monotheistic idea to its extreme cultic consequence.[15]

Kaufmann denied that preexilic Israel recognized the independent activity of gods other than YHWH (his "angels"). But the heart of his quarrel with scholars who deny Israel's monotheism still lies in his approach to the question of what monotheism is. Scholars such as Robinson, Wellhausen, and Widengren defined the term much as did the undergraduate with whose ideas this paper began. They took it literally to imply the nonexistence of gods other than YHWH.[16] Kaufmann allowed the common use of the term to determine its meaning, and in this respect must be allowed the point. It would be irrational to deny that preexilic Israel was monotheistic on grounds that would imply traditional Judaism, Christianity, and Islam were not monotheistic.

Kaufmann's alternative is in the end rather complex, and to summarize it here is to do him an injustice. His criteria to distinguish monotheism from polytheism include attitudes toward angelology/demonology, theogony, cosmogony, magic, and so forth. In each case, his concern is that the attitude in Israel toward this or that aspect of religion should be consonant with the philosophical implications of theoretical monotheism.

Those familiar with Kaufmann's work widely recognize that this approach is more sophisticated than the one adopted by his predecessors. To some extent, this is imputable to Kaufmann's very conservative picture of the history of religion (for example, he insists on an early date for the Priestly Code, and his stance is vindicated only by recent appreciation of the weakness inherent in Wellhausen's religio-historical typology).[17] Kaufmann sought the "mark of monotheism" in "the idea of a god who is the source of all being, not subject to a cosmic order, and not emergent from a pre-existent realm; a god free of the limitations of magic and mythology."[18] Although this description may be controversial in its individual components, it does have the virtue of representing fairly some of the characteristic properties of Western monotheisms. It manages not to exclude monotheism on the basis of their Manichaean or multidivinity proclivities.

In light of this fact, it seems reasonable to break the question of Israel's development of monotheism into segments. It is legitimate to inquire into the origin of the doctrinal, philosophical monotheism Robinson and his colleagues interested themselves in, and which we may characterize as radical monotheism. But this is not to say that one should avert one's gaze from the signs of monotheism to which Kaufmann drew attention. It is important to establish when and in what measure the notion prevailed that YHWH was the god who indisputably mastered the cosmos—this, after all, is the premise from which Kaufmann's specific criteria ultimately flow. We should be helped in our research if we could discover also when the principle of monolatry took hold. Here, we will base our conclusion both on the terms that Kaufmann lays down on the basis of modern monotheism (allowing sacrifice to lesser deities in the chief god's "suite"), and on the concept of radical monolatry (allowing sacrifice directly to YHWH only). Finally, our interest should center on the relationships among such varieties of practice and theory, not on their static existence or their appearance *ex machina* or through untimely and unexplained revelation.

II

There is, as one might expect from the foregoing survey, a considerable body of evidence to indicate that early Israel believed in the existence and even the puissance of deities other than YHWH. Along with numerous allusions in early poetry to YHWH's council of gods, testimonies that Israel at large understood this council to be YHWH's medium for administering the cosmos have generated a substantial scholarly literature on the subject (e.g., Ps. 29:1; 82:1; Deut. 33:2–3[19] and 1 Kings 22:19–22; Job 1—2; 33:23; Isa. 6:1–10).[20] The multiplicity of early Israel's gods has rarely been called seriously into question. Moreover, not all the evidence implies that all the gods were universally regarded as mere extensions of YHWH's will. Kaufmann sees YHWH's battles with such figures as Rahab and Leviathan as isolated vestiges of Israel's Canaanite cultural heritage, but such liturgical specimens as Pss. 74:12–17 and 89:10–15 illustrate how closely bound to cosmogonic myth these battles remained in the Israelite consciousness.[21] Thus, to the primordial era, at least one strain of thought comprised struggles for the mastery of the cosmos. These struggles were not necessarily on the order of those depicted in Babylonian (*Enuma Elish*) or Canaanite myth, but they were nevertheless comparable in type.[22] The reports of these battles do not, of course, imply the existence of a Yahwistic theogony. Still, taken together with the rhetorical comparison of YHWH with the other gods (Exod. 15:11; Ps. 89:7), the texts testify that challenges to YHWH's mastery were, if foredoomed to fail, at least conceivable. This is consonant with the implications in such texts as 1 Kings 22:19–22 and Isa. 6:8 that the heavenly beings actually exerted independent powers of thought (the coup of the Morning Star in Isa. 14:13 may have similar implications). Genesis 6:1–4, that mystifying text which describes the descent of the gods and their miscegenation with primordial women, confirms that in the Israel of the Yahwist (J), independent thought was very much the case among heavenly beings.[23] Of course, this is only to be expected in a tradition that ascribes disobedience to primordial humans ensconced like an angel in YHWH's presence (Genesis 2—4; see also Ezek. 28:11–18 and Psalm 82).

Additional evidence is provided by the study of sacrifices. On the cultic level, all varieties of sacrifice were countenanced in early Israel. Human sacrifice (a proper Yahwistic rite)[24] and other forms of worship later deemed heretical maintained, and there was also sacrifice to gods other than YHWH. *t'rāpîm,* or icons of household gods, figure in a number of texts (e.g., Judges

17:5; 18:14–20; 1 Sam. 15:23; 19:13, 16; Hosea 3:4; Ezek. 21:26; 2 Kings 23:24; Gen. 31:19–35), and these, or icons of more important deities, may be represented in the variety of figurines that periodically come to light from excavations in Israelite levels.[25] While the much-debated *pithoi* unearthed at Kuntillet Ajrud may depict YHWH in the company of a consort, such figurines were generally understood to represent the gods who served YHWH.[26] On the basis of these finds, too, it seems most judicious to understand the cult of the "queen of heaven" not as an imported, debased Mesopotamian cult,[27] but as a hoary folk practice interrupted by the Josianic reform (Jer. 44:1ff.) and construed by its practitioners as a Yahwistic cult (hence 44:16, 26 with YHWH).

The appearance of YHWH's consort at Kuntillet Ajrud, or of a hypostatized sacred precinct, complements other evidence of sacrifice to subordinate members of the pantheon. The suppression of supposedly heterodox regalia by Hezekiah and Josiah is perhaps most suggestive. The former is said to have smashed an Asherah, a cultic pillar, and, notably, the bronze snake reputed to have been made by Moses at which the people had for some time offered incense (2 Kings 18:4). Josiah's purge included altars built centuries earlier by Solomon and dedicated to Chemosh and other foreign gods (2 Kings 23:13); reportedly, he removed sacra of "Baal and Asherah and all the host of heaven" from YHWH's temple (2 Kings 23:4). While the narrator's stratagem of blaming the Babylonian Exile on Manasseh (2 Kings 21:12–15) makes it appear as though these icons' presence resulted from that king's debauchery, G. Ahlström is undoubtedly right to regard it instead as a reflection of the traditional religion of Judah which perhaps followed on a hiatus in the official cult under Hezekiah (2 Chronicles 29—31).[28] The old, traditional homage to subsidiary members of YHWH's assembly was carried on even in Jerusalem, and, to judge from the evidence, even after Hezekiah's otherwise far-reaching reform.

But the strongest indications that non-Yahwistic cult practices existed lie in traces of the ancestral cult, particularly in the pre-monarchic period. Certainly, it is simplest to explain the recollection of the "minor judges" burials (Judges 8:30, 32; 10:1–5; 12:7–15) on the supposition that these served as shrines and oracles. And Rachel's tomb, at the least, must have represented just such a shrine (Gen. 35:19f.; 1 Sam. 10:2; Jer. 31:15). Still it is clear that necromancy thrived in Israel. Indeed, A. Haldar concluded from Isa. 29:4 that the prophet announced an oracle from the underworld in procession at the Jerusalem temple.[29] But 1 Samuel 28, the story of Saul's encounter with the witch of En-Dor, and Deut. 18:8ff., which assails all forms of divination other than prophecy, suggest that the practice was not condoned in the temple cult. Yet at the same time, even those who advocated its suppression did not deny its efficacy, and indeed, in the popular religion, necromancy was never eradicated, but flourished from time to time (see Isa. 2:6–8; 3:2; Micah 3:6–11;

5:11; Isa. 8:19; 19:3).[30] The persistence of funerary societies through the era of the monarchy shows that this assessment reflected popular sentiment (as Amos 6:1–6; Jer. 16:5). And as M. Pope's commentary on the Song of Songs illustrates, the cult of the dead was one to which virtually every preexilic Israelite, especially the upper class, was exposed.[31] Even in this case, to what extent such sacrifice represented an assertion of independence from YHWH is not altogether clear.

The strongest testimony remains that which suggests Israel's gods were understood to lie within YHWH's "suite." Thus the Israelite onomasticon both inside the Bible and without contains names compounded only with the name of YHWH and with epithets attached to YHWH (including *b'l,* a term meaning "lord," and not to be reified as the name of a god).[32] The same condition characterizes Israel's "closest kinsfolk and neighbours," as Wellhausen anticipated. Ammon, Moab, and Edom each adhered to a single national god. In contrast to names stemming from city-states, each of their onomastica contains names compounded only with the name of the national god or with some soubriquet denominating the national god (such as *ēl* or *ba'l*).[33] While inscriptional materials from the Transjordanian states are scanty, and the Deir Alla texts reflect the presence of a pantheon,[34] the Mesha stele is unambiguous. Mesha attributes to his national god Chemosh both defeat and victory (ll. 5–6). The inscription mentions YHWH as Israel's god (ll. 17f.); the only other divinity mentioned is the enigmatic "Ashtar-Chemosh," the recipient of a human sacrifice. At worst, he constitutes an underling or hypostatization of the national god, conceivably syncretized with the Canaanite Athtar.[35]

This distribution of evidence reflects Israel's place among the "Hebrew" successor-states to the Egyptian empire in Asia, all of which crystallized at the close of the Bronze Age along the major trade routes from Mesopotamia to Egypt.[36] These states appear uniformly to have devoted themselves to the worship of the national god. When Jephthah recognizes Chemosh's activity in Judges 11:24, he does so during international negotiation, which is by nature ecumenical. Deuteronomy 32:8–9 too merely reflects shared understanding that while every people has its god, our god is the supreme god.[37] While no biblical text identifies polytheistic Egypt or Greece with a single god, and while even Marduk at Babylon seems to be understood in Israel to have been more an emblematic than a national god, it is worth noting that these texts presume henotheism to have been the normal form of religion. On the Mediterranean littoral, adherence to the cult of a single high god seems to have been taken early as the natural way of things.[38]

This henotheism was early understood to be monolatrous. The Covenant Code, a text commonly dated to the pre-monarchic era, enjoins sacrifice to gods other than YHWH (Exod. 22:19). Whether this was meant to exclude sacrifice to YHWH's retinue or held widespread force in Israel cannot now be determined, but that it was consistent with general opinion is now plain from the fact that Israel devised a theology in which it was in a treaty relationship with YHWH. Such suzerainty pacts characteristically included clauses demanding of the vassal exclusive fealty to the overlord (see Exod. 22:19).[39] How early the covenant form was introduced as a means of expressing Israel's relation to YHWH is uncertain, but we get a clue from Hosean analogy which takes Israel as an adultress on the basis of a contractual relationship.[40] Israel's monarchy was also contractually based, with YHWH a party to the pact.[41] Already, at twelfth-century Shechem, Israel had organized itself around a god who called himself "El of the Covenant" (cf. Judges 2:46) or "the lord of the covenant" (*ba'alb^erît*, Judges 9:4).[42] The likelihood is that the covenantal relationship with YHWH was a notion that early pervaded the nation's thought.

Furthermore, the characteristic name of YHWH and the understanding of his cosmic role present signal indications of monolatrous henotheism—effectively of monotheism. YHWH's name means "he causes to be/happen."[43] In its most primitive longer form, it is coupled with *s^ebā'ôt*, "armies" (so, "he causes the [heavenly] armies [i.e., the gods, of whom the stars are the counterparts, Judges 5:20][44] to be" [1 Sam. 4:4; 2 Sam. 6:2]).[45] And the Yahwist, writing in the tenth century, introduces YHWH in his narrative history by the fuller, probably explanatory name, *yhwh 'lhym*, "he causes the gods/pantheon to be" (not the appositive, "YHWH, God," which would require a definite article before the second member). If exegetical of the older cultic name, this represents YHWH as the patriarch of all the gods, as the universal progenitor.

Kaufmann identified the absence of theogony in Israel and the battle-free cosmogony of Genesis 2—3 as hallmarks of an early monotheism.[46] One point of comparison was the cosmogonic fight in *Enuma Elish* in which Marduk rescued his peers and elders from their mother, the salt-water dragon Tiamat, who sought to avenge on them the death of their father. But it is worth noting the Canaanite evidence not, as Kaufmann did, in the fragments of Sakkunyaton, but in the tablets from Ugarit.[47] On the basis of an analogy to the *Enuma Elish,* some scholars have supposed that the cycle of battles between Baal (Haddu) and Yamm ("Sea") at Ugarit was in fact cosmogonic.[48] Haddu's acquisition of a palace is in type a cosmogonic act.[49] But there is not the faintest hint that the cycle involves creation at Ugarit; indeed, El is repeatedly called "the creator/progenitor of all creatures/progeny,"[50] and "father of man,"[51] and the gods, as in Israel, are called "sons of El." Too, references to villages in the Haddu-Yamm cycle suggest that the conflict is situated after the creation of the world.[52] This is what one would expect, given that El is so much in control of the cosmos that he alone dispenses permits for palace construction while his "sons," Haddu, Yamm, and Mot, administer the regions of land/sky, sea, and underworld under his supervision.[53] Thus, theogony and cosmogonic theomacy may already be absent at Ugarit. While Marduk, the storm-god, defeats Sea and creates from his enemy the cosmos, and YHWH, the patriarchal, tent-dwelling, and eternal deity fashions the world peacefully around his paradisiacal garden, Ugarit's pantheon includes both the storm-god's fight with Sea and the "patriarchal"-type cosmogony. It may represent a sort of middle between the extremes of the Babylonian theogony-cosmogony and the Israelite Genesis.[54] This is not to deny the presence of the themes of cosmogonic conflict in Israel, for myths need not be mutually exclusive even when in mutual contradiction. As noted above, YHWH's defeat of primordial menaces is frequently mentioned. By the same token, the themes of cosmogonic conflict were present in Canaan, and, in Sakkunyaton, those of theogony. However, with antecedents in Ugarit's El that can be dated to the fourteenth century, the Yahwist in the tenth century B.C.E. understood YHWH to have created both cosmos and gods. YHWH, "he causes," is his ultimate cause, a prime mover—what Kant would regard as the inevitable product of the use of reason.

Early Israel was far from homogeneous, and it would be foolish to assume that the Yahwist's latent theology was widely shared. And, if we stretch things, we could add that, in addition to the general references to the cult of the ancestors noted above, Deut. 33:27 could be taken to portray YHWH as "oppressing the gods of old." The context is difficult, still the LXX does reflect the same *Vorlage,* so a vestige of theogonic thought may be present.[55] But even if one embraces speculation based on such pale traces,[56] the broader picture of YHWH as chief and as national god remains. This YHWH is universal in his power, just as Ugarit's El, Babylon's Marduk or Asshur's Asshur. Thus, the notion that universalism developed late in Israel as a product of radical monotheism ignores the implications of YHWH's name, of the primordial history in J, and of the liturgical language of most of the Near East in the millennium before J.[57] Further, the argument that YHWH's universal exaltation, so central to Trito-Isaiah, is late,[58] neglects the universalism inherent in nearly every account of temple construction extant from Mesopotamia.[59] And even within the latest incarnations of this motif, as M. Weinfeld has observed, a particularist program for the exaltation of Zion and Israel remains.[60] Again, Amos's renowned question, "Are you not Cushites to me, children of Israel? . . . Did I not bring Israel up from Egypt and Philistia from Caphtor and Aram from Qir?" (Amos 9:7), has generated no end of assertions that Amos was a "universalist," and perhaps the first universalist.[61] But this claim ignores Amos's equally famous plaint, "You alone have I known of all the families of the earth; that is why I visit on you all your sins" (3:2). The point is, Israel remains specially sacred to YHWH no matter how universal his scope of power or his recognition. Second Kings 5:17, which is coupled with the recognition of YHWH as the only active god, demonstrates this. Naaman still does better to appropriate the soil of Israel for his worship. Here is evidence of special sanctity, not of limitation or an exclusive or reified "particularism." And this is exactly the implication of the J primeval history when coupled with the call of Abraham.

However, this YHWH is from the first a just and gracious god. Indeed, Israel's early psalmody is replete with testimony to the fact (Psalms 24, 29, 82, for example). Such a bias does not surprise us in a culture that conceived of its relationship with its god as covenantal. (The gods of Canaan and Mesopotamia were similarly understood by their votaries to dispense justice.) So there is little evidence of the "whimsical" or "amoral" polytheism in Western Asia of which the Greek philosophers accused the Greeks; the gods are just—they are ethical.[62]

Even Israel's later aniconism, a true hallmark of radical monotheism, has a discernible antecedent in the early period. The J "decalogue" contains an ordinance prohibiting the manufacture of molten images of gods. Like the later (Jerusalem priestly) interdiction against all pictorial or plastic representation (Exod. 20:4, after v. 3), the ordinance is tied to the commandment of exclusive devotion (Exod. 34:14–17).[63] The pre-monarchic legislation of Exod. 20:19–23 begins with an injunction against manufacturing (precious?) metal images of gods. Provided one accepts that the bronze oxen in Solomon's temple were not meant to be gods,[64] and that Jeroboam's golden "calves" were representations of YHWH's steed and not of a god,[65] or were at best the symbol of a god, the nearest violation of these ordinances is said to have occurred when Solomon had the cherubim for the inner sanctum of the temple constructed (1 Kings 6:23–28).[66] These gods were made of wood and plated with beaten gold. Certainly, their construction does not violate the J ordinance; indeed arguably it satisfies the term of Exod. 20:20 as well.

In any event, barring only the illustrated *pithos* from Kuntillet Ajrud, there is no signal indication that YHWH himself was depicted in the cult. There is a strong presumption from silence that other than his ark, no representation of him stood in the Jerusalem temple or in Jeroboam's royal sanctuaries in the north. At least in the state cult, YHWH was from the first an invisible deity. The only known precedent for this distinction lies in the representation of 'Aten by the solar disk at Akhetaten, and that remains a representation, of course.[67]

Again, it should not be disputed that in the popular religion representatives of YHWH may have played a role. And even in the capital YHWH may have been portrayed in ritual. Presumably, it was in part through dialogue with the rural cult that the official cult assumed an identity of its own. Still, virtually no major component of Israel's later monotheism is absent from the cult at the turn of the millennium, with the introduction of the kingship. Had we the evidence, we should probably be in a position to say the same of Moab, Ammon, and Edom. What is absent in these early materials is perhaps philosophically important but practically epicyclical. Early Israelite religion is not self-consciously monotheistic; it defines itself in terms of loyalty to YHWH, in terms of YHWH's incomparability, but not in terms of YHWH's transcending uniqueness. It has as yet no developed notion that being monotheistic, as it is (to use the term as it is applied to modern monotheisms), is central to its identity.

III

A. The philosopher Karl Jaspers characterized the period from 800 to 200 B.C.E. as Axial. He attributed to it the dawn of consciousness ("in which thinking is the object of itself"), distinguishing as the three areas in which this transition was made China, India, and the eastern Mediterranean. In the last, he maintained, the earlier empires did not make the transition, which was mediated by the poets and philosophers in Greece and by the prophets (especially Deutero-Isaiah) in Israel.[68] It would seem that in the case of the development of radical, self-conscious monotheism in Israel, we thus confront an instance of a widespread phenomenon. Still, it is instructive to trace the mechanics of the process that led Israel from monolatrous henotheism—the unselfconscious monotheism of the early first millennium B.C.E.—to philosophical monotheism by the time of the Babylonian Exile. The fates of Dagan, Qaws, Chemosh, and Milcom, not to mention Asshur and Marduk, suggest that contiguous cultures did not undergo the same development. How did it occur in Israel?

Continental scholars have characteristically suggested that YHWH was successively syncretized, assuming the properties of El Elyon (Gen. 14:19–20; 15:1), El Shaddai (Gen. 17:1; Exod. 6:2–3), El himself, Baal, and so forth.[69] But the materials surveyed above make this unlikely. First, YHWH was a fully articulated high god by the time the monarchy was introduced ca. 1030. Given the rhetoric of incomparability in Exodus 15 (probably twelfth century), and YHWH's control over the heavenly armies in Judges 5 (certainly twelfth century), it would not be inappropriate to assert YHWH's full-scale articulation in the thirteenth/twelfth century B.C.E.[70] Second, the understanding on which was based the idea that YHWH absorbed local Canaanite gods and various gods of the patriarchs was dealt a severe blow by F. M. Cross's argument that a variety of epithets need not imply a variety of Els, and that the variety of epithets are just that—epithets. Indeed, far from assimilating the various local *'ēlîm* or even *b^e'ālîm,* YHWH was El, in Cross's view. Perhaps one might say that he was in Israel's pantheon what El was in Ugarit's.[71] We might add that the accretion of storm-theophany language to YHWH should not be interpreted to imply syncretism with Haddu or, still less, with "Baal." It signifies only the accretion of language in keeping with the god's character—especially his character as a warrior. Finally, it violates good sense to hypothesize that the xenophobic Israel which produced such extensive polemics against baals and "alien" worship of any variety in the eighth through sixth centuries was a hotbed of syncretism and assimilation in the eighth century or even slightly earlier (see Hosea and Jeremiah). Rather, the vehemence of the prophets and of kings such as Saul should lead us to expect only the rejection of actually alien worship.[72] Indeed, this is a promising avenue for research to pursue.

B. The proprietary henotheism present in earliest Israel is, with its tendencies toward monolatry, nationalistic in nature. The tendency toward exclusivism is nationalistic, and nationalism entails movement toward exclusivism. Thus, in cases in which the "high" tradition asserts itself (as the exclusion of representations of YHWH from the Jerusalem or Bethel establishments), inner-Israelite customs and traditions may themselves become targets for polemic. This is a process through which the development of the self-conscious monotheism of a Deutero-Isaiah would be possible.

1. The redirection of Israel's xenophobia against native institutions first occurs, as the evidence suggests, with the constitution of the monarchy. At this time non-Levitic, nonprophetic mantics were suppressed, though the kingship unquestionably embraced the broadest spectrum of Yahwistic cults, including a variety of priesthoods (1 Samuel 28; Deut. 18:8ff.). Some scholars have maintained—on the slimmest grounds, unfortunately—that key figures in the sacral establishment of the early monarchy were actually scions of a Jebusite priesthood.[73] This is unlikely even in the time of David, who enfranchised all manner of non-Israelites in his regime, for the same reason that it is unlikely Jeroboam invented the golden-bull iconography. In each instance the state undoubtedly portrayed itself not as a daring innovator but as the mainstay of authentic and untainted tradition. Saul's assault on the non-Israelite populations of Canaan[74] may have reflected fear of Philistine and Ammonite onslaughts, but at the same time it embodied Israel's collective cultic conviction that YHWH, the chief god, has specially elected Israel (1 Samuel 8—14, esp. 10:1;[75] 12:12). The suppression not the adoption of foreign cults would have been the order of the day.

At this time, priestly franchise in the state sacral establishment seems to have been restricted to a single hereditary guild, the Levites, who were constituted as a "tribe."[76] Whether or not this priesthood included elements of earlier, non-Levitic orders (as it did), its very existence and the legislation of its monopoly over the state cult—indeed, the formation of the state cult itself—created an artificial standard and the potential for the alienation of Israel's official cultus from the religion of the people.[77] Moreover, it is clear that, for whatever reason, necromancy and the ancestral cult were stigmatized as alien and as un-Israelite (Num. 23:23; cf. 22:7; much later Isa. 2:6–8). It may be that the centripetal cult of the national god was consciously preferred to the centrifugal, familial, and fragmenting cults of the ancestors for reasons of state. (One could almost imagine such concerns underlying the stance of Saul, in 1 Samuel 20, for instance.) Conversely, the Chinese emperors with their warrior/priest/bureaucrat elite (aristocracy being the natural ground as in Canaan for the cult of the ancestors) made a virtue of the centrifugal ancestral cult by generalizing ancestors. Alternatively, it may have been Saul's or Samuel's intention to suppress the Levite's competitors on the mantic market (see Deut. 18:1–22). Whether or not this was the case, by virtue of its attack on necromancy the early state cult (the forerunner of the establishment that in Josiah's time proved to be the arbiter of the normative) began the process of identifying elements in the religion of the people of Israel as Israelite and as alien.

2. Leaving aside the issue of necromancy, the state cults of Judah and Israel were not always in sync with the popular religion. Under Saul the presumable erosion of the power of non-Levitic priesthoods already distinguished them. Quite early, it was understood that central government meant conducting censuses, conscripting troops and laborers, and constructing fortifications and state buildings such as the temple (1 Samuel 8; 2 Samuel 7 and 24; 1 Kings 6—8). Scholars have long recognized that such innovations, which were supported by the Davidic priesthood, crossed the grain of conservative folk sentiment.[78] Moreover, Solomon's Jerusalem was rife with shrines. This abundance the Josianic historian responsible for the Books of Kings attributes to the demands of international diplomacy and of Solomon's wives (1 Kings 11:1–8), and indeed, it should be noted that after Solomon's death, when the Judahite monarchy was severely reduced in scope and when the number of the king's foreign wives was not so legendary, Solomon's shrines continued to function (2 Kings 23:13). One may therefore justifiably suppose that the shrines represented only a part of an ecumenical, tolerant state policy toward the components of an imperial population. This is consistent with the exaltation of YHWH—the one god to whom Solomon dedicated the temple—as chief of the gods including the gods of the Gentiles (see Deut. 32:8–9).[79] Conversely, the sort of zeal for YHWH exhibited in Saul's persecution of visible minorities (note 2 Sam. 21:2) and in Solomon's construction of the temple complex (which required much conscription) may itself have been foreign to the folk religion. One clue to this situation lies in the early tribesmen's response to taxation. It appalled them, for they not unnaturally took it to amount to tribute (1 Sam. 8:11–18; 1 Kings 12:4; 13:16; Deut. 17:14–20).

The Israelite revolts against Solomon and at his demise sprang from inequities in his political economy (1 Kings 11:29–40 and 1 Kings 12).[80] Still, there is reason to believe that in seceding Jeroboam employed nativist rhetoric of the sort attributed to Ahijah of Shiloh in 1 Kings 11:33. Jeroboam's election of the bull iconography and his erection of two shrines in Dan and Bethel stood opposed to the Judahite cultic establishment with its single shrine and cherub iconography (1 Kings 12:25–33). Despite the polemic leveled against Jeroboam in Kings, he must have been trying to appeal to the Mosaic antecedents and nationalist sentiment of the north.[81] Part of his denunciation of

Solomon must have centered not just on the construction of the massive royal temple (and the demotion of the Shilonite priesthood, which supported a rival pretender at Solomon's accession, see 1 Kings 1—2), but also on the erection of shrines to gods of foreign peoples on the arrival of the new gods in town (cf. Deut. 32:17).

In short, the competition among national gods understood to underlie or embody the competition among nations may in the period of Israel's domination have engendered a tolerant monolatrous polytheism (cf. 1 Sam. 5:15). At the north's secession in an era of competition for independence, this may have been succeeded by a return to the sort of exclusivist nationalism that had characterized Israel's original differentiation as an ethnic state among alien Canaanites. While Solomon may have imported into Jerusalem the pantheon that arose from and was necessary to the administration of his empire, his political foes such as Ahijah seem to have distorted his behavior into an acknowledgment of the claims of the other gods to be YHWH's equals (cf. Exod. 15:11; Judges 11:24).[82] Thus, by repudiation of Chemosh et al. as foreign, rather than as subordinates in YHWH's council assigned by him to the nations, exclusivist sentiment again redefines what is and what is not authentically Israelite.

3. From the time after Solomon, information touching the Judahite monarchy is sparse. Concerning the north, the Books of Kings present considerable narrative, but its reliability is unsure. The sources claim that under the Omrides, whose imperial success in Transjordan and Syria involved them in foreign marital entanglements like those of Solomon, the cult of the Tyrian Baal made missionary inroads into Israel. Kings attributes this success to the patronage of Ahab's wife, Jezebel, daughter of Ethbaal, Tyre's king. It further identifies the revolt under Jehu that brings the Omride dynasty down with the revolutionary program of Elijah and Elisha (1 Kings 19:15–18; 2 Kings 9—10). This program, historically nativist in character, stigmatizes the cult of Tyre's Baal as foreign and conceivably identifies it with devotion to some "baal" known in Israel as YHWH's subordinate (see below). A subsequent coup in Judah, parallel to Jehu's in that it removed the Tyrian-Israelite scion Athaliah from the throne and eradicated the traces of Jehoshaphat's policy of accommodation with the Omrides (the only unification of Israel and Judah between Solomon and Josiah), is said to have issued in the destruction of some cult paraphernalia, including a temple of "the baal" (2 Kings 11:18). But this revolt is staged by the Jerusalem temple priesthood and bureaucracy in isolation from the rural population. While echoing the xenophobia of Jehu's purge, it seems to represent nothing more than a palace coup.

Jehu's coup was bloody, xenophobic (reacting against the tainted Omride foreign alliances, but also against military losses in Transjordan), and monolatrous (Hosea 1:4–5; 2:2).[83] The report in 1 Kings 18 on prophetic conflict with the Omrides has it that the issue was monolatry—even monotheism. In the tale, Elijah taxes the tolerant Israelite laity with exclusivist logic that derives from a complete misunderstanding of the range of meaning inherent in the word "god." He says "How long will you straddle the fence? If YHWH is the god, follow him, and if the baal is, follow him!" (1 Kings 18:21). And the cry "YHWH—he is the god," *yhwh hû hāʾᵉlōhîm* (1 Kings 18:39), which follows Elijah's miracle, may reflect Elijah's own name, "YHWH is my god," and anticipate paronomastically that of the king to come who would suppress the cult of "Baal," *yēhûʾ<*yhw hûʾ*. This is not, however, to say that the authors of the Elijah-Elisha stories or their characters were radical monotheists, since the stories reflect a continuing belief in the activity of heavenly armies and angels (2 Kings 6:17; 2:10–12; 1 Kings 19:5, 7). In any event, it is not clear that these texts antedate by much the time of Josiah's reform when the Books of Kings were assembled, or even, should the texts be older, that they accurately reflect what they report.[84] Consequently, it is unclear even whether Jehu's movement was an assault on traditional folk devotions to gods whose relationship to YHWH was that of subordinates to a suzerain (or, on the somewhat problematic reading of *ʾšrth* in the Kuntillet Ajrud inscriptions as "his concubine/Asherah," of chattels to a master). We cannot know whether the central ideological issue was monotheism versus polytheism as opposed to monolatrous Yahwistic henotheism versus monolatrous Yahwistic henotheism that included the Tyrian baal, or that tolerated that baal's worship, and so on. What we can say is that Israelite xenophobia was turned against certain cults or rites perceived as foreign. As in Jeroboam's time, the hue of YHWH's successful human troops concerned the strangeness of certain aspects of the state cult.

4. The next corpus affording insight into the history of ideas in the northern kingdom stems from a period roughly a century later, with a substantially different political complexion. Omride Israel had engaged in a seesaw conflict with the Arameans of Damascus, contesting possession of northern Transjordan. Together with its neighbors, it stopped Assyria's westward expansion for half a century. Jehu's dynasty therefore inherited the basis for a prosperous realm. Again in the mid-eighth century, Israel enjoyed a sustained ascendance under Jeroboam II (ca. 787–747). But after his reign the tide of Assyrian conquest waxed. There was attendant instability and ultimately political destruction and exile for Israel. It is in this era that the oracles of Amos and Hosea originated.

Prophesying before the death of Jeroboam II, Amos does not seem to have concerned himself overly with the threat of any "baal" cultus—in fact, he does not mention it (7:10–17). A. S. Kapelrud has suggested that the absence of polemic against "Baal" in Amos indicates that in Amos's time YHWH was being syncretized with the universal El. He notes that in the same period Hosea is not virulently opposed to the worship of "Baal" since he condemns the purge of Jehu (1:4–5) and thereby exhibits an attitude more ecumenical than that reported of Elisha.[85] Kapelrud's reconstruction is flawed, however. The problem in hypothesizing syncretism has been noted above, especially in an Israel prone to bouts of nativist xenophobia. Second, Kapelrud has not grasped that polemic against one *ba'al* may not represent polemic against another. Elisha's reputed bête noire was the Tyrian baal; the *ba'al* against whom he believes Jeremiah to have inveighed presumably signifies some other god or gods altogether. The absence of polemic against "Baal" in Amos is in fact an absence of polemic against Haddu, Melqart, Marduk, Asshur, Dagon, and all the other gods—YHWH included—whom that title could denote. Third, Hosea does inveigh against baal-worship, and in a most enlightening way.

In Hosea 1—3, the prophet castigates Israel for her infidelity to YHWH.[86] The image he chooses, a dominant image in the eighth to sixth centuries for such infidelity, is that of the adulteress pursuing her lovers (2:9). This permits Hosea to construct an elaborate pun based on the two words for "husband" in Israelite usage, *'îš* (lit. "man") and *ba'al* (lit. "master," in the sense of "proprietor" or of "lord"). "On that day, says YHWH, you (Israel) will call, 'My man' (*'îšî*) and will no more call me 'My master' (*ba'ᵉlî*)" (2:18). Scholars have long recognized in the second stich of the line a rejection of the very term *ba'al* accompanying the rejection of the baals themselves (though it is tellingly rejected as a designation of *YHWH*). But what is important to note is that while Hosea uses the singular in his pun, and in an unfortunately difficult piece of 2:10, where again the art of his piece seems to demand it (a reference to Exod. 20:23),[87] it is the plural *bᵉ'ālîm*, that he uses when his idiom permits (2:15; esp. 2:19; 11:2). Immediately after the pun in 2:18 he makes it clear he intends to remove from Israel's lips "the names of the baals," not the name of Baal. It is to Israel's patronizing the cults of a variety of deities that Hosea is objecting. So too, later, will Jeremiah (see 2:23). In fact, the term *ba'al* never appears as a proper noun or as the equivalent of a determined noun without a definite article in the MT. For the Israelite, there is no Baal, no Baal-worship, only *bᵉ'ālîm*, "baals."

Who are these baals against the worship of whom neither Amos nor (Proto)-Isaiah utters a word? The possibilities are limited. Either they are the foreign gods such as Melqart, periodically cultivated by the aristocracy and the central regime, or they are the identifiable members of YHWH's assembly, the identifiable troops of the "host of heaven," the big battalions on whose side was YHWH (see 1 Kings 22:19 and 2 Chron. 18:18; Isa. 13:4; 24:21; Josh. 5:14, 15). In a theology that saw YHWH as the god who appointed his minions each over his people, there would be no difference between the two (again, see Deut. 32:8–9). However, this could of course have substantial political implications as "baal"-worship and vassalship or even alliances could very well be equated, the subsidiary deity being at the same time the god of a foreign people (see Hosea 1—3; cf. 7:11, e.g.—the transfer of the harlot imagery to include foreign alliances). At any rate, Zeph. 1:4–5 includes the host of heaven among the "remnant of 'the baal'" that survived Josiah's reform. And Jer. 19:5 identified the human sacrifice as a ritual performed for "the baal," while Jer. 2:23ff. unequivocally establishes that the Judahites regarded the aspects of their cult that Jeremiah attacked as self-evidently (and so unselfconsciously) Yahwistic. More particularly, Jer. 7:31 (cf. Micah 6:7!) indicates that the practice condemned in 19:5 was universally understood to represent homage to YHWH (hence 8:1–3). Human sacrifice in the Mesha stele may entail dedication of the offering to *'aštār-Chemosh;*[88] if so, the references in Jeremiah indicate that a specific baal was the object of sacrifices offered to YHWH through him in the Tophet, the locus of human sacrifice in Jerusalem. Thus, the *b^e'ālîm* would represent YHWH's subordinates, whose worship no later than the period of Josiah's reform was stigmatized as foreign (Deut. 4:19; 17:3; 2 Kings 17:16; 21:3, 5; 23:4, 5; 2 Chron. 33:3, 5; Isa. 34:4; Jer. 8:2; 19:13; Neh. 9:6; Zeph. 1:5; the host of heaven are understood to be the stars in Jer. 33:22; 8:2; Dan. 8:10, and the earlier Ps. 148:1–5, where they are both stars and heavenly councilors; note the related texts Gen. 2:1; Isa. 34:2, 4; 40:26; 45:12; Ps. 33:6). Who "the baal" par excellence was for Jeremiah (Hosea?), if there was one at all, is indeterminate (though for Hosea it seems to have been YHWH). Perhaps the deities mentioned by Amos (5:26) or at Elephantine (cf. Amos 8:14) or Kuntillet Ajrud are candidates.

The obvious advantage in this construction is that the plurality of the baals finds a logical explanation in the plurality of the divinities attending YHWH. Although this is as much as to denote rival gods it is not to recognize their status as high gods. The title in Israel as at Ugarit adheres to prominent but subordinate figures in the heavenly council, in Israel as in Mesopotamia not to the patriarchs as a group but rather to "sons" of the patriarchal generation of gods. It will be objected that the baals and the host of heaven are not regularly juxtaposed. Yet the terms "host of heaven" and "baals" are not proper names. The altars of Jerusalem, located by Jeremiah on every corner (11:13), were dedicated to the host (2 Kings 21:3, 5; 23:4, 5; 2 Chron. 33:3, 5). Second Kings 23:5 is best taken to use the word *ba'al* generically, then to specify in the succeeding apposition "the sun, the moon, the constellations and all the host of heaven" (this is why the conjunction is absent before *lšmš*). Thus, the plasticity of the terminology accounts for the rarity of formal conjunctions of the baals and the host of heaven.

It may or may not be that Hosea, in stigmatizing the *b^e'ālîm,* also identifies their worship as alien to what is authentically Israelite and as tantamount to the worship of foreign gods. This identification, absent from Amos, would seem to be the logical if undrawn implication of the adultery metaphor. The cults of the baals within Israel should have been understood to be equitable with cults of the foreign baals, as Melqart or Haddu. This is the mechanism by which the inner-Israelite practice could have been alienated from itself. Certainly, by the time of Jeremiah (cited above), the strain of thought that identified these cults as alien was fully developed, though it had not by any means eradicated competing and more traditional modes of religion (Jer. 44:1ff.).

One other element in the prophecy of Amos and Hosea relates to the issue of subsidiary deities in the pantheon (again, Amos 5:26; 8:14, with Elephantine and 2 Kings 17:30). Amos assails ritual. He observes that in itself it is useless as a means of propitiating the deity, and that only when coupled with the thorough implementation of YHWH's program for Israelite society is the cult of any (more than symbolic) value (esp. 5:21–25; also 3:8; 4:4–5; 5:5ff., 18ff.; 8:4–6, 10, 14; 9:1). Not dissimilarly, Hosea assails the contemporary cultus as no substitute for wholesale adherence to YHWH's will (6:6; 4:11–19; 8:11–13; 9:15). The cult, he says, is now Ephraim's license to sin, rather than his warrant of fidelity. It has become a technicality for evading responsibility rather than a real emotional *proskynesis* (8:11ff.).

Accompanying Amos's and Hosea's polemic against *pro forma* cultic obeisance of their contemporaries is Hosea's attack on the "calves" of Bethel and Dan and the icons of his people at large (Hosea 2:10; 4:17, 12; 8:4–6; 10:2–5; 11:2; 12:12; 13:2; 14:9). This exhibits the same character as the attack on empty ritual. In each case, the prophet insists that the reality, the organic implementation of the social and emotional homage demanded by the god, not be confused with the representation or symbol of the reality, that the metaphorical expression of the god's power or the worshiper's devotion not be confused with the actuality it is meant to represent. Both in Amos and in Hosea, therefore, the distinction between true and false worship of YHWH, between real and unreal devotion to the deity, is theologically central.

In this connection, Hosea's paronomasia has not fully been plumbed. That YHWH is no more to be called *ba'al* and that the term *ba'al* is to be expunged from Israel's consciousness has long been understood (2:18), but the term by which YHWH is to be addressed is unjustly ignored. YHWH will be called *'îšî* (2:18), "my man," echoing the central element of the names Jesse (*yišāy*), Ishbaal, Eshbaal, and Ethbaal, i.e., **'it*, "YHWH/-Baal/X *IS*," which expresses the god's presence and activity. No longer will YHWH be called baal, the subordinate and impotent and therefore deceptive deity, says Hosea (Hosea 2:10; cf. 1 Kings 18:27). Instead, he will be called the one who "is," who is "present," YHWH, the true provider. Hosea's pun is thus a double double-entendre on the order of "One man's Mede is another man's Persian." In it, we can see the prophet's still-provisional denial of the baal's power taking shape. Later prophets would reify this insight even more than Hosea himself.

5. W. Zimmerli has suggested that the polemic against imagery began with Hosea and that Hezekiah's reform in the south a few decades after Hosea, with its attendant destruction of Nehushtan and similar cultic imagery, reflects a comparable intellectual bent.[89] It is not to be denied, especially in light of 2 Kings 18:22, that Hezekiah did centralize worship, probably because of incorrect expectations that Babylon could destroy Assyria's empire.[90] And certainly the social conditions of Hezekiah's realm would have been conducive to the sort of upheaval Zimmerli posits, for the population of Jerusalem burgeoned, whether because of an influx of refugees from the northern kingdom after the fall of Samaria or because of Hezekiah's centralization and the depopulation of rural Judah during Sennacherib's third campaign.[91]

Naturally, cultic reform was not altogether new in Judah. Asa, Jehoshaphat, and Joash had dabbled in it (2 Chron. 14:2, 4; 15:8–16; 2 Chron. 17:8f.; 19:3–4, 11; 2 Kings 12:5ff.). But Hezekiah achieved a new dimension in reform, celebrating a centralized Passover. The financial aspects of this innovation are not a primary concern in this context, though they must have been significant at the time.[92] What is important is that Hezekiah's reform became programmatic for his successors. His revisionist central temple and his enfranchisement of non-Aaronid Levites in the cult (possibly in an attempt to earn loyalty from rural elements among whom he had no natural constituency, see 2 Chron. 31:15) seem to have responded to or stimulated the rhetoric of Micah, Amos, Hosea, and Isaiah (Micah 1:7; 5:12–14; Amos, above; Hosea, above; Isa. 1:10–17 on the cult; 27:9; 29:13; 1:29–31; 17:7–10; 19:1, 3; 27:9; 30:22; 31:7 on icons, with Isa. 2:9, 16, 18–22; 10:10f.). In short, it seems to be sometime in the period around 715–701 that we speak of the systematic turning of traditional xenophobic rhetoric and monolatrous thought against the traditional religion of Israel. Certain antecedents were present, but the affirmation that the Israelite could sacrifice to his god in one locus only, and the concomitant affirmation that the god had little interest in anything other than the service of his socioethical ideals, together establish that an incunabulary monotheistic consciousness was present, just as together they determined how the rhetoric of those prophets following in Hosea's, Amos's, and Isaiah's footsteps would take shape. The prophetic critique, based on the isolation of the symbol from the represented reality (and flowing into the issue of the entity and its manifestations, thence into the issue of the unity and the multiplicity, on which see further below), entailed the alienation of native practice. This critique stemmed from consciousness of the oneness of the now sometimes alien and forbidden subordinate deities with YHWH which conflicted with their distinction from YHWH. As early as Isa. 6:3, the Jerusalem temple's theologians had begun to conceive the mundane world as a part of YHWH's nimbus, as a reflection of him (so "the fulness of the whole earth is his glory," rather than "the whole earth is filled with his glory").[93] This perspective is reflected in Genesis 1, where man is the reflection of YHWH, or the divine, in a creation that is YHWH's imagination, the reification of his word. Thus reality is a set of manifestations of YHWH flowing from YHWH. Like the now-foreign gods, this manifold reality must be repudiated as different from yet pointing to the underlying causal force, YHWH. Thus a general assault on instantiation (the One and the many) and symbol follows. Consciousness of the otherness of those things that are one with the god leads to the repudiation of all hypostatization (or, in Greece, instantiation).

This critique inevitably produced in Israel a consciousness that had been lacking before the prophets. Naturally, this consciousness had been present in embryo in statements such as Hosea's "I, YHWH, have been your god since the land of Egypt, and no god other than me have you known, nor is there a savior beside me," or in the pun on "man" and "master" (13:4; 2:18). But Hezekiah's demolition of the rural cult followed by Sennacherib's demolition of rural Judah provided a testing ground for the critique's application. That Hezekiah's subjection and humiliation by Assyria was not taken to discredit his policies by all factions, but rather was reinterpreted as a miraculous victory for the king, is a formidable tribute to the intellectual vigor of the proponents of his innovation (Jer. 44:1–30 on Josiah; cf. 2 Kings 18—20; Jer. 26:17–19).[94]

6. The developments of the late eighth and early seventh centuries in Judah do not seem to have kindled the flames of self-consciously radical monotheism itself. While the prophetic critique did achieve a broad distribution to judge from its common occurrence in Amos, Hosea, Micah, and Isaiah, the reign of Manasseh is portrayed as an era of backsliding, although the probably more authentic account of the Chronicler reports a reformation in the middle of his reign (2 Chron. 33:1–19; cf. 2 Kings 21:1–17). This reflects a return to the traditional forms of practice entailing homage to the entire host of heaven the worship of whom had survived Hezekiah's more geographically oriented centralization (cf. 2 Kings 18:4; 2 Chron. 29:3—31:21). In any event, it is, as is commonly observed, at Josiah's reform that the clearest stigmatization of traditional practice as alien takes place.

Like Hezekiah's, Josiah's reform had its political motivations. By the time of Manasseh's death in 642, anti-Assyrian nationalists had grown strong enough in Jerusalem to assassinate the pro-Assyrian successor, Amon, and manipulate the eight-year-old Josiah onto the throne. By 633, Josiah was in revolt against Assyria, allied with Babylon. In short, he was pursuing Hezekiah's old policy.[95] By 629, Josiah was asserting Davidic sovereignty over Israel and pursuing Hezekiah's religious policy. Whether this was also a major foreign-policy goal of Manasseh's regime or not, for Josiah it again entailed cult centralization.

Josiah's reform was, if anything, more bloody-minded than Hezekiah's. It aimed at anything cultic that moved. All apparent public iconography was destroyed. Altars outside that of the temple, altars to subordinate gods—indeed all paraphernalia dedicated to any god whatsoever other than directly to YHWH (e.g., the horses of the sun in 2 Kings 23:11; cf. 2 Kings 11:16–18)—were subject to the proscription. Josiah's reform was the most literally oriented application of the concepts of monolatry and henotheism that could be imagined. This reform was fundamentally, radically, and self-consciously monotheistic.

It is unnecessary here to multiply examples. Suffice it to observe that for the first time homage to the "host of heaven," YHWH's armies, was understood in Josiah's reign to be generically alien (see Deut. 4:19; 17:3). The reform is supposed by scholars to have been bound to the Book of Deuteronomy, a work whose insistence on YHWH's absolute uniqueness is unadulterated (2 Kings 22:3–20; Deut. 4; 6:4).[96] It is precisely in this work that formerly characteristic adulation of YHWH's minions and of YHWH himself is identified as foreign, as equivalent to the worship of competing gods, not gods in "the suite of the One." The book itself, it should be noted, may in part be as old as the time of Hezekiah.

The clearest formulation of the ideological position underlying Josiah's reform and the version of Deuteronomy then promulgated stems from Jeremiah, the priest of Anathoth. Jeremiah sophisticated the prophetic critique to a calculus, understanding YHWH as a generative, life-giving force, "the source of living waters." All other deities, the host of heaven included, he considers "broken cisterns, that don't hold water." They are bad imitations of empty receptacles. To turn from YHWH to any other god is to forsake reality for deception (Jer. 2:10–16).

In maintaining a traditional cultus, Jeremiah's contemporaries understand themselves to be practicing authentic Yahwism (2:23–28). But, reviving the rhetoric-assailing symbol that he inherited from the eighth-century prophets, Jeremiah accuses them of worshiping stones and trees and mistaking idols for gods, much as Cromwell would later accuse the population of Britain and Ireland of mistaking the image for the god (1:16; 2:23–28; 3:7–10; 23; 16:19f.). Jeremiah further accuses the Judahites of swearing by gods that do not exist, of doubting YHWH's puissance, of substituting ritual for real submission, and of angering the YHWH they thought to be in Zion (when the real YHWH was to be present), with icons, alien vanities (5:7; 5:12; 6:19f.; 7:21–28; 8:19). Jeremiah is the most systematic of Israel's prophets in leveling the critique. He attacks his contemporaries for trusting in the "words of deception . . . 'The temple of YHWH, the temple of YHWH, the temple of YHWH!' are they" (7:4–15). It is folly to believe in the symbol, the manifestation of YHWH's protection, when in reality the protection itself has been lost (15:18). Micah perhaps anticipated Jeremiah in the assault on this particular hypostatization (Micah 3:12), but Jeremiah goes further, in fact so far as to indicate that ideally one would dispense even with the ark (3:16). Moreover, Jeremiah adds his own dimension to the critique, accusing the temple establishment in Jerusalem of perverting the law by literalizing it. They reduce it to lifeless writing by executing it in letter but not in spirit (8:7–9).[97] This is certainly the drift of his comment on the "amnesty" for slaves in 34:8–22; since some of the manumitted slaves lack the means to avoid reindenture, the release, whether ritual or actual, satisfies the terms of the law but not the intention it was meant to express. Therefore the release is a fraud. In attacking the hypostatization of the law, its reduction from a metaphor for a complex vision of reality to a literal demand, to writing, Jeremiah renews the assault on symbolism, but at a sort of second degree. He singles out a rarefied and abstract type of representation (verbal rather than visual, even if it is the visible representation of the verbal), of a different order from the symbols singled out by his predecessors.

Jeremiah's chief contribution to the ongoing philosophical development of Israelite religion is thus his systematic assembly of the assault on hypostatization.[98] He assails the hypostatization of icons, of ritual, of the temple, of the ark, of the law, and of the seeming manifestations of YHWH that are understood to be his divine armies (9:12–13; 16:19–20; 19:13). He sedulously avoids anthropomorphism in thought and in language, much as does the Priestly source in the Pentateuch, and he never mentions or implies the existence of angels (false manifestations of YHWH). For him, YHWH is not and cannot be localized; rather, "I fill the heavens and the earth" (23:24). Thus, Jeremiah can say of his prophetic colleagues, "Who has stood in the council of YHWH and seen and heard his word?" with the implication that none of them had (23:18; note 15:17). Nor does Jeremiah himself report a vision involving supernatural actors. For him, in fact, the claim to have seen such an image is a mark of false prophecy (e.g., 23:16, 28). Thus while Micah might speak of the loss of the prophet's vision or Isaiah of the failure or nonrealization of the prophet's vision, Jeremiah understands the true mode of revelation to be the word (Micah 3:6; Isa. 28:18; cf. Jer. 18:18; 23:28; cf. 20:8). For him, in keeping with his notion that any localization of YHWH's presence, whether as god, symbol, or icon, belies (i.e., is fraudulent) YHWH's omnipresence, full intangibility, and transcending unity, epiphany is aural rather than visual.[99] The radical stance against iconography that is linked to monotheism in Jeremiah 10 is thus perfectly consonant with and is indeed the logical corollary of the prophet's other positions. The true god, the source of living waters as opposed to the broken cisterns representing subordinate or competing deities, the living god, as distinct from the dead frauds, this god who suffuses all creation and is himself indivisible and infinite, is the reality underlying a multifarious mundane reality in which that fractured reality has its unity. This god by nature cannot be represented. Indeed the deception or distortion involved in symbolism, the inevitable reification of the symbol and misrepresentation of the reality, makes the representation of the god blasphemous. This is why the language of "deception/illusion" (*šqr, šw', kzb, rmy, hbl*) is so pervasive in Jeremiah's prophecy.[100]

By the time of Deutero-Isaiah, if one does not attribute Jeremiah 10 to the prophet himself, unmistakable formulations of self-conscious monotheism speckle the text. The statements resemble 45:5–7, addressed by YHWH to Cyrus:

> I am YHWH and there is no other; except for me there is no god . . . that they learn from east of the sun and to the west that there is no one/nothing (*'epes*) beside me. I am YHWH, and there is no other; who fashions light and creates darkness, makes well-being and creates evil—it is I, YHWH, who does all this.

Simultaneously, the polemic against cultic imagery reaches its apogee in Deutero-Isaiah's discourses. The *locus classicus* for the polemic against idolatry is in fact Isa. 44:6–20. What succeeds it is a celebration of YHWH the maker, the creator, of YHWH whose creatures live, as distinct from the potter whose creations ("his creatures") are lifeless (44:21–28). The implication may be that human representations are dead whereas YHWH's images live, and that therefore it is illegitimate for humans to create such representations. Indeed, this sort of thinking may already underlie the Priestly source in the Pentateuch, with its notion of *imago Dei* and suppression of all imagery (Gen. 1:26–27; Exod. 20:4–5).[101] Deutero-Isaiah expresses the point somewhat differently in 40:18–31: "To whom will you compare *'ēl* (here, 'God')? What image will you deploy for him?" (40:18). That is, YHWH is limitless, as the context insists, and therefore indefinable. He is "the first and the last" beside whom no god exists, so that the host of heaven seem to be reduced to the status of demythologized stars (40:26). Thus, the radical aniconism derived from the rhetoric of Amos and Micah and the radical monotheism of Josiah's reform remain closely conjoined in the prophecy of Second Isaiah.[102]

Still, Jeremiah's thoroughgoing repudiation of hypostatization, and Josiah's zeal to suppress all but one cult and all regalia that can be reified even in that cult, suggest that Second Isaiah's proud self-conscious monotheism had quite explicit antecedents in the seventh century. Jeremiah, long before Deutero-Isaiah, linked YHWH's creation with his uniqueness and with his special covenantal relationship to his people.[103] This is a natural recourse for the monotheist, for whom the god functions by definition as a prime mover. Moreover, Jeremiah's iconoclasm is as radical as Josiah's applied iconoclasm was. Indeed, it even issues in a denial of visual revelation in favor of the word, whose power is that of a jackhammer (23:16–18, 21:22, 25–29; cf. Deut. 4:11, 15, 32–36). This is the mark of a sophisticated, self-conscious monotheist, and while it is a temptation to deny that Jeremiah's thought was ever so systematic, the critique in its full development, and especially the direction of the critique of the difference between symbol and object to the literal and the spiritual law, suggests the presence of a consistent, systematic theology. The suggestion is corroborated by Jeremiah's insistence on YHWH's illimitability and invisibility.

Jeremiah is a thinker of considerable accomplishment absolutely bent on distinguishing the true from the false. Indeed, Luther's affinity for him is not misplaced, for he stands to the cultic establishment of pre-Josianic Jerusalem much as Luther stood to the Catholic Church of his day. His insistence on circumcision of the heart rather than (or in addition to) that of the flesh—of submission to YHWH's will, not to YHWH's words—anticipates the philosophical position of Karl Kraus and his Viennese circle. Jeremiah must be regarded as a radical monotheist in his own right. It is in fact his work that most explicitly reflects the route by which that self-conscious radicalism was reached.

C. From the time she entered history, Israel seems to have been monolatrous and henotheistic, that is, unselfconsciously monotheistic. Especially before the rise of the Davidic state she was characterized by considerable local heterogeneity. From the tenth through the eighth centuries, however, xenophobic and reactionary elements (particularly active in times of military crisis; consider Saul, Jehu) appealed for fealty to YHWH, for greater and greater zeal on YHWH's behalf. They leveled this rhetoric not just at foreigners but also at elements of the official cultus. Of these, in turn, some may have been foreign in origin or have achieved a somewhat heightened prominence because of their importance in neighboring cultures (as Solomon's altars to Chemosh and so on). Still, it is in the nature of an effective polemic that it is occasionally deployed to tar the soffit along with the roof, and, inevitably, the charge of strangeness came to be laid against institutions that were as Israelite as Israel's Mosaic antecedents. The bulls of Bethel and Dan (Exodus 32; 2 Kings 17), the rural "high places" (1 Kings 3:2–3; cf. vv. 4ff.), the Asherah of YHWH in its various manifestations are all examples. Thus, groups appealing to patriotic fervor came to define authentic Yahwism as a tradition which excluded some of the practices of their political foes. In particular, the tolerant "polytheism" of the royal city offered a target for such attacks, presumably since it included all manner of rites meant to satisfy the diverse constituencies of which the kingdom was composed. Whether Saul's suppression of the necromancers was the first instance of this phenomenon is uncertain, but insofar as it was the first organized attempt to eradicate an "alien" cult, it represents an instance of prime importance.

During the course of the eighth century, at the latest, there developed alongside this "alienating" tendency, this process of narrowing devotion's focus by fits, a second critique which, sometimes unfairly, assailed the confusion of representation with reality in the worship of the deity. The makings of a program are distributed throughout the extant writings of the early prophets, although it remains unassembled there. An icon is not a god, and those who perform obeisance before an icon are accused of worshiping the icon rather than the god; ritual, a symbol of submission, is not submission itself, so that those who participate in ritual can be accused of mistaking the symbol for the act, the temple is not god's literal dwelling, and those who rely on YHWH's presence on Zion are accused of trusting in the temple rather than in the god.

This position was reached by the "alienation" of the baals, the heavenly council, which was now logically understood to include foreign gods (since each nation has a god and the number of nations was correlated to the number of gods). It is predicated on an apprehension of their oneness with and yet alienation from YHWH. Once the pantheon was thus understood both to represent and to belie the god, it was inevitable that the symbol and the individual manifestation would be seen as alien representations of a hidden reality (thus the late *deus absconditus*)—a reality transcendent of but motive in the mundane.

No later than the last quarter of the seventh century, this critique was systematized and applied in the work of Jeremiah, not to mention the other ideologues of Josiah's court (P, after all, avoids all metaphor, angels, and anthropomorphism). The dissonance between metaphor and reality, between language and referent was the premise of the innovation. YHWH was illimitable, free of human attributes, not specially present in any locus. Any symbol of YHWH was a fraud, so any hypostatization (in ritual form or anthropomorphism or, in the case of P or Jeremiah, metaphor included) was a deception.[104]

The repudiation of hypostatization, or hypostatization itself, was a process of alienating the symbol from the symbolized. The logical consequence was that the angels, the localizations of the "living god," were in a sense divisions of the indivisible. The repudiation of hypostatization led to the repudiation of all localizations of the god. It became of central moment that YHWH was one, alone, and all. He was all the numinous that suffused his multifarious creation, the one source of the cosmos. Thus, even the heavenly host that formerly had been allotted to the nations as gods, though subordinate to YHWH, now seem to have been demythologized as the source of signs and portents for the nations, but not for Israel (Jer. 10:2–5; Deut. 4:19; cf. Jer. 10:2; Deut. 4:19). For the first time, they were alien. This demythologization is symptomatic of a larger skepticism.

As the prophetic critique alienated YHWH from his representations, as it strove to apprehend the reality as directly as Israel had on the day YHWH manifested himself at Sinai (Deut. 4:9ff.), it assigned the hypostatized regalia, the cult and the temple, to the category of what was "foreign." YHWH alone was central to the tradition and authentic and authoritative in it. It followed that the now-empty representation, the language that was the cult, was foreign to the authentic culture of Israel. To be Israelite rather than pagan meant to be rid of hypostatizations. To be pagan meant conversely to invest one's self in the hypostatizations to the exclusion of interest in the true god. It followed that non-Israelites believed in the power of the inanimate, the symbol, while Israelites remained faithful to the animate, "living god." Those Israelites tied to the symbol of the cult had lost hold of the authentic faith (a term for the first time applicable, with the cult now removed) and become Amorites, Canaanites, and so on! That this theological position had already been consolidated in Josiah's reign explains more than anything else the survival of Judah and Israel as peoples after the trauma of the temple's destruction and the Babylonian Exile. Simply, in the Deuteronomistic school, the temple had been emptied of content by means of the prophetic critique.[105]

IV

Israel's is not the only culture in which consciousness of the disparity between metaphor and the reality it represents emerged during the Axial Period. Arguably, Buddhism is founded on a similar variety of insight. And certainly the relationship between representation and reality is central to the philosophical program of early Taoism. But it is in the Greek philosophical tradition that the developments most similar to those we have observed in Israel left their marks. The earliest manifestations of movement (after the development of the more just divine administration in the Odyssey) seem to come from Xenophanes, roughly a contemporary of Deutero-Isaiah.

Xenophanes objected to the portrayal of the gods as immoral in Homer and Hesiod, from whom "all have learnt." His concern is that the reader will mistake the Homeric presentation for the reality. Similarly, people err in conceiving the gods as human in form, a fact that can be deduced from every people's habit of portraying the gods as resembling itself; if animals could portray gods, their gods would look like animals. Xenophanes, in short, has already assembled the argument against anthropomorphism.[106]

Xenophanes also has a concept of a single god who is "not at all like mortals," who "sees as a whole, thinks as a whole, and hears as a whole," and who is immovable, omnipresent, and the universal cause.[107] Jaspers suggests that "the one god . . . who rids himself of all form, appears in the forms of the gods," that Xenophanes' one god has no cult, while the many gods have, and that Xenophanes opposed pernicious representations of the gods more than their multitude. Beyond the gods, he found the principle in which to see the unity of the universe, this unifying god being equivalent to the *Weltall*.[108] This is tantamount to saying Xenophanes was a self-conscious monotheist (of a Spinozan turn) who tolerated polytheism and polylatry, and it is not wide of the mark, though it underestimates Xenophanes' stress on the fallibility of human perception, which apprehends appearance only, rather than the underlying truth.[109] He rejects as false multifarious reality when seeking an underlying single cause. It is this concept of an all-pervasive deity, one wholly infracosmic, that is linked with the polemic against anthropomorphism and the issue of representation in Xenophanes' thought (cf. Jeremiah and the extracosmic god of the Jerusalem priesthood).

A bit later than Xenophanes, Heracleitus exhibits a concern for such issues. He too rails against Homer[110] and proclaims speculation concerning the nonempirical risky stuff.[111] He notes the disparity between language and reality, tying it to the idea of a god of whom the term "god" is no apt description[112] since no description is ever apt except in answer to specific concerns.[113] His god is beyond the cult, which horribly misrepresents the god.[114] He is "the purpose which steers all things through all things,"[115] a concept close to that of the god "who causes," even if he does so by causing the gods who dispose of people's proposals to be. In seeking the unity of the cosmos, the philosopher naturally involves himself in the question of the relationship between multiplicity and holism, between metaphor/appearance and reality. Having grasped the principle of causality, the philosopher now seeks the cause, but this is by definition latent in the concrete world of many gods and people. Thus the manifestation must be removed to find what lies behind it.

That the Greek philosophical tradition did not produce intolerant monotheism of the Jeremianic variety is not surprising. Postexilic Judaism, the heir of Jeremiah, went on regarding itself as monotheistic while housing a developed angelology of the sort that surfaces in Enoch and the Talmud, although it managed it rather peripherally in terms of the theology of nonmillenarian Jewish sects. That is, the slogans of radical monotheism were adopted, but the program did not remain ruthlessly in force. (In the same way, Luther's radical iconoclasm could not bring him to abandon the notion of a Lucifer.) The gods may have been alienated from YHWH by Hosea, but they were reunited with him by Ezra. The Greek situation was less conducive to the application of a monotheistic program, and the result was the development of a sort of metatheological discourse the offspring of which would later style itself science. Thus, the history of the two critiques, the prophets' and the philosophers', turns on the difference between a Mosaic Greece rooted in state-supported polytheism and a Mosaic Israel whose state periodically guarded its monotheistic heritage, the articulation of Israel's identity. In neither case was monotheism more than a dogma, a theology, a slogan; it was a different, perhaps more distant perspective on the same world.

Whether the Greek or the prophetic tradition was dependent on external sources for its development of this consciousness about the nature of language and representation is unclear. Certainly, both the reform of Nabonidus and the blossoming of Greek philosophical thought took place well after Israel's reformations under Hezekiah and Josiah. Indeed, the first inklings of the prophetic critique may antedate the eighth-century prophets and lie in the statement of YHWH's ineffability in Exod. 3:14. There, in a ninth-century text, Moses asks YHWH what his name is, and the author provides a folk etymology based in part on the traditional reluctance of gods to produce their names in Israel (Gen. 32:30; Judges 13:17–18).[116] YHWH replies, "I am that I am," which is to say, "My name? Name? Why, I'm me!" (much in the manner of the classic Will Rogers retort when asked at a NRA [National Recovery Administration] office for his birth certificate: "Well I wouldn't be here if I wasn't born, would I?" YHWH is the nameless god, the one who is, and to whom names therefore do not apply.[117] Rather, names necessarily divide and reduce his unitive essence. Heracleitus's hesitation about the name Zeus is not dissimilar.

Still, it is a risky business postulating the diffusion of whole complexes of ideas. If diffusion did occur, it most likely took the form of stimulus to consciousness in conversation; no developed body of theology or philosophy seems to have been transplanted from one locus to another, unless perhaps in the Pythagorean school. Rather, in Israel, for example, consciousness of the difference between reality and representation must have spurred thought in contexts other than that in which it arose. In Greece, as early as the sixth/fifth centuries, the philosophers concern themselves more with the issue of unity and individual manifestation than with repudiating the multiplicity of the universe, as Israel's most radical monotheists do. The Greeks accept it in the form of a pantheon but postulate a unity underlying it. Whether this orientation arose through interplay between interest in metaphor and local problems in contemporary Greek thought, as is not unlikely, or simply arose in the course of the ongoing evolution of Greek thought, is an issue that cannot be resolved. Even had the philosophical insights taken the form of ethnic jokes, in which case the diffusion would have been less limited, we would remain unsure of its direction.

At any rate, it may be that Jaspers is correct in his assessment of the Axial Period; it does seem to be the era from which certain types of self-consciousness first leave traces that survive to the present. But the unconsciousness remains a limited one. In Israel, the limitation is to the dissonance inherent in the need to treat a representation or a representative as a thing in itself, though as a thing in itself it is no longer a symbol. What is most interesting is that that development of a radical critique of symbol seems so wholly to foreshadow Paul's rhetoric deployed against the Jewish followers of Jesus, Luther's rhetoric against the Catholic Church, and more recently, the confrontation between Mach and Planck at the turn of the century. The triumph of a Jeremiah over an Ezekiel, of the cultless god over the god of the cult, is the triumph of the aural over the visual, the abstract over the concrete, that is, of unity over diversity. That triumph is achieved, necessarily, through alienation from the reality—in Jeremiah's case, from the god of the traces of multiplicity, the concrete manifestations. Aniconism, whether Luther's, Cromwell's, or Josiah's, is what one might call applied radical monotheism, applied radical alienation. Interestingly, the Jerusalem priesthood understood alienation to be creation (e.g., Genesis 1; Exod. 26:33; Lev. 11:47; 10:10; Num. 16:9, 21; Deut. 10:8; Ezek. 22:26) and then sanctification. But alienation can lead to the dismissal as well as to the sanctification of what it produces. The temple priesthood ultimately elected to adhere to a synthetic monotheism that sanctified the many; the radical monotheists adopted the opposite course. In either case, the alienation is understood to be the origin of cosmos and, further, is the origin of philosophical consciousness in Jaspers's terms.

The difficulty with radical monotheism was that it lent itself to a second critique, that of the poetic segments of the Book of Job, or, more devastating, Qohelet's. Theodicy in a polytheistic culture is a fundamentally adolescent genre. It reifies a principle such as Justice, and produces in the end, based on the fact that there is no chief god Justice, that most pessimistic of relativist truths, "Life is unfair." In a monotheistic society, however, these issues assume new dimensions. The injustice of the just god produces the same answers as in a polytheistic society. It suggests that human intellect is too limited to penetrate the problem (see also Job),[118] that the gods/god are/is unjust (see Job; also Isa. 45:7), or that either the people are evil and deserve their suffering[119] or the perpetrators of the suffering are evil and will later be punished.[120] None is a satisfactory answer. The most satisfactory answers are these: the first is that underlying apocalyptic—the god once fashioned the world, and will one day return to rectify it. The second is Qohelet's stark implication that one does best to forget about god and live a life of moderation. Each amounts to a practical atheism.

A cynic might see in the way of the Western monotheisms a touch of hypocrisy, as the old polytheists adopted the slogan of radical monotheism (God is One) without changing much else about themselves. But that synthetic monotheism with its rehabilitation of the many gods in the company of a conscious kerygmatic denial of the existence of more gods than one represented a significant innovation in itself. It reconciled the dissipating multiplicity of a polytheism that acknowledged the diversity and distinctness of phenomena with the exclusivism of a monotheism that hypothesized a unity suffusing the cosmos and rendering it unimportant. The result was a balanced outlook that included the causality inherent in monotheism but accepted the diversity of reality. The synthetic monotheism that emerged as the synthesis of polytheism and radical monotheism was in that sense more "scientific" than the former, extrapolating from data, and less mystical, that is, more applied, than the latter. The history of Western monotheism in fact attests to just how adaptive monotheism could be.

Yehezkel Kaufmann was correct in attributing to early Israel a bent most naturally to be characterized as monotheistic. The results of the preceding sketch, however, suggest that his work suffered from two significant imperfections. First, it was fundamentally polemical. Having determined that monarchic and, in his view, pre-monarchic Israel was as monotheistic as any of the modern monotheisms, Kaufmann declined to discover significant movement in consciousness from the earlier to the later periods. Although his approach was markedly historical and diachronic, his view of Israelite monotheism was not; to him, it was a constant rather than a variable, a framework not a datum contained. The second flaw is related. Kaufmann viewed Israelite monotheism as a developed philosophical structure and tended to dismiss or belittle elements out of keeping with its logical consistency. The difficulty is that religion exists only in its implementation by real and very varied people, not in some ethereal Platonic form. Simultaneously, cosmological systems need not be systematic or internally consistent at the literal level of discourse until such consistency is demanded of them. They accumulate, rather, a store of truths in the incommensurable languages of myth, history, paradigm, and dogma. Their ultimate doctrinal or literal coordination always demands reflection and the imposition of the results on an earlier heterogeneity. In short, the nature of the philosophical program one is entitled to seek in the history of any society varies over time and over population. While in its latest manifestations the prophetic critique may have been somewhat closer to folk religion than was the Greek philosophical tradition to which it has here been compared, it will not do to overstate the extent to which it was representative.

What distinguished the monotheism of earliest Israel from that of later Israel was that the former was unselfconscious. An agency central to its evolution was Israel's susceptibility to fits of intolerance. Through a cumulative process of alienation, intolerance generated a self-conscious, radical monotheism. Finally, the earlier, unselfconscious monotheism made its peace with the radical tradition by identifying itself as monotheistic and making attendant adjustments in theology, but without becoming radical. The resultant communal religion remains at the heart of Western culture; the successful socialization of the radical monotheistic insight illustrates the interaction between the theory and the reality. In that sense, synthetic monotheism, as it may be called, was a movement toward theoretical empiricism, toward the "scientific method." It is in that sense that it has contributed most to the progress and the progressiveness of Western thought.

NOTES

1. Read with LXX,

When the Most High propertied the nations,
When he parcelled out the sons of man,
He established the territories of the peoples,
According to the number of the sons of god (*b^{e}nê 'ēl*)
But YHWH's portion is his people,
Jacob is the lot of his inheritance.

Professor F. M. Cross informs me that a Qumran fragment confirms the reading "sons of god," though its text has *bny h'lhym,* not *bny 'l.*

2. See lately E. T. Mullen, *The Assembly of the Gods,* HSM 24 (Chico, Calif.: Scholars Press, 1980), with bibliography.

3. T. H. Robinson, *Amos,* HAT (Tübingen: J. C. B. Mohr [Paul Siebeck], 1938).

4. H. Ringgren, *Israelite Religion* (Philadelphia: Fortress Press, 1966), 99–100.

5. See J. Wellhausen, *Israelitische und Judische Geschichte* (Berlin: Georg Reimer, 1894), 2–3, 73–77.

6. J. Wellhausen, "Israel," *Encyclopedia Britannica* (1883), reprinted in J. Well-

hausen, *Prolegomena to the History of Israel* (New York: Meridian Books, 1957), 440 (a reprint of the Edinburgh, A. & C. Black, edition of 1885).

7. J. Hehn, *Die biblische und die babylonische Gottesidee* (Leipzig: Hinrichs, 1913), 96–99.

8. G. Widengren, *The Accadian and Hebrew Psalms of Lamentation as Religious Documents: A Comparative Study* (Uppsala: Almqvist & Wiksell, 1936), 54–55, 70–72. More recently, note G. Ahlström, *Psalm 89, Eine Liturgie aus dem Ritual des leidenden Königs* (Lund: Gleerup, 1959), 62.

9. B. Baentsch, *Altorientalischer und israelitischer Monotheismus* (Tübingen: J. C. B. Mohr [Paul Siebeck], 1906), esp. 33–34; Hehn, *Gottesidee,* 56ff.

10. Widengren, *Accadian and Hebrew Psalms,* 57–70.

11. V. Nikiprowetzky, "Ethical Monotheism," in *Wisdom, Revelation and Doubt: Perspectives on the First Millennium B.C.E.,* Daedalus 104 (1975), 69–89.

12. Hehn, *Gottesidee,* 64.

13. See A. E. Cowley, *Aramaic Papyri of the Fifth Century B.C.* (Oxford: Clarendon Press, 1923), 22. For a convincing effort to establish that the canard is misguided, see U. Cassuto, *Biblical and Oriental Studies,* 2 vols. (Jerusalem: Magnes Press, 1973–75), 2.240–49. Even if Cassuto is in error, the case would be one of the hypostatization of minor characteristics of the deity at worst. Cf. the speculation of W. Th. in der Smitten, "Vordeuteronomischer Jahwismus in Elephantine?" *BibOr* 28 (1971): 173–74.

14. So, for example, G. E. Mendenhall, *The Tenth Generation* (Baltimore: Johns Hopkins Press, 1973), 19–31 and passim. Mendenhall's ahistorical concept of paganism and his contrast of it with nonpagan religion is fundamentally more extreme than Kaufmann's. One might include also the more moderate work of N. K. Gottwald, *The Tribes of Yahweh* (Maryknoll, N.Y.: Orbis Books, 1979). Other scholars who argue that Israel regressed from revelation, such as R. Kittel (*Geschichte des Volkes Israel* [2d ed.; Gotha, 1912] vol. 1, unavailable to me); ET (*A History of the Hebrews* [London: Williams & Norgate, 1895]), and E. Sellin (*Alttestamentlische Religion im Rahmen der andern altorientalischen* [Leipzig: Hinrichs, 1908] 47ff.) represent the early counterparts of these more modern scholars.

15. Y. Kaufmann, *tôl^{e}dôt hā-'emûnâ hay-yiśrā'ēlît,* 4 vols. (Tel Aviv: Bialik-Dvir, 1937–56), 3:666. The translation is from M. Greenberg's English-language abridgment, *The Religion of Israel* (Chicago: Univ. of Chicago Press, 1960), 137. Subsequent citations are taken from the same volume.

16. This is clearly recognized and formulated by one scholar of this persuasion, B. Balscheit (*Alter und Aufkommen des Monotheismus in der israelitischen Religion* [Berlin: Reimer, 1938]). Balscheit denies that monotheism can evolve or exist without the express repudiation of other gods' existence. He therefore discovers monotheism just where Robinson et al. do. He has in fact only made their narrow criterion explicit.

17. Latterly, see M. Haran, *Temples and Temple Service in Ancient Israel* (Oxford: Oxford Univ. Press, 1978), and M. Weinfeld, *Getting at the Roots of Wellhausen's Understanding of the Law of Israel on the 100th Anniversary of the Prolegomena* (Report 14/79; Jerusalem: Hebrew Univ., Institute for Advanced Studies, 1979). To argue P is late because it assumes centralization, as Wellhausen did, is identical to arguing the United States of America's Bill of Rights must be late because it assumes the manumission of the slaves. It can be done, but the argument bases itself heavily on a conjecture as to what lay between the lines of a document whose overt intentions still defy our psychologizing.

18. Kaufmann, *Religion,* 29; *tôl^{e}dôt,* 2:316.

19. Read,

Yhwh came from Sinai and dawned from Seir upon them,

He shone forth from Mt. Pa'ran;
There came with him myriads of holy ones;
At his right hand marched (*'šrw*) the gods,
Even the pure ones of the peoples.

See further, P. D. Miller, *The Divine Warrior in Early Israel,* HSM 5 (Cambridge: Harvard Univ. Press, 1973), 75–81.

20. See above, n. 2.

21. Kaufmann, *Religion,* 62; *tôl^edôt,* 2.423–25.

22. *CTA,* MRS 10:2; 4; 6; 3; 5 (Ba'l-Yamm, Ba'l-Mot).

23. It is generally accepted that J is to be assigned to the tenth century and, despite the recent challenge, for example, of J. van Seters (*Abraham in Tradition and in History* [New Haven: Yale Univ. Press, 1975]) or of H. H. Schmid (*Der sogenannte Jahwist: Beobachtungen und Fragen zur Pentateuchforschung* ([Zurich: Theologischer, 1976]), this seems to me to be one of the more durable products of nineteenth-century literary criticism. See, recently, W. H. Schmidt, "A Theologian of the Solomonic Era? A Plea for the Yahwist," in *Studies in the Period of David and Solomon and Other Essays,* ed. T. Ishida (Winona Lake, Ind.: Eisenbrauns, 1982), 55–74.

24. Note Isa. 22:1, 5; 30:33; Jer. 2:23a (cf. 2:2); 7:31–32; 19:6, 11–14; 31:40; 32:35; Ezek. 39:11 (cf. Jer. 19:6); Ps. 23:4; 2 Kings 23:10; Deut. 14:1–2; Lev. 18:21; 19:27–28; 20:2–5. The *mulk* (occasionally mistranslated as Molech) is described in the Deuteronomistic History as "passing through fire."

25. See, for example, G. Ahlström, "An Israelite God Figurine from Hazor," *OrSuec* 19/20 (1970): 54-62; idem, "An Israelite God Figurine Once More," *VT* 25 (1975) 106–9; W. F. Albright, *Archaeology and the Religion of Israel,* 3d ed. (Garden City, N.Y.: Doubleday & Co., 1935), 114–15; idem, *The Archaeology of Palestine* (Harmondsworth: Penguin Books, 1960), 104–7. Note also P. Lapp, "The 1968 Excavations at Tell Ta'annek," *BASOR* 195 (1969): 4–44; idem, "The 1963 Excavation at Ta'annek," *BASOR* 173 (1964): 26–32; M. Tadmor, "Female Cult Figurines in Late Canaan and Early Israel: Archaeological Evidence," in *Studies in the Period of David and Solomon,* ed. Ishida, 139–73. Egyptian-influenced figures, some of them much at home in the Israelite iconographic tradition, are found in J. W. Crowfoot and G. M. Crowfoot, *Early Ivories from Samaria,* Samaria-Sebaste: Reports of the work of the Joint Expedition in 1931–1933 and of the British Expedition in 1935, no. 2 (London: Palestine Exploration Fund, 1938), 1:1–3; 2:1, 2; 3:1–2b; 4:1, 2, 3 = 14:2, 15:7; 5:1–3; 6; 7 = 14:4; 11:1, 2–5; 12; 13:2; 14:1 (see p. 18). Cf. F. W. James, *The Iron Age at Beth Shan* (Philadelphia: Univ. of Pennsylvania Museum, 1966), figs. 101:2; 107:1–2, 4–5, 7–8, 10; 109:5 (cf. 111:1–6 and 112:2–3, 5–7); 112:6; 113:9, 10; 115:1–6, 7; 116:2, 1, 5, 3, 4, 6, 7; 117:7, and in Iron II Lahav obj. 645 (photos 680a, b). Other varied figurines, including pillars, occur in O. Tufnell, *Lachish III. The Iron Age* (London: Oxford Univ. Press, 1953), 27:1–7, 8; 28:10, 11, 13, 14; 19:17, 18, 19–22; 30:23, 24, 26; 28:15, 16; 34:12–14, 18–29; 35:30–35 (Tufnell [p. 205] suggests Libyan provenience here); 36:48–51, also Egyptian. Latterly, see T. Holland, "A Study of Palestinian Iron Age Baked Clay Figurines, with Special Reference to Jerusalem: Cave 1," *Levant* 9 (1977): 121–55, and L. E. Stager, "The Archaeology of the East Slope of Jerusalem and the Terraces of the Kidron," *JNES* 41 (1982): 111–21, esp. 119–20, on the nature of Kenyon's "shrine." Further, Y. Aharoni, *Excavations at Ramat Rahel. Seasons 1961 and 1962* (Rome: Instituto di Studi del Vicino Oriente, 1964), pls. 35–36; Y. Yadin, et al., *Hazor II. An Account of the Second Season of Excavations, 1956* (Jerusalem: Magnes Press, 1960), pls. 76; 31:7, 8; 103:1–6; cf. idem, *Hazor I* (Jerusalem: Magnes Press, 1958), 41–42.

26. However one disposes of the problem of the illustrations on the pithoi, hypostatization remains a fact. See most recently P. Beck, "The Drawings from Horvat Teiman

(Kuntillet 'Ajrud)," *Tel Aviv* 9 (1982), 3–68, for the argument that the inscription succeeds the illustrations and that the illustrations themselves stem from several hands. This hardly invalidates the notion that the Asherah is YHWH's concubine; rather, it complicates the situation so as to demand increasing historical-theological sophistication from the critic. In all events, on the finds at Kuntillet Ajrud, see A. Lemaire, "Les inscriptions de Khirbet el Qôm et l'Ashérah de YHWH," *RB* 84 (1977): 595–608; Z. Meshel, *Kuntillet 'Ajrud: A Religious Centre from the Time of the Judaean Monarchy,* Israel Museum Catalogue 175 (Jerusalem: Israel Museum, 1978); M. Gilula, "To Yahweh Shomron and his Asherah," *Shnaton* 3 (1978/79): 129–37; J. Naveh, "Graffiti and Dedications," *BASOR* 235 (1979): 27–30; Z. Meshel, "Did Yahweh Have a Consort?" *BAR* 5:2 (3–4, 1979): 24–34; A. Angerstorfer, "Ašerah als 'Consort of Jahwe' oder Aširtah?" *BN* 17 (1982): 7–16; S. Mittmann, "Die Grabinschrift des Sängers Uriahu," *ZDPV* 97 (1981): 139–52 (cf. W. Dever, "Iron Age Epigraphic Material from the Area of Khirbet el-Kom," *HUCA* 40/41 [1969/70]: 139–204); J. A. Emerton, "New Light on Israelite Religion: The Implications of the Inscriptions from Kuntillet 'Ajrud," *ZAW* 94 (1982): 2–20; W. Dever, "Recent Archaeological Confirmation of the Cult of Asherah in Ancient Israel," *Hebrew Studies* 23 (1982), unavailable to me. Note further M. Tadmor, "Female Figurines in Late Bronze Age Canaan," *Qad* 15 (1982): 2–10. How one resolves the problem of the suffix on the term *'šrh/t* at Kuntillet Ajrud is not crucial. See below for a suggestion.

27. Kaufmann, *Religion,* 144; *tôl^edôt,* 674 (see 662). This treatment ignores the importance of cults specialized to sex in an Israel whose late cult (not early, with an Asherah in the temple to Hezekiah's time) was unrelentingly masculine. In addition, it is difficult to determine on the basis of our largely post-Josianic sources just when the cult of the Queen of Heaven ceased to enjoy the overt sanction of the state authorities.

28. G. Ahlström, *National Administration and State Religion in Ancient Palestine* (Leiden: E. J. Brill, 1982).

29. A. Haldar, *Associations of Cult Prophets among the Ancient Semites* (Uppsala: Almqvist & Wiksell, 1945), 128–29.

30. See Kaufmann, *Religion,* 87–89; *tôl^edôt,* 3.485ff.

31. M. Pope, *Song of Songs,* AB 7C (Garden City, N.Y.: Doubleday & Co., 1973). See on Ugarit, idem, "A Divine Banquet at Ugarit," in *The Use of the Old Testament in the New and Other Essays,* Festschrift W. F. Stinespring, ed. J. M. Efird (Durham, N.C.: Duke Univ. Press, 1972), 170–203; C. E. L'Heureux, *Rank among the Canaanite Gods: El, Ba'al and the Repha'im,* HSM 19 (Missoula, Mont.: Scholars Press, 1979), 201–23. It is the warrior aristocracy that engaged in ancestral worship, as elsewhere—hence its proscription in Israel. This is why the *rp'um* at Ugarit appear to be both chariot warriors and the principals of the underworld, as Isa. 14:9. Note that the term *'^elōhîm,* meaning "God, god or pantheon" means "spirit" in 1 Sam. 28:13, as in so many other cultures. On the suppression of the cult of the dead under Saul, note the archaeological evidence for the discontinuation of funereal figurines during the United Monarchy in Tadmor, "Female Cult Figurines," esp. 170–73.

32. Names compounded with *ba'al* include those of Saul's and David's sons. It is commonly supposed that this reflects the fact that polemic against "Baal" had not yet become necessary, but in fact, like Marduk, Asshur, Haddu, Melqart and, no doubt, others (e.g., the pharaoh in the Amarna letters), YHWH himself was a god called *ba'al.* The polemic directed against the term *ba'al,* no more to be YHWH's epithet (Hosea 2:18), is concerned with the worship not of Baal but of baals. See below.

33. See F. M. Cross, "The Epic Traditions of Early Israel," in *The Poet and the Historian,* ed. R. E. Friedman, HSS (Chico, Calif.: Scholars Press, 1983), 36–37.

34. See recently P. K. McCarter, Jr., "The Balaam Texts from Deir 'Allā: The First

Combination," *BASOR* 239 (1980): 49–60; cf. S. A. Kaufman, "The Aramaic Texts from Deir 'Allā," *BASOR* 239 (1980): 71–74; H. Weippert and M. Weippert, "Die 'Bileam'-Inschrift von Tell Dēr 'Allā," *ZDPV* 98 (1982): 77–103; J. A. Hackett, *The Balaam Text from Deir 'Allā,* HSM 31 (Chico, Calif.: Scholars Press, 1984), and idem, "The Dialect of the Plaster Text from Tell Deir 'Allā," *Or.* 53 (1984): 57–65.

35. *KAI,* 3 vols., no. 181. Cf. Zeus-Amun. Note, though, that Athtar ("the terrible") is a comical figure at Ugarit.

36. See B. Halpern, *The Emergence of Israel in Canaan,* SBLMS 29 (Chico, Calif.: Scholars Press, 1983), 89–91, 101–2.

37. See G. Ahlström, *Aspects of Syncretism in Israelite Religion* (Lund: Gleerup, 1963), 73–74. Any other reconstruction of the understanding of Moab, for example, would be naive in terms of motivation to worship and inconsistent with the epigraphic and onomastic evidence. Mesha, for example, assumes that Chemosh fully controls fate. Any Ashtar-Chemosh would thus have to be thought of as Chemosh's underling. It is critical to recognize that this system of thought is completely inimical to syncretism.

38. The case of Philistia is clouded by lack of evidence. But note 1 Sam. 5:1–5. Tyre is identified with the *ba'al* in 1 Kings 17ff., possibly Melqart, but here an unidentified subsidiary deity (which is how *ba'al* comes to be used in Israel). Perhaps the Tyrian theology involved devotion to an active delegate of El called *ba'al* (= Lord, or the lord) of Tyre.

39. See K. Baltzer, *Das Bundesformular,* 2d ed. (Neukirchen-Vluyn: Neukirchener, 1963); ET, *The Covenant Formulary* (Philadelphia: Fortress Press, 1971).

40. Some scholars, following in Wellhausen's footsteps (*Prolegomena,* 418–19), assign the covenant to a late era. See recently L. Perlitt, *Bundestheologie im Alten Testament,* WMANT 36 (Neukirchen-Vluyn: Neukirchener, 1969). Cf. D. J. McCarthy, *Treaty and Covenant,* 2d ed., AnBib 21A (Rome: Pontifical Biblical Institute, 1978), 22–23.

41. See T. N. D. Mettinger, *King and Messiah. The Sacral and Civil Legitimation of the Israelite Kings,* CBOTS 8 (Lund: Gleerup, 1978); B. Halpern, *Constitution of the Monarchy in Israel,* HSM 25 (Chico, Calif.: Scholars Press, 1981).

42. The scholarly assumption that this chapter treats a Canaanite Shechem is baseless. See B. Halpern, *Emergence,* 28 and n. 35.

43. See, for example, F. M. Cross, *Canaanite Myth and Hebrew Epic* (Cambridge: Harvard Univ. Press, 1973), 60–75; W. H. Brownlee, "The Ineffable Name of God," *BASOR* 226 (1977): 39–46. Cf. S. Mowinckel, "The Name of the God of Moses," *HUCA* 32 (1961): 121–33.

44. On the stars as counterparts of the gods, see the use of *ṣᵉba' haš-šamāyîm* to mean the gods in 2 Kings 23:4 and elsewhere, but the stars and planets in Gen. 2:1, Deuteronomy 4, and Deutero-Isaiah. Further, B. Halpern, "The Ritual Background of Zechariah's Temple Song," *CBQ* 40 (1978): 167–90, esp. 174ff. and Ee 5:1–2.

45. See Cross, *Canaanite Myth,* 69–70, on the antiquity of this form.

46. Kaufmann, *Religion,* 24–31; *tôlᵉdôt,* 303ff.

47. See O. Eissfeldt, *Sanchunjaton von Berut und Ilumilku von Ugarit* (Halle: Niemeyer, 1952); L. R. Clapham, on Sakkunyaton in "Sanchuniathon: The First Two Cycles" (Diss., Harvard Univ., 1969).

48. As O. Keel, *The Symbolism of the Biblical World,* 2d ed. (New York: Seabury Press, 1979), 52; Mullen, *Assembly,* 46, 54, but also 76.

49. On the temple and the cosmos, see M. Eliade, *The Sacred and the Profane* (New York: Harper & Row, 1961), 36–47; B. Halpern, "Zechariah's Temple Song," for later Israel; J. D. Levenson, "The Temple and the World," *JR* (1984): 275–98.

50. As *CTA* 4.2:11; 3:32; 6.3:5, 11; 17.1:25.

51. Ibid. 14.1:43; 3:136, 151; 5:259; 6:278, 297. Cf. "Fathers of Years" in ibid. 1.3:24; 2.3:5; 3.5:16; 4.4:24; 5.6:2; 6.1:36; 17.6:49.

52. Ibid., 4.7:8, 10.

53. See A. S. Kapelrud, *Baal in the Ras Shamra Texts* (Copenhagen: G. E. C. Gad, 1952), 110ff. So latterly Mullen, *Assembly,* 22ff.

54. Note that in Israel, man (*'ādām*) is named for the soil (*'ᵃdāmâ*) from which he is formed (with divine breath), while in the *Enuma Elish,* man is formed from soil (and the blood of the evil god, Kingu) and called LULLU (LÚ.LUx' Sumerian for "man" being LÚ). The same sort of pun on "man" and "soil" as in Israel may thus be the referent in the designation of Ugarit's El's abode as Mt. *ll* (Lullu?). El's mount would then be that out of which man was formed, an element not present in Ee, but developed in Israel. There may be traces of mediation here. Cf. *lullû,* "abundance," and *'dn.*

55. One might translate along the lines "There is none like the god of Jeshurun, who rides the heavens in your behalf, and in his exaltation the clouds, who suppresses the gods of old, and, below, the arms of the underworld." On *'wlm* as underworld, see A. M. Cooper, "Ps. 24:7–10: Mythology and Exegesis," *JBL* 102 (1983): 37–60. See also Ps. 68:20–24, followed by the procession in vv. 25ff., perhaps adducible in Cooper's behalf. For the relationship between YHWH and Sheol, see G. A. Danell, *Psalm 139,* UUÅ (Uppsala: Lundequistska; Leipzig: Harrassowitz, 1951), 26–31.

56. See Cooper, "Ps. 24:7–10."

57. See Kaufmann, *Religion,* 128, 221, and passim.

58. As Widengren, *Accadian and Hebrew Psalms,* 78–79.

59. Starting at least as early as Gudea, Cyl. A (as 8:7–18; 12:1–11). See A. Petitjean, *Les Oracles du Proto-Zacharie* (Paris: J. Gabalda, 1969), 137–42, with the citation from Merodach-Baladan II. Note especially W. W. Baudissin, "Zur Geschichte des Monotheismus bei semitischen Völkern," *DLZ* 35 (1914): 5–13.

60. M. Weinfeld, "The Universalistic and the Particularistic Tendency in the Restoration Era," *Tarbiz* 33 (1964): 1–15; cf. Danell, *Psalm 139,* 31.

61. So Nikiprowetzky, "Ethical Monotheism," 69–89; A. S. Kapelrud, *Central Ideas in Amos* (1956; reprinted, Oslo: Universitetsforlagets, 1961), 23–28, 33–47.

62. See Widengren, *Accadian and Hebrew Psalms,* 50–54, 139–70. Codex Hammurabi is also clear on this point (especially the Prologue). At Ugarit, Haddu also seems to be a moralist (*CTA* 4.3:17–22).

63. On the ascription of Exod. 20:1–17 to P (though the "Decalogue" itself may be somewhat older), see esp. T. N. D. Mettinger, "The Veto on Images and the Aniconic God in Ancient Israel," in *Religious Symbols and their Functions,* ed. H. Biezais, SIDA 10 (Stockholm: Almqvist & Wiksell, 1979), 15–29.

64. 1 Kings 7:23–26. On the significance of the sea, see A. J. Wensinck, *The Ocean in the Literature of the Western Semites,* VNAW 19/2 (Amsterdam: J. Müller, 1918).

65. See W. F. Albright, *From the Stone Age to Christianity* (Garden City, N.Y.: Doubleday & Co., 1957), 199–200. Cf. H. Motzki, "Ein Beitrag zum Problem des Stierkultes in der Religionsgeschichte Israels," *VT* 25 (1975): 470–85.

66. Unless one conceives of the cherubim as steeds only, as in the Meggido ivories (G. Loud, *Megiddo II,* OIP 62 [Chicago: Univ. of Chicago Press, 1948]). I would take Isaiah 6, with seraphim who have the appearance and function of cherubim, to imply that the cherubim are the council of YHWH. Note recently, W. B. Barrick, "The Straight-Legged Cherubim of Ezekiel's Inaugural Vision (Ezekiel 1:7a)," *CBQ* 44 (1982): 543–50.

67. On the disk, see Mendenhall, *Tenth Generation,* 33–56; cf. A. J. Wensinck, *Tree*

and Bird as Cosmological Symbols in Western Asia, VNAW (Amsterdam: J. Müller, 1921).

68. K. Jaspers, *Vom Ursprung und Ziel der Geschichte* (1949); ET, *The Origin and Goal of History* (New Haven: Yale Univ. Press, 1953).

69. See, e.g., Kapelrud, *Central Ideas in Amos,* 33–47; A. Alt, "Der Gott der Väter," *Kleine Schriften zur Geschichte des Volkes Israel* (Munich: C. H. Beck, 1953), 1:1–78; Ringgren, *Israelite Religion,* 19–22, 69, among many others. Cf. Ahlström, *Aspects of Syncretism.*

70. On the dates of these songs, see D. A. Robertson, *Linguistic Evidence in Dating Early Hebrew Poetry,* SBLDS 3 (Missoula, Mont.: Scholars Press, 1972); Halpern, *Emergence,* chap. 2, with bibliography.

71. This is sustained by the position of "the baal" and "the asherah" in texts such as 2 Kings 23:4. See O. Eissfeldt, "Yahweh and El" *JSS* 1 (1956): 25–37.

72. Whose xenophobia was first argued by D. Merkur in a paper presented in seminar in 1981. See further Halpern, *Emergence,* chap. 11.

73. As Haldar, *Cult Associations,* 138–39; H. H. Rowley, "Zadok and Nehushtan," *JBL* 58 (1939): 113–41; C. E. Hauer, "Who Was Zadok?" *JBL* 82 (1963): 89–94. Cf. S. Olyan, "Zadok's Origins and the Tribal Politics of David," *JBL* 101 (1982): 177–93.

74. Halpern, *Emergence,* chap. 11.

75. Read with G^B (OG).

76. Halpern, *Emergence,* chaps. 7–8, 10; idem, "The Uneasy Compromise: Israel between League and Monarchy," in *Traditions in Transformation: Turning-Points in Biblical Faith. Essays Presented to Frank Moore Cross, Jr., on the Occasion of His Sixtieth Birthday,* ed. B. Halpern and J. D. Levenson (Winona Lake, Ind.: Eisenbrauns, 1981), 59–98.

77. B. Halpern, "The Rise of Abimelek ben-Jerubaal," *HAR* 2 (1978): 67–100.

78. Cross, *Canaanite Myth,* 219–65; E. von Nordheim, "König und Tempel. Der Hintergrund des Tempelbauverbotes in 2 Samuel vii," *VT* 27 (1977): 434–53.

79. Cf. Widengren (*Accadian and Hebrew Psalms,* 78) who suggests that YHWH only in Solomon's reign surpassed Jerusalem's city-god, Salem. This is unrealistic. The appeal of the monarchy was based on YHWH's ascendance, and cannot have admitted the superiority of any other god.

80. B. Halpern, "Sectionalism and the Schism," *JBL* 93 (1974): 519–32.

81. See S. Talmon, "Divergences in Calendar-Reckoning in Ephraim and Judah," *VT* 8 (1958): 46–74; Cross, *Canaanite Myth,* 73–75.

82. Nikiprowetzky ("Ethical Monotheism," 79) suggests that at the Solomonic schism, YHWH became a supranational god. This may indeed have been a factor in the development of radical monotheism, but not because it contributed to YHWH's universalization, on which see above.

83. See Mesha's claims to have wrested southern and central Transjordan from Ahab (*KAI,* 181). Note further the reports of continual jockeying with Aram in 1 Kings 20—2 Kings 9. Mesha's xenophobia is worth marking.

84. See on the Josianic date of Dtr^1, A. Jepsen, *Die Quellen des Königsbuches,* 2d ed. (Halle: M. Niemayer, 1956); N. Lohfink,, "Die Bundesurkunde des Königs Josias" *Bib* 44 (1963): 261–88; Cross, *Canaanite Myth,* 275–89.

85. Kapelrud, *Central Ideas in Amos,* 32–34.

86. I take these chapters as a unit, virtually free of redaction. Cf. H. W. Wolff, *Hosea,* Hermeneia (Philadelphia: Fortress Press, 1974), and D. N. Freedman and F. I. Anderson, *Hosea,* AB (Garden City, N.Y.: Doubleday & Co., 1982), ad loc.

87. G^B adds "and silver and gold" before *'św lb'l,* and reads the verb as a singular.

MT is preferable. The reference is to *a,* not *the* baal, I take it. This may be an assault on the manufacture of icons.

88. *KAI,* 181:14–17, and above.

89. W. Zimmerli, "Das Bildverbot in der Geschichte des alten Israel (Goldenes Kalb, Eherne Schlange, Mazzeben und Lade)" in *Schalom. Studien zu Glaube und Geschichte Israels,* Festschrift A. Jepsen, ed. K.-H. Bernhardt (Stuttgart: Calver, 1971), 86–96; Cf. Mettinger, "Veto."

90. B. Oded, "Judah and the Exile" in *Israelite and Judaean History,* ed. J. H. Hayes and J. M. Miller (Philadelphia: Westminster Press, 1977), 441–46, presents a convenient assembly of the data.

91. See M. Broshi, "The Expansion of Jerusalem in the Reigns of Hezekiah and Manasseh," *IEJ* 24 (1974): 21–25; idem, "La populations de l'ancienne Jérusalem," *RB* 82 (1975): 5–14.

92. For Josiah's period, see W. E. Clayburn, "The Fiscal Basis of Josiah's Reforms," *JBL* 92 (1973): 11–22. Cf. Diaz's, Mirabeau's, and Nabonidus's centralizations, all in eras of crisis, and note M. Weinfeld, "Cult Centralization in Israel in the Light of a Neo-Babylonian Analogy," *JNES* 23 (1964): 202–12.

93. So J. D. Levenson, *Sinai and Zion: A Path into the Jewish Bible* (New York: Crossroad, 1983). Note the linkage of this concept, with its implication that creation = sanctification = differentiation, to the theology of P, especially in Genesis 1. Perhaps the original formulation needed reinterpretation to reach this stage of meaning.

94. But the alleged apostasy of Manasseh's reign may reflect more widespread sentiment.

95. In his eighth year, with 2 Chron. 34:3. Kings has suffered a haplography from "8th" to "18th" (2 Kings 22:3), possibly in its *Vorlage.*

96. Scholars have questioned the date of segments in Deuteronomy 4 (see J. D. Levenson, "Who Inserted the Book of the Torah?" *HTR* 68 [1975]: 203–33; but cf. R. E. Friedman, *The Exile and Biblical Narrative,* HSM 22 [Chico, Calif.: Scholars Press, 1981], 20–22). The chapter's resemblance to Jeremiah 10 is so stark that it is difficult to imagine the authors of the two were unacquainted with one another. The result is, the tendency has been to date Jeremiah 10 late. See M. E. Andrew, "The Authorship of Jer. 10.1–16," *ZAW* 94 (1982): 128–30. But as a part of the scroll of 605 B.C.E. (Jeremiah 1—25), Jeremiah 10 is the evidence for an early date of Deuteronomy 4. Both chapters are intellectually coherent and consistent with the thought of Jeremiah. See below.

97. Given the trend of Jeremiah's thought, this is the preferred meaning. See J. Bright, *Jeremiah,* AB 21 (Garden City, N.Y.: Doubleday & Co., 1965), ad loc; already J. Skinner, *Prophecy and Religion* (London: Macmillan & Co., 1922), 103.

98. The only extant deviation from this position occurs in Jer. 17:21–27, which appears to hypostatize the sabbath. Whether this is purely rhetorical or real is unclear; it is at least inconsistent.

99. So much was recognized by S. Mowinckel in "The 'Spirit' and the 'Word' in the Pre-exilic Reforming Prophets," *JBL* 53 (1934): 199–227. Mowinckel went too far, however, in ascribing a similar theology to Hosea. Wolff (*Hosea*) follows Mowinckel only by disallowing the "angel" in Hosea 12:5 on the grounds that no such concept elsewhere appears in Hosea, and by taking *q^edōšîm* in 12:1 to refer to people (prophets), not gods, on the grounds that nowhere else does such a concept appear in Hosea. At any event, the very visual Ezekiel attacks Jeremiah on this point (13:2) on grounds that are summarized in 1 Kings 22:15ff. There, Micaiah claims that he is privy to the workings of YHWH's council (as Isaiah in chap. 6 or Ezekiel in chap. 1), whereas the other prophets depend on revelation by the intermediary "spirit." They are thus susceptible to being deceived, while he actually participates in all such decisions. Visual

revelation is direct (22:17, 19). Thus, when Zedeqiah asks Micaiah, "How did the 'spirit' of YHWH pass from me to speak with you?" he has missed the entire point; Micaiah's revelation is neither audial nor of the "spirit," but visual and direct. Micaiah's response that Zedeqiah "will see" indicates the position poignantly (22:24–25). Inspiration by the "spirit" is not the same as firsthand experience of YHWH.

100. Cf. T. W. Overholt, *The Threat of Falsehood. A Study in the Theology of the Book of Jeremiah,* SBT 2/16 (London: SCM Press, 1970).

101. Note R. J. Clifford, "The Function of the Idol Passages in Second Isaiah," *CBQ* 42 (1980): 450–64. Second Isaiah did have P before him, on which see A. S. Kapelrud, *God and His Friends in the Old Testament* (Oslo: Universitetsforlaget, 1979), 23–27.

102. Whether Second Isaiah admits of the existence of a heavenly council or not (and in P only the "we, us" of Gen. 1:26) is moot. F. M. Cross ("The Council of Yahweh in Second Isaiah," *JNES* 12 [1953]: 274–77) maintains he does, and that 40:1 is addressed to them. But this may refer to the people in Babylon who intend to return as the central cultic and royal establishment. Note R. J. Clifford, *Fair Spoken and Persuading. An Interpretation of Second Isaiah* (New York: Paulist Press, 1984), 56–58.

103. See H. Weippert, *Schöpfer des Himmels und der Erde: Ein Beitrag zur Theologie des Jeremiabuches,* SBB 102 (Stuttgart: Katholisches Bibelwerk, 1981).

104. Note esp. J. Dus, "Zur bewegten Geschichte der israelitischen Lade," *Annali* 41 (1981): 351–83, with the insight that those who localize YHWH's presence are not members of the "Deuteronomistic" movement.

105. Note that the other model for the development of monotheism is present in M. Smith, *Palestinian Parties and Politics that Shaped the Old Testament* (New York: Columbia Univ. Press, 1971). His concept of an old "YHWH-alone" party confronting the syncretizers seems ahistorical and displaces in a sense the issue of how much sentiment developed.

106. See K. Freeman, *Ancilla to the Pre-Socratic Philosophers* (Oxford: Basil Blackwell & Mott, 1956), 22.

107. Ibid., 23.

108. K. Jaspers, "Xenophanes" in *Aneignung und Polemik. Gesammelte Reden und Aufsatze zur Geschichte der Philosophie,* ed. Hans Ganer (Munich: R. Piper, 1968), 32–42. The quote is from p. 37.

109. Freeman, *Ancilla,* 22.18; 24.34, 35, 36. Cf. H. Frankel, "Xenophanesstudien II," (*Hermes* 60 [1925]: 174–92), for the view that Xenophanes was an empiricist. Xenophanes' monotheism proves otherwise. He was a relativizer of knowledge and of perception, and a causalist.

110. Freeman, *Ancilla,* 27.42, 40; 32.105.

111. Ibid., 28.47, 55.

112. Ibid., 27.32, 41. Cf. G. S. Kirk and J. E. Raven, *The Presocratic Philosophers* (Cambridge: Cambridge Univ. Press, 1963).

113. Freeman, *Ancilla,* 28.49a, 56.

114. Ibid., 25.5.

115. Ibid., 27.41.

116. See A. Jenks, *The Elohist and North Israelite Tradition,* SBLMS 22 (Missoula, Mont.: Scholars Press, 1977), on E.

117. See above, n. 43.

118. See above on Xenophanes, and Jaspers, "Xenophanes," 39; Widengren, *Accadian and Hebrew Psalms,* 160–61, on Mesopotamia.

119. See J. L. Crenshaw, *Prophetic Conflict* (Berlin: Walter de Gruyter, 1971), 36–38.

120. Widengren, *Accadian and Hebrew Psalms,* 165–70.

6 ALEXANDER ROFÉ

THE BATTLE OF DAVID AND GOLIATH: FOLKLORE, THEOLOGY, ESCHATOLOGY

I

David's battle with Goliath, in 1 Samuel 17, rests on two pivotal themes, each expressing a different concept of the conflict between the two heroes.

The first thematic contrast comprises the unknown little shepherd boy and the heroic giant of renown who is armed from head to toe. Through his resourcefulness, quick thinking, and the sort of daring that comes from an unfamiliarity with the horrors of war, the shepherd boy overcomes the giant. His pathetic equipment (slingshot, five smooth stones, and a shepherd's staff as the last resort) proves his superiority over the giant armed with brass helmet, breastplate of mail, brass greaves, javelin, sword, and shield—this last carried ahead by a shieldbearer.

Such a contrast frequently occurs in fairy tales,[1] which often regale listeners with the amazing victories of the underdog, and is central to most of our story. David is described as Jesse's youngest son, a lad who generally spends his time tending the sheep. Then his elderly father sends him to check on his brothers' well-being and take them provisions (vv. 12–14, 17–20). So it happens that David chances upon Goliath. All this characterizes David as the sort of lowly youth who makes an ideal fairy-tale hero. And this characterization is driven home when Eliav sharply rebukes David for being an idle, bloodthirsty good-for-nothing (vv. 28–29). Again, the first two rewards promised by the king to the man who defeats the giant are glittering prizes from the treasure house of the fairy tale. The king promises great riches, the hand of the princess in marriage, and freedom from royal service (v. 25). Saul's conversation with David (v. 33) also runs along fairy-tale lines. As Saul says, David is a mere boy, whereas the Philistine is "a man of war from his youth." Still, David is a shepherd and has been tested through fights in the open with wild animals (vv. 34–35)—this is why he goes to battle in his shepherd's gear, and not in the military gear which Saul presses upon him (vv. 38–46). And so, "with a slingshot and a stone," David vanquishes the Philistine even though "there was no sword in David's hand" (vv. 49–50). Only when the boy returns "carrying the Philistine's head in his hand" does he emerge from anonymity, and this, too, indicates his lowly origin: "Whose son are you, boy?" asks the king, and David answers, "I am the son of Jesse of Bethlehem" (vv. 57–58). At last, the unknown boy becomes the darling hero of the entire people.

The second pivotal theme comprises the contrast between the uncircumcised Philistine who "has taunted the armies of the living God" (vv. 26, 36) and "the Lord of Hosts, the God of the armies of Israel, whom you have taunted" (v. 45). Thus, the defeat of the Philistine testifies not to the superiority of shepherds' slingshots over battle armor, but to David's faith. David fights and will win "that all the earth might know that Israel has a God and that all who are here might know that God does not save through the sword and the spear—the war is the Lord's" (vv. 46–47). Here we have certain tenets of faith (to be explained by us later on), and David's victory serves to prove their veracity. The contrast no longer involves the folkloristic portrayal of fairy-tale heroes. Rather, it is a theological confrontation between two antagonists of different faiths—and one of them, at least, puts his beliefs to the test in a contest of champions. Although this confrontation is not central to the story, it does recur from time to time (as we have seen, in vv. 26, 36, 45–46).

By identifying these two pivotal themes we can develop a hypothesis concerning our story's historical development. Clearly, each theme belongs to a different area and a different stage of literary creativity; the fairy tale is popular and universal, whereas theology is an intellectual domain and the preserve of a specific group of believers. For these reasons, the most natural explanation of the ambiguity in the story's theme must be this: the story originated as a popular fairy tale told, perhaps orally, in order to entertain the simple folk. Later, it was reworked from a theological angle by thinkers and teachers who wished to ascribe to it their own religious principles.[2]

Of course, this description is nothing more than a hypothesis, but two pieces of evidence support it. First, as we have seen, most of the story revolves around the folkloristic theme, with the theological theme playing only a minor role. Second, the theological elements sometimes appear in a way that interrupts the narrative flow of the story. In v. 26 David asks "What will be done for the man . . . ?" and continues "Who is that uncircumcised Philistine that he dares defy the ranks of the living God?" But the question "What will be done for the man . . . ?" has already been answered in v. 25.[3] Similarly, in v. 36 David proclaims "Your servant has killed both lion and bear; and that uncircumcised Philistine shall end up like one of them for he had defied the ranks of the living God," and his words are all but duplicated in v. 37: "David said, 'The

Lord, who has saved me from the lion and the bear, will also save me from that Philistine.' And Saul said to David, 'Go, and may the Lord be with you.'" It seems that v. 36 was inserted in order to emphasize Goliath's sin from a theological standpoint and also to give David's answer a fitting measure of assurance—he was not speaking merely of saving his own skin, but of dealing the Philistine a fatal blow. A third example of such reworking occurs in vv. 45–47. Certainly we have no reason to question the aptness of David's long speech given as Goliath draws nearer and nearer (vv. 45–47, esp. 41, 48), yet it is impossible to ignore the way in which a contrast between the Philistine and the shepherd boy with his "sticks" (vv. 40–43) is transformed (from v. 45 onward) into a confrontation with the Lord God of Israel. Indeed, a subtle artistry underpins this transformation. Whereas the Philistine believes David was coming against him with sticks (v. 43), David says "I come against you in the name of the Lord of Hosts, the God of the ranks of Israel, whom you have defied" (v. 45). Had the Philistine even wished to concede defeat at this point, then, he would have been too late.

II

Our discussion thus far on our two themes and their role in the story's historical development leads us to address the difficult and even vexing question of the relationship between chapter 17's MT and its LXX translation. In the original LXX, reflected first and foremost by Codex Vaticanus,[4] 17:12–31, 41, 48b, 50, and 17:55—18:6a, are not represented. Scholars continue to debate which source is the original or is closer to the original—the longer version of MT or the shorter version of LXX.[5] In my opinion, MT constitutes the primary source, while LXX represents a secondary, abridged version. Why?

What supports my distinction between the two texts? First, one cannot ascribe any theological tendency whatsoever to the material included in MT and omitted in LXX. Of David's three theological statements (vv. 26, 36, 45–57), the last two are also found in LXX, and the statement in v. 36 is even longer in LXX than in MT.[6] Were MT the secondary source, we would expect its expansions to be of a theological nature in accordance with our secondary pivotal theme, thus befitting later authors. Instead, we find numerous traces of the fairy-tale theme: David is described as young (v. 14), as a shepherd boy (vv. 20, 28), and as bringing his brothers food (vv. 17–18). On his errand, he happens to hear the Philistine giant's challenge (vv. 23–24) and the king's promise to whomever kills the giant (v. 25). His elder brother sharply rebukes him as an idle thrill-seeker for his interest (v. 28). Then the king has him brought over (v. 31). Still, he remains anonymous until the end of the battle (vv. 55–58) when he is taken into the king's service (18.2). Because of their folkloristic nature, these traces appear to be original. Indeed, they cannot be considered later elements in the story as we have it in MT since they are also hidden deep within the shorter version. In LXX, too, David appears as a shepherd (v. 34) who is unable to wear armor, a bronze helmet, or a sword, and instead goes into battle with his shepherd's gear (vv. 38–40). Thus, the longer story of MT must be seen as the original story.

At the same time, we can see how and why the shorter version came into existence. It must have been created in order to make the story of David and Goliath consistent with the stories which precede it. David was anointed "*in the presence of his brothers*" (1 Sam. 16:1–13); therefore it is unlikely that Eliav would rebuke him for his impudence and wickedness (17:28–29). Moreover, David has already been brought into Saul's court as "a stalwart fellow and a warrior" (16:18), so he cannot be described as a lad who tends Daddy's sheep and brings food to his big brothers (17:17–18), who is completely unknown to King Saul (17:55–58), and who is brought into the court only after he has vanquished Goliath (18:2). What we have here are ancient attempts at harmonization within the narrative of David's rise to power.

Certain other small omissions in LXX can also be explained as the result of a harmonizing process. For example, MT v. 41 (lacking in LXX), "The Philistine, meanwhile, was coming closer to David, preceded by his shield-bearer," duplicates MT v. 48a, "When the Philistine began to advance toward David," and does not provide an adequate interval for the exchange in vv. 43–47. As for the shield-bearer, he may be mentioned in v. 7, but he is not really compatible with a contest of champions. Verse 48b, "David quickly ran up to the battle line to face the Philistine," duplicates v. 40b, "he went toward the Philistine." Verse 50, "David overcame the Philistine with a stone and a slingshot; he killed him, and there was no sword in David's hand," duplicates v. 51 which also describes the killing and decapitation of the Philistine with his own sword.

Harmonization continues in chapter 18, where the following verses are missing in LXX: 1–6a*α*, 10–11, 12b, 17–19, 21b, 29b–30. In the first group of verses (1–6a*α*), v. 2 conflicts with the story of David's coming to Saul in 16:19–22, and the story of Jonathan's love for David comes at too early a point in the narrative, as does that of David's appointment to head of the warriors. But most importantly, the passages interrupt the account of the day's events. The Israelites return from pursuing the Philistines (17:53), David takes the Philistine's head and brings it to Jerusalem (17:51), and then "the women of all the towns of Israel [come] dancing out to greet *David*(!) with timbrels and cymbals and great rejoicing" (18:6, according to LXX). Also Saul's attempt to spear David (18:10–11) is described somewhat prematurely (since David's marriage to Saul's daughter is still to come). Further, it is repeated in 19:9–10. And if Saul's failed attempt is omitted, there is no need to say that "God was with [David] and departed from Saul" (18:12b). As for the puzzling story of David's marriage to Merab (18:17–19), clearly an alternative version of the marriage to Michal, it disappears along with Saul's peculiar comment in v. 21b, "Today you shall become my son-in-law through two (daughters)." For our final example, let us consider 18:29b–30, "And Saul bore David a continual enmity. The Philistine leaders went out to battle, and whenever they went out, David proved more successful than any of Saul's other men, and he made a great name for himself." This passage duplicates 18:9, 13–15. Furthermore, this verse interrupts the continuity between 18:28–29a and 19:1: "When Saul saw that the Lord was with David and that *all Israel*(!) loved him, he began to fear David more and more and told his son, Jonathan, and all servants to kill David." Thus both this new story of a Philistine war (18:30) and Saul's "continual" enmity disrupt the flow of the narrative from the time when Saul is gripped by fear of David until he plots to have him killed.

Opposing the hypotheses that the shorter version of LXX developed from a need to harmonize the text, scholars commonly argue that if this were indeed the case, certain other anomalous details should have been dealt with. For example, Saul calls David a "boy" (17:33), and David himself admits that he has never worn battle armor (17:38–40). Still, the fact that David is young does not contradict anything in chapters 16 and 18—19. As for the battle armor, this episode cannot be omitted without destroying the story as a whole. Can we expect the harmonizer to describe a fully armed David fighting Goliath on equal terms? We must conclude that he removed the obvious and disturbing contradictions and duplications but was unable—and most probably unwilling—to delve into contradictions inextricably woven into the basic story. The two perceptions of David comprise such a contradiction. On the one hand, David is a "warrior" who becomes Saul's "arms-bearer" (16:18, 21), and on the other, he is a shepherd whose weaponry consists of a staff, a slingshot, and "five smooth stones from the river" (17:40). Further, we must acknowledge that the harmonizer, for all his perspicacity, could not master the entire corpus of material in his hands. So, for example, he omits the pact between Jonathan and David (18:3), but nevertheless retains a later allusion to it (20:8).[7] In this way, he actually leaves us traces which evidence his work and which confirm the secondary nature of the shorter version.

We should not be in the least surprised that efforts were made to harmonize these chapters. The original written material was so variegated and, once assembled, produced such noticeable contradictions, it became imperative to reconcile them. In MT, however, we find a different sort of harmonization. In 17:12 we read, "David was the son of this Ephrathite of Bethlehem in Judah, named Jesse." The added word, "this" (*hazzeh*), links the story to the preceding events in 1 Samuel 16, where David and Jesse are introduced to the reader. By means of 17:15, "David would go back and forth from Saul to tend his father's sheep in Bethlehem," the harmonizer of MT brings David from Saul's court back to his home and his sheep, and it is from there that Jesse sends him out to the valley of Elah. In 18:11, "But David eluded him twice," the word "twice" justifies the repetition of the spear episode in 19:9–10.

Apparently, Saul's words, "Today you shall become my son-in-law through the two (daughters)" (18:21), are intended to solve the problem of a duplicate tradition concerning David's marriage to Saul's daughter by suggesting a double wedding.[8] Here, then, we have clear evidence of the biblical writers' sensitivity to difficulties inherent in their text and of their efforts to smooth out the narrative as much as possible.

What is unusual about the LXX translation to 1 Samuel 17—18 is the way in which the text was reworked. Unlike MT, it was not harmonized by means of explanatory additions. Instead, it was boldly and thoroughly abridged. Although such a reworking might appear highly irregular, an examination of its components makes it quite understandable.

Even the Book of Chronicles was completely reworked. First Chron. 20:5 relates that Elhanan, son of Ya'ir, killed "*Lahmi* the brother of Goliath the Gittite," and thereby removes the contradiction between our story and the passage in 2 Sam. 21:19 which attributes the victory over Goliath to Elhanan son of Ya'ir the Bethlehemite. And one by one, 1 Chronicles does away with the contradictions found in the story of the pestilence in 2 Samuel 24. First, it deals with the duration of the pestilence, then the way in which it was halted, and finally, with the reason why Araunah's threshing floor was consecrated as a place of worship.[9] There exist also examples of drastic abridgment in Chronicles. For instance, it omits Ish-boshet's entire reign (2 Samuel 1—4) and, no doubt in order to enhance David's image, it fails to mention the scandals at his court (2 Samuel 9—20).[10]

What is new about the shorter version of 1 Samuel 17—18 is neither that it was harmonized nor that it was abridged, but that, here, the two processes went hand in hand. The harmonization was achieved by means of a comprehensive abridgment. Yet this sort of phenomenon should not be seen as some completely unreasonable freak occurrence in Scripture. Rather, we thus conclude that MT is closer to the original, whereas the shorter LXX version consists of a later abridgment. From all indications, what was abridged was a Hebrew text which later came into the hands of the Greek translator.[11]

From the interplay of folkloristic and theological elements, and from the discrepancies in its narrative flow, we have learned something about the historical development in the David and Goliath story. By examining contradictions between it and 1 Sam. 16:14–23, and with the help of the shorter version found in LXX, we can see what happened to the text after it was incorporated into the Book of Samuel. But none of this helps us to determine authorship and dating of the story itself.

Determination matters for several reasons. First, as we have seen, the stories contain unequivocal theological pronouncements. If we are to describe accurately the development of Israelite religion in the biblical period, these must not only be understood, but also dated. Second, David, who will one day become king of Israel, utters these pronouncements. If we wish to understand the historical David—as either warrior and ambitious courtier, banished from Saul's court to become the leader of a band of outlaws, or innocent and pious shepherd boy upon whom the spirit of the Lord alights to help him perform wonders—we must take a stand on the origins and authenticity of the story before us. Third, despite its fairy-tale elements, the story of David and Goliath contains many details concerning military and administrative *realia*. We hear of armor worn by Goliath and by Saul, the military strategies of Israel and Philistia, the practices surrounding recruitment and supplies, and the nature of the subject's duties to the monarch. It is up to us to appraise the value of such testimony. As our first step toward accurately appraising it, we must date the source.

III

Scholarly criticism has hardly precipitated radical reassessment of the David and Goliath story's origins. Tradition viewed the story as an accurate report of the battle in the valley of Elah written around the time the events took place or, at the very latest, within a generation or two.[12] Scholarly criticism has not deviated very far from that point of view. Opinions on the authorship of our chapter are mere byproducts of the prevailing opinion on the authorship of Samuel as a whole. In the heyday of the documentary hypothesis (which was also used to explain the authorship of the Former Prophets), the story of David and Goliath was attributed to the E document, written in the eighth century, prior to the fall of Samaria.[13]

According to this theory, the Elohistic writer took what was either a historical account or a hero tale concerning the battle and embellished it along the lines of the *legenda,* which evaluate reality from the perspective of the believer. When scholars deduced that the Former Prophets had their own character and differed from the Pentateuch in both source material and method of redaction, the traditio-historical approach associated with Martin Noth became dominant.[14] Now, the story of David and Goliath was considered part of a relatively early source at the disposal of the Deuteronomic redactor who, in the sixth century, following the destruction of the Temple, produced his *magnum opus* on Israel's history. In time, this theory was rounded out through the influence of Leonhard Rost's thesis on the Succession Narrative. The existence of an analogous narrative running from 1 Samuel 16 through to 2 Samuel 5 and describing David's rise to power was posited. According to this idea, this narrative was compiled from early sources and modeled on the Succession Narrative. It was compiled shortly after the Succession Narrative—that is, at the end of the tenth or at the beginning of the ninth century—and then, in the later period of the monarchy, was to some extent reworked by prophetic or Priestly redactors.[15] According to these theories, the story of David and Goliath was also written during the First Temple period. It preserves certain historical recollections from Saul's war with the Philistines and reflects the political and military realities of the monarchy. Furthermore, it expresses the principal tenets of Israelite religion prior to the exile and possibly even before the appearance of classical prophecy.

If I now question this scholarly consensus, I do so on the basis of two methodological principles which, as I have argued elsewhere, must be upheld in biblical criticism.[16] The first principle requires that criticism of any individual text should never be subsumed under some broad theory concerning the composition of biblical literature. On the contrary, each detail should first be examined on its own merits and independent of any preconceived molds or structures. Only then can we get to the bottom of the subject, be equipped to determine its origins, and understand it from a philological point of view. In the case of our story, we must put aside any theories about the formation of the Book of Samuel or of the Former Prophets in general until we have fully examined the story itself. The second principle requires the scholar to free him- or herself from the standard notion that a connection exists between the time at which events occur and the time at which they are related. This is generally accepted so far as the creation stories are concerned, but is somewhat less widely acknowledged in relation to stories from Israel's history.

We must assert nonetheless that the Hebrew Bible was completed within a period of a thousand years—between the twelfth century B.C.E. (when the Song of Deborah was composed) and the second century B.C.E. (when the four visions of Daniel 7—12 were written during the period of Seleucid oppression). In the case of the Pentateuch and the Prophets (including the Former Prophets) we can reduce the period of composition to some eight hundred years, or up to the fourth century B.C.E. There is no reason to assume that most of this literature was formed at the beginning of the period; on the contrary, what we know from inscriptions and seals concerning the proliferation of Hebrew writing from the eighth century on indicates that much of the Pentateuch and the Former Prophets was set down in writing after the eighth century. Moreover, there is no evidence that the Pentateuch or Former Prophets were closed books by the end of the monarchy. It is not up to the scholar to disprove those who believe that the story of David and Goliath was taken down as the testimony of an eyewitness. Rather, he or she must fix a date of composition for the story, and that date must fall somewhere between the eleventh and fourth centuries—most likely nearer the latter.[17]

It is through these two methodological principles that we approach the story and examine our findings. What, then, is our obligation? We must consider each and every piece of evidence, no matter how isolated, as we try to determine when the story was written. One may argue that isolated pieces of evidence cannot be used as proof of late authorship, since even very ancient works later passed through the hands of Second Temple writers who could, and did, alter the texts in accordance with the literary conventions of their day.

But this is not the case here. The scribes of the Second Temple period, whose foremost skill was the copying of Scripture, took great pains to transmit their text accurately. In matters of language, for example, they were acquainted with every aspect of classical biblical Hebrew, with its orthography, morphology, lexicon, and syntax. They were well aware of the differences between their language and that of the First Temple period; they did not tend to combine the two. When they did alter the biblical text in front of them, they were more likely to archaize the language than bring more ancient forms up to date. Indeed, popularized texts such as the first Isaiah scroll from Qumran must be considered exceptional. As a rule, the trend was the reverse; the classical diction of biblical texts was zealously preserved.

What is true of the scribes is all the more true of the writers who, during the Persian period at least, attempted to imitate the classical Hebrew of the First Commonwealth. Some of them were highly successful in their attempts. These men had a remarkably broad knowledge of the ancient texts, to the point where they were able to recite them by heart. They could incorporate idioms and complete sentences from these texts into their own writings or even pattern their words after linguistic models which they had memorized. This supports our argument that the late composition of a biblical text can be determined on the basis of even a few pieces of evidence.[18] As we shall see, the story of David and Goliath provides many more than a few pieces of evidence.

IV

We start our attempt to date the story by examining those elements in it which first attracted my attention—those outward signs which led me to linger over the text and ask myself whether these might not indicate lateness.

The story's first unusual aspect is its length. According to the Christian division of the text, it runs to fifty-eight verses. Verse 18:2 must be added to these verses: "Saul took him that day and would not let him return to his father's house" clearly follows upon the events of 17:55–58, where the victorious David is brought before Saul and tells the king his name. Verse 18:5 may also form part of the story. "David went out and was successful wherever Saul sent him, and Saul put him in charge of the soldiers. This pleased all the people, including Saul's men" also is something of a continuation; David is appointed commander of Saul's army following his heroic achievement. This version conflicts with the story that David was originally appointed to play the lyre in Saul's court (16:14–23), and that Saul got rid of him by making him an officer in the army only after his attempt to kill him had failed (18:10–13). On the other hand, although it begins "When they came home [and] David returned from killing the Philistine" (18:6), the episode of the rejoicing women in 18:6–9 does not constitute an integral part of the David and Goliath story. It introduces Saul's nascent envy of David at too early a point, and its content, "Saul has slain his thousands, and David, his tens of thousands," pertains to David's success as a military commander, not as a single combatant. This is confirmed by the quotation of the refrain by the Philistines (21:12; 29:5—note the frequentative "ya'ănû"). The love between Jonathan and David and the pact they make (18:1, 3–4) are also related prematurely and are not organically linked to the story of David and Goliath. Thus, in its present position, the story of David and Goliath occupies the following sixty verses in the Book of Samuel: 17:1–58 and 18:2, 5.

A story of such length would be highly irregular for classical biblical literature but not for literature of the later period. For example, Rebecca's betrothal takes up Gen. 24:1–67, and the war between Israel and Aram runs through 1 Kings 20:1–43. But the question is not one of long or short stories. What concerns us is not merely the number of verses the story occupies. Certainly, classical biblical writers excelled in writing short stories (such as the story of the war of Jabesh in 1 Sam. 11:1–13), but they were well able to produce longer stories with more elaborate plots (cf. the battle from Michmas to Ayalon, 1 Sam. 13:16—14:46, some fifty-four verses). What makes our chapter and the other late stories mentioned above special is the extensive setting provided for a relatively simple and, on the whole, static plot. This aspect of the story of David and Goliath is the first indication that the story may have been written in the postclassical period of biblical literature.

Our puzzle at the story's length must grow stronger still when we consider the literary form it takes. It is remarkably paradigmatic. This paradigmatic quality can be seen, first and foremost, in the portrayal of David as a paragon of virtue. The portrayal differs entirely from that found in most of the other, earlier stories in this unit (1 Samuel 16—2 Samuel 6). David is idealized, developed, in part, by being presented as an exemplary figure, the personification of faith and courage. Primarily, however, the paradigm arises from the story's explicit message. Goliath has taunted the ranks of the living God; God, therefore, will hand him over to David so that all might know there is a God in Israel and that the battle is the Lord's. This is not to say that classical biblical literature lacks a kerygmatic quality; it does not. But those messages are implicit in the story; if they are spelled out, it is often by secondary characters. Here, the message cannot be ignored, proclaimed, as it is, with great ceremony by David as he stands between the two camps. This highly paradigmatic quality clearly indicates late authorship, as Genesis 24 or the stories in Daniel 1—6 testify.

Our story of David and Goliath resembles also tales concerning the hero's beginnings, stories which consider the nature of his charisma and ask where it came from and how it came to be revealed. The question itself assumes that this charisma is already well known through the many other stories on the subject current among the people.[19] Our story describes the revelation of charisma also. David's charisma is revealed at a time when all "the Israelites who saw the man were terrified and fled from him" (v. 24). From that moment,

David's presence and authority are recognized, and he goes on, without any difficulty, to become commander of a thousand men, leader of his own company of men, ruler of Ziklag, and ultimately king of Judea. All his later exploits, which are already recorded, are explained by this great victory. Likewise, the other story about David's origins, comprising his anointment by Samuel (1 Sam. 16:1–13), is a classic story of beginnings. Anointment explains the source of David's charisma. The trouble is that this story is completely unknown to the rest of the Book of Samuel and is not even alluded to in Chronicles. It appears only in a very late source, Psalm 151, which is found only in LXX and the Dead Sea Scrolls. So this story must represent a final layer in the saga of David's rise to power. As for the story of David and Goliath, it is mentioned a few times in Samuel, but nonetheless cannot be considered integral to the David narrative. David's marriage to the daughter of the king (18:17–28) is connected to his bravery in fighting the Philistines (but there, the fight has nothing to do with the events in the valley of Elah). When David fled to Gath, the Philistines were suspicious of him, but there was no indication that they saw him as the killer of a famous Gittite hero (21:11–17; 27). Furthermore, the collection of stories about the warrior's deeds in 2 Sam. 21:15–22 and 23:8–23 ascribes the victory over Goliath to Elhanan, the son of Ya'ir the Bethlehemite (2 Sam. 21:19).[20] It seems that the writer of this collection was unaware of the story linking this deed to David, son of Jesse.

This brings us to a question which may, at first, seem surprising. Who is David's opponent? We are accustomed to the words "the battle of David and Goliath," and I have even used them to entitle this article. But as many exegetes have pointed out, the name "Goliath" appears only twice in our story, in vv. 4 and 23. In v. 23, the words "Goliath the Philistine was his name, from Gath" interrupt the natural flow of the verse "and then the champion stepped up from the Philistine ranks. . . ." Proper biblical syntax would demand something like "And then the champion stepped up from the Philistine ranks; his name was Goliath the Philistine from Gath . . ." (*wĕhinnēh 'îš habbēnayim 'ôleh mimma 'arkôt pĕlištîm golyāt happĕlištî šĕmô miggat*). In this verse, at least, the Philistine's name appears to be a later insertion into the text. Indeed, as opposed to these two verses (and two additional mentions in 1 Sam. 21:10; 22:10), twenty-nine times between 17:8 and 19:6 the opponent is called "the Philistine."

Of course, one might argue that the writer speaks from the point of view of the Israelites on the second battle line. They saw only an unknown foreign fighter coming toward them.[21] But this cannot be every time "the Philistine" appears. Certainly, it cannot apply when the giant presents himself and says, "I am the Philistine" (17:8). In the verbal exchange preceding the battle, during the battle itself, and in the events that follow (17:41–57), it would seem only right—given the rapprochement of those involved—that the man be called by name, yet he is not. David's foe, who has taunted the ranks of Israel, remains "the Philistine." We must conclude that the naming of the man is secondary and that, originally, the Philistine hero was anonymous. The Philistine's anonymity could be explained as yet another fairy-tale ingredient included in our story, since fairy tales delight in anonymous characters. In my opinion, however, this explanation does not suffice. On the Israelite side, for example, everyone is named. We meet Jesse, David, Eliab, Saul, and Abner. Further, most of the fairy-tale elements are to be found on this side of the battlefield. Thus, the enemy's anonymity is not connected in any integral way to the folkloristic motifs in our story. We had better seek the explanation elsewhere.

Late biblical legend, which was markedly paradigmatic, excelled in the use of anonymous heroes. Consider, for example, "Abraham's servant" in Genesis 24, "the man of God" and "the old Prophet" in 1 Kings 12:33—13:32, and the prophets in 1 Kings 20.[22] We speak here not of the secondary characters which abound in ancient storytelling, but of characters central to the plot. Elsewhere, I have already proposed the following explanation for this phenomenon: paradigmatic stories such as these proliferated in the Second Temple period and carried on the tradition of prophetic historiography, which often delivered its message via *anonymous prophets.*[23] The "prophet" (*'îš nābî'*) who chastises Israel during the period of Midianite oppression (Judges 6:7–10) and the "man of God" (*'îš 'ĕlōhîm*) who rebukes Eli because of his sons' transgressions (1 Sam. 2:27–36) are only one step away from the prophet who keeps returning to guide the king in times of crisis (1 Kings 20:13, 22, 28) or the (apparently) different prophet who chastises the king and prophesies punishment from God (1 Kings 20:35, 38). Taking that step involves actually bringing the prophet into the plot of the story. This, in turn, allows further developments. The man of God can provide an example not only in word, but in deed (as in 1 Kings 13). But instead of presenting an ideal divine messenger the story might portray a complete "anti-prophet"—an uncircumcised Philistine who taunts the ranks of Israel, for example. Thus, as far as we can tell, the anonymous antagonist too arises from the paradigmatic fiction of the Second Commonwealth.[24]

V

Linguistic evidence may be classified in ascending order of importance from the areas of orthography, lexicon and idioms, semantics, morphology, and syntax.

In our story, late orthography can be seen in the word *dob.* It occurs twice in the *plene* spelling (*dwb*—vv. 34, 36), and is only once written defectively *db*—v. 37). In the Hebrew Bible, nouns in the qŭṭl form taken from geminate verbs are usually spelled without *matres lectionis.* We thus find *db* (8 times), *ḥq* (38 times), *ḥm* (12 times), *kl* (approximately 700 times), *'z* (some 40 times defectively, as opposed to *plene 'wz* found twice), *'l* (21 times), *rb* (some 110 times; twice with *plene* spelling), *r'* (18 times), and *tm* (6 times). *Plene* spellings are infrequent, and usually occur in the later books, as for example, *'wz* (Ps. 84:6; Prov. 31:17) and *rwb* (1 Chron. 4:38; 2 Chron. 31:10). In the writings of the Qumran sect, the spelling is almost always *plene.*

The spelling *cly'* with an 'alep is now familiar to us from Qumran documents[25] and, as has already been noted, it is a clear indication of late biblical authorship.[26] *Nqy'* (*plene*) appears only twice in the Bible (Joel 4:19; Jonah 1:14), as opposed to 32 examples of the defective spelling *nqy.*[27] The *qly'* of our passage is a unique example, as the word is written *qly* in four other cases.

The verb *bĕrû* in Goliath's challenge, *bĕrû-lākem 'îš wĕyēred 'ēlāy* (v. 8), is lexically striking. The unexpected use of this word in classical biblical Hebrew has led commentators either to amend it to *baḥărû*[28] or to connect it to the noun *bĕrît.*[29] The natural solution, however, would be to parse the word as coming from the root *brr,*[30] in which case, according to normative biblical grammar, the imperative form should be *bōrû.* The verb *brr,* in the sense of "to choose," appears only in late biblical books and then in Qumran texts and Rabbinic literature as a substitute for the classical biblical root *bḥr.*[31] That this verb appears in our story proves its late authorship.

In v. 16, we read *wayyiggaš happĕlištî haškēm wĕha 'ărēb wayyityaṣṣēb 'arbā'îm yôm.* This adverbial use of the infinitive absolute of the *Hip'îl* (*haškēm weha 'ărēb*) appears to be irreproachable classical Hebrew usage. Yet we find that the denominative verb *ha'ărîb* (in the *Hip'îl*), whether in the sense of the setting of the sun,[32] the bringing on (by God) of evening,[33] or the performing of some act in the evening,[34] is not to be found in biblical Hebrew, while it is Rabbinic usage par excellence![35] There is also an idiomatic aspect to this lexical point, since the phrase *lĕhaškîm ûlĕha 'ărîb* is characteristic of Rabbinic Hebrew. Thus, we find in *m. Baba Meṣi'a* 7:1, "One who engages laborers and demands that they commence early and work late (*wĕ'āmar lāhem lĕhaškîm ûlĕha 'ărîb*): Where the local custom is not to commence early or work late. . . ." This phrase is repeated in *Sifrē* and in *Baraitot* in the Babylonian Talmud.[36] The classicists of Qumran avoided this usage and retained the biblical phrase "When night and morning depart, I will recite his precepts" (*w'm mwṣ' 'rb wbwqr 'mr hwqyw*). (See 1QS 10:11; and cf. 1QM 14:4 on the basis of the phrase in Ps. 65:9).

In the category of idioms, we must mention the diachronic chiasmus, a phenomenon that Professor Avi Hurvitz has already defined and implemented in the dating of biblical literature.[37] Certain phrases in classical biblical Hebrew, such as "silver and gold," "small and large," or "from Dan to Beersheba," are transposed in the Second Temple period. They become "gold and silver," "large and small," and "from Beer-sheba to Dan." We find this phenomenon in our chapter. Verse 11 reads, "When Saul and all Israel heard the words of the Philistine, they were dismayed and very much afraid" (*wayyēḥattû wayyir'û mĕ'ōd*). But in normative classical usage, we find this: "Fear not and be not dismayed" (*'al-tîra' wĕ'al-tēḥāt;* in Deut. 1:21 and elsewhere). Our story contains the only example in the entire Bible where this phrase has the word order *yr'—ḥtt*. Such a word order appears to signify late usage.

Semantic innovation occurs in the phrase *r'lbb*, when Eliab says to David, *'ani yādaʿti 'et-zĕdōnĕkā wĕ'ēt rōʿa lĕbābekā* (1 Sam. 17:28). In biblical Hebrew, expressions such as *ṭûb lēb* and *rōʿa lēb* indicate happiness and sadness.[38] Only in Neh. 2:2–3, when Artaxerxes believes that Nehemiah "looks bad" because of *rōʿa lēb*, and Nehemiah becomes "very frightened," does the context make it clear that the phrase indicates evil intent.[39] In *'Abot* 2:9, the phrases *lēb ṭôb* and *lēb raʿ* convey the sense of good and evil intent.[40] As far as we can tell, this semantic change characterizes only later literature, although this literature (Chronicles, Esther, Qoheleth) also retains the early meaning of the idiom. Thus, the idiom *rōʿa lebābekā* further indicates the late authorship of our story.

As far as morphology goes, we find late language in the form *yĕhôšîʿa* ("will save," in v. 47). As Driver notes, "The retention of *hē* of the Hifʿil, after the preformative of the impf. is rare and usually late: Jer. 9,4; Is. 52,5; Pss. 28,7; 45,18; 116,6 (as here); Job 13,9; Neh. 11,17; Ez. 46,22 (*Hof.* ptcp.). . . . The form occurs also regularly in Biblical Aramaic, as Dan. 7,16 [as the reference should be], 24."[41] Suggestions to emend this unusual form are irrelevant, given the other examples of late language in this chapter.

A number of syntactic phenomena further testify to the lateness of our story's language. The use of prepositions constitutes one such phenomenon. In v. 39 we read, "David girded his sword *over* his armor" (*wayyaḥgôr Dāwid 'et-ḥarbô mēʿal lĕmaddāyw*). The pleonastic phrase *mēʿal lĕ* for *ʿal* is characteristic of late sources.[42] Another syntactic example is the use of a definite demonstrative pronoun together with an indefinite noun in *waʿăśārâh leḥem hazzeh* (v. 17). This phenomenon occurs in Rabbinic Hebrew, as in *t. Yebamot* 5:4. There we find *pānûy hazzeh* (twice).[43] It appears that this form developed by analogy to the use of a definite adjective with an indefinite noun, such as *yēṣer hāraʿ* and *kĕneset haggĕdôlâh.*[44] Of course, this use of the definite article does appear in biblical literature, as in *yôm haššiššî*, but there it is much less frequent.[45]

Also, in vv. 34–35, David describes his valor as a shepherd. We read *ûbā' hā'ărî wĕ'et-haddôb wĕnāśā' śeh mēhā ʿēder: wĕyā sā'tî 'ahărā wĕhikkitîw wĕhiṣṣaltî mippîyw wayyāoom ʿālāy wĕheḥĕzaqtî bizqānô wĕhikitîyw wahămîtîyw.* If a frequentative sense were intended, it would be necessary to shift the stresses and read the verbs as follows, in the consecutive perfect: *wĕyāsā'tî´ . . . wĕhiṣṣaltî´*, etc.[46] However, *wayyāqom*, in v. 35, does not fit this pattern. Apparently, the Masora preserved the original reading and the verbs are in the regular perfect. This conforms to the use of tenses in Rabbinic Hebrew. Classical biblical Hebrew would read, *wayyābō' . . . wayyiśśā' . . . wā'ēṣe' . . . wā'ak . . . wā'aṣṣîyl . . . wayyāqom . . . wā'āhăzek . . . wā'ak . . . wā'amîtēhû.*

Finally, the temporal clauses in vv. 55 and 57 (*wĕkirĕ'ôt šā'ûl 'et-dāwid . . .* and *ûkĕšûb Dāwid mēhakkôt 'et-happĕlištî*) are particularly characteristic of late biblical Hebrew. Driver comments, "It is the tendency of the earlier Hebrew, in the case of temporal or causal clauses . . . either (a) to postpone them somewhat, or (b) to prefix *wayĕhi*: it is the later Hebrew, that is apt to introduce them at the beginning."[47] Of the many examples which Driver presents, one of the most instructive is the following: 1 Kings 8:54 reads, *wayĕhî kĕkallôt šĕlōmōh lĕhitpallēl . . . qām millipnêy mizbaḥ YHWH* . . . 2 Chron. 7:1 reads, *ûkĕkallôt šĕlōmōh lĕhitpallēl wĕhā'ēš yārĕdāh mēhaššāmayim wattō'kal*. . . .

Without doubt, so far as syntax goes, this sentence approximates more closely the language of Chronicles than of the early historical writing or even the Deuteronomic historiography from the end of the First Commonwealth.

VI

An examination of the term "free" (*ḥopšî* from v. 25: "and will make his father's house free in Israel") falls into the category of *realia*, not philology. Abundant evidence from the Amarna letters, from Assyrian documents, and from the Ugaritic texts suggests that the term *ḫubšu* and *ḫbṯ/ḫpṯ* indicate social class, be it that of native citizens, landowners, freehold farmers, or land tenants. Of course, findings are not uniform, and scholarly opinion on the subject is divided.[48] But in spite of this, most scholars here take the word to signify the granting of a defined social status or position, or else permission to enter a military unit, all within a second-millennium context.[49] This supports the early dating of the term, and, incidentally, of the entire story.

It seems to me that the literal meaning of *ḥopšî* in our text derives from the basic meaning of the adjective and verb as they are found in the Bible (and also in Phoenician), that is: the freeing of a person from slavery.[50] Third Isaiah's "to let the oppressed go free" (*ḥopšîm*, in Isa. 58:6) suggests that the definition was extended to signify freeing for other oppressed groups such as aliens, laborers, and debtors. A still broader definition appears in Sir. 13:11, where we read, "Venture not to be free (*lḥpš*) with him" (with the rich man).[51] Undoubtedly, in our passage the term refers to the permanent exemption of David's family from the royal levy or conscription. Evidence suggests that this type of levy began with the reign of Solomon (1 Kings 5:27–28; 12:4, 18), ran through the days of Asa (1 Kings 15:22), and no doubt continued during the First Commonwealth and on into the period of Assyrian, Babylonian, and Persian domination. The declaration of those who made the covenant in Ezra and Nehemiah's time testifies to the practice's continuation. These are their words: "behold, we are now servants . . . the kings . . . control our bodies and our cattle as they please, and we are in great distress" (Neh. 9:36–37). The allusion in our story to compulsory service does not point to any period more specific than the span between the tenth and fourth centuries. However, the use of *ḥopšî* in its broadest application appears more appropriate to late sources than to early legal codes.

The description of Goliath's armor (vv. 5–7) makes an important contribution to the story's realism. Five items are listed for us: we are told of a brass helmet, brass mail armor, brass greaves for the legs, a brass sword, and a wooden spear with an iron hand.[52] If we consider the story a reliable historical source, we can use it to learn about the weaponry of Aegean or, at any rate, Philistine warriors in the time of David.[53] The problem is that we cannot rely on a military description which has passed through the hands of storytellers and, later, theologians. In fact, Philistines of the twelfth century B.C.E. must have looked completely different from Goliath; they wore neither greaves nor brass mail, and their heads were covered not with brass helmets but with sweeping locks of hair (or, in the opinion of others, hats made of feathers). It seems, then, that this description consists of a random assortment of items intended to create a terrifying picture of an armed giant.[54]

Another possible means of dating the story lies in calling Goliath *'îš habbēnayim* (17:4; 17:23). Ugaritic sources indicate that the word *bēnayim*, derived from the preposition *bēyn*, may be early.[55] The problem, however, is not the etymology of this *hapax legommenon*, but rather its meaning in the context. In my opinion, we must understand the word (as it was understood already in the nineteenth century) as a Hebrew parallel to the Greek *τὸ μεταιχμίον*, "which is between the spears," i.e., the area between the battle lines.[56] In the Qumran War Scroll (1QM), we find the terms *'nšy hbynym* and *dgly hbynym*. However, the terminology in 1QM does not depend on our passage. There, the terms refer not to heavily armed individual fighters, but to light units which would be sent out into the field between the two armies to provoke and skirmish with the enemy.[57] Therefore, the semantic connection between *'îš habbēnayim* in 1 Samuel 17 and *'nšy/dgly hbynym* in 1QM being recondite, the use of the same term in the two texts is not a case of one imitating the other in a later period; it seems rather to result from historical proximity. Both the external Greek analogy and the currency of the term within the Qumran sect support the theory that *bēnayim* as a military term arises in its entirety from the Second Commonwealth.

Greek history provides an analogy to the battle fought by David and Goliath. Using biblical and other evidence, scholars have shown that single combat was widely practiced (consider the exploits of David's warriors in 2 Sam. 21:18–22; 23:21).[58] The single combat described in our story differs, however. It is a contest of champions in which each combatant represents his people; the outcome of the battle will determine the fate of the warring nations. That, at any rate, is the original intention behind the duel (17:8–9); later on in the story it appears to be forgotten (vv. 51–52). This type of single combat is very rare. It appears in two famous sources, our chapter and the third book of the *Iliad*, where the contest between Paris and Menelaus is described.[59] We must ask is there any connection, and if so, what type of connection, between these two renowned battles.

Two possible connections exist. First, the parallel could have resulted from contact with the Sea Peoples (Philistines) who had recently traveled to the land of Israel and who came to control considerable portions of the land. The Israelites adopted a few of their customs and retained them for some time,[60] and when the Philistines proposed a contest of champions, the Israelites understood immediately what was involved and responded accordingly. It is also possible, however, that the connection is literary, not historical. The literary influence of one people upon the other may have included the theme of a contest of champions. Of course, there is a third possibility. There may be no connection between the stories. Each culture may have developed the tradition of such a contest independently. If this is the case, we must seek a common reason for such a tradition. We must seek shared social and cultural conditions—such as an aristocratic society like that of Homeric Greece; a warrior elite, like that found in David's court; or a feudalistic society, like that of medieval Europe—in the two peoples.

If it were true that the exploits of the warriors in 2 Samuel 21 and 23 represent a contest of champions,[61] we would have evidence of a historical connection or of an independent tradition related to similar conditions within the two societies. But the contest of champions occurs only in 1 Samuel 17, which, on the basis of considerable evidence, appears to be a late, Second Commonwealth composition. Thus, given the long interval between the period of contact and the date of authorship, the possibility of a historical connection based on contact between the two peoples is no longer relevant. It is even less likely that an independent tradition comprising a contest of champions could have arisen in a society where Jews, led by their high priest, lived under foreign domination. We must therefore favor our second possibility and assume a literary connection whereby, in this late period, Israel came under Greek influence.

The story's development may be reconstructed as follows: during the Davidic period, and in particular the years of David's reign, single combat was a very popular form of warfare; duels and other heroic exploits involving individuals (2 Sam. 21:17; 23:8, 9–10, 11–12, 13–17, 18–19, 20) won attention and patronage from the king, indeed, David had his own "military" past as leader of a band of outlaws who lived by the sword, and he turned what remained of this band into an elite unit of fighters, the "warriors"; the names of outstanding warriors were recorded (2 Sam. 23:8–39), but the people lost track of them; in time, popular storytellers attributed the deeds of unknown heroes to the renowned and beloved king of Israel (shifting the story's protagonist from an insignificant, anonymous character to a great hero follows a well-known historical pattern). The folk tale preserved only two elements of the original story, (1) the contest between two fighters; (2) David (and David, as we have seen, was reworked into a sort of fairy-tale hero). In the Second Temple period, the story assumed its final form. We cannot specify a date of authorship, but the many signs of lateness in the story point to the fourth century B.C.E., at the end of the Persian period. It was in this period that the first contacts between Judea and Greece were established; the Greeks in Asia Minor had already been incorporated into the Persian Empire before the fall of Babylonia. During the war with Greece, in the days of Darius and Xerxes, contact was maintained. Greek merchants visited and Greek mercenaries encamped in the land. Signs of the material Greek culture could be found in the cities of Judea.[62] These contacts made it possible for a Jewish storyteller at the end of the Persian period to take the theme of a contest of champions between "Europe" and "Asia" and adapt it to his story. He did not need to have read the *Iliad* in order to do so; he need only have heard the foreigners tell of their forefathers' valor. It seems, therefore, that the connection is literary and late. The idea of a contest of champions, which appears only in vv. 8–9, was included in the story through the influence of the legend found in the *Iliad*.

VII

Our conclusion thus far that the story of David and Goliath was written during the Second Commonwealth, probably in the late Persian period, can help us to understand the theological concepts embedded in it. These concepts, once clarified, seem most likely to have originated and flourished in the fourth century B.C.E.

Time after time, David denounces "the uncircumcised Philistine . . . who has taunted the armies of the living God," *'ĕlōhîm ḥayyim* (vv. 26, 36; cf. v. 45). What is the theological significance of "living God"? Even within the context, the words clearly are meant to contrast with "the uncircumcised Philistine." Thus they suggest that the gods of this uncircumcised Philistine are not "living," but "dead." If we examine other biblical passages in which the term appears we shall find evidence to support our idea.

The terms *'ĕlōhîm ḥayyim, 'ĕlōhîm ḥay*, and *'ēl ḥay* occur infrequently, and in a variety of contexts.[63] In Deut. 5:23, "For what mortal ever heard the voice of the living God (*'ĕlōhîm ḥayyim*) speak out of the fire, as we did, and lived?" the term tells us that the living God's vitality and power are so tremendous that human beings cannot hear this God and live. This verse does not fit in with the passage as a whole—it even contradicts it. No doubt it forms a later addition to the description of the theophany at Sinai contained in Deuteronomy 5. In Deut. 4:23 and 36 we also find insertions of this sort which, as additions to what is already a very late chapter in Deuteronomy, appear to represent the final stage in the book's composition. As I have tried to show elsewhere,[64] the addition to 4:33 should be emended, in accordance with the Samaritan Pentateuch and LXX, to read, "Has any people heard the voice of the *living* God speaking from out of the fire. . . ."

In Josh. 3:10, Joshua says, "By this you shall know that a living God (*'ēl ḥay*) is in your midst and will dispossess for you the Canaanites, Hittites. . . ." Here, the term expresses God's power to perform "such wonders as have not been wrought"; the crossing of the Jordan upon dry land is to symbolize the miraculous victory over the seven Canaanite peoples. We may not easily put a precise date of authorship to the passage in Josh. 3:9–10.

In Hosea 2:1, we read, "The number of the people of Israel shall be like that of the sands of the sea, which cannot be measured or counted; and instead of being told, 'You are Not-My-People,' they shall be called 'Children-of-the-Living-God' (*bĕnê 'ēl-ḥay*)." These verses of consolation (2:1–3) were added to soften both Hosea's condemnation of the people and his prophecies of divine retribution. Yet it is hard to reconcile the phrase "living God" with its context here. Perhaps we should understand it to mean that, along with the change in the relationship between God and Israel ("Call your brothers 'My People' and your sisters 'Lovingly Accepted'"), God will reveal (as in Josh. 3:10) all of his redemptive power: "And I will give them victory through the Lord their God. . . . The people of Judah and the people of Israel shall assemble together and appoint one head over them and they shall arise over the land" (Hosea 1:7; 2:2). The unleashing of this power is the revelation of the living God.

A rather different meaning of the term occurs in Jer. 23:36. There we find, "But do not mention 'the burden (*maśā'*) of the Lord' any more, for the burden of every man's own word, [?] and you have perverted the words of the living God (*'ĕlōhîm ḥayyim*), the Lord of Hosts, our God." Given v. 33's "and I will cast you off," and, further on, v. 39's "And I will forget you (*wĕnāšîtî 'etkem*) . . . and cast you off," we can assume that the writer is denouncing the people for mocking prophecies. He plays on the words *mś'/nś'* in the sense of burden and *mšh/nšh* in the sense of forgetting. It used to be, says the writer, that his prophecy from God (*mś'*) was given to all the people, but they transformed the Word of God into a burden and forgot it. "The words of the living God" are contrasted with what the people made of them, a burden and a thing forgotten.[65] Apparently, this passage was written not by Jeremiah but by one of the book's later editors, an editor who was careful to remove the term *mś'* from the rest of the book. The use of the verb *wahăpaktem* instead of the *wattahpĕkû* of classical biblical Hebrew testifies to the text's lateness.

In Psalms 42—43, the term "living God" (*'ēl-ḥāy*) has yet another meaning. The psalm itself is difficult to date, however. It contains a wealth of divine epithets, such as "the living God" (*'ēl-ḥāy*), "the God of my life" (*'ēl ḥayyāy*), "God, my rock" (*'ēl sal'î*), "God, my refuge" (*'ĕlōhê mā'uzzî*), "God, my exceeding joy" (*'ēl śimḥat gîlî*). "The living God" appears at the beginning of the psalm, where the image of thirst for water articulates the poet's longing to come before God in the sanctuary. It reads, "As a doe (*'ylt*) longs for flowing streams, so longs my soul for Thee, O God. My soul thirsts for God, for the living God. When shall I come and behold the face of God?" To this image of thirst is added the salty tear: "My tears have been my food day and night, while men say to me continually, 'Where is your God?'" If the longing is like thirst, then the Lord is like a source of fresh water (*mĕqôr mayim ḥayyim*); cf. Jer. 2:13; 17:13). This makes the term *'ēl ḥāy* all the more appropriate.[66] Verse 3 brings in another contrast, that between the poet, who is aware that he worships "the living God," and his enemies, who constantly say to him, "Where is your God?"

We find this contrast also in fairly late passages, where the term "living God" is used to distinguish YHWH, unique and true God, from pagan gods who have no life whatever. A prime example is Hezekiah's prayer at the time of the revolt against Sennacherib (2 Kings 19:15–19, esp. v. 16). This prayer appears to have been written during the Babylonian Exile by the editor of the story.[67] The Assyrian enemy has taunted (*ḥrp*) the "living God" (*'ĕlōhîm ḥāy*) and has compared him to the pagan gods (18:32–35; see also 19:4). The Davidic king answers that pagan gods are "the work of human hands, wood and stone"; only YHWH is God.

Jeremiah 10:1–16 expresses the same contrast. Wood and metal, gold and silver make pagan gods. They are adorned and clothed in blue and purple, but they are not alive. YHWH stands in contrast to them. He is "King of the nations" (v. 7), "the living God (*'ĕlōhîm ḥayyim*) and the everlasting King" (v. 10).

Textual criticism may help us to understand the historical development of this contrast. In LXX and the Jeremiah scroll from Qumran, chapter 10 reads as follows: vv. 1–5a + 9 + 5b + 11ff. Verses 6–7 and 10, which praise YHWH, and v. 8, which mocks idols that go up in smoke, are lacking altogether! It is impossible to discount the testimony of LXX, which in the case of Jeremiah often appears to reflect an older and more authentic text.[68] We must also remember that the polemic against man-made gods is most characteristic of the vision of Second Isaiah (44:6–20; 46:1–7). Indeed, scholars consider that the later writer-editor of Jer. 10:1–15 took this polemic from Second Isaiah—and we see that Isaiah 40—53, like most of the passages which call pagan gods mere wood and stone, does not present any contrast with "the living God." These other passages are Hab. 2:18–20, the late layers of Deuteronomic literature (Deut. 4:28; 28:36, 64; 29:16), and Pss. 115:4–8 and 135:15–18. We must therefore conclude that the contrast between pagan gods and the living God is a later development in the polemical battle against idols.

Second Commonwealth texts which set "the living God" in contrast to dead gods include the late psalm, 106.[69] Verse 28 reads "Then they attached themselves to Ba'al Pe'or and ate sacrifices offered to the dead" (*zibḥê mētîm*). As many have noted, "the dead" here are synonymous with *Ba'al Pe'or,* and describe pagan gods in general.[70] Numbers 25:2–3, the source for this psalm, reads as follows: "The Moabite women invited the people to the *sacrifices for their god*(s), and the people *ate* and bowed down to their god(s). Thus Israel *attached itself* to *Ba'al Pe'or.*" Another example of a contrast between Israel and pagan nations can be found in Daniel 6. King Darius calls Daniel, who has refused to worship the king and worships only YHWH, "servant of the living God" (*'ăbēd 'ĕlāhā' ḥayyā',* v. 21). The king then commands that all his subjects "fear and be in awe of the God of Daniel, for he is the living God, enduring for ever; his kingdom shall never be destroyed, and his dominion shall be to the end" (v. 27). How faithful this is to Jer. 10:10, "He is the living God and the everlasting King"!

Apocryphal literature also contains a short paradigmatic story on the subject of who is the living God, the tale of "Bel and the Dragon." Preserved only in Greek, this story was apparently written in Hebrew at the end of the Persian era or the beginning of the Hellenistic period.[71] Theodotion's translation presents this central issue very clearly: Daniel is obliged to worship Bel but responds that he worships only the living God and not man-made gods. He sets out to prove that Bel does not really eat the food that is set before him and therefore cannot be a living god (ζῶν θεός). Once Bel worship has been eliminated, the question of the Dragon arises. "You cannot say that this god is not alive," the king tells Daniel. But once again, Daniel responds that he will worship his God, YHWH, who is the living God. With the very food that was used to prove that the Dragon lives, Daniel kills the monster and shows that only YHWH is the living God.

Our look at the biblical sources thus seems to indicate that calling YHWH "the living God" is a late development. As part of the polemic against idol worship, the term appears in the later layers of biblical literature; however, the earliest example occurs in Hezekiah's prayer (sixth century). In the Persian and Hellenistic periods, God-fearing Jews composed polemics against heathenism; this constituted the theological context for David's declaration that Goliath "has taunted the living God."

We may also understand David's declaration that "all the earth will know that Israel has a God" in this context. What is the significance of a pronouncement so entirely alien to early biblical literature? The natural Gentile response to the Jewish claim that their enemies had "mute gods" (Hab. 2:18), gods who had "mouths but do not speak . . ." would be "better mute gods than no god at all." No doubt the Jews were mocked for having no god, since no symbols of YHWH were manifest. David's declaration, then, constitutes a straightforward response to this mocking and slander; through David, YHWH will reveal that he does exist. Henceforth, "all the earth will know that Israel has a God."[72]

David also calls YHWH "the Lord of Hosts and God of the armies of Israel." This phrase, too, contains theological elements. These we may examine from three aspects. First, we may consider them in the context of Israel's early religious traditions. The term "Lord of Hosts" (*YHWH ṣĕbā'ôt*), which appears to mean "creator of hosts" (from the verb *h.w.h.*), is first connected to the sanctuary at Shiloh and the ark which was taken from Shiloh into battle (1 Sam. 1:3, 11; 4:4; 2 Sam. 6:2, 18; 7:8). We see from its full formulation, "Lord of Hosts, enthroned on the Cherubim" (compare also Psalm 80), that the term expresses a belief in the invisible army of the warrior God on high. This army is alluded to in the fragmentary story of Joshua's encounter with the *śar-ṣĕbāʾ-YHWH* (Josh. 5:13–15). It also arises through the admittedly late references to the "angels"/"hosts" (*malʾākāyw/ṣĕbāʾāw*) of the Lord in Pss. 103:20–21; 148:2.[73] With the outside influences of the Assyrian rule in the eighth and seventh centuries, worship of the heavenly hosts became more widespread (compare Deut. 17:3; 2 Kings 17:16; 21:3, 5; 23:4–5). In reaction to such practices, the vitality and power of these heavenly hosts was denied, and the hosts were relegated to the level of inanimate forces of nature (Deut. 4:19–20). This reaction was carried over into the Second Commonwealth, when the word "hosts" as part of a divine epithet was removed from certain biblical books. Undoubtedly, we have here the reason why "Lord of Hosts" is missing from the Hexateuch, Judges, Ezekiel, and most of LXX to Jeremiah.[74] As a corollary to censoring "Lord of Hosts," the Priestly writers reinterpreted the concept and applied it over and over again to the Israelites, the hosts of YHWH (Exod. 7:4; 12:41; cf. also Exod. 6:26; 12:17).

If we then examine the phrase "Lord of Hosts, God of the armies of Israel" within this context, we see that the term is self-defining. What is the Lord of Hosts? The God of the armies of Israel. This definition points out the dialectical relationship between our story and previous biblical literature. In the story of David and Goliath, the term is no longer censored. On the other hand, care is taken to give it a this-worldly, nonmythological meaning in accordance with the later outlook characteristic of the Priestly writers who described the exodus from Egypt.

The question of the Lord of Hosts brings us to a second aspect of the story, the theological perception of the war. In what way is the Lord of Hosts the God of the armies of Israel? The victory over Goliath answers the question. Once Goliath has been beaten, "all who are here will know that God does not save through the sword and the spear, for the war is the Lord's." We have here a particular conception of victory. It is neither the understanding found in late, Ephraimite historiography (e.g., Joshua 24; 1 Samuel 7; 12) nor that in Hosea (13:4, 9–11). These, negating human activity completely, attribute all victory to God. Nor is it the understanding of Deuteronomic historiography, which sees God fighting alongside Israel every step of the way (Deuteronomy 1—3; Joshua 1—11; 23). Rather, the understanding here most resembles that of the Chronicler. Israel goes out to battle, but victory is somehow attained through divine intervention. This is how the Chronicles describe the victories of Abijah, Asa, and Jehoshaphat, and the saving of Jerusalem in Hezekiah's time. In this case, there also may exist a dialectical relationship with the two earlier historiographical schools. But our writer may have been influenced by both, and may favor now one, now the other view of victory.

The resemblance between 1 Samuel 17 and Chronicles can be seen in the literary style of the two. David says "for the war is the Lord's" (*kî laYHWH hammilḥāmâh*), and we find much the same thing in Chronicles. In 1 Chron. 5:18–23, we read that when the Transjordanian tribes went to war with the Hagri'im, "they were assisted and the Hagri'im and all their allies were given over to them. For, during the battle, they cried out to God, and their request was granted since they trusted in him." The writer concludes "for the war was from God" (*kî mēhā'ĕlōhîm hammilḥāmâh*). Again, Jehoshaphat and his people went to war with Ammon, Moab, and Mount Seir; Jahaziel the Levite proclaimed, "Fear not and be not dismayed because of this mass of people, *for the war is not yours, but God's*" (*kî lō' lākem hammilḥāmâh kî l'ĕlōhîm*) (2 Chron. 20:15).

A third aspect worth investigating is the story's theology in the context of its political background. What did the victory of David, the shepherd boy, over the heavily armed giant, Goliath, communicate to members of a tiny Jewish province under the dominion of a Gentile world empire? Is there not some resemblance between the stone which felled the Philistine and the stone in Daniel 2 which, cut without hands, smashed a mighty and terrible image?[75] In other words, what is David if not the archetypal future savior of Israel, and what does Goliath represent if not the Gentile empire? It is difficult to believe that the words "God does not save through the sword and the spear—the war is the Lord's" refer solely to the days of David and Goliath. They suggest an element of expectation—expectation that Judea will be miraculously redeemed from its domination by kings imposed "because of our sins" (Neh. 9:37). Indeed, David's concluding words, "for he will give you into our hands" (*wĕnātan 'etkem bĕyādēnû*, 1 Sam. 17:47), seem to express that very expectation. These words do not mean "we shall rule over you," as demanded by the context, that of a contest of champions to decide which of two warring nations will have dominion over the other. They mean rather "we shall beat you," and are completely out of context. All of a sudden, the subject of the story is a future war against all the Philistines. This is a war that will establish a new monarchy that will never be destroyed or surrendered to another people.

VIII

If there are indeed indications of Second Commonwealth messianic expectations in our text, we must ascertain whether they conform to visions of redemption in the literature of the period. Unfortunately, the origins of many of those visions transmitted to us in the prophetical books are dubious. This makes it difficult for us to reconstruct the messianic idea's development in Israel.[76] We shall draw our evidence from only a few works, whose origins can be traced with some degree of certainty.

In the sixth century, expectations of redemption took many different and mutually exclusive forms. In Obad. v. 21, we read, "Saviors (*môšî'îm*) shall go up to Mount Zion to judge Mount Esau; and the kingdom shall be the Lord's." The focus of salvation is Zion, but the idea of a Davidic monarchy is not introduced. The ideal monarchy is that of the Lord, who sends "saviors"/ "liberators" to Israel.

Such terminology originates in the editorial layer of the early Book of Judges (Judges 3—16; 1 Samuel 1—12), where the saviors, Gideon and Samuel, express their strong opposition to the idea of an earthly king (Judges 8:23; 1 Sam. 8:7; 10:19; 12:12, 17). According to Second Isaiah, Israel's redemption will be brought about by Cyrus, the Lord's anointed, and by Cyrus alone. God has turned matters over to him so that he may rebuild God's city and redeem God's exiles (e.g., Isa. 44:24—45:25). It is YHWH who rouses Cyrus and facilitates his progress, but he himself is a "hidden God" (Isa. 45:13, 15). Redemption is to be realized within a historiopolitical sphere, and will lead to the Gentiles' recognition of YHWH. Yet the Lord will not reveal himself; he will remain hidden.

An opposing view occurs in the words of Haggai and Zechariah. In the second year of Darius's reign (519/518 B.C.E.), the prophet Haggai announces that the Persian Empire will fall and that the new king, Zerubbabel, will be like "the signet of the Lord." (Compare Jer. 22:24, where the phrase "signet of my right hand" is used with reference to King Coniah.) Zechariah also sees Zerubbabel playing a key role in the rebuilding of the Lord's house (Zech. 4:6–9). In a few prophecies, he mentions "my servant the Branch" (*'abdî ṣemaḥ,* 3:8) and "the man whose name is the Branch" (*'îš ṣemaḥ šĕmô,* 6:12). Undoubtedly, like Haggai, Zechariah alludes to Jeremiah's "I will raise a righteous branch of David's line, and he shall reign as king and prosper" (Jer. 23:5–6; cf. 33:15–16). Apparently, at this point, expectations of redemption come to be most clearly identified with the Davidic dynasty. This is so for a variety of reasons. One, the pathetic end to which the Judean monarchy had come was forgotten, whereas the golden memories of the empire glowed brightly, and the old court style, which praised and glorified the kings of little Judea out of all proportion, was revived by the new generation. Two, the first twenty years under Persian rule had probably lessened somewhat Israelite enthusiasm for Cyrus, the Lord's anointed.

We do not know what became of Zerubbabel, but clearly the Persian monarchy did not fall, and no Davidic kingdom arose in its place. Indeed, the reality was the complete reverse of what Jews had desired. No one from the Davidic line took Zerubbabel's place as the focus of expectations that the monarchy would be restored. Persia, on the other hand, was stabilized under Darius's leadership and went on to become a world empire of dimensions hitherto unknown in the East. As a result, the nature of the Jewish concept of redemption underwent a fundamental change. Until now, hopes of salvation had been rooted in the actual, historical sphere and had centered on real personalities and events, i.e., Cyrus and the fall of Babylonia, Zerubbabel and the rebuilding of the Temple. Now, they became metahistorical.

Reality guarantees nothing; it is only the Lord's miraculous intervention which, bringing an end to the natural course of history and utterly transforming the universe, will save Israel. This is an eschatological view of redemption. The means by which it is to be attained put this salvation beyond history; that it will be everlasting puts it at the end of history.

Trito-Isaiah (Isaiah 54—66) is the first outstanding exponent of this eschatological view of redemption. According to his prophecy, the Lord will reveal himself, will fight the Gentile nations without any assistance or representative (cf. Cyrus in Second Isaiah), and will trample and destroy Israel's enemies (63:1–6; 59:16–18). Then a redeemer will come to Zion (59:20), which will be transformed into the glorious capital of a universal kingdom (60). Those who mourned for Zion shall be called "Priests of the Lord . . . the attendants of our God," and they shall consume "the wealth of the nations" (61:6). In them, the covenant with David, "And I will make an everlasting covenant *for you,* the true and steadfast love of David," will be realized. David's promised role as "*ʿēd* [judge] to the peoples, leader and commander of nations" is to be fulfilled in the Lord's faithful ones, and they will be served by faraway nations which have not previously heard of them (55:1–5).[77] It seems that a Davidic scion plays no part in this prophecy; rather, those who obey God (55:2–3) will inherit David's covenant to establish a world rule. The prophet does not identify the "redeemer" who will come to Zion (59:20).[78]

Nevertheless, the Davidic line came to occupy a focal position in expectations of redemption. Those who put Zion at the center of their prophecies could not obliterate the fact, acknowledged even by opponents and enemies, that "there once were mighty kings over Jerusalem, who ruled all the province of Beyond the River" (Ezra 4:20), and that these kings were from the House of David. Indeed, an awareness of the Davidic dynasty's preeminence was already deeply ingrained in prophecy. (See Isaiah ben Amoz in Isa. 9:6 or the words attributed to him by his followers in 2 Kings 19:34 and 20:5–6 in psalmody [Pss. 78; 89; 132], and historiography [2 Samuel 7; 1 Kings 8; etc.].)

In this context, four prophecies are of particular interest to us. They come from three prophetic books and speak of David himself as the future king of Israel.

> Jer. 30:8–9 states:
> In that day—declares the Lord of Hosts—I will break the yoke from off your neck and I will rip off your bonds. Strangers shall no longer make slaves of them; instead, they shall serve the Lord their God and David, their king whom I will raise up for them.

> Ezek. 34:23–24 reads:
> Then I will appoint a single shepherd over them to tend them—my servant David. He shall tend them, he shall be a shepherd to them. I the Lord will be their God, and My servant David shall be a ruler among them—I the Lord have spoken.

> Ezek. 37:23–25 continues:
> . . . and I will be their God. My servant David shall be king over them; there shall be one shepherd for all of them. . . . My servant David shall be their prince for all time.
>
> Finally, in Hosea 3:5, we read:
> Afterward, the Israelites will turn back and will seek the Lord their God and David their king—and they will thrill over the Lord and over His bounty in the days to come.

That the three books prophesy in a similar style ("David their king," in Jeremiah and Hosea, and "My servant, David . . . prince/king" in Ezekiel) suggests that these prophecies represent a single stage of reworking in the prophetic books. The rabbis already asserted that "the same words come to many prophets, yet no two prophets prophesy in the same words" (Sanh. 89a). Insertions in a style characteristic of one prophet within the book of a second are a well-known phenomenon in the criticism of prophetical books.[79] For example, in Hosea 2:20 (not far from our passage in 3:5), we read, "On that day, I will make a covenant for them with the wild beasts . . . and I will allow them to lie down in safety." This passage has nothing to do with its context; it is, however, worded very much like Ezek. 34:25, where we read, "I will make a covenant of peace with them and will put an end to dangerous beasts, and they shall live safely in the wilderness and sleep in the forests." It appears that the Book of Hosea underwent some sort of reworking by the school of Ezekiel.

We learn even more about the secondary character of these passages from a critical examination of Hosea 3 and Ezekiel 34. Scholars have recognized that the content of Hosea 3:5 does not correspond to the prophet's chastisement of the people; Hosea would never rebuke Ephraim for turning away from Judah and the House of David.[80] A contrasting example appears in 14:2–9, an original Hoseanic message of consolation which exhibits, both in style and content, features typical of this prophet. In Ezekiel 34, we can distinguish between the original prophecy (vv. 1–16, 31) and its secondary reworking (vv. 17–30),[81] and the resumptive repetition of v. 17 (*wĕ'attēnâh ṣo'nî*) in v. 31 (*wĕ'attēn ṣo'nî*) makes the distinction all the more clear. In the original prophecy (1–16, 31), the shepherds are condemned for not tending their sheep, which are then scattered and preyed upon. The Lord will dismiss the shepherds and tend the sheep himself (v. 15). In the reworked prophecy (vv. 17–30), the fat sheep have sinned by plundering the choice pastureland, drinking the water, and then trampling or muddying what they leave behind. The Lord will pass judgment on the individual sheep—here he is judge, not shepherd—and will appoint his servant, David, to tend them (v. 23). Here, everything—sinner, sin, and corrective—has been changed. Whereas the original prophecy expressed disillusionment with earthly rulers by presenting the alternative that "I myself will graze my flock, and I myself will let them lie down—declares the Lord God,"[82] the secondary reworking harks back to what once was—David the shepherd. So it is in Ezekiel itself, where the motif of David the future ruler seems most deeply embedded (compare the title *nāśî'* customary in this book), that we find evidence suggesting this idea to be secondary and late. And if this is the case with Ezekiel, a fortiori with the other prophecies. Evidently, a concept that has been attributed to the classical prophets belongs in fact to the redactional stage of their books.

The text also contains an indication of the period in which this redactional layer was written. The fat sheep are further indicted thus: "Because you pushed with flank and shoulder against the feeble ones and butted them with your horns *until you scattered them abroad.*" Clearly, this is a sociopolitical indictment; plunder and oppression within the land force the poor to emigrate or, worse still, through plunder and oppression, the poor are being forced into slavery and are being sold abroad. This brings to mind Nehemiah's charges against the noblemen of Judea. There, we read, "As far as we were able, we bought back our Jewish brothers who had been sold to the nations—yet will you sell your brothers so that they be sold to us?" (Neh. 5:8). This similarity between the two texts confirms that we have here a redactional layer like those added to other prophetic books in the fifth century, when prophecies already began to be assembled.

In the fifth century B.C.E., then, prophecies announce that the Lord will appoint David over Israel (Jer. 30:9; Ezek. 34:23); the Lord will be their God and David will be their king (Jer. 30:9; Ezek. 34:24; 37:23–24; Hosea 3:5). Who is this David who will be brought back for Israel?

Some have interpreted "David" in this context as "the House of David," a collective term for the entire dynasty and for each of its members.[83] This does not, however, make the use of the name by itself any the less surprising. There is no dearth of collective references elsewhere in these prose texts (e.g., "a lamp for David," in Jer. 23:5 and 33:15; "There shall never be an end to men of David's line who sit upon the throne of the House of Israel," in Jer. 33:17; ". . . only then could my covenant with my servant David be broken—so that he would not have a descendant reigning upon his throne," in 33:21). Why, then, do we find "David" himself in these passages?

The possibility that the text should be taken literally, and that David will indeed be the king, may at first seem difficult to accept, since this sort of belief seems uncharacteristic of biblical thought. Yet we should not rule it out. At around the same time, the Book of Malachi was closed with the proclamation, "Behold, I am sending you Elijah the prophet" (3:23).[84] Thus, Elijah is alive and about to make a comeback. The foundation for this sort of belief is already laid in the Priestly Document, where Enoch is presented as a mythical figure who is taken up by God (Gen. 5:22, 24). Clearly, Ezekiel's vision of the dry bones (37:1–14) is intended as an allegory for the "resurrection" of Israel; nevertheless, it provided an opening for a belief in the physical resurrection of the dead. The final song of the Suffering Servant lyrically describes the Servant as dead and buried, and then as someone who "will see offspring and have long life" (Isa. 53:10). Thus, there are indications that already at the beginning of the Second Commonwealth there appeared a belief in the resurrection of the dead, perhaps related to Persian religion.[85] Perhaps, at first, resurrection was only a possibility for exceptional personalities. David, who had merited an everlasting covenant with the Lord, whose descendants reigned for eighteen generations, was considered such a personality. It is David brought back to life, *David redivivus,* as scholars would put it, who will return to rule over Israel![86]

These messianic expectations, if we have understood them correctly as such, provide the context for the David and Goliath story. David the shepherd boy, who vanquishes the Philistine giant, who removes disgrace from Israel (1 Sam. 17:26), who proclaims in the midst of the armed camps "that Israel has a God . . . and that God does not save through the sword and the spear—the war is the Lord's, for He will give you into our hands" (vv. 46–47), is not even a prototype for the Davidic descendant destined to be revealed. It is this very David, and none other, who will appear. He will bring down the uncircumcised giant, the pagan world empire, in one fell swoop—and with its downfall he will usher in Israel's redemption. "Strangers shall no longer make slaves of them; instead they shall serve the Lord their God and David, their king whom I will raise up for them."

NOTES

1. *Märchen,* in German. Indeed, the present story is about a known hero who acts in well-defined historical circumstances. Therefore it has transcended the bounds of the fairy tale; cf. H. Jason's study. Jason defines it as a "romantic epic," in "The Story of David and Goliath: A Folk Epic?" *Bib* 60 (1979): 36–70.

2. A different analysis has recently been offered by Stoebe and Krinetzki. Stroebe posits an original, historical hero tale, later reworked as a popular pious legend, while Krinetzki assumes that the first recension tended to theology, and its secondary reworking to folk tale. See H. J. Stoebe, "Die Goliathperikope 1 Sam. XVII 1—XVIII 5 und die Textform der Septuaginta," *VT* 6 (1956): 397–413; idem, "Gedanken zur Heldensage in den Samuelbüchern," *Festschrift L. Rost,* BZAW 105 (Berlin: Töpelmann, 1967), 208–18, esp. 217; idem, *Das erste Buch Samuelis,* KAT (Gütersloh: Gerd Mohn, 1973) 315; L. Krintezki, "Ein Beitrag zur Stilanalyse der Goliathperikope (1 Sam. 17, 1—18, 5)," *Bib* 54 (1973): 187–236. In my opinion, neither hypothesis starts where it should, within the story's internal tensions and discrepancies; besides, both overestimate the evidence of LXX in the present chapter.

3. A. B. Ehrlich was at pains to explain away this discrepancy by interpreting *mh y'šh l'yš* of v. 26 as if David expressed his wonder at why such a high price was offered for killing the Philistine when the latter had already exposed himself by insulting the living God. See Ehrlich, *Randglossen zur hebräischen Bible,* Band 3 (Leipzig: Hinrichs, 1910), 227.

4. The longer text of MS A does not represent the original LXX; see N. Peters, *Beiträge zur Text- und Literaturkritik sowie zur Erklärung der Bücher Samuel* (Freiburg im Breisgau: Herder, 1899), 36–40.

5. There is no need here to review the rich literature on this subject. Convenient

summaries were offered from time to time by Thenius (below, n. 56) in 1842, Driver (below, n. 28) in 1913, and, recently, by J. Lust, "The Story of David and Goliath in Hebrew and in Greek," *EThL* 59 (1983): 5–25. Lust also describes in detail the changes which occur in J. Wellhausen's position. Among those who prefer the shorter version, special attention is due to W. Robertson-Smith, *The Old Testament in the Jewish Church,* 2d ed. (London: A. & C. Black, 1982), 119–24, 431–33.

6. In the LXX, v. 36 is rendered as follows: "Your servant smote both the lion and the bear, and the uncircumcised Philistine shall be as one of them: shall I not go and smite him and this day remove insult from Israel? For who is this uncircumcised one who has insulted the ranks of the living God?"

7. As already realized by A. Kuenen, *Historisch-kritische Einleitung in die Bücher des alten Testament,* trans. from Dutch (Leipzig: Reisland, 1890), 1/2: 61–62.

8. On these ancient harmonistic interpolations, see I. L. Seeligmann, "Hebräische Erzählung und biblische Geschichtsschreibung," *ThZ* 18 (1962): 305–25, also 312:14, 321 n. 35.

9. Alexander Rofé, *Israelite Belief in Angels in the Pre-exilic Period* (diss., Jerusalem, 1969; reprinted, Jerusalem: Makor, 1979), 186f.

10. The sharp-eyed editing of the Chronicler may arouse the envy of the modern philologist. In 1 Sam. 31:6, we read: "So Saul died and his three sons, and his armor bearer, and all his men, that same day together." A fourth son, Ishboshet, survived and was made king by Abner. The Chronicler, who denied the reign of Ishboshet and considered David the legitimate heir to Saul's kingdom, rewrote the verse to read: "So Saul died and his three sons and *all his house* died together" (1 Chron. 10:6)!

11. E. Tov, "The Composition of I Sam. 16—18 in Light of the Septuagint Version," in *Empirical Models for Biblical Criticism,* ed. J. H. Tigay (Philadelphia: Univ. of Pennsylvania Press, 1985), 97–130. My thanks to the author for his permission to read the manuscript. Professor Tov presents adequate evidence that the Greek translator did not edit the Hebrew, but faithfully translated his *Vorlage*—a shorter Hebrew text. On the other hand, his argument that this Hebrew text represented the original account of the David and Goliath contest does not follow, in my opinion.

12. The notorious *baraita* in *b. Bat* 14b–15a, attributed the whole book to Samuel; the Emoraim (see 15a) maintained that the book was finished by the prophets Nathan and Gad. See also Don Isaac Abravanel's introduction to his commentary to Samuel (reprinted, Jerusalem: Tora Vada'at, 1964).

13. K. Budde, *Die Bücher Richter und Samuel* (Giessen: Ricker, 1890), 210–17; P. Dhorme, *Les livres de Samuel,* EtB (Paris: Lecoffre, 1910), 5–6, 167–68. In the last generations this trend was outstandingly represented by O. Eissfeldt, *Die Komposition der Samuelisbücher* (Leipzig: Hinrichs, 1931). Pfeiffer and Fohrer conceived of E as supplementary to J; see R. H. Pfeiffer, *Introduction to the Old Testament* (New York: Harper & Bros., 1941); G. Fohrer, *Introduction to the Old Testament,* trans. D. Green, 10th ed. (Nashville: Abingdon Press, 1968).

14. M. Noth, *Uberlieferungsgeschichtliche Studien,* 3d ed. (Tübingen: Niemeyer, 1967), 1–110, ET: *The Deuteronomistic History,* JSOTSup. 15 (Sheffield: JSOT Press, 1981).

15. H. V. Nübel, "Davids Aufstieg in der frühe israelitischer Geschichtsschreibung" (Diss., Bonn, 1959); F. Mildenberger, "Die vordeuteronomistische Saul-David-Ueberlieferung" (Diss., Tübingen, 1962); R. L. Ward, "The Story of David's Rise: A Traditio-Historical Study of I Samuel XVI 14—II Samuel V" (Diss., Nashville, 1967); R. Rendtorff, "Beobachtungen zur altisraelitischen Geschichtsschreibung anhand der Geschichte vom Aufstieg Davids," in *Probleme biblischer Theologie,* Festschrift G. von Rad (Munich: Kaiser, 1971), 428–39; J. H. Grønbaek, *Die Geschichte vom Aufstieg*

Davids (1 Sam. 15—2 Sam. 5): Tradition and Komposition (Copenhagen: Prostant apud Munksgaard, 1971); J. T. Willis, "The Function of Comprehensive Anticipatory Redactional Joints in I Samuel 16—18," *ZAW* 85 (1973): 294–314; N. P. Lemche, "David's Rise," *JSOT* 10 (1978): 2–25.

16. A. Rofé, "The Betrothal of Rebekah—A Historico-Literary Study," *Eshel Beer-Sheva—Studies in Jewish Thought,* Vol. I (Beer-Sheva: R. Mass, 1976), 42–67 (in Hebrew); also, *The Book of Balaam (Numbers 22:2—24:25). A Study in Methods of Criticism and the History of Biblical Literature and Religion* (Jerusalem: Simor, 1979) (in Hebrew).

17. Therefore, I cannot share the excessive caution of my colleague, Prof. Avi Hurvitz, in identifying postexilic works. See his recent "The Hebrew Language in the Persian Age," in *The History of Israel: The Restoration—The Age of Persian Rule,* ed. H. Tadmor (Jerusalem and Tel Aviv: Am Oved, 1983), 210–33, 306–9 (in Hebrew), with earlier literature. Moreover, one should not isolate the linguistic evidence from the other evidence usually accepted in all historico-literary criticism, i.e., anachronistic hints, history of the literary genres, search for the tendency, legal history, history of thought and of religion. See, e.g., "The Zohar I. The Book and its Author," in G. G. Scholem, *Major Trends in Jewish Mysticism,* rev. ed. (New York: Schocken Books, 1946), 156–204; V. A. Tcherikover, "The Third Book of Maccabees as a Historical Source of Augustus Time," *ScrHie* 7 (1961): 1–26; D. Flusser, "The Author of the Book of Josippon: His Personality and His Age," *Zion* 18 (1953): 109–26 (in Hebrew); also, idem, *The Josippon (Josephus Gorionides),* Jerusalem: Bialik, 1980), 2.74–120 (in Hebrew).

18. But evidence must be adduced! *Pace* Pfeiffer, who apodictically marked out dozens of "midrashic additions" to Samuel; cf. R. H. Pfeiffer, "Midrash in the Books of Samuel," in *Quantulacumque: Festschrift Kirsopp Lake* (London: Christopher, 1937), 303–16.

19. Alexander Rofé, "The Classification of Prophetical Stories," *JBL* 89 (1970): 427–40, esp. 435–40.

20. There have been various attempts to harmonize this contradiction. The first, no doubt, being 1 Chron. 20:5, where Elhanan, son of Ya'ir, slew *Lahmi, the brother* of Goliath the Gittite. A modern variation of this proposal is offered, e.g., by M. H. Segal, *The Books of Samuel* (Jerusalem: Kiryat Sefer, 1956) cxxxv–cxxxvi (in Hebrew). Since David's antagonist is generally called "the Philistine" (see below), one assumes that his identification with Goliath is secondary. In any event the compiler of the "Acts of the Heroes" (2 Sam. 21:15–22; 23:8–23) clearly was not acquainted with the David and Goliath story in its present form. The alternative proposal, interpreting the name David as *dawīdûm* ("leader"), was abandoned after Tadmor found the latter to be but a dialectical form of *dabdûm* ("defeat"); see H. Tadmor, "Historical Implications of the Correct Rendering of Akkadian dâku," *JNES* 17 (1958): 129–41. For the meaning of the same David (*dôd*), see J. J. Stamm, "Der Name des Königs David," *VTSup* 7, Congress Volume, Oxford, 1959 (Leiden: E. J. Brill, 1960), 165–83; reprinted, H. Tadmor, *Beiträge zur hebräischen und altorientalischen Namenkunde,* Orbis Biblicus et Orientalis 30 (Freiburg: Universitätverlag; Gottingen: Vandenhoeck & Ruprecht, 1980), 25–43.

21. This phenomenon in biblical narrative has been treated at large by Professor Meir Weiss in his "Einiges über die Bauformen des Erzählens in der Bibel," *VT* 13 (1963): 456–75.

22. On Genesis 24, see A. Rofé (above, n. 16). For the story of "The Man of God in Bethel," see idem, *The Prophetical Stories* (Jerusalem: Magnes, 1982), 144–54 (in Hebrew). I hope to deal with 1 Kings 20 in a forthcoming study.

23. Besides the passages noted in my "Betrothal of Rebekah," 55–56, we may mention that anonymous prophets still appear in the Chronistic historiography; see, e.g., 2 Chron. 25:6–11, 15–16; 36:15–16.

24. This pattern did not last long. In Rabbinic legend, one finds the opposite, an avoidance of anonymity; see I. Heinemann, *The Methods of 'Aggadah* (Jerusalem: Magnes-Masadah, 1950), 28–32 (in Hebrew).

25. E. Y. Kutscher, *The Language and Linguistic Background of the Isaiah Scroll (1QIs[a])*, STDJ 6 (Leiden: E. J. Brill, 1974), 178–92.

26. E. Qimron, "The Language of Jonah as a Dating Indicator," *Beth Miqra'* 25 (1979/80): 181–82 (in Hebrew).

27. The Samaritan Pentateuch spells *nqy'* everywhere. Indeed, its *plene* writings are notorious. Yet in this case I wonder whether the Samaritan had an original *nqy'* in the late story of Genesis 24 which made it adhere to that same spelling throughout the work.

28. S. R. Driver, *Notes on the Hebrew Text and Topography of the Books of Samuel,* 2d ed. (Oxford: Oxford Univ. Press, 1913), 140; K. Budde, *The Books of Samuel; Critical Edition of the Hebrew Text Printed in Colors Exhibiting the Composite Structure of the Book, with Notes,* trans. from German (Leipzig: Hinrichs, 1894), 65.

29. See Krinetzki and Stoebe (above, n. 2).

30. On the absence of *b.r.h.* (meaning *b.r.r.*) in Hebrew sources, and its late appearance in deeds from the Middle Ages, see E. Y. Kutscher, *Studies in Hebrew and Aramaic* (Jerusalem: Magnes, 1977), 424–25 (in Hebrew).

31. Isa. 52:11; Ezek. 20:38; Ps. 18:27 = 2 Sam. 22:27; Qoh. 3:18; 9:1; Neh. 5:18; Dan. 11:35; 12:10; 1 Chron. 7:40; 9:22; 16:41. Actually, everything datable in this list proves to be late. See, further, Jub. 23:23 (Hebrew MS: A. Rofé, "Further MS Fragments of the Jubilees . . . ," *Tarbiz* 34 [1964/65]: 333–36 [in Hebrew]); CD 10:4; 1QH xiii:20; xv:20; xviii:4; 1QS i:2; iv:20.

32. Like *m. Neg.* 14:3 and *t. Par.* 3:8, *h'ryb šmšw.*

33. In the evening prayer, *hm'ryb 'rbym.*

34. See below.

35. This absence was pointed out to me by my student, David Kōhēn-Ṣemaḥ, Jerusalem.

36. See *Sifre Deut.* 31 (53); *b. 'Erub.* 21b; *b. Meg.* 15b = *b. Sanh.* 111b; *b. Hor.* 13b; *b. Ber.* 62a; *b. Git.* 7a; the morning prayer: *'šrynw, ks'nw mškymym wm'rybym bbty knsywt.* Later, a denominative from *š.ḥ.r.* came into being: *mšḥyr wm'ryb; Lev. Rab.* 19.

37. A. Hurvitz, "'Diachronic Chiasmus' in Biblical Hebrew," *Bible and Jewish History Studies,* ed. Jacob Liver (Tel Aviv: Univ. of Tel Aviv, 1971), 248–55 (in Hebrew).

38. Y. Muffs, "Joy and Love as Metaphorical Expressions of Willingness and Spontaneity in Cuneiform, Ancient Hebrew and Related Literature: Divine Investitures in the Midrash in the Light of Neo-Babylonian Royal Grants," *Studies for Morton Smith at Sixty,* ed. J. Neusner (Leiden: E. J. Brill, 1975), 3.1–36, esp. 9–10.

39. Rightly so, Pseudo-Rashi. Most commentaries accept the usual meaning of *r' lb,* "sadness," which makes no sense here. Is it possible that in 1 Sam. 17:28 and Neh. 2:2 we have a Persian calque in late biblical Hebrew? Professor Shaul Shaked (Jerusalem) kindly informed me on "bad heart" meaning evil intent in (later) Persian.

40. But in *b. Qidd.* 66a (*'yš lṣ lb r'wbly'l*) the word *lb* does not appear in the Munich MS. Erlich realized the extraneous meaning of *r'lbbk* in our passage, and therefore read here *rea' l[e]babka,* "your thoughts."

41. Driver, *Notes on the Books of Samuel,* 147.

42. Driver (ibid., 146) refers to the BDB, 759a §e, which, in turn, quotes Gen. 1:7; Jonah 4:6; 1 Chron. 13:4; 24:20; 26:19; Neh. 12:31 (2x), 37, 38 (2x), 39.

43. See further *t. Sot.* 2:3, *spq hzh; t. Ta'an.* 4:7, *mšwbk hlz šlpny; t. Tohar.* 7:8, *mṣd hlz; Mek. b^eŠallah* 5:2 (to Exod. 17:14), *mḥyy 'wlm hzh wmḥyy 'wlm hb'; Sifre Num.* 65 and 142, *mmšm' hzh.* See also the use of *hllw, mwmym hllw* (*m. Ket.* 7:8); *šlwšh dbrym hllw* (*m. 'Abot.* 5:19). See G. B. Sarfatti, "L'uso dell'articolo determinativo in espressioni del tipo Keneset Ha-Gedola," *Annuario di Studi Ebraici* 10 (1980–84): 219–28.

44. Cf. E. Y. Kutscher, *A History of the Hebrew Language* (Jerusalem and Leiden: E. J. Brill, 1982), 130f., with reference to M. H. Segal, "Mišnaic Hebrew and Its Relation to Biblical Hebrew and to Aramaic," *JQR* 20 (1908): 647–737, esp. 663–67.

45. S. R. Driver, *A Treatise on the Use of Tenses in Hebrew,* 3d ed. (Oxford, 1892), 281–83.

46. Driver, *Notes on the Books of Samuel.*

47. Ibid. A wider application of this rule has been proposed by A. Hurvitz, "The Date of the Prose-Tale of Job Linguistically Reconsidered," *HTR* 67 (1974): 17–34, esp. 28–30.

48. W. F. Albright, "Canaanite *Ḥofši,* 'Free' in the Amarna Tablets," *JPOS* 4 (1924): 169–70; J. Pedersen, "Note on Hebrew Ḥofši," *JPOS* 6 (1926): 105; W. F. Albright, "Canaanite Ḫapši, and Hebrew Ḥofši again," *JPOS* 6 (1926): 107; I. Mendelsohn, "The Canaanite Term for 'Free Proletarian,'" *BASOR* 83 (1941): 36–39; H. L. Ginsberg, *The Legend of King Keret,* BASORSup. 2–3 (1946), 16; J. Gray, "Feudalism in Ugarit and Early Israel," *ZAW* 64 (1952): 49–55.

49. Against this accepted interpretation, see A. F. Rainey, "Institutions: Family, Civil and Military," in *Ras Shamra Parallels,* ed. L. R. Fisher (Rome: Pontificium Institutum Biblicum, 1975), 2:103–4.

50. Cf. Exod. 21:2, 5, 26, 27; Lev. 19:20; Deut. 15:12, 13, 18; Jer. 34:9, 10, 11, 14, 16; Job 3:19; 39:5; Sir. 7:21. See further, C. F. Jean and J. Hoftijzer, *Dictionnaire des Inscriptions Sémitiques de L'Ouest* (Leiden, 1965), s.v. The meaning in Ps. 88:6 (cf. 1QH viii:28–29; x:32–33) and in 2 Kings 15:5; 2 Chron. 26:21 (cf. Ugaritic *bthptt*) appears to be a euphemism; see W. Baumgartner, *Lexikon zum AT* (Leiden, 1967), 1.328; A. Schoors, "Literary Phrases," in *Ras Shamra Parallels,* ed. Fisher (Rome: Pontificium Institutum Biblicum, 1972), 1.27–28.

51. In Qumran and Rabbinic Hebrew, the root seems no longer fertile. 1QH (cf. preceding note) depends on Ps. 88:6, and the rabbis on the laws in Exodus 21; Leviticus 19; Deuteronomy 15. Cf. also the homilies in *b. Shab.* 30a; 151b; *b. Nid.* 61b; *b. B. Bat.* 85b.

52. G. Molin, "What Is a Kidon?" *JSS* 6 (1956): 334–37.

53. As wished by Y. Yadin, *The Art of Warfare in Biblical Lands in the Light of Archaeological Study* (London: Weidenfeld & Nicolson, 1963), 265, 354–55. However, the dates of his illustrations do not fit. The Aegean warrior with a bronze helmet and bronze greaves dates from the fifth century B.C.E.; the scale breastplate belonged to Pharaoh Sheshonk, of the tenth century B.C.E.

54. I follow hereby K. Galling's conclusions in his "Goliath and seine Rüstung," *SVT* 15 (1965): 150–69.

55. See W. F. Albright, "Specimens of Late Ugaritic Prose," *BASOR* 150 (1958): 36–38, esp. 38 n. 12.

56. See O. Thenius, *Die Bücher Samuels, Erklärt,* KEHAT (Leipzig, 1842): 66.

57. See J. Carmignac, "Précisions apportées au vocabulaire de l'Hébreu Biblique par la Guerre des fils de lumière contre les fils de ténèbres," *VT* 5 (1955): 345–65, esp. 354–57; J. van der Ploeg, "La règle de la guerre: traduction et notes," *VT* 5 (1955): 373–420, esp. 396. The terms "skirmishers" and "skirmishing battalions" are used by Chaim and

Batya Rabin in their translation of Y. Yadin, ed., *The Scroll of the War of the Sons of Light against the Sons of Darkness* (New York: Oxford Univ. Press, 1962), 156ff.

58. See R. de Vaux's extensive survey, "Les combats singuliers dans l'Ancien Testament," *Bib* 40 (1959): 495–508; ET, *The Bible and the Ancient Near East* (Garden City, N.Y.: Doubleday & Co., 1971), 122–35. In contrast, Lanczkowski considers the single combat of David and Goliath as continuing the knights' tradition of the *mariannu,* first attested in the fight of Sinuhe; see G. Lanczkowski, *Die Geschichte vom Riesen Goliath und der Kampf Sinuhes mit dem Starken von Retenu,* Festschrift Hermann Junker, MDAI. K 16 (Wiesbaden: Harrassowitz, 1958) 214–18.

59. On the other hand, the fight of Ajax and Hector, in Book VII, is not a representative contest of champions. The distinction between simple, single combat and a representative contest of champions was rightly introduced by H. A. Hoffner, "A Hittite Analogue to David and Goliath Contest of Champions?" *CBQ* 30 (1968): 220–25. However, even in Hoffner's opinion, the Hittite parallel is not certain.

60. This is the position of C. H. Gordon, "Homer and the Bible," *HUCA* 26 (1955): 43–108, esp. 87.

61. They are posited as such by Y. Yadin (Sukenik), "'Let the Young Men . . . Arise and Play Before Us'," *JPOS* 21 (1948): 110–16. In his opinion, the fight of the twelves at Gibeon (2 Sam. 2:12–16) was also a contest of champions. Actually, it was merely single combat (well illustrated by Yadin with the Gozan bas-reliefs). From Joab's reply to Abner, in v. 27: " . . . if you had not spoken, from this morning the people would have parted from each other," it is clear that the fight of the twelves was *not* a contest of champions intended to end a fight, but a daring *jeu des armes* which lighted up the spirits and started a full-scale war.

62. E. Stern, *Material Culture of the Land of the Bible in the Persian Period, 538–332* B.C. (Warminster, Wilts.: Aris Phillips, 1982).

63. Important material has been gathered by H. J. Kraus, "Der lebendige Gott," *EvT* 27 (1967): 169–200. I cannot, however, accept Kraus's conclusion (p. 189) that the epithet *'lhym ḥyym* is old, having originated in hymnic psalmody.

64. A. Rofé, "The Monotheistic Argumentation in Deut. IV 32–40: Contents, Composition and Text," *VT* 35 (1985): 434–45.

65. N. H. Tur-Sinai, *The Language and the Book* (Jerusalem: Bialik, 1950), 2.265–74 (in Hebrew).

66. Therefore Ps. 84:3, which describes longing for the "living God" without any metaphor of thirst, probably depends on Ps. 42:2–3.

67. See Rofé, *Israelite Belief in Angels,* 203–18.

68. E. Tov, "L'incidence de la critique textuelle sur la critique litéraire dans le livre de Jérémie," *RB* 79 (1972): 189–99.

69. Elaine Adler, my student, provided this insight.

70. As correctly interpreted by Ibn Ezra, RaDak, and, in modern times, H. P. Chajes, *Commentary on Psalms,* A. Kahana Series (Kiev, 1903) (in Hebrew). Chajes, however, also considered correcting *mtym* into *mhym.* A. F. Kirkpatrick, *The Book of Psalms,* CB (Cambridge: Cambridge Univ. Press, 1903), rightly pointed out the same expression in Wis. 13:10; A. B. Ehrlich, *Die Psalmen, neu ubersetzt und erklärt* (Berlin, 1905), offered his usual ingenious (but sometimes far-fetched) explanation: *mtym* = *morituri.*

71. Cf. T. W. Davies, "Bel and the Dragon," in *APOT* (New York: Oxford Univ. Press, 1913), 1.652–64, esp. 652–57.

72. R. Knierim, "The Messianic Concept in the First Book of Samuel," in *Jesus and the Historian,* ed. F. T. Trotter (Philadelphia: Westminster Press, 1968), 20–51, compared David's declaration with that of Elijah on Mount Carmel, ". . . it will be known today that you are God in Israel . . ." (1 Kings 18:36). In my opinion the two

declarations are distinct. Elijah wished to make it clear that the Lord, and not Baal, is God *in* Israel (cf. v. 39); as for David, he wished everyone to know that "there is a God *to* Israel," contra those who believed that Israel was a people without God. Knierim's article has a clear typological trend; the Messiah, after being anointed by the Prophet (1 Samuel 10 and 16), proves his charisma with an act of salvation (1 Samuel 11 and 17). But Knierim has rightly observed that David acts here as a confessor to the Lord.

73. Ross's attempt to demonstrate that the Lord of Hosts is a royal epithet does not convince; see J. P. Ross, "Jah. Ṣᵉba'ot in Samuel and Psalms," *VT* 17 (1967): 76–92.

74. No less important is the absence of *Ṣᵉba'ot* from 2 Kings 19:15, 31 (in the latter *qᵉre weᵉla' kᵉtib*), while it obtains in the parallel Isa. 37:16, 32. See also W. Kessler, "Aus welchen Gründen wird die Bezeichnung 'J. Zabaoth' in der späteren Zeit gemieden?," *WZ(H).GS* 7/3 (1958): 767–71.

75. Dan. 2:34–37: "As you looked on, a stone was hewn out, not by hands, and struck the statue on its feet and crushed them. All at once, the iron, clay, bronze, silver and gold were crushed, and became like chaff of the threshing floors of summer; a wind carried them off until no trace of them was left. But the stone that struck the statue became a great mountain and filled the whole earth" (NJPS trans.).

The analogy between 1 Samuel 17 and Daniel 2 is even more striking if one accepts Samuel Deem's interpretation that David's stone did not hit Goliath's forehead, which was protected by a bronze helmet (v. 5), but sank into his greave (*miṣḥah,* v. 6). He stumbled and fell forward "on his face" (v. 49); then David came, stood over him and killed him with his own sword (v. 50). Deem's suggestion was related by his daughter; see A. Deem, "'And the Stone Sank into His Forehead': A Note on 1 Samuel 17:49," *VT* 28 (1978): 349–51. The suggestion, however, conflicts with v. 50, the absence of which from the LXX is no argument against its originality; see above.

For the relatively early date of Daniel 2, see D. Flusser, "The Four Empires in the Fourth Sibyl and in the Book of Daniel," *Israel Oriental Studies* 2 (1972): 148–75; J. J. Collins, *The Apocalyptic Vision of the Book of Daniel,* HSM 16 (Missoula, Mont.: Scholars Press, 1977), 33–65. Flusser maintains that an original Iranian scheme of three kingdoms was enlarged after Alexander's conquest in order to suit anti-Macedonian propaganda. Is there any relation between 1 Samuel 17 and Daniel 2 in its present or earlier form? The answer would affect the dating of 1 Samuel 17.

76. In this matter I cannot subscribe to the views by several eminent Israeli scholars, e.g., J. Klausner, *The Messianic Idea in Israel,* trans. W. F. Stinespring (London: George Allen & Unwin, 1956); Y. Kaufmann, *Mikkibšonah šel Hayyeṣirah Hammiqra'it* (Tel Aviv: Dvir, 1966), 185–96; Y. Zakovitch, "Poor and Riding an Ass," in *The Messianic Idea in Jewish Thought,* in Honour of G. Scholem (Jerusalem: Israel Academy of Sciences and Humanities, 1982), 7–17 (in Hebrew).

77. Isa. 55:5 finds its explanation in Job 19:16. It is the servant's duty to answer his master's call.

78. The identity of this redeemer, to be inferred from the context, will be the object of a separate study.

79. For instance, Hosea 2:20 which reflects the style and ideas of Ezek. 34:25, or Amos 9:4 which sounds like Jer. 21:10; 24:10.

80. It is possible, indeed, that the words "and David their king" in Hosea 3:5 are a secondary addition, as maintained by some commentators. But this does not affect our argument.

81. The first step toward this distinction was made by K. Begrich, "Das Messiasbild des Ezechiel" (Diss., Altenburg, 1904), 21–22. Perhaps even the secondary layer is not a single piece and the text was expanded again in vv. 25–31; see G. Hölscher, *Hesekiel, der Dichter und das Buch,* BZAW 39 (Giessen: Töpelmann, 1924), 169–71; G. A.

Cooke, *Critical and Exegetical Commentary on the Book of Ezekiel,* ICC (New York: Charles Scribner's Sons, 1937); J. W. Wevers, *Ezekiel,* NCBC (London: Thomas Nelson & Sons, 1969). In my opinion, neither Hammerschaimb nor Rembry succeeds in establishing the unity of the chapter; see E. Hammerschaimb, "Ezekiel's View of the Monarchy," *Studia Orientalia Ioanni Pedersen Dicata* (Hauniae: Munksgaard, 1953), 130–40, esp. 136–38; J. G. Rembry, "Le théme du berger dans l'oeuvre d'Ezechiel," *Liber Annuus* 11 (1960/61): 113–44.

82. As usual in biblical Hebrew, the pronoun preceding the finite verb strongly emphasizes the subject. See the translations of NEB and NJPS: "I myself. . . ."

83. E. König, *Die messianischen Weissagungen des Alten Testaments,* 2d and 3d eds. (Stuttgart: Kohlhammer, 1925), 180–81, 259; A. Mowinckel, *He That Cometh,* trans. G. W. Anderson (Nashville: Abingdon Press, 1956), 161–64. König relies on 1 Kings 12:16 and Ps. 132:16, but do these passages truly confirm his view? As for Mowinckel, see below.

84. Mowinckel (*He That Cometh*) rejects the comparison of David with Elijah, since Elijah did not die but ascended to heaven. His argument, however, seems to be an overrationalization of the rules of the future state.

85. See S. Shaked, "The Influences of the Iranian Religion on Judaism," in *The History of Israel,* ed. Tadmor, 236–50, 315–7, esp. 241.

86. H. Schmidt, *Der Mythos vom wiederkehrenden König im AT,* 2d ed. (Giessen: Töpelmann, 1933); H. Gressmann, *Der Messias,* FRLANT 43 (Göttingen: Vandenhoeck & Ruprecht, 1929), 232–72. This belief was noted in postbiblical times by G. F. Moore, *Judaism in the First Centuries of the Christian Era, the Age of the Tannaim,* 3 vols. (Cambridge: Harvard Univ. Press, 1927–30), 2.325–26; E. Schürer, *The History of the Jewish People in the Age of Jesus Christ (175 B.C.–A.D. 135),* ed. G. Vermes et al., 2 vols. (Edinburgh: T. & T. Clark, 1973, 1979), 2.521–23; P. Volz, *Die Eschatologie der jüdischen Gemeinde im neutestamentlichen Zeitalter* (Tübingen: J. C. B. Mohr [Paul Siebeck], 1934), 206–7. See the texts in *b. Ros Has.* 25a; *b. Sanh.* 98b; *Y. Ber.* 82:4.

Part Three

LITERATURE

7 STEPHEN A. GELLER

"WHERE IS WISDOM?": A LITERARY STUDY OF JOB 28 IN ITS SETTINGS

I

Set into the Book of Job, in chapter 28, we find a beautiful poem on the hidden place of wisdom.[1] As in all poems, however, the real topic is beauty itself. Since, as Goethe said, poems, like stained-glass windows, reveal their true beauty only from the inside, we aim in this study to penetrate beyond the standard biblical exegesis into the luminous interior of the poem.[2] This we will accomplish through literary analysis of the poet's integration of form, meaning, and effect.[3] Of course, the primary witness to a poet's success must necessarily be the poem itself; still, ultimately we may manage to place the piece in the larger contexts of Job and the traditions of wisdom literature.

Biblical windows are much darkened by age, they frequently miss panes, and they are full of cracks. Not surprisingly, the text of Job 28 needs some judicious restoration. In the following text and translation, changes from the Masoretic version are, I hope, limited to those which will facilitate analysis but not arouse in anyone suspicions that I have made the text conform to my explication.

v. 1 Now,[4] silver has a source[5] / and there is a place for gold which is refined;[6]
v. 2 Iron is taken from the earth / and copper from the hard rock.[7]
v. 3 (Man) sets an end to darkness[8] / and searches out to the utmost extremity / The stone of darkness and thick gloom.
v. 4 - - - - -[9]
v. 5 A land which produces bread, / overturned where it stood by fire,[10]
v. 6 Whose stones are a place of lapis lazuli / and which has dust of gold.[11]
v. 7 A path which vultures do not know / and the hawk's eye never scanned,
v. 8 Which reptiles[12] have never traced[13] / nor serpents[14] traversed.[15]
v. 9 He has attacked the hard rock, / overturned mountains from their base;

v. 10 He has cleft channels in the rocks,[16] / so that his eye sees all precious things;
v. 11 He has bound[17] the sources of the streams[18] / so that he may bring the hidden to light.
v. 12 But wisdom,[19] whence does it *go forth*[20] / and what is the place of understanding?
v. 13 Man does not know *the path to it*[21] / nor is it found in the land of living.
v. 14 The Deep says, "It is not in me," / and Sea says, "It is not with me."
(v. 15 Bullion[22] cannot be exchanged for it / nor silver weighed out as its price;
v. 16 I cannot be bought[23] for the gold of Ophir / for precious onyx or lapis lazuli;
v. 17 Gold or glass cannot be compared to it, / nor can it be exchanged for vessels[24] of fine gold;
v. 18 Corals and crystal need not be mentioned; / for better a bag[25] of wisdom than of pearls!
v. 19 The topaz of Cush cannot be compared to it, / nor can it be bought for pure gold.)
v. 20 But wisdom, whence does it come[26] / and what is the place of understanding?
v. 21 It is concealed[27] from the eyes of all the living / and hidden from the birds of heaven.
v. 22 Abaddon and Death say, / "We have heard (but) a rumor of it."
v. 23 God understands its path; / he knows its place,
v. 24 For he looks to the ends of the earth / sees everything under heaven,[28]
v. 25 To set[29] the wind's weight, / the water he's meted out by measure;
v. 26 When he fixed the rain's rule[30] / and a path for the thundershower,[31]
v. 27 Then he saw it and mustered it[32] / *understood it*[33] and searched it out.[34]
(v. 28 And he said to man, "The fear of the Lord is wisdom / and rejection of evil is understanding.")

The only truly obscure verses here are 4 and, to a lesser extent, 5. But in both cases a glimmer of light shines through. Potentially more obstructive to literary analysis are the several emendations. The most serious of these is *darkāh,* "the path to it," for MT's *'erkāh,* "its value," for I assign the term *derek* great weight in the structure of the poem. But the greatest problem is the suggested omission of vv. 15–19 and, even more importantly, v. 28 (implied above by parentheses). These verses have been declared guilty without trial. Eventually, a good lawyer's case must be made for such cursory treatment; however, analysis will proceed without these disputed passages.

If we omit v. 28 in particular, even a first reading of Job 28 produces a fairly clear impression of the meaning. It may be presented in the following sentence, which expresses basic contrasts: man can search out and acquire even the remotest precious stones, but only God knows where wisdom is, for he used it at creation.

The poet's art lies in how he presents and develops this basic meaning. First, he gives the poem good, solid bones, for the essential contrasts are set by a nuclear equation—a skeleton so to speak—of four core verses:

v. 1 Now, silver has a source / and there is a place for gold which is refined;

v. 12 But wisdom, whence does it *go forth* / and what is the place of understanding?
v. 13 Man does not know *the path to it* / nor is it found in the land of the living.
v. 23 God understands its path; / he knows its place.

The basic oppositions are two. In vv. 1 and 12, precious stones are set against wisdom, and in vv. 12 and 23 man is set against God. The nuclear equation is formed by simply interlocking the contrasts as follows: man : precious stones :: God : wisdom. Over this taut frame the poet has stretched the sinews, the poem's imagery, to produce the following tripartite structure:

Section One: Man's Search for Jewels
(vv. 1–11)

a. Precious ores have a place of origin (vv. 1–2)
b. Man searches the remotest regions to find gems (vv. 3–8)
c. He penetrates the lowest depths to mine them (vv. 9–11)

Section Two: Where Is Wisdom?
(vv. 12–14; 20–22)

a. But where is wisdom to be found? (v. 12)
b. The way to it is unknown to man and the Sea (vv. 13–14)

(vv. 15–19)

c. Where is wisdom?[35] It is unknown to beasts and birds.
Even the underworld knows of it only by hearing (vv. 20–22)

Section Three: God the Creator Knows Where Wisdom Is
(vv. 23–27)

a. God knows wisdom's path, for He sees everything (vv. 23–24)
b. When He created the world he searched out wisdom utterly (vv. 25–27)

(v. 28)

We shall attempt to follow the play of poetic effects as the poem proceeds, section by section.

Section One

Verses 1–2 form an intricately structured introductory quatrain. Its lines are linked by the semantic parallelism of the ores, which are arranged in word pairs of partial (v. 1) and total (v. 2) chiasm.[36] Striking also is the alliteration. This occurs chiefly through nasals (m/n), velar stops (k/q), and sibilants (s/z/ṣ). For example, la*kk*esep *m*ôṣā' / ū*m*ā*q*ô*m* la*zz*āhāb yā*z*ō*qq*û / bar*z*el *m*ē'āpār yu*qq*aḥ / wĕ' ebe*n* yāṣû*q* *n*ĕḥûšâ. Some of these devices serve in part to isolate the quatrain from what follows, thus making it an effective introduction to the poem. Syntax strengthens this sense of disjunction, for the structure of v. 2b reverses either the syntactic functions or positions to effect a strong sense of closure.[37] The poetic justification for these disjunctive devices is that they underscore the function of vv. 1–2 in the nuclear framework of the poem. This function is established by *lakkesep* and its parallel complements, the other ores. *Lakkesep* is placed in an emphatic position in its clause. Since emphasis implies contrast, the reader awaits a partner for *lakkesep*. He finds it only in *wĕhaḥokmâ,* "but wisdom," of v. 12.[38]

Yet v. 2 serves more specifically as an introduction to section one, for it is difficult not to hear in it a subtle shift in emphasis from the metals themselves to their place of origin, the theme of vv. 3–11. The effect is a kind of pointed specification. Now, precious metals have a place of origin, and that place is the dust and stones of the earth. Here too alliteration plays a role, as it is impossible to miss the phonetic link of v. 2b, and through it of 1–2a, to v. 3: 'ebe*n* yāṣûq *n*ĕḥûšâ/*q*ēṣ śām ('ĕ*n*ôš?) la*h*ōšek. This integration of form, content, and effect makes a memorable beginning to the poem.

After v. 2 we naturally expect a description of the process of acquiring precious stones. Such is, in fact, the content of vv. 3–11. Commonly, scholars see in them an attempt realistically to describe certain aspects of mining. So "[man] puts an end to darkness" (v. 3) is often read as a reference to miners' helmets with attached lamps; the depths of the earth "overturned [as if] by fire" (v. 5) supposedly refers to the ancient practice of shattering rocks by heating them; "binding the streams" (v. 11) is interpreted as referring to underground damming and draining. Even obscure passages like 4c are pressed into use; there, *dallû mē'ĕnôš nā'û,* often translated as "they hang far from men, they swing to and fro," or the like, supposedly refers to either daring or hapless miners suspended in vertical shafts, and the like.

In my opinion, it is far from the poet's intention to write a treatise on mining technology; "realistic" meaning is submerged in a vibrant complex of imagery. All its constituent metaphors are presented or implied in v. 3. The following levels of meaning may be distinguished: (1) there is a "realistic," narrative plane comprising a description of how jewels are found and mined; (2) there exists also the poetically dominant plane of metaphor and associations. The poet, then, constructs his real meaning from the flow of complementary and contrasting images. The effect is almost impressionistic. It is astonishing that the metaphorical, allusive plane does not dissolve the poem but, on the contrary, tightens its underlying framework. In fact, the images directly relate to the basic skeleton of the poem. They therefore operate as the play of living flesh over bone.

Of course, v. 3 certainly describes some activity associated with mining—but which? Since *hôqēr,* "he searches out," can refer to spying, and since in vv. 7–8 the poet still talks of the road to the mines, I agree with S. Byington who sees here a description of prospecting rather than of mining itself.[39] Mining does not begin until man enters the subterranean world (vv. 9–11). Here, the poet describes the region of mines as remote and desolate, though fabulously rich. The road to it is beyond the ken of even the most far-ranging, far-seeing creatures—except for man.

Verse 3's *Qēṣ śām laḥôšek,* "[man] sets an end to darkness," an otherwise unattested phrase, by its parallelism to *lĕ(kol) taklît . . . ḥôqēr,* "he seeks out to the utmost extremity," calls to mind the phrase in 26:10, *'ad taklît 'ôr 'im hôšek,* "to the extremity of light and darkness."[40] Likely, the latter phrase means, as E. Dhorme suggests, the place where light and darkness meet, the horizon. The "realistic" sense of the verse is, then, that in his quest for jewels man reaches the ends of the earth.

This narrative meaning is, as I have said, overwhelmed by the images and associations. In particular, the divine overtones of the metaphor are so potent that Jewish tradition was deceived into applying the entire passage to God.[41] For instance, *Ḥôqēr* itself is prominently used to refer to divine powers of intellectual penetration (cf. Pss. 139:1, 23; 44:22; Jer. 17:10; etc. [often with *lēb,* "heart, mind," as object]). "Light" and "darkness" also appear in divine contexts (cf. 26:10, cited above). They bear connotations of creation, when the first act comprised God making light, "putting an end" to the "darkness over the surface of the Deep."

So the poet's tactic in section one is to describe a human activity in terms which echo godhood. This form of hyperbole will culminate in verses 9–11. Its effect is twofold. Certainly it is ironic and extreme, and these terms apply to the poem's imagery as a whole, as we shall see. The poet likes to hone contrasts to merisms. But the main purpose is to prepare the reader for that basic opposition of the poem's nuclear equation opposing man and God which will not appear overtly until vv. 13 and 23. When it does appear, its profile will be sharper because we will remember the metaphors of vv. 3–11. Verse 3, then, introduces this strategy.

But the riches of v. 3 are not yet exhausted. Corresponding to the narrative level of meaning with its divine resonances there exists, as we have noted, a metaphorical plane. In this verse, the object of man's godlike search comprises "stones of darkness and thick gloom." Of course, this is literally true of underground mining, but again, the realism is swallowed up by the imagery. By natural association, mining taps one of the richest lodes of biblical metaphor and allusion, underworld motifs. For these, terms like "darkness" and "gloom" are especially characteristic (cf. Ps. 88:7; Job 10:21ff.; etc.).[42] Indeed, *'āpār,* "dust" (v. 2), has already anticipated underworld themes, since it too is prominent in such contexts (cf. Isa. 29:4; Job 17:16; Ps. 22:16; etc.).[43]

Again, the image functions hyperbolically. In his greed for gems man approaches the realm of the dead, the undermost part of the earth, *šĕ'ôl taḥtît,* "nethermost Sheol" (Deut. 32:22). This picture resembles that in Ps. 141:7, which I also take as drawn from mining. There we read *kĕmô pōlēaḥ ûbōqēaʿ bāʾāreṣ / nipzĕrû ʿăṣāmēnû lĕpî šĕʾôl,* "like those who hack and cleave into the earth (or netherworld), so are our bones scattered at the entrance to Sheol." Job 3:21 rests on the similar image, *hamḥakkîm lāmāwet wĕʾenennû / wayyaḥpĕrūhû mimmaṭmônîm,* "who wait for death but it does not appear, who dig for it more than for treasures." In our passage, the underworld motifs introduced in v. 3 climax in vv. 9–11, paralleling these divine themes.

Yet a third complex of associations arises from this wonderful verse to culminate in vv. 9–11. Often, *ḥôqēr* refers to penetrating intellectual activity and is used in conjunction with wisdom terms like *ḥākām,* "wise," *yādaʿ,* "know," *(hē)bîn,* "understand," and so on (cf. Deut. 13:15; Isa. 40:28; Ps. 139:1, 23; Job 29:16; Prov. 28:11; etc.). But by clever play of association, the object of *ḥôqēr* in Job 28:3 is not the "heart" or knowledge itself, but "stones"!

Ḥôqēr's wisdom associations are augmented by allying it with *taklît,* "extremity." This conjunction recalls Job 11:7, *haḥēqer ʾĕlōah timṣāʾ / ʾim ʿad taklît šaddai timṣāʾ,* "can you find out the hidden place of God; find him out to the extremity?" Here, too, the imagery is spatial; subsequent verses present merisms of the heights of heaven, the depths of the underworld—the vertical dimension of the cosmos, as it were—and the width of the earth, depth of the sea—a mixture of horizontal and vertical. Moreover, the context of 11:7ff. is definitely that of wisdom. Consider, for instance, *ta ʿălūmôt ḥokmâ,* "hidden things of wisdom," in 11:6.

No doubt even the darkness imagery of Job 28:3 strengthens the overtones of wisdom. "Darkness" is a standard biblical image for everything negative, as "light" is for the positive. They can be extended also to include ignorance and knowledge, respectively, especially since "reality" reinforces the image; only what is bathed in full light can be clearly seen and known—it was only because God created light first that he could see that it was good! But what is sheathed in darkness is hidden, secret (cf. Qoh. 2:13–14; Pss. 82:5; 139:11–12; Prov. 7:9; and, esp., Job 38:1, *maḥšîk ʿēṣâ,* "he who darkens counsel," equivalent to *maʿlîm ʿēṣâ,* "he who obscures counsel," in 42:3). Therefore, "putting an end to darkness" may itself be heard as a metaphor for attaining recondite knowledge.

Here again, a theme introduced in section one (the wisdom theme) culminates in vv. 9–11. *Taʿălūmâ yōṣîʾ ʾôr,* "he brings the hidden to light" (v. 11b), certainly evokes *ḥokmâ,* although its grammatical and "realistic" object, as in v. 3, is gems, treasure—the *kol yĕqār* of the parallel in v. 10b.

As with divine themes, the tone here is ironic. While man has the skill (and also a sense of *ḥokmâ*) to snatch jewels from the depths, he nonetheless lacks hidden wisdom. Moreover, just as with the divine themes, the echoes of wisdom prepare the ground for the following basic equation which will be formulated in v. 12: the precious stones are set against wisdom. And here again reverberations of 3–11 will strengthen the contrast in the reader's mind. Verse 3, then, prospects all these rich meanings.

A "stone of darkness and thick gloom" provides an apt metaphor for v. 4, as niggardly with meaning as v. 3 is extravagant. Nevertheless, this general sense seems to emerge: the region of wadies man penetrates to find mines is remote, "forgotten by the foot," "poor in men." While it is possible that the underworld imagery of v. 3 continues, I think it more likely that the poet has shifted from the vertical dimension to the horizontal, and that the poet refers here to the location of mines in trackless deserts at the ends of the known earth.[44] This interpretation corresponds to the reality of most ancient mining, for aside from copper, most precious ores and stones came from truly remote regions. Gold came from Nubia and Ophir, for example, and lapis from Afghanistan.[45] But I suspect that also here "reality" bows to metaphor; and that the prime intention of the poet is to introduce the desert, yet another complex of common biblical motifs.[46] Deserts, as etymology states, are precisely the untraveled regions v. 4 seems to be describing. Consider, for instance, Jer. 2:6: *hammôlîk 'ōtānû bammidbār / bĕ'ereṣ 'ărābâ wĕšûḥā / bĕ'ereṣ ṣiyyâ wĕṣalmāwet / bĕ'ereṣ lō' 'ābar bāh 'îš / wĕlō' yāšab 'ādām šām,* "(God) who led us in the desert, a land of steppe and pits, a land of dryness and thick gloom, a land through which no man has ever passed, nor any man dwelt"; cf. Jer. 51:43.

Also significant in this passage is the use of *ṣalmāwet,* "thick gloom," for the desert is often linked to the underworld by terms of darkness, as follows: *midbār* ("desert") // *'ereṣ ma'pēlyâ* ("land of gloom"), in Jer. 2:31; *mĕqôm tannîm* ("place of jackals") // *ṣalmāwet* ("thick gloom") in Ps. 44:20; *tōhû lō' derek* ("chaos without roads") // *hōšek lō' 'ôr* ("darkness without light"), in Job 12:24–25. Now, the desert glare is hardly Stygian gloom. Rather, its "darkness" is metaphorical. Indeed, the desert is sometimes termed *tōhû,* "chaos," as in Job 12:24 and Isa. 45:15, and so on, because, like primordial Tehom, it is unproductive and formless. It is also like the underworld, to which similar language may be applied (cf. Job 10:22, *ṣalmāwet wĕlō' sĕdārîm,* "[a land of] thick gloom, without order"). Like the primeval ocean, the desert is unpierced by God's creative light. Thus, the underworld motif of v. 3 is not very removed from the postulated desert theme of v. 4; "darkness and thick gloom" of v. 3 can refer to both.[47] Discerning the latter in v. 4 adds the horizontal dimension to the vertical; all extremities of nature are encompassed in man's exploration for wealth.[48]

Verse 5 also proves difficult. However, it clearly forms a quatrain with v. 6. A return to key terms from vv. 1–2 (*māqôm,* "place"; *'āpār,* "dust"; *zāhāb,* "gold") highlights the significance of this passage. Further, v. 5's *yēṣē'* links with *môṣā'* in v. 1. The point arising from these verbal ties seems to be that the "land" of vv. 5–6 is the "source" and "place" of ores alluded to in v. 1. Although the syntactic link between vv. 5–6 and v. 4 is uncertain, perhaps owing to corruption in the latter verse, they do seem to describe the mining region. Verse 6 definitely refers to its extreme wealth in precious stones, and I read v. 5 as contrastive, taking up the themes of vv. 3–4 and presenting the place of gems as a desolate, fire-blasted land.

Indeed, language points to sites that function as paradigms for divine destruction, Sodom and Gomorrah. The desert motif frequently occurs in relation to places destroyed by God (cf. Jer. 51:43; 50:12f.; Isa. 13:20f.; Ezek. 35:7ff.). Isa. 34:9 employs terms strongly reminiscent of the annihilation of the cities of the plain. It reads *wĕnehepkû nĕhālehâ lĕzepet / wa'ăpārāh lĕgoprît / wĕhāyĕyâ 'arṣāh lĕzepet bō'ērâ,* "her wadies will turn to pitch, her dust to brimstone, and all her land will become burning pitch." *Hāpak,* "overturn," is in fact almost a technical term for the overthrow of Sodom (cf. Gen. 19:25; Deut. 29:22; Amos 4:11; Isa. 13:19; Lam. 4:6; Jer. 49:18; Zeph. 2:9–10; etc.). Its use in Job 28:5, in such a context of desolation, is at the very least suggestive. The sense of the verse should then be "fruitful, bread-producing land, (now) overturned by fire."[49]

A Sodom motif is totally appropriate. That site was proverbial for its extreme fertility, "like the garden of God, like the land of Egypt" (Gen. 13:11; cf. Ezek. 16:49). Its later "overturning" was therefore merismatic; from the pinnacle of fertility it plunged to a state of salt-drenched sterility, a proper penalty for the extreme wickedness of its inhabitants (cf. the similar idea in Ps. 107:34, *'ereṣ pĕrî limlēḥâ / mērā'at yôšĕbê bāh,* "[God made] a fruitful land a salt desert on account of its dwellers' evil"). Such hyperbolic extremism is, as we have seen, characteristic of the poem's imagery. The place of mines is as desolate and as hot as hell—such would be the later way of putting the poet's point.[50] And the metaphor's beauty lies in its realism, as any visitor to ancient mines can attest.

Verse 6 operates contrastively; the "fertility" of this sterile region lies not in its fruit but in the abundance of gold and jewels. Surprisingly, this aspect too may connect with Sodom and Gomorrah. In Wayyiqra Rabba 5:2, Sodom appears thus, as a place rich in precious stones: "When one of them (the Sodomites) would go to a garden to buy vegetables for a coin, he would find gold in the dust on them." Interestingly, this is a comment on Job 28:6. But whether it alludes to the Sodom motif of v. 5 or not, v. 6 sounds like ancient hyperbole—like Ashurballit's statement to Pharaoh in the Amarna Letters that "in your land gold is as dust" (*ḫurāṣu ina mātīka eperu šū*).[51] This idea of a place whose very dust is precious points to yet another range of metaphor, paradise.

Ezekiel 28 portrays an Eden quite unlike that of Genesis. Here, a cherub walks about amidst "stones of fire" (*'abnê 'ēš*) in a "garden of God" also termed, apparently, "the holy mountain of God" (*har qōdeš 'ĕlōhîm,* v. 14). Despite the grave textual difficulties, we can clearly see that Eden, here uniquely called the divine mountain, is studded with jewels;[52] nine are enumerated. Since messianic motifs commonly reflect paradise themes, on Gunkel's principle of *Endzeit gleicht Urzeit,* indirect evidence for a bejeweled Eden may also come from Second Isaiah's future Jerusalem set in gems, with all its territory studded by precious stones (Isa. 54:12). Even the largely demythologized Genesis 2 has a hint of the fabulous wealth of paradise. One of the rivers flowing from it circles the land of Havilah, "whose gold is good."[53] And this motif luxuriates even into apocalyptic literature; Enoch's visions reveal the gem-encrusted hills.[54] The contrast of desolation and mineral "fertility," Sodom and Eden, could hardly be more merismatic.

But now imagery has become bewildering; underworld, desert, Sodom, and paradise motifs have succeeded each other, intertwined, and merged. The motifs retain the fluidity of the mythological concepts from which they are surely derived. For example, the divine-mountain = paradise link is attested through the literature of the ancient Near East to Jewish apocalyptic.[55] Perhaps, too, these verses echo epithets for the Mesopotamian underworld (*šad ḫurāṣi,* "mountain of gold"),[56] for Ereshkigal's palace of lapis lazuli in the infernal regions,[57] and for *apsû,* the watery home of Ea-Enki, the Mesopotamian god of wisdom, a place also described as rich in gems.[58] Certainly, Canaanite Baal's house of silver and gold on Zaphon reverberates in the imagery,[59] and, El's mountain in the midst of the deeps may do likewise.[60]

This paradise motif blends with the divine themes of the previous verses, strengthening in an almost imagist manner the overall effect. The perceptual meaning is something like the following: in an inhospitable desert region man, laboring with almost divine skill, finds a netherworld Eden of preternatural wealth. But the rapid succession of complementary (underworld-desert-Sodom), partially conflicting (desert-paradise) motifs also intimates meanings that prose could never achieve with such startling simultaneity. Above all, the themes of desolation and death implicit in the concepts of Sodom and the underworld cast a negative pall over man's achievement. Even to find riches, digging into Sheol must bear a dark meaning.

Moving on to v. 7, we find it belongs to a quatrain, vv. 7–8, which is linked to vv. 5–6 by the similarity of structure in their respective first lines. Verses 7–8s' lines are themselves welded by grammatical and semantic parallelism. All depend on initial *nātîb,* "the road," isolated by *casus pendens.* The dominant device is surely the repeated negatives. They assert that the road to treasure is unknown to the cited beasts. It is likely that here, too, merism is involved. The birds of v. 7, creatures of the sky famous for their keen-sighted vision, are most effectively contrasted with the denizens of the earth, that is, snakes or, at least, reptiles. As we have noted, S. Mowinckel makes a good case for such an interpretation of *šaḥal,* and it is likely that its phonetic complement (*bĕnê*) *šaḥaṣ* has a similar meaning. Snakes are, as the Midrash says, "experts in the earth," and far more fitting to the context than "lions," which symbolize strength and ferocity rather than subterranean sinuosity. Moreover, serpents (and other reptiles) are associated with buried riches in many folklores, and their endowment with wisdom and cunning is known to everyone. That man outdoes both far-seeing birds and deep-delving "gliders in the dust" (Deut. 32:24) fits the hyperbolic nature of the poem's metaphors. Yet simultaneously, the sequence of negatives anticipates that of section two where, ironically, man is to be included among the ignorant.

Section one climaxes in vv. 9–11. Verse 9 is bound to v. 8 by (chiastic) alliteration (*lô*' 'ādā '*ālāw šaḥal* / baḥ*allāmîš šālaḥ* yādô), and to vv. 10–11 by the probably formulaic pair *hallamîš* and *ṣûr*.[61] But the height of formal integration is achieved in vv. 10–11, a quatrain of alternating parallelism. All four lines consist of noun phrase plus verb phrase which, in the case of the B and D lines, is formed by the compound expressions *rā'ătâ 'ênô,* "his eye sees," and *yōṣî' 'ôr,* "he brings to light," respectively. This structure functions as a tight housing for a remarkable set of wordplays on the words *rā'ā,* "see," and *'ôr,* "light." The former occurs in the phrase from 10b just cited. The latter appears only in 11b, in final, climactic, position. Two members of the pun refer to water channels. *Yĕ'ōrîm,* which contains within itself the key word *'ôr,* normally refers to the Nile and its channels (it is the Egyptian for "river"), and was undoubtedly chosen here for the wordplay;[62] *Nĕhārôt,* "streams," echoes *nĕhārâ,* "light," (cf. Job 3:4).[63]

The aim of these plays on words is certain. They mark the verses as the culmination of the passage which began with v. 3; *'ôr,* especially, is the complement of *ḥōšek* from that verse. *Mĕgallê 'ămūqôt minnî ḥōšek / wayyōṣē' lā'ôr ṣalmāwet,* "He uncovers hidden things from darkness, He brought thick gloom into the light" (Job 12:22), refers to God's works of creation, and as noted above, vv. 9–11 bring the themes of vv. 3ff. to completion. Man's mining activities thus mimic divine creation, splitting, crushing, overturning (cf. v. 5), and so on.[64] Like God, man displays wisdom in bringing things to light, so the divine motifs of section one climax in language that clearly recalls creation; man penetrates to the primeval waters which, like God, he "binds," and brings out not hidden wisdom but *yĕqār,* "treasure."[65] The link between divine wisdom and the physical acts of creation—paradoxically destructive—is similar to that in Job 9:4ff., *hăkam lēbāb wĕ'ammîṣ kōaḥ . . . hama'tîq hārîm . . . 'ăšer hăpākām bĕ'appô* "(God is) wise and mighty in power . . . the mover of mountains . . . which he overturned in his wrath. . . ." The ultimate allusions are to God's battle with the Sea, the monster Leviathan. This was perhaps the reason for the use of *bĕnê šahaṣ* in v. 8, since that term occurs elsewhere (41:26) only to note Leviathan as their king. So powerful are the divine creation motifs in vv. 9–11 that they totally submerge the narrative, "realistic" plane of meaning. In obtaining jewels man mimics, and perhaps mocks the creator.

Section Two

If man has any pretensions of competing with the divine, vv. 12–13 put him in his proper place. Verse 12 states that what he has acquired by his efforts are riches, not wisdom; v. 13 places him firmly within the circle of created beings. For good measure, v. 14 says that the underground primeval waters he has reached, the *ḥēqer,* "hidden place," of the netherworld, are also ignorant of the place of wisdom.[66] Physical penetration of the deep, then, has nothing to do with deep wisdom. Verse 20 repeats v. 12, and v. 21 echoes v. 13 (*kol ḥay,* "all the living," -*'ereṣ hahayyîm,* "the land of the living").[67] The passage ends in this merism: neither the birds of the heavens (echoing v. 8) nor the underworld itself (paralleling the subterranean waters of v. 14) knows the site of wisdom.[68] All nature, man included, knows not its place.

Section two's message appears totally negative. Every line contains some negative term except v. 22, and its negative import is implicit in its context. To be sure, "hearing" is itself positive (cf. Ps. 44:2), and may appear with "seeing" as a kind of hendiadys for "perceiving" (cf. Job 13:1; 39:11). But contrasted with "seeing," "hearing" is negative (cf. 1 Kings 10:6–7). This is the purport of those key words in Job's "recantation" (42:4), "I had heard of you (only) by the hearing of the ears, but now (*wĕʿattâ*) my eye (actually) sees you!" The contrast to 28:22 occurs in 28:24: the underworld may only have heard of wisdom, but God sees everything. *Šāmaʿ* of v. 22 is thus a transition to vv. 23ff. Poetically, the point is clearly this: the underworld, despite its geographic propinquity to what one might suppose, on the basis of metaphor, might be the home of wisdom, knows of it only by rumor, a shadow of the real thing. Just so, man's skill in obtaining jewels mimics real *ḥokmâ.*

Moreover, given that rhetorical questions are commonly negative in import, even the questions of vv. 12 and 20 reflect the theme of total ignorance. One has no reason to think wisdom has a "place" of any kind! Perhaps it is totally beyond the ken of all creation.

Together, these sections, one and two, make a fine poem. All the major themes of section one are taken up by two, and all its implicit structures are completed. Precious stones have been compared, to their detriment, with wisdom; man's pretensions have been deflated. As it stands, the poem is rich and complex. One has no reason to expect anything more.

Section Three

So unexpected is it, the initial *'ĕlōhim* of v. 23a, backed by the emphatic *hu'* of 23b, is almost as much a theophany as the divine speech out of the whirlwind. Light from this sudden revelation immediately transfigures the preceding parts of the poem. The second nuclear equation, man-God, implicit in the earlier divine motifs, now springs actively to life, as the reader hears in v. 23 the complement to v. 13.

Verses 12 and 20s' "negative" questions, amazingly, now appear not rhetorical at all, but literal and positive in import; wisdom does have a "place."

But with lightning speed, almost before the reader can follow it, this lively poem makes a new swerve, this time from the spatial dimensions (vertical and horizontal) that have hitherto dominated it to the temporal. The "place" of wisdom is not where, but when, and "when" lies in the distant past, at the time of creation. The creation motifs of section one are now revealed as more than mere poetic conceit. They are essential to the poem's dialectic. In section three they leap into the foreground. Even as they do, a new level of meaning emerges which centers on shifts in the meaning of *darkāh* in vv. 13 and 23. We shall attempt to follow these maneuvers.

The temporal shift from present to past is effected by grammatical parallelism—the syntactic correspondence of vv. 25a and 26a (preposition plus infinitive), reinforced by repetition of the verb *ʿāśâ.* Verse 25a depends on v. 24, whose tense is presumably present; *laʿăśôt* is either, as translated "purpose," or it continues the action of the finite verbs of v. 24, as noted above. Yet the actions recounted are those of creation. The wind is weighed, the water measured. Moreover, the tense of *tikkēn* may already signal a change in the temporal focus to past. Verse 26a removes all ambiguity. It forms a temporal clause with v. 27, and 27 seals the shift from present to remote past by *'āz* ("then"), and the staccato sequence of four perfect verbs. It forms a strong closure to the poem. The initial *rā'âh,* "he saw it," echoes *yabbîṭ* // *yir'eh* of v. 24 and, ultimately, the wordplay on "light" and "seeing" in section one.

These devices, which reinforce the temporal shift, imply that the "place" of wisdom is in the primeval past. That is why creation does not know of it; since God used it to create the world, it existed prior to any part of nature. Thus, the wisdom man cannot attain is cosmic. *YHWH bĕḥokmâ yāsad 'āreṣ kônēn šāmayim bitbûnâ,* "God founded the earth with wisdom, he established the heavens with understanding" (Prov. 3:19; cf. Jer. 10:12; Ps. 104:25; Isa. 40:12ff., 28; etc.).[69] The message is so common as to be almost trite.

II

Yet any accusation of banality seriously underestimates the poet's skill. The poem contains such striking plays on words and themes, evoking such diverse levels of meaning, as to be one of the most original and impressive in the Bible. *Derek* provides the focus for the key wordplay. In v. 13 (as emended) it means "the way to it"; the pronominal suffix is objective. Initially, this is also its sense in v. 23, parallel to *mĕqômāh,* "its place." But, as the reader perceives in vv. 23ff. a shift from a spatial to a temporal dimension, so one also apprehends a change in the nuance of *derek* from literal and geographical to figurative. In the context of creation, *darkāh* must be reanalyzed as "its path," that is, "its manner of conduct, its way of acting," even "its nature." The pronominal suffix is then subjective: "the way wisdom takes."[70]

One clue to this shift lies in the parallelism between *derek* and *ḥōq,* in v. 26. Although, as M. Pope suggests, *ḥōq* may here have its etymological meaning of "groove," or the like, that sense itself is surely a pun.[71] In creation contexts the expected nuance is "law or statute" of nature that may not be violated (cf. Job 3:22; Prov. 8:29; Jer. 31:35; and so on).

Plays on the literal and figurative meaning of *derek* underlie Prov. 30:18ff. The things "too wonderful" to comprehend are the *derek* of an eagle in the sky, of a snake on rock, of a ship in the sea, of a man with a woman. The first three are literal, the last certainly figurative.[72] The play on words is precisely what makes the saying memorable.

Therefore, when a reader hears the creation motifs of vv. 25ff., he or she is probably supposed to reinterpret the meaning of 23a retroactively and supported by 26b as "God understands its (wisdom's) way, its nature." This interpretation conforms to the ancient understanding of the link between knowing the origin of things and having control over them, an inner magical bond of intellect and primal causes of secret knowledge and great power. Because God knows the *môṣā',* the "source" of wisdom, he is all-wise; because man does not and cannot know it, he can never achieve divine wisdom.

Evidently, Job 28 provides the site for a dialectic of negatives and positives that may be represented schematically as follows:

Section One:	man's skill	(positive)
Section Two:	man's ignorance creation's ignorance	(negative)
Section Three:	God's wisdom God's skill (creation)	(positive)

Section one thus presents man's skill in finding jewels as a kind of hymn to human ingenuity. Despite the implicit negative overtones we noted above, the overall effect is positive. Section two, on the other hand, is totally negative. There, ignorance replaces skill, and man's domination of nature is replaced by his dependence upon it. Nothing in creation, even man, knows where wisdom is. Section three is again positive. Here, God does know wisdom's "path"; he used it skillfully in making the world. Taken together, the sections produce a mixed but positive effect, for if man can never have divine wisdom, he nonetheless receives its benefits. He can trust that the cosmic order is good and just, since it reflects hidden wisdom.

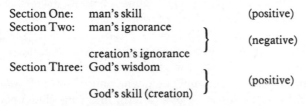

The positive tone emerges forcefully in the final couplet, vv. 26–27, for rain is the special sign of divine providence. Surely it is no accident that *derek lahăzîz qōlôt,* "a path for the thundershower," occurs also in 38:25–26, which many commentators consider a key passage in the later divine speeches. There we read *mî pillag laššeṭep tĕʻālâ / wĕderek lahăzîz qōlôt lĕhamṭîr ʻal 'ereṣ lō' 'îš / midbār lō' 'ādām bô,* "Who channeled a ditch for the flood, a path for the thunderstorm / to make it rain on uninhabited regions, deserts without people?" That God provides for "useless" desert plants and animals is perhaps the ultimate sign of his goodness; that he knows their needs attests to his supreme wisdom (cf. Ps. 104:10ff.; Job 5:10–11).[73]

Such care for unpeopled regions clearly indicates the differences between divine and human viewpoints. Human *mišpāṭ,* "justice," is not necessarily the same as God's *mišpāṭ,* his governance of the cosmos.[74] This is the point of another famous passage which, significantly, also connects providence with rain as evidence of the divergence between human and divine perspectives. Isaiah 55:8ff. (note also the use of *derek*) reads: "For my thoughts are not like your thoughts, nor my ways (*dĕrākay*) like your ways . . . for just as the heavens are above the earth so are my ways above yours. . . . Just as the rain and snow come down from heaven and do not return unless they water the earth, make it give birth and sprout, producing seed for sowers and bread for the eater, so the word which comes from my mouth does not return to me empty handed. . . ."

The emphatic *rā'âh,* "he saw it," of v. 27, confirms the essential nuance of v. 26 as providence. "Seeing" is of course the literal sense of providence. A classic passage connecting rain and divine providence is Deut. 11:10ff., where rain is declared a barometer of Israel's covenant loyalty. That Canaan, unlike Egypt, is a land dependent on rainfall, signifies that God *dôrēš 'ôtāh / tāmîd 'ênê YHWH . . . bāh,* "He cares for it (literally, inquires about it), his eyes are on it constantly." It is literally the special object of providence.

We can now understand how the plays on *'ôr,* "light," and *rā'â,* "seeing," that we noted in section one, prepare for the positive, providential nuance of section three. These terms connect the wisdom and creation themes of the poem. *Rā'â* is at first, in v. 24, a term implying divine omniscience (// *yabbîṭ*), but in v. 27, filtered by v. 26, it has become a term implying divine beneficence; all the while retaining its echoes of creation. Such is the poet's great art.

Now we can easily perceive how the theme of divine providence represents a kind of resolution of the negatives and positives underlying the poem. In structural terms, the basic oppositions man-God and ignorance-wisdom are "mediated" and resolved by providence, the wise ordering of the world by a good God for the benefit of his children. Thus, the poem ends on a note that seems to be pietistic, for what can man do but obey the wise laws of this good God? He must trust in him. If man cannot know more than this, he knows at least that this is so.

If the poem indeed implies such quietism, the poet has at least acted decisively to counter any deadening effect it might have by introducing a startlingly unorthodox overtone already in v. 13, and also involving the word *derek: lō' yāda' 'ĕnôš darkāh / wĕlō' timmāṣē' bĕ'ereṣ hahayyîm,* "man does not know the path to it / its path, nor can it be found in the land of the living." Surely an Israelite could not have heard such a statement without surprise if he or she was knowledgeable in wisdom traditions, for it seems to contradict some of the fondest platitudes of pietistic wisdom literature. The admonition to "walk in the path(s) of wisdom," to "follow her paths," are practically omnipresent. "Path" (*derek, nātîb, maʿăgāl, ʾōraḥ*) is almost a code term for piety.[75] Similarly, the command to "find" (*māṣāʾ*) or "acquire" (*qānâ*) wisdom is a commonplace of ordinary piety.[76] *Māṣāʾ*, "find," appears prominently in Job 28 not only in its explicit use in v. 13, but also as a pun in *môṣāʾ* of v. 1 and (emended) *tēṣēʾ* of v. 12. And *hayyîm*, "life," of vv. 13 and 21 is also familiar from wisdom contexts. He or she who finds wisdom finds life, its paths are paths of life, and so on.[77] Against this background one can appreciate the potential heresy or at least the shock value of a statement like v. 13.

Moreover, even the basic metaphor of the poem is rooted in a theme dear to pietistic, "practical" wisdom, the comparison of wisdom to precious stones—the very pattern of vv. 15–19. One can easily find the germ of the sentiment of Job 28, and much of its language, in a passage like Prov. 3:13–18:

ʾašrê ʾādām māṣāʾ ḥokmâ / wĕʾādām yāpîq tĕbûnâ
kî ṭôb saḥrāh missĕhar kāsep / ûmēhārûs tĕbûʾātāh
yĕqārāh hîʾ mippĕnînîm / wĕkol hăpāṣêkā lōʾ yišwû bāh . . .
dĕrākêhā darkê nōʿam / wĕkol nĕtîbōtêhā šālôm
ʿēṣ hayyîm hîʾ lammahăzîqîm bāh . . .

Happy the man who finds wisdom, and the man who obtains understanding;
For trade in her is better than trade in silver, and her income than gold;
She is more precious than rubies, none of your goods can compare to her . . .
Her ways are beautiful ways and all her paths peaceful;
She is a tree of life to those that hold on to her . . . [78]

These echoes of piety have a remarkable perceptual effect. When he or she hears v. 13, an Israelite reader may reasonably suspect, presumably to his or her horror, that the poet intends to deny the possibility of piety. His or her anxiety is not finally relieved until the providential overtones of the last couplet become evident; providence is unthinkable without piety, and both are aspects of creation's cosmic order. These unorthodox overtones serve to enliven the poem and, along with the wordplays discussed above, help to turn a seemingly banal message into something poetically interesting.

III

Plays on words and themes provide the poem with internal drama. Certainly striking devices, but I think they are also clues to a larger meaning. To determine what that might be, we must extend our examination beyond the boundaries of Job 28 to the wisdom tradition as a whole and, specifically, to the Book of Job.

Key to the understanding of Job 28 is the role played by nature in wisdom. Wisdom teachers were expected to make their arguments from study of the natural and human order, hence the famous absence of reference to Israel's covenantal and cultic traditions until the late period. Wisdom had no traffic with revelations aside from dreams.[79] Rather, it tried to elucidate the inner, hidden relationship between things by demonstrating that the laws of human behavior reflected cosmic order.[80] For this reason the scholarly distinctions between "practical" wisdom (*Lebensweisheit*) and "speculative" wisdom would have seemed deeply false to the ancients. The theme of wisdom as an intellectual tradition was the unity of order.[81]

Order and chaos are also themes of the Book of Job, a debate between wise men. Job's friends argue that since cosmic order is immutable, his sufferings must result from sin. From effect, they deduce a cause. Job, however, knows he is innocent. The effect therefore has no cause. This violates moral and, in the view of wisdom, natural order, threatening cosmic chaos.[82] In his anguish, which is intellectual as well as emotional, Job even portrays God as a kind of anti-God, a vicious demon.[83]

But the divine speeches of chapters 38ff. remove the threat of chaos. God himself appears to assert in a series of rhetorical questions that the world was created with a wisdom that cannot be discerned by wise men like Job and his friends. Moderns often find these speeches brutal because they seem to crush Job into insignificance. Such readers fail to understand, first, that encounters with the divine are, according to the universal testimony of those who have experienced them, overwhelming events, and second, that they are a sign of Job's victory. His "repentance" of 42:1–5 represents his vindication because his constant demand has been that God appear to justify himself. The friends have argued that no man can compel him to do so (22:4), yet Job has. Man has overcome God and wrested a reply from him. The duality of Job's final speech, a humble shrinking back of man before the numinous even as he defeats it, characterizes the highest art.

Moderns are often further disappointed because God does not seem to address himself directly to Job's complaint *hôdi'ēnî 'al mah tĕrîbēnî,* "tell me why you are contending with me!" (10:2). They expect a theodicy to contain logical arguments in the manner of a philosophical or theological treatise. They also dislike the resumption of the pious "folktale" of Job in chapter 42. They think it demeaning that Job be rewarded materially for his courage.

These modern reactions are ingenuous. The first fails to take into account that for the wisdom tradition any statement about the natural order has moral implications also. As perceptive commentators notice, the issue of the divine speeches is providence.[84] Such a point would not have to be told to the wise; to wisdom all statements of order imply benevolence. Both Job and his friends would understand this automatically.

The second reaction results from a failure to apprehend the ancient technique of making intellectual arguments through juxtaposition rather than through logical exposition.[85] Whether composed by the author of the dialogue or not, the resumed story of the pious Job is a brilliant device, for this "repentant" Job is far from the casuistic savant represented by his friends, and equally distant from the quietist who merely trusts God out of simplicity or inertia. He is a man who has challenged God and won. His piety rests on a new ground which, because of the unity of natural and moral order, represents also a new reaction to nature.

What is this new ground of piety? Traditional wisdom, represented by Job's friends, viewed nature as a source of analogies or models for human behavior. The goal was for man to act in harmony with cosmic order. "Fear of God" and "knowledge of God," both meaning "piety," rested on this ground. This order is wrecked for Job. Just as he sees the threat of universal chaos, so he is immune to ordinary fear of God (9:35; 13:15). This is what makes him so bold in his challenge. God has done his worst to him; even death would be a relief, as he often says.

The poet could not make this point more clearly: Job's submission results not from fear but from awe, a closely related though quite distinct emotion. Awe is a complex, sophisticated reaction to the terrible, standing in relationship to fear more or less as sublime majesty does to naked power. It must clearly be separated from that flattery of divinity that fills ancient hymns, and even from the fear of God. Fear involves primarily an awareness of self and of a threat of extinction. Awe adds to it a contradictory reaction, loss of self-awareness through direct experience of sublimity. Here is the second reason for Job's submission: it rests not in confident assumptions about universal order, like the piety of the old wisdom, but in the experience of revelation. The ground of the new wisdom's piety is to be a new cause and effect, revelation and awe.

One can trace the development of this essential message by examining the changing contexts surrounding the key term *niplā'ôt,* "wonders." Traditionally, *niplā'ôt* referred either to God's miraculous rescues of Israel through history (the crossing of the Red Sea, the conquest of Canaan, etc.),[86] or to his great acts of creation, the wonders of nature.[87] Wisdom, of course, could appeal only to the latter, for its proper sphere was outside both history and revelation.

Niplā'ôt occurs three times in the main dialogue of Job[88]—in Eliphaz's first speech, 5:9; in Job's first direct indictment of God, 9:10; and in his "repentance," 42:3. Eliphaz's speech (5:8–27) is a cunning example of wisdom casuistry. Eliphaz argues from the axiom of cosmic order in nature to moral order to Job's specific case, employing several clever rhetorical devices in the process. God, he says, does wondrous things (*niplā'ôt*) without number, for example, he provides rain—the model of providence. He makes the low high (*lāśûm šĕpālîm lĕmārôm*)—a reference to mountain building—and provides help for the suffering (*wĕgōdĕrîm śāgĕbû yešaʿ*)—a shift to the divine management of the moral order. God punishes the wicked, here pointedly called the "wise"—a barb at Job?—and rescues the poor man (*'ebyôn*). The implications for Job are thus: his fancied wisdom has led him astray; it is the root of his "wickedness." Yet Eliphaz's reasoning is subtle. Job is also the oppressed "poor man," crushed by his own sin. If one repents, divine punishment really is no more than "correction," so "happy the man whom God corrects." Repentance will automatically result in reward and prosperity. This, Eliphaz says, is what "we have fathomed (*ḥăqarnûhā*), it is true (*ken hî'*)." Eliphaz's lively sophistry represents the case of traditional wisdom, from the "wonders" of created order in general to specific cases, inexorable cause and effect.

Job's bitter speech turns these arguments against God. He cites, probably sarcastically, the same words used by Eliphaz, *'ôśeh niplā'ôt 'ad 'ên mispār,* "(God) does wonders without number" (9:10 = 5:9). Now, they signify not providence but raw, brutal power.[89] God is so strong no one dares call him to account. The chief device here is the famous *double-entendre* on the "forensic" and "moral" meanings of *ṣaddîq* and *rāšā',* "innocent-guilty" and "righteous-wicked," respectively. Even if man could call God into court, he could never win his case. God would force his accuser's own mouth to declare him guilty (*rāšā'*)—even if he were innocent (*ṣaddîq*). So a righteous man (*ṣaddîq*) cannot win against God, who, by implication, is wicked (*rāšā'*). There could be no more damning statement of moral chaos. The cosmos rests on force, not on right. *Niplā'ôt* (9:10) is part of this radical accusation.

In 42:1–5, Job "repents" thus: "I have spoken—but did not comprehend—things too wonderful for me (*niplā'ôt mimmennî*) that I did not know." These words have long been considered problematic, for Job seems to do no more than finally espouse the position tediously reiterated by the friends that man cannot know the ways of God.[90] Yet it is the friends whom God rebukes, declaring that they have not spoken the truth (*nĕkônâ*) about him like Job!

In fact, the very similarity between Job's argument and his friends' serves as the poet's conclusive device highlighting the essential difference between the friends and Job. It acts as a kind of poetic "distinctive feature." The friends have argued as wise men by analogy and inference, from cause to effect and vice versa. Job's "repentance" results not from their argumentation, but from the direct experience of revelation. The content of the divine speeches is not crucial, although the device is brilliant—the rhetorical questions both reveal and conceal the wonders of nature from Job.[91] Rather, the circumstance dominates. Through Job's accusations, God has been compelled to reveal himself.

Thus ironies are those of the greatest art. Job alone has spoken the truth. He has maintained the world is out of kilter and that nothing less than a divine explanation will be acceptable. This challenge to God paradoxically threatens his reputation while defending his honor. Behind the fervent pieties of the friends, however, lies a true threat to God's freedom. Their view of order is so mechanistic that God himself is constrained by it. Even he is bound by natural law, so to speak. Job, on the other hand, forces God to break his own rules, and in context, this serves to assert his supremacy. Fittingly, God's response is correspondingly ironic. It functions both to rebuke Job's impudent challenge and to signal the ultimate divine favor that Job could never have achieved had he remained pious like the wise. We have here proper divine compensation for the cruelty of the "test."

Job is struck dumb with awe, not fear.[92] His new piety results from revelation, not deduction. If this is the primary message in Job, it represents a partial assimilation by wisdom of covenant religion's experiential basis. The use of a primary theophany theme (the "whirlwind") clearly signals this as the author's intention.

Yet although the poem remains firmly in the wisdom tradition of seeking answers from nature rather than history, it also attacks the position of standard wisdom. Its exponents are the friends, and they are shown to be fools. Surely, this is the primary effect of the "test." Readers know the casuistic arguments of the friends are totally false; Job has not sinned. Nothing could make the poet's indictment of old wisdom clearer. Its dogma that the moral order is so directly related to nature as to be part of it, implicitly binding even God, simply is wrong. There can be no "science" of piety. Wise men thus turn out to be a gaggle of gurus learnedly discoursing on the equine nature of the camel.

We must understand chapter 28 in the context of this polemic against wisdom's traditional view of nature's role in piety. The poem's true topic concerns the relationship among man, nature, and God. Section one presents man as lord of creation; man reigns supreme in nature by virtue of his almost divine wisdom (the search after jewels metaphorically manifests the attainment of knowledge). But section two thrusts man back into ignorant nature, and section three contrasts both with the wisdom of God as creator. The poem aims to assert the duality of man's position. Man dominates over nature, he stands closer in wisdom to God than any other creation, but still he can offer no challenge to God so far as obtaining the ultimate knowledge of natural order is concerned.

Psalm 8 shares this duality. It translates "When I see your heavens, the work of your fingers, the moon and the stars you established—What is man that you should even mention him, a human that you should even consider him? Yet you have made him little less than divine (*mĕʿaṭ mēʾĕlōhîm*) and crowned him with glory and majesty!" The sense of awe in this statement recalls that of Job. At best, it is implicit in chapter 28. The main point appears negative; the heaped-up negative statements of section two and, on the allusive level, the plays on words and themes discussed above, make it inescapable. Now, these verbal and thematic flourishes may be understood not merely as enlivening devices but as central elements in the author's strategy. The denial by all parts of nature that they know where wisdom is to be found directs itself against traditional wisdom's claim that one can draw lessons from natural and human order. Thus, the allusive implication of v. 13 that "man cannot know the path of wisdom" serves as no mere rhetorical turn; it manifests the real intention of the poem. Any wise Israelite would recognize it as an explicit denial of wisdom's iron casuistries. And the related play on *derek*'s meaning also plays a key role. As "nature," rather than just "path," it cuts to the heart of wisdom's claims; "man cannot know the nature of wisdom."[93]

Probably, chapter 28 is intended as a partner to the divine speeches, that is, it operates as an integral part of the book. For a long time, scholars have considered its relationship to the speeches a sign of its unoriginality, for it seems to anticipate so much of their purport as to make them almost superfluous, a glorious anticlimax. But once again, the very similarity isolates the crucial differences. Chapter 28, as we noted, lacks the message of awe and revelation which we posited as the essential element of Job's "repentance." These elements come from the divine speeches alone, and could hardly appear in chapter 28. So chapter 28 ought rather to be viewed as a preparation for the book's climax. It is a meditation far removed in tone from the passionate arguments of the dialogue. Whether originally placed in Job's mouth or not, it represents the author's comment on the friend's position as exponents of traditional wisdom's piety of confident order.[94]

Yet this negative message accounts for only half of man's duality, his ignorance. His wisdom still reigns supreme in nature provided—and this is also central to the poem—it understands itself as created by God's overwhelming wisdom. In this sense, Job 28 also serves to prepare for the message of awe in the divine speeches.

If we can reasonably interpret Job 28 thus, then v. 28 can form no part of the passage. To be sure, piety is the poet's ultimate point, but it must not appear until the divine speeches have laid the necessary ground of awe. Even then, it will be conveyed through subtle juxtaposition, the resumption of the pious "folk tale." Here it is premature, for Job 28 is only a harbinger of the book's climactic meaning.

Verse 28 is superfluous even if one views chapter 28 as an independent poem inserted by an editor. Literarily, it is misplaced, for we have seen from internal analysis of the poem that the poet makes his meanings by metaphor and allusion, associations and perceptions. Verse 28 is altogether too bold and bland a statement of traditional piety for such a subtly orchestrated context. To these arguments of content one may add those of form. As noted above, v. 27 makes a strong conclusion to the poem not only in its effective sequence of four verbs (cf. also 3:26), but also in its cunning resumption of key terms (*rā'āh* echoes the *Leitwort* of vv. 9–11, etc., and final *ḥăqārāh* returns to *ḥôqēr* of v. 3). Not that v. 28 is utterly unjustifiable, of course. One may allow that a poet who has displayed the greatest art may suddenly stumble with both feet. I prefer to see in v. 28 the addition not, as Duhm suggested, of a "foolish reader," but, on the contrary, of a wise man who understood all too well the negative import of the chapter for his philosophy and consequently sought to neutralize it by an echo of 1:1.[95]

Verses 15–19 we can more easily defend, for they construct a clever irony;[96]

even if man were to possess all the riches he mines in section one, they would be useless in buying wisdom. This may represent the twisting of the common theme in traditional wisdom literature that the value of wisdom is above jewels (cf. Prov. 3:13ff. and the other passages cited above). Elsewhere, the point is that one would not exchange wisdom for wealth; here, it is that one literally cannot, for wisdom is absolutely unattainable. This twist worthily manifests the poet's subtlety.

Still, another stronger literary argument refutes this last. The poem's theme concerns man's relationship to nature and to God. Verses 15–19 simply comprise a digression from this main topic, separating as they do the listing of the parts in nature ignorant of wisdom's place. They serve to distract—a mortal poetic sin. Even as clever irony they weaken the primary argument of what is otherwise a tightly constructed poem.[97]

Here, too, form buttresses content, for vv. 15–19 make up the very physical heart of the poem, its center. They are artfully framed by vv. 12–14 and 20–22. Poetically, they fill a highly emphatic position. Yet they are secondary to the main line of poetic logic. Without them, section two itself properly fills this central position. Perhaps, then, some reader found the basic metaphor of the poem distracting and thoughtlessly inserted a beloved traditional theme—"foolish reader" is here appropriate—or perhaps the same editor who cunningly added v. 28 was again at work, hoping to distract other readers from the poem's unorthodox message.

IV

That a feeling of swelling awe at the divine wisdom manifest in nature can overcome the pain of suffering is a proposition not for the masses but for the chosen few. Like Stoicism and other philosophical religions it is for the wise, not Everyman—but then Job is hardly Everyman! And not everyone can receive a divine revelation. Ordinarily mortals—even wise men—presumably must move themselves to awe by mere contemplation of nature's wonders. This would seem preeminently a doctrine for scientists. Indeed, we must remember that wisdom was a kind of proto-science. Job's author has presented an "answer" to suffering intrinsically no more or less convincing than any other, but it is at least consonant with wisdom's focus on nature rather than history and—his essential contribution—congruent with Israel's insistence that piety be rooted in the freedom and fullness of divine revelation (though a complete vision might be granted only to those who have suffered as much as Job, that is, no one).[98] Job's unique reward is equivalent to his extreme pain. In this respect, he is as singular among wise men as Moses is among the prophets; there exists none like him on earth (1:8).

Qoheleth presents a contrasting answer, also rooted in wisdom. It perhaps represents a direct continuation of old wisdom's attempt to link piety directly to observation of natural order. Qoheleth studied everything under the sun to find a unifying principle and found only this: all is nothingness. Wisdom is, after all, too far, too deep to find (7:23ff.). Thus, since God has made piety part of the natural order (3:14), it is best for man to be conventionally pious, but let him not overdo it (7:16)! This reasonable, gentle cynicism stands at the opposite pole from Job's passion.[99]

Finally, however, neither Job's nor Qoheleth's answer won. Rather, wisdom itself was absorbed by and identified with covenant, in the form of Torah. We can observe the earlier stages of this development in Deut. 4:6 and Proverbs 1—9; its termination may be witnessed in Psalm 119 and Ben Sirach. One major result from this transition was that nature itself was ousted from wisdom subsumed by law: *'Ābîṭâ niplā'ôt mittôrātekâ*, "I espy wonders from thy law!" (Ps. 119:18; cf. v. 27). Nature became anathema, a forbidden mystery, as in Sir. 3:21–22:

> Do not inquire into what is too wonderful for you, (*bĕmuplā mimmĕkā*)
> Or delve into what is hidden from you.
> Consider only what you are allowed;
> You have no truck with secret things.[100]

Cosmic wisdom herself testifies that her "place" is now in Israel as its Torah:

> Then the creator of all things commanded me;
> He said, "Let your dwelling place be in Jacob,
> Make your inheritance in Israel." (Sir. 24:8)[101]

Eventually even wonder at the beauty of a tree would be excoriated—if it distracted one from Torah.

Yet awe itself did not disappear, for the few, though it turned from wisdom to revelation and from creation to the creator to find its final resting place in the mystical vision of the divine Presence.[102] The ecstasy of the mystics is a strange but undoubted heir to the wonder that moved Job to silence.

NOTES

1. Chapter 28 is assigned to Job and is supposed to be a continuation of his speech in chap. 27. There he says he will maintain his innocence, giving as a reason the unhappy fate of the wicked (vv. 7ff.), the negative argument for piety. Chapter 28, which, like 27:1, begins with *kî*, "because," starts the positive argument. The wealth of the wicked had played a prominent role in chap. 27 (cf. vv. 16–19). Job now says, "Why should I give up my faith? Wisdom is above all earthly gain!" Such is the interpretation of Jewish tradition (cf. Rashi). It has had a modern defender (E. Konig), but is a tortured response at best. Chapters 27 and 28 are only tenuously connected, and scholars commonly recognize that the third cycle of the dialogue is disarranged. Both 27 and 29 begin with formulae which seem to underscore their discontinuity with what preceded. The Elihu speeches are secondary. Job's final speech, 29—31, likewise enjoys no clear role. On my suggestion for the arrangement of the book, see n. 94. Here, it suffices to note that after 27:7 there are no impious words in the book. Probably this confusion in the book's

core arises from an attempt by later editors to soften or negate the unorthodox tone of the original dialogue. Certainly, by later Jewish (and Christian) tradition, Job had become pious again. Once more we see the proverbial paragon of long-suffering patience, the original patient Job of the folk tale. The radical hero of the dialogue, accusing God of the worst crimes, is domesticated and denatured.

Usually, chap. 28 is considered unoriginal to Job. The main reasons for this are literary. First, its reflective tone differs sharply from the passionate, *ad hominem* arguments of the dialogue, of which it shows no awareness. Second, its message agrees so much with that of chaps. 38ff. that it removes all force from the divine speeches, making them anticlimactic. The former objection may be countered by viewing chap. 28 as a kind of pause, a meditation (cf. Dhorme, *Job,* p. li; Gordis, *Job* [full references appear in the Bibliography below]). But the second objection is more serious, for it is strange to make God into an afterthought. On this problem, see the discussion below.

Even if independent, Job 28 must have been composed by the author of Job or by a close imitator, for many of 28's phrases recall those elsewhere in Job (cf. on v. 3b, 11:7; 26:10; on vv. 10–11, 12:22; on 10b also 9:5; on 11b, 11:6). Many have noted the especially close link to chap. 38—so, the use of *māqôm* (28:1, 12, 23; cf. 38:12, 19); the alternation of the prepositions *bě* and *lě* plus infinitive construct (28:25–26; cf. 38:7, 9, 13, 26–28); 28:11 and 38:16; the use of *môṣā'* in 28:1 and 38:27; the parallelism of *ḥokmâ-bînâ* in 28:12, 20, 28, and 38:36; the use of *spr* in a rather strange way in 28:27 and 38:37; the conjunction of *yṣq* and *'pr* in 28:2 and 38:38; most importantly, the identity between 28:26b and 38:25b. At the end of this study we shall have to return to the question of the relationship of 28 to the rest of the poem and particularly to chaps. 38ff. For the present, it will be treated as an independent poem.

2. Gedichte sind gemalte Fensterscheiben!
Sieht man vom Markt in die Kirche hinein,
So ist alles dunkel und düster;
Und so sieht's auch der Herr Philister . . .
Kommt aber nur einmal herein,
Begrüsst die heilige Kapelle!
Da ists's auf einmal farbig helle,
Geschicht' und Zierart glänzt im Schnelle . . .

3. On the approach, see my "Through Windows and Mirrors into the Bible: History, Literature and Language in the Study of Text" in *A Sense of Text: The Art of Language in the Study of Biblical Literature,* Supp. to *JQR* (Winona Lake, Ind.: Eisenbrauns, 1983).

4. *Ki* is asseverative. I have translated it as "now," a term which implies a more limited degree of assertion than "surely" or "certainly." It presupposes no necessary link to chap. 27.

5. M. Pope's "smelter," based on a hypothetical root **yṣ'* < *w*ḍ',* "be clean," is possible but unnecessary. In 23:10b we find a similar connection between refining metals and *yṣ',* and the semantic extension from "to extract" or the like seems natural (cf. Jer. 15:19). *Môṣā'* is employed in Job 28 as in 1 Kings 10:26; 2 Kings 2:21; and Job 38:27.

6. The chiastic structure of this and the following verse indicates that *yāzōqqû* probably should be taken with *zāhāb* as a relative clause rather than with *māqôm,* as "a place where they refine gold." The site where metals are refined may, but need not be, the site of the mine. In any case, the poet is interested in the "place" not the act of refining, which is irrelevant to the context.

7. This verse recalls Deut. 8:9cd. Here, our main problem lies in *yāṣûq.* As it stands *yāṣûq* may be either a passive participle of the *qal* of the root *ysq,* or a *qal* imperfect of a

root *ṣwq* (there is no reason to emend to *yiṣṣōq* or old *qal* passive *yūṣaq*). *Ysq* occurs in Job 41:15–16 (three times! cf. 38:38); *ṣwq* occurs only in Job 29:6. My rendering follows 41:15–16, with reservations. *Eben* is masculine only here and in Qoh. 10:9, whose evidence is, however, suspect, since gender is indicated only by a resumptive pronominal suffix (*bāhem;* cf. Ges. 135o). The other passage usually cited, 1 Sam. 17:40, proves nothing, because masculine *ḥămiššâ* and *'ōtām* refer to *ḥălluqê,* not *'ăbānîm.*

8. The subject of the verse is certainly man. Although, as R. Gordis notes, a stated subject for the verb is not essential, it is desirable. *'Ĕnôš* is perhaps the best term, since it occurs in v. 4 and, especially, in v. 13, part of what we shall term below the "nuclear framework" of the poem. Its loss is also easily explained as vertical haplography from *'ĕnôš* of v. 4 and, partially, from *nĕḥûšâ* of v. 2. So *'ĕnôš śām qēṣ laḥōšek* or, better, *qēṣ śām 'ĕnôš laḥōšek,* seem possible reconstructions, although it is not necessary to raise them to the level of definite emendations. In any case, *'ĕnôš* in v. 3a is far preferable to the common emendation of *hû'* in 3b to *hā'ādām.* The relationship between hypothetical *'ĕnôš* and *hū',* then, partially parallels that between *'ĕlōhîm* and *hū'* in v. 23—also, as we shall see, part of the poem's "nuclear framework." Alternatively, one may simply take *śām* as indefinite (cf. Ges. 116t if *śām* is a participle, 144d if it is a perfect).

9. The verse manifests a notorious crux. The versions offer no help because they clearly had their own difficulties. Commentators have produced a zoo of emendations, none of which, in my opinion, rests on more than the merest speculation. I shall cite only the most popular, H. Graetz's *pāraṣ nĕhālîm 'am gēr,* "a foreign people breaks open shafts" (a supposed reference to the use of slave labor, often war captives, in mines). I shall limit my comments to what seems germane to this study.

The common translation of *naḥal* here as "shaft, tunnel" is a guess (but note that Akk. *naḫlu/naḫallu* is glossed by Sumerian words that mean "cave," "mine" [hole in the ground]; cf. *CAD,* 125). *Gār* as "inhabitant" is unusual but possible if one takes it as a *qal* participle of *gwr;* cf. *šāb* in Zech. 7:14, *wĕhā'āreṣ nĕšammâ . . . mē'ōbēr ûmiššāb,* "the land is desolate . . . (devoid of) travelers (lit.: 'passers by and returner')"; cf. also 9:8. *Hanniškaḥîm minnî regel,* "forgotten by the foot-travelers" (synecdoche), conforms to biblical idiom (cf. Ps. 31:1, *niškaḥtî . . . millēb;* Deut. 31:21, *tiššākaḥ mippî;* etc.). *Dallû* as "hang down, dangle," a common rendering, is problematic. As it stands the verb is *qal* perfect of *dll* (Ges. 67bb). The root means "to be poor, lowly." Evidence for "hang down, suspend" is weak—a supposed Arabic cognate, *daldala,* "to dangle, vacillate"; and several dubious Hebrew words, of which the best may be *dalyû,* of Prov. 26:7. *Dallû* of Isa. 38:14 is quite obscure and of little help. In later Hebrew, *dal min* means "to be poor in," as in *dallû min hammiṣwôt,* "they were poor in good deeds." Besides, hanging would presumably be done in vertical shafts, while the ancients seem to have had mainly horizontal ones (cf. R. J. Forbes, *Ancient Technology,* 7:115ff.). Vertical shafts were known, however (de Jesus, *Development of Prehistoric Mining,* 101). Still, the general sense of the verse seems to emerge as follows (I do not venture to call this a translation): "They have broken through (or spread out into) wadies far from habitation, they have wandered through (those) forgotten by travelers and poor in men." This involves the change of *naḥal* to plural or *niškāḥîm* to singular, both explainable as dittography. The point is that the region of mines is an uninhabited, untraveled desert (on this, see the discussion below). Note that *naḥal* is also used of the underworld (cf. 21:33; 2 Sam. 22:5).

10. The relationship of vv. 5–6 to v. 4 is obscure, probably owing to the corruption of the latter verse. As they stand, they may be taken as parallel to the structure of vv. 7–8, a term in *casus pendens* (*'ereṣ*) on which the rest of the clauses, with their resumptive suffixes, depend. But see the following note. *Leḥem* here surely denotes "bread, food"; *lĕḥûm,* Job 20:23, is obscure, but see Gordis. *Taḥtehâ* may, of course, mean "nethermost parts," in which case *nehpāk* may be emended to *nehĕpākîm* (haplography). The

above translation reflects another common meaning of *taḥat*, "in its place, where it stood" (cf. Exod. 16:29; Lev. 13:23, Josh. 5:8; 6:20; Zech. 12:6; etc.). Note also the Vulgate's *in loco suo*. *Kĕmô* of 5b is literally "as by fire." On this pregnant use of *kĕ*, see Ges. 118w (cf. Isa. 1:25, *kĕbōr*—but before *beth*!). The Vulgates *igni* seems to suggest *bĕmô*.

11. The feminine suffix of *'ăbānêhā* returns to *'ereṣ*, while the masculine suffix of *lô* depends on *māqôm*. Perhaps the error is orthographic. The feminine suffix, spelled *lh* = *lāh*, may have been mistaken for the masculine, in the older spelling also *lh* = lô, and then at some time erroneously normalized as *lw*. The most likely cause, I think, is confusion in regard to the syntactic position of *mĕqôm sappîr*. Perhaps it was first analyzed as simple construct ("a place of lapis"). The suffix of *'ăbānêhā* then returns to *'ereṣ*, as expected ("a land, its stones are a place [= source] of lapis"). Then v. 6a was analyzed as a relative clause, since *māqôm* is often in construct with a following relative (cf. Gordis), i.e.: "a place whose stones are lapis and which has gold dust." The suffix of the preposition, so remote from *'ereṣ*, succumbed to this second analysis and was attracted to *mĕqôm*. In many languages people have difficulty with relative clauses. In any case, the verse should not be emended. Gordis notes that *māqôm* seems to be feminine in Job 20:9 and 2 Sam. 17:12 (*kethib*). He even posits simple confusion of suffixes. The least satisfactory suggestion is that *lô* refers to *sappîr*, "lapis, which has gold dust," in a supposed reference to pyrites in lapis. While the image of a land so rich even its lapis has gold is certainly striking, it seems decidedly odd.

12. *Bĕnê šaḥaṣ* occurs elsewhere only in the discussion of Leviathan which, in 41:34, is called *melek bĕnê šaḥaṣ*. Usually, scholars translate this as "proud beasts" (Pope: "proud beings"). LXX and the Vulgate guess "vagabonds, hucksters"; the Peshitta simplifies to "beasts"; so also the Targum, which in one version has "lion," paralleling *šaḥal*'s normal sense, and in another, "men." Mowinckel argues from his interpretation of *šaḥal* (see n. 14) and from the context of 41:34 that *bĕnê šaḥaṣ* refers to some sort of mythological reptilian creatures, like Leviathan, their "king."

13. *Drk* in Hebrew may show the same range of meaning as its Akkadian semantic equivalent *kabāsu*, which in the G stem means "tread" and in the D and Š stems "tread down" or the like. However, I find no biblical examples in which the *hiphil* does not have some possible causative nuance (Isa. 11:15 is no exception since God is the subject; Jer. 51:33 may be exceptional, although the text is uncertain). Possibly, *hidrîk* here has the Aramaic nuance "to trace, overtake." The latter may be the meaning in Jud. 20:43 (see Moore in the ICC in *Judges*; note also the *hiphil* of *rdp*)! Interestingly, Syriac *aph'el* means also "to find, apprehend, understand," a sense appropriate, perhaps as a pun, to Job 28. The parallel term, *'ādâ*, seems to be an "Aramaism."

14. On this rendering, see Mowinckel, "*šaḥal*." In the main, his case convinces; his attempt to relate all possible roots (*šḥl-nḥš-lḥš*, etc.) is forced. To the evidence cited by Mowinckel one may add the following:

a. Egyptian Arabic *siḥlīya*, "lizard."

b. Job 12:7. MT's *śîah lā'āreṣ* is commonly emended to *zōḥălê 'ereṣ*, (cf. Micah 7:17) because of the context, a listing of creatures of earth, sky, sea, and underworld (*'ereṣ*). *Šaḥal(ê) 'ereṣ* would require only a vocalic emendation. *Šḥl* and *zḥl* may be related roots.

c. Note *derek nāḥāš 'ălê ṣûr* (Prov. 30:18), a collocation of themes similar to Job 28:7–8.

d. Later Hebrew *šāḥal*, "move in a hollow space," *hišḥîl*, "pass through a hollow space" (M. Jastrow). It is used for looping rope, threading needles, and tracing one's way through caves, and sounds most serpentine (cf. Akk. *saḫālu*, "durchbohren" [*AHw*]).

e. Note also the Akkadian *šahan* (Ass. *saḫan*) as a divine name according to the equivalence of [d]MUS—*Šaḫan,* the snake god; see H. Wohl, "Niraḫ or Šaḫan," *JANES* 5 (1973): 442–43.

f. The targumic translation of Job 28:8b, *wĕlā' sĕṭā' 'ălôhî ḥiwyā',* "nor did a serpent twist over it." Note also Ug. *šḥlmmt*—"serpent of Death" or the like? See Clifford, *Cosmic Mountain,* 84.

15. *'Ādâ* occurs elsewhere only in Prov. 25:20, a difficult verse. The root is well attested in Aramaic; in the Targum it often translates Hebrew *'ābar.* Interestingly, this probable "Aramaism" is here translated *sĕṭā'* by the Targum.

16. The feminine plural of *ṣûr* is by no means impossible; many words take endings of both genders (cf., as Dhorme points out, *nĕhārôt* of 11a, another plural of which is *nĕhārîm*). Four of the five times *hallāmîš* occurs, parallels, or is in conjunction with *ṣûr,* so *baṣṣûrôt* may well mean, as translated here, "in the rocks."

However, Theodotion and the Peshitta read *bĕsûrôt,* "fortified places." This raises the possibility that *bĕsûrôt yĕ'ōrîm* may be a construct parallel to *mabbĕkê* (MT: *mibbĕkî*) *nĕhārôt* of 11a—the quatrain displays alternating parallelism. "Fortified places of the channels" may be correct, given the mythological battle motifs alluded to in this section. Even better would be *nĕṣûrôt,* "secret places." Jeremiah 33:3 reads *wa'aggîdâ llĕkā gĕdōlôt // ûbsūrôt lō' yĕda'tām,* "I shall tell you great things, 'fortified things' you don't know." The Targum translates by *nṭryn* and, as Kimhi noted, clearly read *nṣrwt.* Isaiah 48:6 is very similar and does read *ûnṣūrôt lō' yĕda'tām.* Jeremiah 4:16 probably manifests a reverse case. MT read *nṣrym,* but the Targum translates with a form of *qṭp,* showing, as Kimhi again noted, that it read *bṣrym.* These may be either simple textual errors (*beth-nun* similarity) or represent a semantic convergence of the root meanings of *nṣr,* "guarded" → "secret" :: *bṣr,* "fortified" → "*secret.*"

A slight emendation in Job 28:10, either vocalic to *bĕṣûrôt* or consonantal to *nĕṣûrôt,* yields "fortified, secret places of the channels." This meaning fits the context, for it could refer to the hidden, inaccessible places under the earth which miners penetrate, to subterranean channels viewed, in terms of the mythologically rooted imagery, as strongholds of the sea monster defeated by the regnant deity. The link to *ḥallāmîš* would then operate as a pun, and the grammatical parallelism to *mabbĕkê nĕhārôt* would be striking. But perhaps the main attraction of this emendation is that it offers a parallel to the Ugaritic passage Keret C vi (*CTA,* 16), (albeit not in an underworld context): *bt krt bu tbu / bkt tgly wtbu / nṣrt tbu pnm.* Pope translated as follows (*El,* 16) "Keret's house she enters / *bkt* she penetrates and enters / the secret chamber she enters within." For his rendering of *nṣrt* as "secret chamber," he cited only *nĕṣûrîm* of Isa. 65:4, parallel to *qĕbārîm,* "graves." Job 28:10, especially if one reads *nĕṣûrôt,* would provide a better parallel for the Ugaritic passage. Is *bkt* somehow connected with *mabbĕkê,* the parallel to a putative *b/nĕṣûrôt* in 28:11? It is also worth noting a possible pun of *bṣrt,* in whatever form, to *beṣer* "ore," or the like (cf. Job 22:24, *wĕšît 'al 'āpār bāṣer / ûbṣûr nĕḥālîm 'ôpîr*).

17. MT's *mibbĕkî* is now universally vocalized as *mabbĕkê* or something similar, since the term is known from Ugaritic (*mbk nhrm*) to refer to the sources of streams (cf. Pope, *Job*). Thus, the miner has reached the nethermost waters in his search for jewels. That the earth rested on water is well known from a host of poetic references (Pss. 104:6; 136:6; etc.) as well as from Ugaritic and Mesopotamian cosmologies. The proximity of Sheol to this underground water, plus the fact that it may itself have been surrounded by a river, led to the association of *tĕhôm* and other water terms with the underworld (cf. Job 26:5; Ps. 18:5 = 2 Sam. 22:5; Ps. 88:7; Ps. 71:20; Job 33:22 [reading *lmy mwtm,* "the waters of death," with Pope]; Job 2:6–7; and so on). Note also that in Rabbinic literature *tĕhôm* means the center of the earth; *qeber tĕhôm* is a "deep grave," etc. For Mesopotamian connections, see Tallqvist, *Sumerisch-Akkadische Namen,* 8, where *apsû* is associated with the underworld, although the two are distinct.

18. Most emend MT's *ḥibbēš,* "bind," to *ḥippēś,* "search out, investigate," following the LXX's *anekalypsen* (which properly means "uncover, reveal" and might better point to *ḥāśap*). I think emendation unnecessary if one recognizes a pun. B/p interchange is well attested—note especially Ezek. 27:20, a reverse example in a similar phonetic environment. It reads *bigdê ḥōpeš lĕrikbâ,* "saddle-cloths for riding." *Ḥōpeš* almost certainly is equivalent to *ḥōbeš,* "binding." Moreover, the pronunciation of *śin* and *shin* may still have been close enough to facilitate the pun. "Binding" is appropriate to the mythological motif of overcoming and restraining primeval waters. The intellectual nuance of *ḥibbēš* = *ḥippēś* fits the allusive wisdom level of the poem's meaning. Note that *biqqēa',* the parallel to *ḥibbēš* = *ḥippeś* may also be a pun (albeit an Aramaic one) on the roots containing *bq* meaning "investigate, search out," *bq'* and *bqr.*

19. The definite article of *hăḥokmâ* is generic, implying no hypostatization of wisdom. It simply corresponds to the definite article (also generic) of *lakkesep* and *lazzāhāb* in v. 1. These terms relate contrastively with *hăḥokmâ.* The definite article occurs with *ḥokmâ* in other passages (cf. 1 Kings 7:14; etc.) without any discernible special nuance.

20. With most commentators, I suspect MT's *timmāṣē'.* Verse 20 seems to repeat v. 12, so some follow the reading of Ken. 150 and read *tābō'* here also. Ken. 157's *tēṣē'* seems preferable. MT's *timmāṣē'* can be explained through v. 13's influence. A verb of motion does seem to be required with *mē'āyin* (but cf. Hosea 14:9, *mimmennî . . . nimṣā'*).

21. Reading *darkāh,* with the LXX. MT's *'erkāh* is not impossible. In Exod. 40:4, 23 *'ērek* seems, uniquely, to mean "arrangement," like *ma'ărākâ,* and not "value." There is a slim chance it means something like "position" here (*'erkô* of Job 41:4 is hardly illuminating). This possibility ("its abode"), accepted by Pope in later editions of *Job,* may perhaps be strengthened by the association—hardly parallelism—of *b'lt bhtm* and *b'l 'rkm* in a Ugaritic list (for *Ugaritica* V, Text 12:3–4, see M. Dahood, review of Maria Giulia Guzzo Amadasi's *Le incrizioni fenicie* in *Or.* 38 [1969]: 158–60, and "Hebrew-Ugaritic Lexicography VII," *Bib* 50 [1969]: 355). But the other texts cited by Dahood are inconclusive since *'rk,* a root with cultic associations in the Bible, may mean "arrangements" of a cultic rather than a spatial nature. The supposed biblical "parallelisms" of *bayit* and *'ārak* are spurious (i.e., 2 Sam. 23:5; Prov. 9:1–2; Ps. 23:5–6). In any case, *'ērek* does not parallel *bayit* in Job 28:13. Dahood's brand of reasoning would, I suppose, assign some meaning like "place" to *derek* itself in Job 28:23 (and 38:19) because of its (undoubted!) parallelism there to *māqôm.* And the latter fact offers prime evidence for the correctness of *derek* in Job 28:13. Context and literary form must speak louder than any other evidence here. Rather, *'ērek* probably results from the influence of the list of metals in vv. 15–19, in which *ya'arkennā* occurs twice.

22. For a good discussion of the precious materials in vv. 15–19, see G. Holscher. My own comments will be kept to a minimum. Usually, scholars emend MT's *sĕgôr* to *sāgûr* (1 Kings 6:20; 7:49; 10:21; etc.; cf. Akkadian *ḫurāṣu sagru*). "Bullion" follows Pope. On the chiastic arrangement of vv. 16–19, see A. Ceresko, *Job 29—31,* 152.

23. *Tĕsulleh* seems to have a cognate in ESA *sl',* "pay," *sl'm,* "tribute." Dhorme makes an attractive suggestion that it may be a denominative of *sal,* "basket," the latter being used as measurements of grain in barter trade. The form occurs only here, though *mĕsullā'îm* of Lam. 4:2 is certainly related.

24. Vocalizing plural *kĕlê* following Theodotion and the Targum.

25. Following L. Köhler's argument that *mešek* here and in Ps. 126:6 means "bag, bundle." Some such meaning seems assured for Akkadian *mašku,* even though *AHw*'s *m.* (*ḫurāṣi*) seems unattested (cf. *CAD, sub mašku,* 379).

26. We have no reason to emend MT's *tābō'* to make it conform to the verb of v. 12. *Tēṣē',* of the latter, was sufficient to take up the link to *môṣā'* of v. 1. Here the poet uses

the variation *tābō'*, thereby producing the idiomatic pair *yāṣā'-bô'*. In fact, *bô'* is the verb most commonly used with *mē'āyin*. The LXX's *timmāṣē'*, in both vv. 12 and 20, proves nothing. The other versions support the use of two verbs (the Vulgate is enabled to use the pleasant pun *invenitur* (v. 12)-*venit* (v. 20).

27. The initial *waw* is probably a vertical dittography from v. 20.

28. The versions generally rearranged the unusual phrase *taḥat kol haššāmayim* to a more normal *kol taḥat haššāmayim*, but 37:3 and 41:3 vouch for the idiom's genuineness.

29. The common emendation of *la'ăśôt* to *bā'ăśōtô* to conform to v. 26 is unnecessary. The preposition *lĕ* indicates purpose, as translated, or it may indicate merely continuance of the action of the previous verb. See, in a similar context, 5:9 and 11, also 38:7, 26, 27, where it seems to be used in the same sense as the *bĕ* which heads many clauses (cf. Ges. 114o).

30. On Pope's *ḥōq*, "groove" (parallel to *tĕ'ālâ*, "channel" in 38:25), see below.

31. The etymology of *ḥāzîz* (also 38:25b) is unclear. In Zech. 10:1, parallel as here to *māṭār*, it seems to mean simply "rainstorm."

32. *Piel sippĕrāh* is used here as in 38:37 and Ps. 22:18 in the sense of the *qal*, "number," i.e., "muster" or the like (cf. also Rabbinic Hebrew). J. Reider connects it with Aramaic *sbr*, perhaps another example of b/p interchange (cf. *ḥibbēš* of v. 11).

33. MT's *hĕkînāh* can be defended, but its association with at least two verbs of cognition suggests that *hĕbînāh*, the reading of five Ken MSS, is correct.

34. Note the similarity to Sir. 1:9. In fact, the reverse order might be more logical, i.e., first God "searched it out," then "comprehended it," then "mustered it," and finally "approved it," taking *rā'āh* in that sense as perhaps an echo of *wayyar' kî ṭôb*, Genesis 1.

35. Some see in v. 20 a refrain marking the commencement of a new section of vv. 20–27(28). More likely, it marks only the resumption of the main argument after the digression and, I think, insertion of vv. 15–19 (see n. 94). In this case v. 20 might be a secondary addition also. Its removal would "solve" a minor problem, the initial *waw* of *wĕne'elmâ* of v. 21, which would then be directly after v. 14 (see n. 27).

36. *Kesep-zāhāb* is the common order, but *barzel-nĕḥûšâ* (*nĕḥōšet*) and the reverse seem to be about evenly distributed.

37. Syntactic positions, in that *'eben yāṣûq*, "firm rock," forms a prepositional phrase with ellipsis of the preposition (cf., in the A line Ps. 89:6: *šāmayim*, "in the heavens" // *biqhal qĕdōšîm*, "in the assembly of the Holy Ones"). It may be a reversal of syntactic functions if one takes *yāṣûq* as predicate, "the rock pours out copper." The former possibility produces this striking double chiasm of ores and places: (*kî yeš*) *lakkesep môṣā'* / *ûmāqôm lazzāhāb* (*yazōqqû*) // *barzel mē'āpār* (*yuqqaḥ*) / *wĕ'eben* (*yāṣûq*) *nĕḥûšâ:* A B / B' A' // A" B" / B"' A"'. On chiasm in the verse, see Dahood, "Chiasmus in Job," Job 28:2.

38. As Dhorme points out, the structure in this respect is precisely that of 14:7ff., *ki yeš lā'ēṣ tiqwâ* . . . (v. 10) *wĕgeber yāmût wĕyeḥĕlaš*, "for there is hope for a tree . . . but man dies and utterly fails . . ."

39. Cf. Judges 18:2; 2 Sam. 10:3; 1 Chron. 19:3.

40. Note also the conjunction of *kol tiklâ* and *qēṣ* in Ps. 119:96: *lĕkol tiklâ rā'îtî qēṣ* // *rĕḥābâ miṣwātĕkā mĕ'ōd*. Surely the meaning relates to the image of Job 28:3, and may be translated as "I have seen the extremity of every end but your commandment is very wide." The sense is that God's law is more spacious than any conceivable geographical dimension; man may come to the limit of other things, but not of God's commandments, for they are very wide, i.e., the most spacious things of all.

41. Cf.the Targum, Rashi, etc., which took God as the actor in v. 3 and in most of

the poem. Among modern commentators M. Houtsma and N. H. Tur-Sinai follow the Rabbis' lead. Now tradition may interpret these verses as applying to God because it treats the Bible atomistically, but the scholars mentioned are forced to feats of tortured exegesis to fit their reading of these verses into that of the poem as a whole. Houtsma rips chap. 28 apart and reassembles it into a mosaic more pleasing to him. Tur-Sinai produces what one must term a fantastic midrash.

42. See esp. Tromp, *Primitive Conceptions of Death.*

43. See Tallqvist, *Sumerisch-Akkadische Namen,* 37, on *bīt epri,* "house of dust," and *bīt eklēti,* "house of darkness," as epithets of the underworld.

44. More likely is that both dimensions eventually become one, i.e., at the horizon. At the ends of the earth, beyond the mountains which support the sky, one may find the entrance to the netherworld. Consider Gilgamesh's journey beyond the Mushu mountains to find the underworld. There he finds trees whose boughs bear jewels (tablet 9, col. 5).

On the *Nachleben* of these motifs, see esp. I. Friedlander, *Die Chadirlegende und der Alexanderroman.* The useful indices (326ff.) give references to the important motifs—see, above all, those cited on pp. 331 n. 28, and 37 n. 1 for the Babylonian parallels. For similar references in legends on the source of the Nile, see Byington, "Hebrew Marginalia II," 205–7.

45. On ancient mining sites, see the commentaries of Holscher and Fohrer, which contain bibliographies on the topic; Forbes, *Ancient Technology,* esp. 126ff; Muhly, *Copper and Tin.*

46. See esp. Talmon, "The 'Desert Motif,'" 43–44, 51–52.

47. Note also that some of the terms used in Jer. 2:6, cited above, recall the underworld—not only *ṣalmāwet,* "thick gloom," but also *ṣiyyâ,* "dryness" (the underworld also in Mesopotamia is a place of thirst), and probably *šûḥâ,* related to *šaḥat,* "pit," with its synonyms *bôr,* etc., common underworld terms (cf. Pss. 16:10; 55:24; Job 33:24; etc.). On Akkadian *būru* and *šuttu,* see Tallqvist, *Sumerisch-Akkadische Namen,* 3, and, in general, Tromp, *Primitive Conceptions of Death.*

48. Note also that in Mesopotamia the underworld may be termed *ṣēru,* "steppe" (cf. Tallqvist, *Sumerisch-Akkadische Namen,* 17ff). On Ugaritic *šd,* see Clifford, *Cosmic Mountain,* 83.

49. Cf. Ps. 104:14, *lehosi lehem min ha'ares,* "to bring forth bread from the earth." Note the similar conjunction of motifs in Deut. 32:22.

50. Note here the similar complex of themes in Mesopotamia; the underworld may be termed a "ruin," "waste" (*ḫarbu, karmu, namūti*). See Tallqvist, *Sumerisch-Akkadische Namen,* 17, 22–23. The association of desert and underworld may have been reinforced in Israel by the Dead Sea region—hence its name! On the great heat of the Egyptian mines in Sinai, see *ANET,* 229.

51. J. A. Knudtzon, *Die El-Amarna Tafeln* (Aalen: Otto Zeller, 1964; reprint of 1915 ed.), 16:14; cf. Zech. 9:3; Job 22:24.

52. Clifford views this identification as secondary for no solid reason (p. 172 n. 94). Note that *'abnê 'ēš,* "stones of fire," in Ezek. 28:14, may somehow be connected with *'ēš* of Job 28:5b.

53. The Targum took Job 28:6 to refer to the Garden of Eden.

54. See esp. Enoch 24. In the extreme northwest Enoch is shown, beyond a range of seven fiery mountains, seven other hills of stone "magnificent and beautiful." The seventh of these, whose "summit is like the throne of God" (25:3), is covered with beautiful trees. It is clearly Paradise—the mountain of God. In 18:6ff. Enoch sees seven mountains, to the east of which lies the Garden of Eden. They are in a place which "burns day and night," and are made of colored and precious stones. The middle

mountain reaches to heaven "like the throne of God," and its summit is lapis lazuli ("sapphire"). Somehow the desert is part of this confusing mélange. In Enoch 8:1, Azazel teaches men to make weapons, and ornaments, and the art of working metals "and all kind of precious stones"; in 10:4ff. he is ordered to be bound and cast into darkness through an opening made in the desert. The (demythologized?) link between Azazel and the desert is of course found in Lev. 16:8, 10, 21.

55. See Pope, *El*, chap. 7. He identifies El's mountain with the *ḫuršānu*, the infernal mountain of the Mesopotamian underworld. But see Clifford, *Cosmic Mountain*, 23ff., 37ff., for justified criticism.

56. See Lewy, "Tabor," 385, for sources. Note also the ancient idea that mountains gave birth to metals, 384–85.

57. See Heidel, *Gilgamesh Epic*, 172.

58. See the hymn to the Enki temple, Falkenstein and von Soden, *Sumerische und Akkadische Hymnen*, 135ff.

59. See Clifford, *Cosmic Mountain*, 112.

60. See Pope, *El*, chap. 7. Clifford points out that there is no reason to think the *mpk nhrm* and *'pq thmtm* were underground (p. 50).

61. *Ḥallāmîš* may or may not be cognate with Akkadian *elmēšu* (*CAD* suggests rather *hašmal*). Intriguing also is a possible link to Akkadian *ḫulamīsu*/*ḫallamīšu*, "chameleon"(?), a term associated with *nēš qaqqari*, "lion of the earth." See Mowinckel, "*šaḥal*,", 98. Is there a pun in Job 28:9 on *hallāmîš*, "rock," and a hypothetical *hallāmîš*, *"reptilian"? After šaḥal* it is not impossible. Note also *šāmîr*, the Targum's translation for *hallāmîš* here. In later legend it is viewed as a worm capable of cutting the hardest rock, and considered one of the wonders of creation. The mythological complex deserves further study.

62. In Isa. 33:21 it seems to have lost all Nilotic connections; so also Dan. 12:5, 7, where *yĕ'ôr* seems to mean just "river, stream."

63. An "Aramaism," like *yĕqār* of 10b. *Hārîm* of 9b may be part of the chain of wordplays also.

64. Cf. Prov. 3:20; Micah 1:4; Job 9:4; Isa. 48:21; Ps. 114:8. On God's "bringing things to light," aside from Job 12:22, see Dan. 2:22, quite similar to the complex of themes here in Job 28.

65. Cf. Ps. 104:9; Job 38:8–11; Prov. 8:29; Jer. 5:22. *Ḥibbēš* itself does not occur, but note *tĕšabbĕḥēm*, of Ps. 89:10, and *mašbîah,*, of Ps. 65:8 (probably "restrain, still" or the like—metathesis?). On "netting" Sea, see Greenstein, "Snaring of Sea," 207, for a recent discussion of Tur-Sinai's suggestion in Job 26:13, as well as a treatment of the mythological motif. *Šbm*, Ug. "muzzle," may occur in Ps. 68:23; see Dahood, *Psalms II*. For a good treatment of the divine motifs in Job 28 in general, see Niccacci, "Giobbe 28," 42ff.

66. Is there an echo here of *apsu*, watery subterranean home of Ea, Mesopotamian God of wisdom?

67. Section two parallels section one roughly chiastically—so *tĕhôm* and *yam* of v. 14 // *yĕ'ōrîm* and *nĕhārôt* of vv. 10–11, *kol ḥay* and *'ôp* of v. 21 // *bĕnê šaḥas*, *šaḥal* and *'ayit*, *'ayyâ* of v. 7; *'abaddon*, *māwet* of v. 22 correspond to the underworld motif of v. 3 and perhaps even 4–5 (cf. *taḥtêhā* of v. 5, if taken as "nethermost parts"; even *'ereṣ* may mean "underworld" in certain contexts).

68. Note that *yam* of v. 14 may imply not depth, like *tĕhôm*, but horizontal extension. See Deut. 30:13 and esp. Job 11:8–9; Ps. 139:8–9.

69. Whatever its possible connection with Proverbs 8, here no hypostatization or even personification of a "metaphysical" wisdom is implied, *pace* Dhorme, *Commentary on Job*, 414. The use of the definite article does not mean we are dealing with a special form of wisdom. See n. 19.

70. The "figurative" or even "theological" meaning need not be limited to the plural.

71. It parallels *tĕʿālâ,* "channel," in 38:25, but is purely a pun also there, as it certainly is in Prov. 8:29 (cf. 27).

72. Probably, a similar play on the meanings of *derek* underlies Exod. 33:12–16 and 17–25, passages joined in such a way as to highlight certain parallelisms. (See *wahănīḥōtî lāk* of 33:14 and *wĕḥannōtî 'et 'ăšer 'aḥōn* of v. 19.) The effect is to isolate the similarity of Moses' request *hôdī ʿēnî nā' 'et dĕrākêkā,* "make known your ways (in the desert) to me!" (v. 13), and *har'ēnî nā' 'et kĕbōdêkā,* "show me your glory!" (v. 18), and to show the consequent correspondence between the divine answers *pānay yēlēkû* (v. 14), "my Presence will proceed," and *'anî 'aʿăbîr kol ṭûbî ʿal pānêkā,* "I shall let my 'goodness' pass before you" (v. 19). One senses that an editor has collocated a narrative of the wandering in the desert and a revelation to Moses with, to build puns, *dĕrākay* as "paths, roads," and "nature, character," or the like (equivalent to *tûb* here; cf. Rabbinic Hebrew *ṭîb,* "form, nature, character"). See N. Waldman, "God's Ways—a Comparative Note." That Ug. *drkt,* "dominion," or the like, has any relevance to Job 28 is to be doubted, whatever the situation may be in regard to Prov. 8:22 (see Albright, "Some Canaanite-Phoenician Sources," 7). *Derek* may, however, have a more specific connotation of "act(ivity) of creation," to judge from the occurrence of the phrase *rē'šît darkê 'ēl* in reference to *bĕhēmôt* in Job 40:19, and the phrase wisdom uses of herself in Prov. 8:22, *re'šît darkô.*

73. See also Job 36:27ff., and David's curse of Gilboa in 2 Sam. 2:21, "May no dew or rain fall upon you," i.e., may you be cursed by being cut off from the chief sign of divine favor.

74. This is the general sense of *špṭ* in the so-called Enthronement Psalms (cf. Ps. 96:13; 98:9).

75. Prov. 3:17; 4:11; 9:6; etc.

76. Prov. 2:5; 3:13; 4:5, 7; 8:17, 35; etc.

77. Prov. 2:19; 3:18; 6:23; etc. (26 times in Proverbs).

78. Prov. 2:4; 8:10–11; 17:3; 22:24; etc. See also 31:10.

79. Cf. Job 4:12ff.; 33:15–16. Note also 7:13–14.

80. See von Rad's classic discussion, *Old Testament Theology,* 1:418ff., esp. 424ff. Note also Elihu's statement in 35:11.

81. Literary evidence comes from the frequent conjunction of "cosmic" wisdom and piety (see Prov. 3:3–18 and 19–20; Psalms 19; 104, vv. 24 and 35; etc.; and perhaps even Psalm 139, which ends on a repellent but undoubtedly pietistic note). Proverbs 8 itself should probably be included in the list.

82. Such seems to be the sense of 18:4, which reads: "For your sake shall the earth be abandoned, the rock removed from its place?"

83. Von Rad, *Old Testament Theology,* 1:413.

84. Some even translate *ʿēṣâ* of 38:2 and 42:3 as "providence" (Pope, *Job*).

85. See von Rad's comments, *Old Testament Theology,* 1:409–10. I think he underestimates the logical coherence of the speeches in the dialogue.

86. Exod. 34:10; Job 3:5; Judges 6:13; Pss. 78:4, 11; 106:27, 22. This is by far the more common usage.

87. Prov. 30:18; Pss. 139:14 (cf. 6); 136:4; Job 5:9; 9:10; 37:5, 14; Ps. 107:24. Note that in Job 42:3 it provides a kind of pun, for *hippālē' min* means "to be too difficult for one." The wonders of nature are too difficult for Job to comprehend.

88. Excluding the Elihu passages.

89. Note the special violence of the acts of creation in 9:5–7.

90. An echo of ancient Near Eastern wisdom. Consider Ludlul, where we read, "Who knows the will of the gods in heaven? Who understands the plans of the

underworld gods? Where have mortals learned the way of a god?" (See Lambert, *Babylonian Wisdom Literature,* 40–41.) The friends basically represent traditional ancient wisdom.

91. The questions may go back to an old teaching device (see von Rad, *Old Testament Theology,* 1:425).

92. He places his hand over his mouth (*yādî śamtî lĕmô pî*). Silence is both a sign of powerlessness and of wonder. The negative sense of "putting one's hand over one's mouth" appears clearly in Micah 7:16 (// *yēbōšû*) and Job 21:5 (// *hēšammû*). But in 29:9 it seems to signify amazement (cf. Isa. 52:15). And in 31:27, if *tiššaq yādî lĕpî* means the same thing, it may indicate wonder, even awe. Hebrew has no proper term for "awe"—*tmh* is "astonishment"—but silence in such a context speaks for itself. Of course, one might like some specific indication of Job's emotions—a hymn of praise like Psalm 104, for instance—but only if one is the sort of reader who is annoyed with Shakespeare for not clearing up what *Hamlet* is all about, and who does not realize that part of the reason Job and *Hamlet* are supreme works of literature is precisely because their authors know how to keep silence.

93. Westermann also recognized the "radical, polemical thesis" of Job 28. See his *Structure of the Book of Job,* 137.

94. With trepidation I suggest the following schema of the book as a working hypothesis:

a. The prologue: chaps. 1—2. A pious "folk tale" either composed or cited by the author. Its essential information is that Job's suffering is a trial. As noted, this knowledge of the reader highlights the inanity of the friends' sophistries. At the same time the cruelty and unfairness of the test point up Job's accusations better than any other possible device.

b. The dialogue: chaps. 3—27. Somewhat disordered in its third cycle, but essentially composed of well-reasoned arguments, if we knew how to interpret them. Unfortunately, the language is so difficult, the text probably so corrupt in spots and, above all, the disputants so fond of irony and quoting each other's opinions sarcastically, that following it is itself a Jobian trial.

c. A meditation: chap. 28, the subject of this study. Probably it is the author's negative comment on the friends' position, while at the same time it prepares for chaps. 38ff.

d. Job's final speech: chaps. 29—31. A classic complaint, followed by a long oath.

e. The divine speeches: chaps. 38—41. This is the dramatic climax of the book, simultaneously a rebuke and vindication of Job, as discussed above.

f. Job's repentance: 42:1–5. The theological climax of the book, its essential meaning of awe at revelation of nature is achieved by context and by silence.

g. The resumption of the pious "folk tale": 42:6–17. Again, we have an example of meaning through juxtaposition and context, for Job's piety now rests on a new, highly untraditional ground. That the unwary may think he has merely returned to his former state (*šāb šĕbût,* v. 10) is the author's joke on them.

The tedious Elihu speeches are unworthy of such an author. A wise man was eaten by rage at the seeming inability of the friends to rebuke Job properly. His anger is directed quite as much at them as at Job. He has cleverly tried to co-opt the message of the book by ending on a note of awe. In 37:5 he refers to God's *niplā'ôt* (cf. also 37:14ff.). The result is, he hopes, that God will appear to come at Elihu's bidding! The embarrassing divine rebuke to the friends in 42:7 is also defanged, for Elihu has already lambasted them. God is not angry at what they said but at what they didn't say. No doubt the "truth" of Job is to be taken only as his "repentant" words of 42:1–5. This artless artfulness is at least instructive on how a later reader tries to distort a detested meaning.

95. To these reasons one may add the others usually cited: the key terms of the verse are clichés (Prov. 1:7; 9:10; Ps. 11:10; Qoh. 12:13; etc.), *'ădōnāy* is oddly used in Job; there is no definite article before *ḥokmâ*, which here may be significant (cf. Dhorme).

96. Though even if they are retained they must surely be shortened. Verse 19 especially, of which a seems to repeat 17a and b 16a, should certainly be stricken. The versions made a hash of the passage. On the other hand, if one removes the whole section, then one might also delete v. 20, which may have been added by the same inserter (see n. 35).

97. The essential circularity of these arguments is freely conceded, but with the observation that they do not exceed the degree of legitimate circularity required in all interpretation, and (in light of our scholarly knowledge of the imperfection of the biblical text) in biblical interpretation specifically.

98. The idea that Job is a non-Israelite book is baseless. Its language is peculiar in many respects, but should serve as a warning to those who underestimate the resources, especially in vocabulary, of biblical Hebrew. Job's noncultic content reflects the intellectual stance of wisdom literature.

99. Agur appears to be a pocket Qohelet (Prov. 30:1-6), although his questions sound very much like Job, too. This is the utter despair of a wise man.

100. Sir. 3:21–22, cited in Ḥagigah 13 a. Psalm 131:1 may reflect the same attitude.

101. So also in the later passages dealing with "cosmic wisdom," at least by implication (Sir. 1:1-10; 24; Wis. 6:12—9:18, esp. 7:15-22; Enoch 42 and Bar. 3:9—4:4). Note that Sirach's great nature hymn ends on such a note (43:33).

102. As well as passages in apocalyptic literature, especially the "natural science" themes in Enoch. These descend directly from wisdom's interest in nature, although it has become transmuted into something strange.

BIBLIOGRAPHY

Albright, W. F. "Some Canaanite-Phoenician Sources of Hebrew Wisdom." In *Wisdom in Israel and the Ancient Near East* (Rowley Festschrift). VTSup 3:1-15. Leiden: E. J. Brill, 1955.

Ball, C. J. *The Book of Job.* London: Oxford Univ. Press, 1922.

Byington, S. "Hebrew Marginalia II: Job 28." *JBL* 61 (1942): 205-7.

Ceresko, A. *Job 29—31 in the Light of Northwest Semitic.* Rome: Biblical Institute, 1980.

Clifford, R. J. *The Cosmic Mountain in Canaan and the Old Testament.* HSM 4. Cambridge: Harvard Univ. Press, 1972.

Dahood, M. "Chiasmus in Job: A Text-Critical and Philological Criterion." In *A Light Unto My Path* (Myers Festschrift). Ed. H. N. Bream et al., 119-30. Philadelphia: Temple Univ. Press, 1974.

———. *Psalms II.* AB 17. Garden City, N.Y.: Doubleday & Co., 1968.

de Jesus, P. *The Development of Prehistoric Mining and Metallurgy in Anatolia.* Oxford: B.A.R., 1980.

Dhorme, E. *A Commentary on the Book of Job.* Trans. H. Knight. Nashville: Thomas Nelson & Sons, 1984.

Falkenstein, A., and W. von Soden. *Sumerische und Akkadische Hymnen und Gebete.* Zurich-Stuttgart: Artemis, 1953.

Forbes, R. J. *Studies in Ancient Technology.* Vol. 7. Leiden: E. J. Brill, 1963.

Friedländer, I. *Die Chadirlegende und der Alexanderroman.* Leipzig: Teubner, 1913.

Gordis, R. *The Book of Job.* New York: Ktav, 1978.

Graetz, H. *Emendations in plerosque sacrae scripturae V. T. libros.* Breslau: Schlesische Buchdrückerei, 1892–94.
Greenstein, E. L. "The Snaring of Sea in the Baal Epic." *Maarav* 3/2 (October 1982): 195–216.
Heidel, A. *The Gilgamesh Epic and Old Testament Parallels.* 2d ed. Chicago: Univ. of Chicago Press, 1949; reprinted, 1963.
Holscher, G. *Das Buch Hiob.* 2d ed. Tübingen: J. C. B. Mohr (Paul Seibeck), 1952.
Houtsma, M. *Textkritische Studien zum Alten Testament I: Das Buch Hiob.* Leiden: E. J. Brill, 1925.
Jastrow, M. *A Dictionary of the Targumim, the Talmud Babli any Yerushalmi, and the Midrashic Literature.* 2 vols. New York: Pardes, 1956.
Köhler, L. "Hebräische Vokabeln II." *ZAW* 55 (1937): 161–62.
König, E. *Das Buch Hiob.* Gütersloh: Evangelischer Verlag, 1929.
Lambert, W. G. *Babylonian Wisdom Literature.* London: Oxford Univ. Press, 1960.
Lewy, J. "Tabor, Tibar, Atabyros." *HUCA* 23 (1950–51): 357–86.
Mowinckel, S. "*šaḥal.*" In *Hebrew and Semitic Studies. Presented to Godfrey Rolles Driver.* Ed. D. Winton Thomas and W. D. McHardy. London: Oxford Univ. Press, 1963).
Muhly, J. D. *Copper and Tin: The Distribution of Mineral Resources and the Nature of the Metals Trade in the Bronze Age.* Hamden, Conn.: Shoe String Press, 1976.
Niccacci, A. "Giobbe 28." *StBiFranc* 31 (1981): 29–58.
Pope, M. *El in the Ugaritic Texts.* Leiden: E. J. Brill, 1955.
______. *Job.* AB 15. 3d ed. Garden City, N.Y.: Doubleday & Co., 1973.
von Rad, G. *Old Testament Theology.* Vol. 1. Trans. D. M. G. Stalker. New York: Harper & Row, 1962.
Reider, J. "Etymological Studies in Biblical Hebrew." *VT* 2 (1952): 113–35.
Tallqvist, K. *Sumerisch-Akkadische Namen der Totenwelt.* StudOr 4. Helsingforsiae, 1934.
Talmon, S. "The 'Desert Motif' in the Bible and in Qumran Literature." In *Biblical Motifs.* Ed. A. Altmann. Cambridge: Harvard Univ. Press, 1966.
Tromp, N. J. *Primitive Conceptions of Death and the Netherworld in the Old Testament.* Rome: Pontifical Biblical Institute, 1969.
Tur-Sinai, N. H. *The Book of Job: A New Commentary.* Jerusalem: Kiryath Sopher, 1957.
Waldman, N. "God's Ways—a Comparative Note." *JQR* 70 (1979): 67–72.
Westermann, C. *The Structure of the Book of Job.* Trans. C. A. Muenchow. Philadelphia: Fortress Press, 1981.

8 ROBERT ALTER

STRUCTURES OF INTENSIFICATION IN BIBLICAL POETRY*

There is a certain affinity, let me suggest, between the formal properties of any given prosodic system or poetic genre and the kinds of meaning most readily expressed through that system or genre. I have, of course, triply hedged my bets in this formulation with the evasive "affinity," the qualifying "certain," and the limiting "most readily," but such caution is called for because original poets in most eras often devise ways, whether quietly or ostentatiously, to work successfully against the grain of inherited form. Nevertheless, given form does tend to invite a particular orientation in the poetic ordering of the world. The Shakespearian sonnet can lend itself to love poetry, reflections on life's transience, celebrations of the power of art, and a good deal else, but whatever the topic or mood, a writer using this form can scarcely avoid organizing his or her statement in a sequence of three equal and balanced blocks, usually with an implied progression from one to the next, and concluding in a pithy summary or witty antithesis embodied in the couplet that follows the three quatrains. The artifice of form, in other words, becomes a particular way of conceiving relations and defining linkages, sequence, and hierarchies in the reality to which the poet addresses him- or herself. A poet who felt moved, let us say, to celebrate the teeming variety and vastness of the human and natural landscape would not get very far with the sonnet form, would need a kind of poetic vehicle that was more expansive, allowing for free-flowing catalogues and effects of asymmetry and improvisation—would need, in short, something like Whitmanesque free verse.

In the case of biblical poetry, the two basic operations of specification and

*From *The Art of Biblical Narrative* by Robert Alter. © 1981 by Robert Alter. Reprinted by permission of Basic Books, Inc., Publishers.

heightening within the parallelistic line lead to an incipiently narrative structure of minute concatenations, on the one hand, and to a climactic structure of thematic intensifications, on the other hand. The astute reader will perceive that in point of poetic fact these two hands are sometimes tightly clasped, especially because, as we have seen, narrative progression in biblical verse often moves up a scale of increasing intensity, and because in practice it is sometimes hard to distinguish between a "focusing" which specifies and implies temporal sequence and one which is chiefly a stepping-up of assertion. There is no special reason to insist on simon-pure categories—one rarely encounters them in literature—but I do think the general distinction between the two different generative principles in biblical poetry is useful. There are, that is, many biblical poems in which any implied events, even metaphoric ones, are secondary while what is primary is a predicament, an image, a thematic idea which is amplified from verset to verset and from line to line. Poetic form acts in these cases as a kind of magnifying glass, concentrating the rays of meaning to a white-hot point. This means, to translate that static image back into the sequential mode in which the literary text works, that the progression of intensifying thematic particles is brought to a culminating flare-up, or compels resolution by a sharp reversal at the end. This kind of poetic structure lends itself beautifully to the writing of a psalmodic plea for help, a prophetic denunciation, or a Jobian complaint, but not to the aphoristic poise and the sense of cunning interrelation that are at home in the sonnet or to the rhapsodic feeling for the lovely heterogeneity of things that is readily expressed in Whitmanesque verse.

As an initial illustration of the structure of intensification, let us consider a brief and very simple psalm—powerful in its simplicity in a way we may understand better if we try to follow closely the operation of thematic focusing in the text. Psalm 13, in six compact lines, offers a strong model of the supplication—intoned "in straits" or "out of the depths"—which is one of the important genres of psalm. (The translations that follow are all my own.)

To the Leader, a Psalm of David

1 How long, Lord, will you forget me perpetually,   how long will you hide your face from me?
2 How long will I cast about schemes in my mind,   grief in my heart all day?
How long will my enemy be over me?
3 Look, answer me, Lord my God,   give light to my eyes,
lest I sleep death.
4 Lest my enemy say, "I have him,"   my foes exult when I slip
5 But I trust in your kindness,   my heart exults in your saving might.
6 I will sing to the Lord   for he has requited me.

In discussing narrative verse, I drew attention to the importance of incremental repetition and of ways of advancing meaning that may ultimately be derived from incremental repetition. Psalm 13, like many of the psalms of supplication, uses a very different mode of repetition—anaphora, which is to say, the rhetorically emphatic reiteration of a single word or brief phrase, in itself not a syntactically complete unity. In incremental repetition the restatement, with an addition, of a clause in itself complete as a unit of syntax and meaning, often produces an overlap effect where we perceive an action flowing into a related and subsequent action: "Between her legs he kneeled and fell, / where he kneeled, he fell, destroyed." Anaphora, on the other hand, shifts the center of attention from the repeated element to the material that is introduced by repetition, at once inviting us to see all the new utterances as locked into the same structure of assertion and to look for strong differences or elements of development in the new material. There is, in other words, a productive tension between sameness and difference, reiteration and development, in the use of anaphora.

If we are rigorous about the way poems articulate meanings, we would have to conclude that the repeated word or phrase in anaphora never means exactly the same thing twice, that in each occurrence it takes on a certain coloration from the surrounding semantic material and from its position in the series. This general point about repetition has been nicely formulated by the Russian semiotician, Jurij Lotman:

> Strictly speaking, unconditional repetition is impossible in poetry. The repetition of a word in a text, as a rule, does not mean the mechanical repetition of a concept. Most often it points to a more complex, albeit unified, semantic context.
>
> The reader accustomed to the graphic perception of a text sees the repeated outlines of a word on paper and assumes that he is looking at the mere duplication of a concept. In fact he is usually dealing with another, more complex concept, that is related to the given word, but whose complication is by no means quantitative.[1]

Lotman goes on to offer a telling illustration of the principle, an instance of emphatic repetition. When one encounters a line of verse like "Soldier, bid her farewell, bid her farewell," every reader realizes that the second "bid her farewell" could not be identical in meaning with the first. For the soldier is not being urged to say goodbye twice to his girl but, obviously, is being reminded of the poignancy of the leave-taking, the dearness of his beloved, the possibility he may never see her again, the dreadful imminence of the departure, or any combination of such implications. Let me propose that in our psalm the anaphoric series of four times "how long," while clearly informed by what Lotman calls a "unified semantic context," reflects an ascent on a scale of intensity, the note of desperate urgency pitched slightly higher with each repetition. Heightening, as in many other instances, is in part associated with a movement from cause to effect and from general to specific statement, but here without any real development of narrative momentum.

The rising movement is clear, compact, and, as I have suggested, exemplary of the supplication as a form of Hebrew verse. Initially, the speaker complains of being perpetually forgotten (or "neglected") by God; in the parallel verset this plight of neglect is imagined more personally and concretely—in a way, more terribly—as God's hiding his face from the supplicant. The second, triadic line translates the general condition of abandonment into the inward experience of the speaker, who flounders devising futile schemes and, what is more, is in the constant grip of grief—because, as we finally learn in the third verset, his enemy is winning out against him. It is worth noting that this last "how long" in the anaphoric series ("How long will my enemy be over me?") not only introduces a specification barely hinted at in the preceding statements but also has a virtual causal force absent in the previous occurrences of the selfsame syllables (i.e., How long is my distress to continue?—for this is the reason for it). It thus nicely illustrates how verbatim repetition in a poetic text is not to be equated with total identity of meaning.

At this climactic point of desperation (at the end of line 3), the speaker breaks away from the anaphora and pronounces three imperative verbs—the only such verbs in the poem—addressed to God: "*Look, answer* me, Lord my God, / *give light* to my eyes, lest I sleep death." The looking, which is heightened in the second verset into giving light to the eyes—presumably the effect of God's gaze—is obviously a prayer for the reversal of that awful hiding of the divine face evoked in line 1. The third verset, a subordinate clause, is linked to the second verset by an association of thematic and causal antithesis: either you make my eyes shine by turning toward me at once or they will close forever in the sleep of death. At this point, the poet complements the initial anaphora of "how long" which stressed his persisting anguish with an anaphoric insistence on "lest" which stresses the critical precariousness of his present condition. The "lest" at the beginning of line 4 unfolds the meaning of its counterpart in the last verset of line 3: "lest I sleep death"—which is to say, lest my enemy, who has long had the upper hand over me, be granted his final triumph (to cry out *yekholtiv,* "I have him," or more literally, "I have prevailed over him"). This picture of defeat is then emphatically rounded out in the second verset of line 4, with the representation of the foes exulting as they behold the speaker tottering, about to topple.

The general complaint, then, of being forgotten by God with which the poem began has been brought to a painfully vivid culmination in which the speaker imagines his own death both as a subjective state—sleeping the sleep of death, where God's gaze will never be able to light up his eyes—and as a dramatic scene—going down for the last time with his enemies crowing in triumph. This is the white-hot point to which the magnifying glass of the structure of intensification has concentrated the assertions of desperate need. At the moment of the imaginative enactment of death, the speaker swings away sharply into a concluding affirmation of faith, introduced by a strongly contrastive "but I," *va'ani* (in the Hebrew, all the previous occurrences of "I" and "me" are by way of suffixes and prefixes in declined or conjugated forms, and this is the sole instance of the pronoun proper). He trusts in God's kindness, or faithfulness (*ḥesed*), and what is more, his heart exults in God's deliverance, in a precise antithetical response to the enemies who were imagined exulting over his death. The poem that began in a cry of distress to a neglectful God ends (line 6) in a song of praise to God, whose deliverance of those who trust in him is already considered an accomplished fact.

Structurally, the countermovement of the last two lines functions differently from the concluding couplet of a Shakespearian sonnet, which reflects a tendency of the speaker to stand back contemplatively from his or her own preceding assertions and, even when an antithesis to them is proffered, to tie up the meanings of the poem with a certain sense of neat resolution. In the psalm, there is less resolution than surprising emotional reversal impelled by the motor force of faith. In this respect, the uses that later religious tradition made of Psalms are very much in keeping with the spirit of the original poems, even though the psalmist conceived being "saved" in more concrete and literal terms than have most postbiblical readers. (In our text, it is not altogether clear whether the battle imagery is literal or figurative, but in any case the supplicant is complaining of tottering on the brink of death in a world of human action, not of spiritual symbolism.) The speaker, that is, finds himself plunged into a fierce reality where things seem to go from bad to worse to the worst of all. There is no "logical" way out of this predicament—it is an image in small of the general biblical predicament of threatened national existence in the dangerous midst of history—as there is no discursive means in verse to imagine anything but its ominous intensification, except for the sudden, unaccountable, paradoxical swing of faith which enables the speaker at the nadir of terror to affirm that God will sustain him, indeed has sustained him. Generically, the supplication has been transformed in a single stroke into a psalm of thanksgiving.[2]

Perhaps the most brilliant elucidation ever written of this psalmodic structure of concluding antithesis is in the Sea Poems of the twelfth-century Hebrew poet Judah Halevi, which are among the most remarkable lyric achievements in any language of the Middle Ages. Halevi, a virtuoso stylist who has profoundly assimilated, along with other antecedent Hebrew texts, the poetic dynamic of the Psalms, conjures up in these poems about his voyage to the land of Israel the roiling chaos of the sea about to engulf him; and, typically, he effects a sharp turn of faith at the end of each poem in affirming his trust in the God who will pluck him from the wave-tossed "plank" to which he clings and set him down in the courts of Jerusalem. Transposed into another, more intricately elegant poetic mode, Halevi's Sea Poems perfectly capture the underlying movement of our psalm and of a good many like it. One chief reason for the success of Psalm 13 in giving such a resonant voice to a soul in distress—in its own time and for posterity—is that its spare, compact assertions of critical need, which at first glance may seem merely a series of equivalent statements, in fact generate a rising line of tension, reaching the pitch of ultimate disaster which then triggers the sudden turn and resolution of the believer's trust at the end.

While biblical poets often prefer this strong linear development of the structure of intensification, even for longer poems, there are also many instances of more intricate variations of the structure. Psalm 39 is a particularly instructive text in this regard because it offers three different patterns of thematic development which are cunningly interwoven.

To the Leader, to Juduthun, a Psalm of David

1 I said: let me keep my way from offending with my tongue, / let me keep a muzzle on my mouth,
as long as the wicked is before me.
2 I was mute, in stillness, / I was dumb, cut off from good,
and my pain was stirred.
3 My heart was hot within me, / in my thoughts a flame burned,
I spoke with my tongue.
4 Let me know, Lord, my end, / and what is the measure of my days,
that I may know how fleeting I am.
5 Bare handbreaths you made my days, / my existence is nothing to you,
mere breath each man stands.**
6 In but shadow man walks about / mere breath his bustlings,
he stores up, knowing not who will gather.
7 And so what can I expect, O God? / My hope is in you.
8 From all my transgressions deliver me, / make me not the scorn of the fool.
9 I was mute, did not open my mouth, / for yours was the doing.
10 Take away from me your plague, / from your blows I perish.
11 In chastisement for sin you afflict a man, / melting like a moth what he treasures.
Mere breath are all men. selah.
12 Hear my prayer, O Lord, / give ear to my cry,
to my tears be not silent.
13 For I am alien with you, / a resident like all my forefathers.
14 Look away from me so I may recover,** / before I go off and am not.

This, too, is a psalm of supplication, but the speaker's definition of his own plight and of his relation to God is manifestly more complicated than what we encountered in Psalm 13. He, too, is in great straits, but except for the rather oblique reference to the presence of the wicked at the end of the first line, this situation of acute distress is not spelled out in the poem until lines 8–11, and considerable space is first devoted to an introspective meditation on the

**Indicates textual problem in Hebrew.

transience of human life. Moreover, here there is no sharp turning point of faith after the cry of anguish. The speaker introduces the idea that God is his only hope almost as a logical conclusion of desperation, at the exact middle of the poem (line 7). But then he must try to argue God into having compassion on him, using language and ideas strikingly reminiscent of Job as he has just used language reminiscent of Qoheleth in lines 5–6 (whether these are anticipations or echoes of Job and Qoheleth there is no way of knowing), and ending on a disquieting note in an evocation of his own imminent extinction. The supplicant of Psalm 13 wants God to turn toward him; the supplicant of Psalm 39 wants him to have mercy and turn away.

In order to follow these complications of meaning more clearly, we will have to attend to the formal articulations of the poem. It is worth noting at the outset that triadic lines are not merely interspersed, as in other texts we have examined, but actually predominate here. The first six lines of the poem are all triadic, the first dyadic line occurring only when the speaker arrives at the crucial statement that God is his sole hope (line 7), and two more triads appear in the second half of the poem. In most of the triadic lines, moreover, there is an element of imbalance in the semantic parallelism, and one suspects that is precisely why the triads are used. This imbalance is especially clear in the first three lines (in my schematic paraphrase, I will indicate the three versets as a, b, and c):

1 (a) resolution to keep silent; (b) more concretely worded resolution to keep silent; (c) presence of the wicked;

2 (a) report of having been silent; (b) amplified report of having been silent; (c) confession of pain;

3 (a) report of heated thoughts; (b) more metaphorically vivid report of heated thoughts; (c) report of the fact of speech.

In each of these three lines the third verset stands in some relation of tension to the two preceding versets, retrospectively casting a new light on them, and in the case of line 3 also following consequentially from them in a way that involves an element of surprise. In Psalm 13 the speaker's world is desperate but stable: the movement of intensification focuses in and in from being forgotten by God to the image of the supplicant's death, and then is displaced by the concluding affirmation of trust. In Psalm 39, on the other hand, the speaker flounders in a world of radical ambiguities where the antithetical values of speech and silence, existence and extinction, perhaps even innocence and transgression, have been brought dangerously close together. I do not want to propose, in the manner of one fashionable school of contemporary criticism, that we should uncover in the text a covert or unwitting reversal of its own hierarchical oppositions; or more specifically, that silence is affirmed and then abandoned in consequence of the poet's intuition that all speech is a lie masquerading as truth because of the inevitably arbitrary junction between signifier and signified, language and reality. On the contrary, the ancient Hebrew literary imagination reverts again and again to a bedrock assumption about the efficacy of speech, cosmogonically demonstrated by God (in Genesis 1) who is emulated by man. In our poem the speaker's final plea that God hear his cry presupposes the efficacy of speech, the truth-telling power with which language has been used to expose the supplicant's plight. The rapid swings between oppositions in the poem are not dictated by an epistemological quandary but by a psychological dialectic in the speaker. Let me try to explain how this dialectic movement unfolds by tracing the three thematic patterns which together constitute the poem's complex structure of intensification.

The speaker begins by saying that he had intended—the initial *'amarti* can mean either "say" or "think"—to keep his mouth shut, and this because of a very specific circumstance: he is within earshot of the malicious, and if he audibly complains he will become a target for their jibes, a point made explicit in line 8. The actual exposition of the speaker's particular predicament is postponed until the middle of the poem (lines 8–11), which has the effect of blurring his special fate of suffering—line 10 indicates that the specific affliction is physical illness—into the general vulnerability of the human condition evoked in lines 4–6. At the beginning there is an indication, in the last verset of line 2, that he is in pain, but this might be construed in immediate context as the pain of pent-up complaints. Similarly, the speaker begins by professing a desire to avoid "offending" (or "sinning," *ḥat'o*) but in immediate context this seems to refer merely to an offense in the realm of public relations in giving the wicked something to crow about. The first two lines present a clear development of intensification of the theme of silence—from a resolution not to offend by speech, to muzzling the mouth, to preserving (in a chain of three consecutive synonyms) absolute muteness. The realized focal point of silence produces inward fire, a state of acute distress that compels a reversal of the initial resolution and issues in speech. But the content of the speech is something of a surprise. Instead of the formulaic "How long, O Lord" that we might expect, and that might play into the hands of the malicious eavesdropper, the speaker undertakes a meditation on the transience of human life, asking God to give him the profound inner knowledge of his own brief span. This meditation of transience is a second movement of intensification without the poem, beginning with the general "my end," moving on to the "measure of my days," to the speaker's "fleeting" nature, then from "handbreadths" to mere "nothing," to empty "breath" (*hevel,* the reiterated key word in Qoheleth traditionally rendered as "vanity"). The center of this intensifying movement is nicely defined by a shrewd piece of wordplay: in the last verset of line 4, the speaker wants to understand how fleeting, *ḥadel,* he is; in the middle verset of line 5, his existence, *ḥeled,* is as nothing in the eyes of God.

Once the transience theme has been brought to its white-hot point—man is nothing, he can hang on to nothing, can truly know only his own nothingness—the climax compels a reversal, as we have seen elsewhere, and the speaker affirms his hope in God. This in turn leads him to admit to having sinned and to speak of the suffering that has visited him because of it (lines 8–11). The sin-suffering conjunction, however, is less confession than simple admission and, unlike the themes of silence and transience, it is not developed in a pattern of intensification. The reason for this difference is clear: suffering-because-of-sin is what the speaker begs to be rescued from, not anything he wants to conjure up as an intensifying process; while he does want to put heavy stress on both his quandary as a person who needs at once to be silent and to cry out and on the sobering perspective of man's terrible transience. The poet nicely subsumes the whole sin-suffering segment under the two more salient themes by paradoxically reaffirming silence at the beginning of the segment (line 9, first verset) and reintroducing the theme of transience at the end of the segment (the last word of line 10, the last two versets of line 11). By now it would appear also that silence means something different from what might have been supposed at the beginning: "I was mute, did not open my mouth"—that is, I did not give the "fool" (of the preceding line) a chance to deride me: I did not complain about your justice, only asked to understand the ephemerality of my own existence, a condition that might be taken as grounds (the next line) for your withdrawing the terrible weight of your hand from the melting mortal stuff of which I am made.

The last three lines of the poem begin with what momentarily looks like the formulaic conclusion of a supplication—"Hear my prayer . . . , give ear to my cry"—but the third verset of the triadic line once more introduces an unexpected element: "to my tears be not silent." The poet's third synonym for "complaint" is a metonymy, "tears," which, unlike the two others, is mute, while God is asked not to listen or give ear or look but to be not silent—in perfect thematic counterpoint to the speaker himself, who emphatically pledged silence but, under the sharp cutting edge of suffering, had no recourse but speech.

Having thus resumed the theme of silence and speech, the poet returns to the theme of transience in the last two lines, bringing it to a strategically telling culmination. The power of line 13 is more evident in the Hebrew than in translation because the line turns on what is known in biblical scholarship as a "breakup pattern." That is, two words that are ordinarily a bound collocation, or more specifically a hendiadys (two words to indicate one concept, like "hue and cry" in English), are broken up and made into parallel terms in the two versets of a line of poetry. In this case, the hendiadys *ger vetoshav*, "resident alien," is split into *ger* in the first verset and *toshav* in the second, the effect being to defamiliarize the common idiom and bring to the fore the sense of temporary, tolerated presence of someone who does not really belong. "Like all my forefathers" reinforces this implication by placing the speaker in a rapidly moving chain of generations while aptly connecting his own transience with that of all humanity, in keeping with the generalizing perspective of lines 5–6. The poet then concludes, on a very Jobian note, by begging God to turn away from him while he still has his paltry moment to live. The last word of the poem, *'eyneni,* refers to the speaker's death not as a metaphoric idea (to sleep the sleep of death) or as a dramatic scene (my enemies exult as I fall) but as a flat fact of extinction—"I am not," like the "nothing," *'ayin,* to which he compared his existence before God, the two words in the Hebrew being ultimately the same word, *'eyneni,* a declined form of *'ayin.* The final term of intensification, then, in the vision of human transience falls into place with the last word of the poem: what had been before a strong metaphor ("mere breath") or simile ("My existence is *as* nothing before you") now becomes an unqualified statement in the first-person singular of a fact about to be accomplished. The "I said" that was the first word of the poem terminates, in an ultimate convergence of the theme of silence and theme of transience, in the irrevocable cancelling-out of the sayer.

As with the other texts we are considering in this connection, my intention is not to offer an exhaustive analysis of the poem but to indicate certain underlying possibilities of poetic structure manifested in the poem. The impulse of semantic intensification, as we observe it working from verset to verset and line to line, would lead us to expect a continuous linear development to a climax, or to a climax and reversal. Though that pattern is in fact extremely common in biblical poetry, Psalm 39 illustrates another possibility: two different lines of intensification are prominent in the poem; each is displayed intermittently, being interrupted and resumed; each qualifies and complicates the other; and the meaning of both patterns is not fully realized until they are brought together at the end. Obviously, I do not mean to suggest that the Hebrew poets consciously manipulated rhyme patterns. The orientation toward a stepping-up of meaning was, for reasons I have tried to make clear, built into the poetic system. It was in all likelihood quite knowingly perceived on the level of the line and in relatively brief sequences of lines. In regard to larger structural units, I would guess that the tendency to work one's way up a scale of intensity was intuited as a natural way to proceed from line to poem rather than explicitly recognized as a "device." In any event, given the prevalence of this particular mode of moving forward in a biblical poem, it is understandable that a poet might well choose to interarticulate two or more patterns of intensification if his aim was to express something more than usually ambiguous, more multifaceted, more contradictory, more fraught with dialectic tension, or whatever the case might be.

In several ways the most profound development of the structure of intensification occurs in what is arguably the greatest achievement of all biblical poetry, the Book of Job. When we move from the prose frame-story in chapters 1 and 2 to the beginning of the poetic argument in chapter 3, we are plunged precipitously into a world of what must be called abysmal intensities. It is only through the most brilliant use of a system of poetic intensifications that the poet is able to take the full emotional measure and to intimate the full moral implications of Job's outrageous fate. The extraordinary poem that constitutes chapter 3 is not merely a dramatically forceful way of beginning Job's complaint. More significantly, it establishes the terms, literally and figuratively, for the poetry Job will speak throughout; and when God finally answers Job out of the whirlwind, the force of God's response will be closely bound with a shift introduced by his speech in the terms of the poetic argument and the defining lines of poetic structure. What I am suggesting is that the exploration of the problem of theodicy in the Book of Job and the "answer" it proposes cannot be separated from the poetic vehicle of the book, and that one misses the real intent by reading the text, as too often has been done, as a paraphrasable philosophic argument merely embellished or made more arresting by poetic devices. For the moment, however, it will suffice to see how the poetry unfolds step by step in Job's first speech (Job 3:3–26):

1 Perish the day I was born   the night that said, "A man has been conceived."
2 That day, let it be darkness,   let God above not seek it out,
let no brightness shine on it.
3 Let darkness and deep gloom claim it,   let a pall dwell over it,
let what darkens the day cast terror on it.
4 That night, let blackness seize it,   let it not join with the days of the year,
let it not come into the number of months.
5 That night, let it be desolate,   let no sound of joy come into it.
6 Let the doomers of day curse it,   those destined to undo Leviathan.
7 Let its twilight stars stay dark,   let it hope for light and have none,
let it see not the eyelids of dawn.
8 For not blocking her belly's doors,   to hide suffering from my eyes.
9 Why did I not die from the womb,   out from the belly expire?
10 Why were there knees to receive me,   or breasts for me to suck?
11 For now would I lie, be at peace,   I would sleep and find rest.
12 With kings and counselors of the earth,   who build ruins for themselves,
13 Or with nobles who have gold,   who fill their houses with silver,
14 Or like a buried stillborn, I would be not   like infants who never saw light.
15 There the wicked cease to trouble,   there the exhausted rest.
16 Prisoners are utterly tranquil,   no longer hear the taskmaster's voice
17 Small and great are there,   the slave free of his master.
18 Why does he give to the sufferer light,   and life to the bitter of soul,
19 Who wait for death and it comes not,   who dig for it more than for treasure,
20 Who rejoice to exultation,   and are glad to find a grave,
21 To a man whose way is hidden,   whom God has hedged about?

22 In place of my bread my groaning comes,   my roars pour out like water.
23 For I feared a fear—it befell me,   and that which I dreaded came on me.
24 I was not quiet, was not at peace,   did not rest, and trouble came.

Because the author of Job is one of those very rare poets, like Shakespeare, who combine awesome expressive power with dazzling stylistic virtuosity, the translation dilutes the original even more than for other biblical poems. The original has a muscular compactness that is extremely difficult to reproduce while finding honest equivalents for the Hebrew words in a Western language,[3] and makes repeated and sometimes highly significant use of soundplay and wordplay. Let me offer a transliteration of just the first line, which begins the poem with a strong alliterative pattern: *yóvad yom iváled bó / vehaláylah 'amár hórah gáver;* and let me just mention the rhymed antithesis of *'ananáh* ("pall," in line 3) and *renanáh* ("sound of joy," in line 5), and the weighted sequencing of *qéver,* "grave," and *géver,* "man," at the very end of line 20 and the very beginning of line 21. Nevertheless, since the development of the poem depends more on an intensification of semantic materials than on an elaboration of phonetic and syntactic patterns (however much the latter are tied in with meaning), much of the poetic movement is still perceptible in English, especially if the translation preserves (as mine, whatever its defects, as done) the same lexical equivalents for recurring words in the Hebrew.

The poem begins with an obvious and, so it momentarily seems, quite conventional complementary parallelism of day and night (there are abundant lines of biblical verse in which "day" appears in the first verset followed by "night" in the second). But this conventional pairing undergoes a startling development, both within the line and in what follows. If, as we have seen elsewhere, intensification between versets is often allied with temporal sequence, here Job, who wants to cancel out his own existence, goes *backward* in time, first cursing the day he was born, then, nine months previous, even the night he was conceived. This line is one of the most striking instances in biblical poetry of how the second verset in a line with a double-duty verb is emphatically not a "ballast variant" of the first. Since the initial verb "perish" governs both clauses, the poet has the space in the second verset to invent a miniature dramatic scene, and one quite flagrantly founded on a fantastic hyperbole: that at the moment of conjugal consummation, the night or perhaps even the future father himself, cried out in triumph, "A male [in the translation above, "man," *géver,* the same word that begins line 21] has been conceived." The day and night of the first and second versets, which are introduced as complementary terms on a scale of intensity defined by the difference between blotting out birth and blotting out conception, are then split into binary oppositions, and the interplay between those oppositions constitutes the entire first section of the poem, to the end of line 8.

This section might be described as a kind of "conjugation" of the semantic poles of light and darkness in the grammatical mode of imprecation, which means, of course, that every flicker of light invoked is wished into darkness, swallowed up by darkness, or cancelled into nonbeing by the chain of *not*'s and *none*'s that runs down the poem. Let me stress that these lines reflect not merely a piling on of images of darkness engulfing light but, as so often elsewhere in biblical poetry, a rising line of intensity in the articulation of such images.

The rising line is generally evident between versets, as for example in line 3, where in the first verset darkness and gloom merely "claim" (or, in another construal of the Hebrew verb, "besmirch") the day, and by the third verset "cast terror" over it. But the rising movement is still clearer from line to line. First Job wants the day of his birth to be totally swathed in darkness (lines 2–3); then he asks that the night of conception also be seized by blackness and desolation (lines 4–5), thus raising the inherent darkness of the night, one might say, to the second power, and that the fatal night be expunged from the very calendar. (By now, a sequence of day, night, months, year has been worked into the poem, all to support Job's wish that he had never been brought into the cycle of time.) The "sound of joy" at the end of line 4 that is to be cancelled out not only echoes the sound of the Hebrew for "pall" in line 3 but also takes us back to the second verset of line 1, where a joyous announcement of the conception of a male was made.

Having brought the scale of curses to this pitch, Job steps up his statement still further by invoking in line 6 mythological and cosmogonic imagery: a mere human hex is not enough, and so those cosmic agents designated to disable the primordial sea beast Leviathan must be enlisted to curse the moment that saw Job into the world and, implicitly, the initial movement backward in time now reaches across eons to the world's beginnings. "Doomers of day," which I am afraid I have made sound rather Anglo-Saxon in my translation, is a terrific piece of compressed wit in the Hebrew because "doomers" or "cursers," *'orerei,* puns on *'or,* "light," and so introduces a spectral echo of the thing being blotted out in the word indicating the agents of obliteration. Finally, line 7, which is the last moment in the series, conjures up an image of literally hopeless longing for light in a world where the first twilight star will never show, the dawn never begin to glimmer. This climax then leads to a summary and interim conclusion in line 8 which bracket the seven preceding lines: may all these curses fall on that day and night for not blocking up the womb in which I was to lie (an image that picks up the preceding images of being totally enveloped in darkness), for not hiding suffering (or "trouble") from my eyes. A newborn child sees light (compare line 14), but by this point Job has established a virtual equation between light or life and anguish, so the substitution of "suffering" for "light" at the end of the segment has a brilliantly concise recapitulative function.

Now all along I have been speaking of "structures" of intensification, conceding to common critical usage and for want of a better metaphor, but structure suggests an image of static form extended in space, like a building, and I would like to correct that implication by reminding readers that what we think of approximately as structure in literature is, by the serial nature of the medium, dynamic movement unfolding sequentially. If we try to imagine this for a moment not in terms of the finished product we experience in our reading but rather as the process the poet initiates in his making of the poem, we might well speak of a generative principle of intensification. The thematic-imagistic terms of day and night, light and darkness, are introduced, set in sharp opposition, and then the possibilities of that opposition are strongly developed from image to image and line to line, until the speaker can imagine no more than the concrete picture of his own nonbirth, shut up forever within the dark doors of the womb. The momentum of intensifying this whole opposition, making the darkness more and more overwhelming in relation to the light, is what carries the poem forward step by step and what in some sense generates it, determining what will be said and what will be concluded.

The grimly comforting picture of enclosure in the womb in turn triggers a second major development in the poem, the evocation of the peace of the grave that runs from line 9 to line 21. This represents a transfer of the wish for extinction expressed in the first eight lines from a cosmic to a personal scale and so reflects the movement of specification or focusing that also operates within smaller compass in the poem. The blocked doors of the belly of line 8 lead to a more realistic image of stillbirth in line 9, and only now is the wish for extinction translated into explicit words for death, here repeated with synonymic emphasis ("die" and "expire"). Line 10 is then a further concretization of the birth that Job wishes never had been, moving along a temporal axis: he comes out of the womb, is greeted by knees (either the mother's knees parted in birth or, as some scholars have proposed, the father's knees on which the newborn may have been placed in a ceremony of legitimation), and then is given the breast. Though womb and tomb are not a rhyme in Hebrew, they are at least an assonance (*rêḥem, qêver*), and in any case the archetypal connection between the two would seem to be perfectly evident to the imagination of the poet, who has Job go on from the womb he never wanted to leave to the grave where he would have found lasting rest. Perhaps because rest is intrinsically a condition of stasis, the development of this theme is cumulative rather than crescendo, proceeding through a series of near-synonyms: to lie, be at peace, sleep, rest, be tranquil.

Meanwhile, the catalogue of all those who find repose in the grave has the effect of locating Job's suffering as only one particularly acute instance of the common human condition. Old and young, the mighty and the oppressed, all end up in the grave, and all find respite from the "suffering" (*'amal*) of existence—an idea beautifully summarized in the last line of the catalogue, line 17, "Small and great are there, / the slave free of his master," where all verbs are suppressed ("are" being merely implied in the Hebrew) as befits the place where all actions and disturbances cease.

The picture of earthly existence implied by the catalogue of course confirms Job's vision of life as nothing but trouble. Kings and counselors rebuild ruins in the cycle of creation and destruction that is the life of men—or perhaps, since Hebrew has no "re" prefix, the phrase even suggests, more strikingly, that what they build at the very moment of completion is to be thought of as already turning into ruins. Because of the interlinear parallelism between lines 12 and 13, the houses storing silver and gold stand themselves under the shadow of ruin, an image of the futility of all gathering and getting as one would find in Qoheleth. The catalogue, beginning at the top of the social hierarchy, evokes a world where men are set against men, poor against rich, criminal against law enforcer, slave against master, with prisons, exhausting labor, and coercion the characteristic institutions. The third of these six lines introduces the zero-degree instance of existence and hence, from Job's viewpoint, the happiest—the stillborn infant; this both defines the lower limit of the catalogue and pointedly links up with Job's personal wish in lines 11–13 that he had died at birth.

Lines 18–21 sum up the meaning of the catalogue and effect a transition back from the general plight of man to Job's individual case. The smoothness and strength of the transition are reflected in the fact that the four lines, unusual for biblical verse, constitute a single continuous grammatical sentence. "Why does he give the sufferer light, / and life to the bitter of soul . . . ?" Here two of the key words of the poem, *'ameil* and *'or,* "sufferer" and "light," are placed side by side, perhaps even explicitly reminding us of that strategic substitution of *'amal* for *'or* at the very end of the first half of the poem. Now the equation between light and life that underlay the first half of the poem is unambiguously stated, and, appropriately, in the chiastic shape of the line, "light" and "life" are the inside terms, boxed in by "sufferer" and "bitter of soul."

The sufferers (line 19) waiting for a death that will not come, seeking it more than treasure, invite an ironic glance backward both to the night awaiting a dawn that will never come and to the nobles storing up actual treasure that will not avail them. Line 20, picking up the digging image at the end of the preceding line, focuses the just-stated longing for death in the concrete action of rejoicing over the grave. (This effect is still stronger if one makes a small emendation of *qal* for *qil* in the word I have rendered as "exultation," which would then yield: "Who rejoice over the gravemound [or, pile of ruined stones], / who are glad to find a grave.") Line 21 then slides from the plural to the singular, as Job, in a concluding maneuver of focusing, inserts himself in the general category of the embittered who long for death, and prepares to enunciate three final summarizing lines in the first-person singular. There are several verbal clues in this line that connect its still rather generalized third-person utterance to Job's predicament as articulated both in the poem and in the frame-story before the poem: "To a man whose way is hidden, / whom God has hedged about." Job calls himself man, *géver,* the same word he imagined in line 1 being cried out on the night of his conception. (The fondness of biblical writers for this sort of closure of literary units through envelope structures hardly needs to be demonstrated.) He would have wanted trouble to be hidden from his eyes, to remain himself hidden in the darkness of the womb/tomb, but instead his own way has been hidden from him, he is lost in the darkness of life. The adversary in the frame-story had complained that God showed favoritism by setting up a protective "hedge" around Job and his household (Job 1:10); here the very same idiom is used to suggest entrapment, the setting up of dire obstacles. With its echo of the frame-story, this line is also the first and only time that God is mentioned by name in the poem, as if Job found it almost too painful to refer to or address the resented source of his sufferings (the pronominal presence of God at the beginning of line 18 is indicated in the Hebrew by nothing more than the conjugated form of the verb "to give" in the third-person singular).

With the final move of the transition from general to personal effected by line 21, Job now speaks out again in the first person, as he did both at the beginning of the poem (line 1) and at the beginning of the second half of the poem (lines 9–11). The form of these three concluding lines, as we would expect at the end of a large movement of intensification, is powerfully emphatic. In line 22, while "bread" and "water" are complementary terms, "groaning" is stepped up into "roaring," "comes" into "pours out." The obvious emphasis of the next line is in its heavy insistence on the lexicon of fear: "For I feared a fear—it befell me, / and that which I dreaded came on me." The climactic power of the line, however, is less in its formal configuration than in its location as a psychological revelation just before the end of the poem. From the start, Job had made it clear that he was in great anguish, but only now does he reveal that he has been living in a state of dread—dread before the catastrophes, dread which bitter experience has made into a virtual equivalent of life. The final line then completes a strong closural effect by doubling semantic parallelism, each verset internally as well as the line as a whole being built on the bracketing of equivalent terms: "I was not quiet, was not at peace, / did not rest, and trouble came." All these terms, of course, recapitulatively take us back by way of contrast to the tranquility and repose of the grave evoked in lines 11–17. The last word in the line and the poem in the Hebrew is *rógez,* "trouble," breaking the pattern of the three first-person singular verbs that preceded it and reminding us of that from which even the wicked cease in the grave (line 15).

And finally, the simple verb "to come" at the end ties up in this image of turbulence a developmental thread that has been running through the poem. "To come" in biblical idiom, depending on both context and the preposition with which it is linked, has a wide variety of meanings. The ones reflected in our poem are: to be included or counted (line 4), to enter (line 5), to substitute or serve as (line 22), to overtake (line 23), and to arrive or simply to come (line 24). In a most cunning use of the technique of *Leitwort,* this seemingly innocuous word becomes a sinuous hide-and-seek presence in the poem, first attached to subjects Job tries to control verbally in his curse, then to Job's own groaning, and climactically, to the dreaded disaster that overtakes him, and to the state of unremitting turbulence that comes to him inwardly in place of the tranquility for which he yearns. This fine verbal thread, then, is a formal realization of the sense of terrible inexorability upon which Job's complaint is founded.

In everything I have said about this fundamental generative principle of intensification in biblical poetry, I have not intended to claim that this is a feature of poetics entirely unique to ancient Hebrew verse. The fact is that poetry in general involves, necessarily, a linear development of meaning, which means that in one respect it is a linear form of thinking or imagining. "Those images that yet / fresh images beget," Yeats wrote in one of his most famous poems about art and the imagination, and that, approximately, is the way most poems would seem to work: one image suggests a related one, or a further manifestation of the same underlying image; one idea leads to a cognate or consequent one; one pattern of sound, interinvolved with a particular semantic direction, leads to a similar pattern that reinforces some underlying similarity or suggestive antithesis of meaning. Since we tend to expect development of meaning in the specially significant form of discourse that is poetry, it is hardly surprising that poems in many literary traditions will begin with some general notion or image and by stages bring it to a pitch of intensity, or to a sharp focus. Having cited the sonnet at the outset of this discussion as a counterexample to biblical verse, I should add now that one can certainly find sonnets—in English, some of those of Gerard Manley Hopkins come to mind—that evince something like a structure of intensification. There are, however, important differences of degree in the way poets in different traditions may exploit this structure, and differences in what I referred to earlier as the orientation toward reality encouraged by a particular poetic system. Because, as we have abundantly seen, the very prosodic conventions on which the lines of biblical poetry were shaped led poets to a focusing of statements and a heightening of emphasis, they were repeatedly drawn to articulating whole poems and segments within poems as pronounced, often continuous progressions of mounting intensities.

There are surely other possibilities of structure explored by the ancient Hebrew poets, but from Job to Psalms to the Prophets, the axis of intensification, along which meanings and feelings are focused in and in, is very often the line to watch in order to take in the distinctive power of these remarkable biblical poems.

NOTES

1. J. Lotman, *The Structure of the Artistic Text,* trans. Ronald Vroom (Ann Arbor, Mich.: Ardis, 1971) 126–27.

2. I am grateful to Nitza Kreichman for this observation about the reversal of genres.

3. A striking approximation, however, of this compactness has been achieved by Stephen Mitchell in his bold translation of Job, *Into the Whirlwind* (New York: Doubleday & Co., 1979).

9 RICHARD ELLIOTT FRIEDMAN

THE HIDING OF THE FACE: AN ESSAY ON THE LITERARY UNITY OF BIBLICAL NARRATIVE

We have two channels through which to find out what we want to know about the Bible and the world that produced it. These are the archeological and the literary. I mean "archeological" in its broadest sense, including the use of discovered languages and documents, art and architecture, skill in epigraphy, and the field archeologist's full load of tools and skills, from the spade to the macrophotograph. I mean "literary" in its broadest sense as well, signifying text—and the tools and skills for interpreting it. "History of Israel" studies derive from and depend upon these two channels, as do "History of the Religion of Israel" and biblical theology, along with sociological, psychological, and anthropological studies. Thus, when J. Wellhausen sought *Die Geschichte Israels,* and Y. Kaufmann sought *twldwt h'mnh hyśr'lyt,* the literary-critical enterprise was a cornerstone for both of them, while perhaps the greatest challenges and refinements to their models have derived from archeological finds.

One difference between the archeological and literary enterprises worthy of note is that archeology is more undividedly a tool (it is used in order to arrive at knowledge) while the literary enterprise has the value of being a tool (it can help us to acquire historical, theological, or sociological information, for example) but also has its own intrinsic value—the appreciation of the literature itself. Let us say its ends are both knowledge and edification. The dig can be intrinsically pleasurable as well, of course, but that joy of archeological search and discovery is more the equivalent of the joy that a literary scholar (or, for that matter, any scholar) may take in his or her own avenues of search and discovery. Literary study thus still seems to possess one added dimension of intrinsic worth all its own.

Given the obvious importance of the text either as an end in itself or as an avenue to other ends, it is amazing that literary study of the Bible is so young and limited an activity in the biblical field. It is not just that in biblical scholarship history, not literature, has been queen science. In the study of the Bible, the very term "literary criticism" has had a more restricted meaning than in the study of perhaps any other book. So widely has it been held to refer strictly to analysis of authorship that the Fortress Press Guides to Biblical Scholarship series was forced to include the two similar titles *Literary Criticism of the Old Testament* (N. Habel) and *The Old Testament and the Literary Critic* (D. Robertson) in order to treat the two different activities. For one of the oldest surviving books, literary study is among the youngest scholarly approaches. With the text itself still the primary channel of inquiry, the field as a whole still does not regard the skills of literary analysis as of primary importance.

This is an ironic state of things, but not a completely negative one. On the contrary, the considerable neglect of literary scholarship, the delay in developing it as a major area in our field, means that those of us who value and delight in this study have the opportunity to enter upon it in its infancy and to address questions of method and approach with a forethought that was largely lacking in the formative periods of other subdisciplines. We can propose, challenge, and seek agreement to techniques for fathoming text. Further, we come to build a field of study with a century of groundwork behind us. We do not have to replace Mowinckel and Noth with Derrida and Ricoeur. We can use what we have learned through source criticism and so on in the service of our work. Indeed, this is an advantage held by literary critics in biblical and classical studies over their counterparts in the corresponding incipient stages of most other national literatures. We have inherited a fortune of scholarship of many types on which to draw. Indeed, it is difficult to imagine literary study of the Bible without the groundwork. To state it methodologically, adopting a literary approach to the Bible does not excuse one from learning and using all the tools of elucidating a text, namely, historical, linguistic, epigraphic, text-critical, source-critical study, and so on. The rubric "literary" cannot be a shortcut. Structural or structuralist or deconstructionist analyses cannot be an excuse for not undertaking the complete scholarly research.

We should include—minimally—first, rigorous knowledge of the languages of the text. Let English literature professors beware. The King James Version is a masterpiece of translation. It is a model for study of what can result when a great work has the rare good fortune to come into the hands of translators who are both artists in their own right and reverent toward the integrity of the original text. But the days of "King James was good enough for Paul, and it's good enough for me" are over. One who cannot work in biblical Hebrew, Aramaic, and Greek—as well as in the cognate Semitic languages—cannot be certain of the text, of the range of its idioms, of the implications of its nuances, and therefore of the accuracy of his or her analysis.

Second, knowledge of the history of Israel is necessary. I mean this, too, in its largest sense, to include knowledge of the culture that produced the text—its political, economic, religious, and social institutions—and knowledge of other ancient Near Eastern cultures as well.

Third, we require knowledge of the literary history of the text. The conclusions of any analysis of narrative voice, narrative strategy, paronomasia, or character development in a text—to mention but a few categories—hang uncertainly in the balance as long as the critic does not come to terms with the authorial and editorial process that produced that text. The history of the transmission of the text is crucial as well. As long as the scribal interchange of the homonyms *lōʾ* and *lô* occurs to remind us that scribal error can add or remove the word "not" from a sentence, the critic must feel bound to do his or her text-critical homework in any serious literary study.

Still, many of those who pursue literary analysis of the Bible have ignored the tools of their trade, source analysis especially. In some cases, the reason for the omission may be that the scholar does not want to give up a traditional mode of exegesis. In the case of Jewish biblical scholars, this takes the form of a reluctance to give up the process of midrash or, at least, the process of *pᵉšaṭ* in its traditional sense, that is, the interpretation of the plain meaning of the text as it stands. For example, in the case of the second patriarchal wife-sister story, Genesis 20, formerly the interpreter could ask why Abraham misrepresents his wife as his sister to a king a second time, given the trouble that he had the last time he did it, Genesis 12 (if you consider getting rich to be trouble). Once it was recognized that the first wife-sister story is J and the second is E, however, this question became pointless, perhaps even foolish. There was nothing wrong with Rashi's asking it, but what is the literary or historical value of asking it after the nineteenth century? And so the critics who still want to ask it say, "I am taking an ahistorical approach," and they get to ask it anyway. But what is the use of asking—and answering—it now? When Rashi, Ibn Ezra, and Ramban asked it their interest was more than literary, and it was anything but ahistorical. It is an ironic twist that interpreters have taken an approach that is anathema to the tradition precisely out of their desire to ask the traditional questions. They would do better to regard their traditional questions as just that, traditional questions, now of interest insofar as they shed light on former interpreters. And let them then say that they are doing history of interpretation, not biblical analysis. Or let them use the information that the last few centuries have produced so as to go on to new and harder questions.

Another justification offered for ignoring the text's literary history is the claim that the interpreter is focusing on the redactor's work. The unity that was broken when J, E, P, and D replaced Moses is restored by focusing on R. Some have even jokingly referred to R as "Rabbenu," which is a curious new incarnation of the rabbis' once having dubbed Moses "Rabbenu." But one cannot just take up a position that assumes a murky, virtually omnipotent redactor. At minimum, those who wish to take this approach to the text should feel bound to undertake a rigorous discussion of intentionality. If we assume that intention does not matter, then why bother to set up this dependence on the redactor in the first place? If we assume that intention does matter, then we must do the work of redaction criticism. We must study each redactor's method and product and determine what each redactor's relationship with his or her sources was. How much was he or she governed by them; how free did he or she feel to "tamper" with them, to delete a word or a paragraph, to impose a historical or theological direction upon them, to favor one source over another, or to rewrite? Accepting the redactor's final product cannot be just an attempt to circumnavigate (which is to say circumvent) historical criticism. That means navigating between a Scylla of new criticism and a Charybdis of philology, one or the other of which must be faced. I believe that analyzing the interplay of all the layers—the composition of the parts, the redaction of the parts into a unity, unity itself—can produce an incomparably rich appreciation of the text.

I do not mean to suggest that nonspecialists cannot make meaningful contributions to the field. The oft-cited first chapter of Erich Auerbach's *Mimesis*[1] and recent contributions from Dan Jacobson,[2] Robert Alter,[3] and Northrop Frye[4] on literary study of the Bible contain useful insights. Indeed, biblical scholars have generally been more receptive and hospitable to such contributions from outside the field than scholars in almost any other field. Yet as it grows, this field of inquiry will make ever-greater demands upon its practitioners to prepare themselves in a double range of skills. They will need both the established skills of biblical research and the skills necessary for literary research in general. The double burden of preparation is tremendous, but it is in proportion with the opportunity. Biblical scholars acquire a new avenue of learning this text; literary scholars enjoy the fruits of a readymade bank of information acquired through the traditional modes of scholarship.

It is only fair that the literary scholar of the Bible should have this advantage of a readymade foundation. That scholar has to deal, after all, with a multi-authored, multi-aged, multi-genred, religiously charged, and very long book. To state it methodologically, a primary concern of this work must be, what are those literary problems which are unique to the Bible? Or to formulate it from the other side of the cover, what are those aspects of the Bible which contribute to its unique character?

The answer to this question must include at least the following: first, the singular literary history of the text. Whatever specific views we each hold with regard to the sources and redaction of the Torah, the Deuteronomistic History, and the Chronicler's History, as well as the prophetic and poetic books and the remaining writings, we must recognize a rich, complex construction resulting in powerful literary combinations, exegetically rich ironies, and even ambiguities that call out *daršēnî*. It is a book with a hundred fifty authors and no author. Its literary history is so complex and so well hidden that major pieces of the puzzle remain unsolved in source-critical scholarship over a hundred years after Wellhausen.

A second aspect of the Bible which contributes to its unique character is that its prose (and often its poetry) is both literature and history. The very existence of discussions of whether biblical narrative is historicized prose or fictionalized history is to the point. The book is neither so historical as, say, a volume of Salo Baron, nor as fictional as one of the historical plays of Shakespeare.

Third, the Bible is sacred literature by virtue of origin and authority. With regard to origin, it has been considered divinely conceived, written, dictated, revealed, or inspired—or at least composed in dedication to or in service of divinity. With regard to authority, it is a book that combines legislation with narrative, admonition with poetry. Its legislation has been taken as normative and its narratives as didactic. Not every reader—nor even all the authors—of the Bible has held these views of its origin and its authority. But the community of faithful has been so large and has played so far-reaching a role in the interpretation of the book for millennia that we hardly come to it in a vacuum. We embrace the tradition or reject it or hold it in abeyance, but rarely do we ignore it.

The last aspect contributing to the Bible's particular character is the composite nature of its text. The Bible is one book, and it is many books. It includes prose, poetry, and law. It is a literature as well as a book. In this essay I want to focus on this last feature, the Bible's composite character, but my discussion will necessarily involve the other three as well. I want to look at biblical narrative as a unity, but with a consciousness of the compositional and editorial processes that produced it.

The Hebrew Bible comprises thirty-nine books. Its authorship is multiple, it houses diverse literary genres, it covers hundreds of characters (or, let us say, persons) in generations spread over millennia, and yet there is unity, continuity, plot. Thus it is appropriately called both by the plurals *Holy Scriptures* and *biblia* and by the singular *The Bible.* Perhaps the Hebrew *tanak,* conveying by acronym its parts and its sum, best communicates its *e pluribus unum* character.

The reason why biblical scholars, teachers, and lay people so rarely regard the book as a whole—as opposed to nearly every other book—seems to me to derive largely from the traditional mode of study of the Bible, namely, verse-by-verse analysis. This mode derived in turn, first, from the regard for each word and line of the text as sacred, and second, from the nature of the rabbinical sermon in the Midrash's formative years. The rabbis concentrated each week on a small portion of the text. This verse-by-verse mode of exegesis reached a high point in Rashi, whose commentary became the model and norm, at least in Jewish scholarship. It is perhaps ironic that Rashi's commentary should have contributed to this result, since Rashi himself seems rarely to have lost sight of the forest for the trees. He had remarkable control over the full text of the *tanak,* as we clearly see in his treatment of Gen. 1:1. There he draws on one passage each from the Prophets and the Writings to shed light on a verse of the Torah. Indeed, the Midrash itself, in *midrāš tᵉhillîm* for example, develops this same interrelationship of *tōrāh, nᵉbîʾîm,* and *kᵉtubîm* in reflecting sermons based on a weekly selection from each. The modern Christian or Jewish sermon generally focuses on a single point in a story, but the fact remains that one can also read an ongoing story in the biblical narrative books from Genesis to Esther.

Why is this possible? I believe that the answer is partly editorial and partly conceptual. First, I would say, it owes to the skill of the editors (redactors, tradents, *mᵉsaddᵉrîm*) of the larger corpora of biblical narrative, for they designed structures that could comfortably house diverse, duplicating, or even contradicting texts. As I have described elsewhere, the Deuteronomistic Historian(s) set out to bring together in a continuous account the diverse legal, narrative, and occasional poetic materials that now comprise the books of Deuteronomy through Kings.[5] They entered into a literary partnership, as it were, with the authors of their inherited texts, seeking to produce a meaningful, ongoing story rather than the sort of annals that their Mesopotamian neighbors were producing. To summarize the process, the Josianic Deuteronomist took a corpus of old legal materials (Deuteronomy 12—26), added an introduction and conclusion which cast the text as the farewell address of Moses and tied that corpus to the JE accounts by means of direct allusions to them in Moses' reminiscences (the JE accounts were either joined to the Deuteronomistic work or presumed by it—which amounts to virtually the same thing), gathered historical materials for the periods of conquest, judges, and monarchy from sources which he sometimes identified and sometimes did not, arranged them chronologically, and constructed an *inclusio* of parallels between Moses and Josiah. The book that is set beside the ark at the command of Moses is found, read, and carried out at the command of Josiah. Distinct parallels of action and of wording compose the Moses-Josiah *inclusio.* The historian then added a series of statements which unified and explained this historical account, the most prominent of which were: (1) he rated each of the kings of Israel as good or bad in the eyes of Yahweh based, above all, on his fulfillment or nonfulfillment of the law of centralization of worship in the place where Yahweh causes his name to dwell (thus, all the rulers of the Northern Kingdom are berated, and all the Southern rulers [except Hezekiah and Josiah] devalued in part or entirely); (2) he included ten depictions of prophecies with notations of fulfillment in subsequent passages in the work, as Gerhard von Rad has described;[6] (3) he set regular comparisons of the monarchs to David and developed the Davidic covenant as backdrop to their actions. The result was a work covering some eight centuries with narrative continuity that was extended by an exilic Deuteronomist to deal with subsequent events down to the exile.

The Priestly redactor of the Torah achieved at least as successful a continuity despite drawing on a far more complex group of sources, including blatant doublets and mutually contradicting texts. Using the ten *tôl^e^dōt* rubrics and twelve rubrics drawn from the Numbers 33 list of stations of Israel's wilderness journey, as Frank Cross has described,[7] and a plagues framework, as I have described elsewhere,[8] he brought his sources together in a united, ongoing narrative from *b^e^rēšît* to the arrival of Israel at the border of the promised land.

With the Book of Deuteronomy as the link, the Torah and Deuteronomistic History naturally came together to form what David Noel Freedman calls the primary history, from the creation to the exile. The Chronicler's History of course shows no less redactional skill in bringing together historical sources, genealogies, and poetry into literary synthesis.[9]

The result of these three major syntheses is a continuous portrayal of the relations of Yahweh with the human community from the first day of the world to the time of the Jews' restoration under the Persian Empire. One may read the other narrative books—Ruth, Daniel, Esther—easily locating them in their proper chronological settings in this continuous portrayal. One may similarly "locate" the prophetic and poetic books with only occasional difficulty.

Still, there must be more than editorial structure involved in the production of a coherent story from Genesis to Esther. Besides this external structure, which brings the various texts together in a sensible chronological progression, there are unifying components of plot which provide the commonality necessary among the texts themselves to enable them to join in meaningful continuity. The Bible grew out of (and contributed to) an ongoing religious and historical tradition, after all, and so certain central tenets of the faith of Israel also became central literary components of the Bible's plot.

First among these is monotheism. It is not necessary to review here the debates concerning at what point the religion of Israel became properly monotheist. The fact is that those who wrote the works which became parts of the Hebrew Bible consistently focused on one God, either because they did not recognize the existence of other gods or because they were not interested in writing stories about them. Either way, monotheism provides an obvious unity for diverse stories spread over centuries—a unity which a pagan milieu cannot so easily provide and which no pagan culture in the ancient Near East did provide. If the biblical writers had dealt with many gods, then the literary product would have been a collection of myths, not a continuous narrative.

The national character of the materials provided the second unifying component. They concerned one people and one land. Even when events temporarily made them about two peoples in the lands, Israel and Judah, they were still conceived as really one by the redactors of the Deuteronomistic and Chronicler's histories. The Deuteronomist wove the originally separate documents that told the histories of each kingdom around each other like a DNA molecule, and the Chronicler never recognized the division as legitimate. Nationalism plus monotheism meant that almost any story could be conceived as fitting into a narrative that was broadly about the two constants, Yahweh and Israel.

Third, there was a historical sense among the biblical writers. Again, there is no need to enter here into the debates as to how unique ancient Israel was in this regard or whether the historical sense was conceptually linked to Israel's break with pagan-mythical notions of time. The point is simply that the biblical writers did have a sense of linear progression of events through time, and this sense made it possible to arrange a diverse group of stories and records into a sensible sequence.

The mechanism through which the sequence of relations between Yahweh and Israel was pictured was covenant. The E text pictured a covenant between God and Israel at Sinai, the J account added an Abrahamic covenant, the Josianic Deuteronomistic Historian developed the Davidic covenant, and the Priestly narrative added a covenant with Noah. These four primary covenants, the Noahic, Abrahamic, Mosaic, and Davidic, provided a narrative framework in which legal, historical, legendary, poetic, and so on, materials could meet. The four-covenant structure has sufficient conceptual breadth and versatility to be able to encompass a wide range of genres and multi-centuried chronology of stories and personalities while at the same time having sufficient consistency and integrity as a system to be a meaningful housing for those texts. It provides interpretative foci through which one can relate various accounts to the thread of the unfolding narrative of Yahweh's relations with humans in general and Israel in particular. Thus the Exodus account commences with the notation "God remembered his covenant with Abraham, Isaac, and Jacob" (Exod. 2:24). The leitmotif passage for the Book of Judges characterizes the crux of Israel's fortunes in the pre-monarchic age explicitly as their transgression of the Israelite covenant (Judges 2:20). The loss of the Northern Kingdom after Solomon is ascribed to the king's nonfulfillment of the Israelite and Davidic covenants (1 Kings 11:4, 11), while the ongoing retention of the Southern Kingdom is ascribed to the power of the Davidic covenant despite the crimes of Solomon (11:12–13, 34–36), Abijah (15:3–4), and Jehoram (2 Kings 8:18–19). The peroration on the fall of the Northern Kingdom traces that event to its rejection of the Israelite covenant (2 Kings 17:15), and the portrayal of the fall of the Southern Kingdom, even though it lacks an explicit peroration, casts the final events in Judah as fulfilling the covenant curses of Deuteronomy (Deut. 28:64; 2 Kings 25:26) and resulting from the transgression of specific covenantal commands. The renewal of covenant is depicted at critical junctures in the development of the narrative: Moses rehearses the covenant in the Plains of Moab on the eve of entry into the land (Deuteronomy); Joshua brings the conquest to culmination in the Shechem covenant renewal (Joshua 24); Josiah establishes the *sēper tōrâ* as authoritative in Judah in a covenant renewal at Jerusalem (2 Kings 23); Ezra and Nehemiah bring the restoration to culmination in the covenant renewal at the water gate (Nehemiah 8; 9).

With the Noahic covenant promising the stability of the cosmic structure, the Abrahamic covenant promising people and land, the Davidic covenant promising sovereignty, and the Israelite covenant promising life, security, and prosperity, the biblical authors and editors possessed a platform from which they could portray and reconcile nearly every historical, legendary, didactic, folk, and the like, account in their tradition. If we could delete all references to covenant—which we cannot do, precisely because it is regularly integral to its contexts—we would have an anthology of stories. As it is we have a structure that can house a plot.

Still, all of these factors together (monotheism, nationalism, the historical sense, and covenant) would not have produced a continuous literary work. Monotheism and nationalism provided the necessary components, the historical sense provided the mechanism for continuity, and covenant provided the structure. But that only amounts to a collection of related units. What was still needed was to make the collection into a continuous story—in literary terms, a plot. The record of the relations between Yahweh and the human community provided the plot. Specifically, the major unifying component of the biblical plot is the phenomenon of the continually diminishing apparent presence of Yahweh among humans from the beginning of the book to the end, the phenomenon of *Deus absconditus* or, in the book's own terms, *Yahweh hammastîr pānâw.* I have made a source-critical study of this phenomenon in the Torah and *nᵉbî'îm rî'šōnîm* elsewhere.[10] In this essay, I want to offer in summary a picture of the shape of this phenomenon as it appears in the biblical authors' and editors' final narrative product. (I intend to treat the phenomenon as it appears in biblical prophecy and poetry in a separate study.)

The narrative begins in Genesis 1 and 2 with Yahweh involved in word and action in the creation of heaven and earth. In creating humankind, Yahweh personally fashions Adam and Eve, himself breathes life into the man's nostrils, plants the garden, forms the animals, walks in the garden, speaks directly to the humans, and even makes their clothing. He demands less from them than from their descendant of the tenth generation, Noah. Noah must build his own ark. Still, a sense of Yahweh's presence and personal involvement in human affairs persists through the *Urgeschichte.* Yahweh himself shuts the ark, and he brings the cosmic crisis, the breaking of the portals which hold back the water that is above the sky and below the earth. Here, in the most cosmic depiction of his power outside of the creation, and at the same time in a particularly personal picture of his attention to the creatures in the ark, the narrative conveys Yahweh's continuing immanence in the world that he has created, though his involvement is here less intimate than with Adam and Eve in Eden.

In Noah's descendant of the tenth generation, Abraham, the human share of responsibility in the narrative action grows in a lifelong testing, from the first *lēk lᵉkā,* in which Abraham gives up his father's house, to the latter *lēk lᵉkā,* in which he takes his son to Moriah. Again, the portrayal of the growth of human responsibility shares context with the development of signs of divine involvement in human affairs. Angels enter the narrative as at least two of the visitors to Abraham at Mamre (some scholars take the third to be Yahweh in human form) and elsewhere. The divine presence is manifest in a flame of fire in the Genesis 15 depiction of the covenant ceremony and in an unspecified form in the Genesis 17 covenant account. In this world of awesome visible displays of divine presence, the human Abraham nonetheless raises questions to his covenant partner concerning the latter's plans for Sodom and Gomorrah (Genesis 18), and even Lot successfully acquires a divine reprieve for the city of Zoar (Gen. 9:17–21). Strikingly, in the latter case Yahweh responds, "Escape there quickly, because I cannot do a thing until you arrive there" (v. 22). Even Abraham's servant himself chooses the sign by which he wishes Yahweh to identify the appointed woman for Isaac (Gen. 24:12ff.).

Something is happening. For whatever reason, Yahweh is transferring (relinquishing?) ever more control of the course of human affairs to members of the human community. It is Yahweh who chooses Isaac as covenantal heir, despite Abraham's explicit request for Ishmael (Genesis 17), but it is Jacob who chooses Jacob. He manipulates the birthright and the blessing in a manner which has taxed exegetes for millennia, yet Yahweh honors the succession. Jacob fights with a man? an angel? Yahweh in some human form? and demands a blessing. A divine power, the interpretation of dreams, resides in Joseph in such a way that he must continually protest to all that it is Yahweh and not himself operating (Gen. 40:8; 44:16; 45:5, 7, 8, 9).

This phenomenon of the divine deposit of power in a human's apparent control, itself an important stage in the developing metamorphosis of the divine and human roles, reaches a new level in the accounts of Moses. Moses so controls the timing and performance of miracles that he appears as a god to humans (Exod. 4:16; 7:1). Like Joseph, he continually has to say that Yahweh has sent him (Exod. 16:8; Num. 16:11, 28). He speaks to the deity in a manner unlike that of any predecessor, challenging divine decisions concerning the destruction of the people of Israel at Sinai (Exodus 32) and in the matter of the spies (Numbers 14), and protesting Yahweh's treatment of him in general (in the matter of the quails, Numbers 11). The text has come a long way from Abraham's humbly worded questions in the Sodom/Gomorrah dialogue to Moses' arguments and protests. Most interesting here is the second story of

Moses' striking a rock (Num. 20:2–13). The divine commission is to speak to the rock; Moses strikes it. But the miracle works. Moses has power to alter a miracle. He is punished, true, but the very severity of the punishment dramatizes the significance of what Moses has done.

In the midst of this growth in the human stance in the narrative come two accounts which depict pinnacles of divine immanence: first, the declaration of the covenant in the hearing of all the people at Sinai (Exodus 19; 20) and, second, Moses' personal experience at Sinai (Exodus 34) in which he actually sees Yahweh. From one perspective, these two episodes are exceptions to the otherwise diminishing immanence of Yahweh in the narrative. In context, however, they serve precisely to dramatize that process. The people's response to hearing the deity's voice at Sinai is to tell Moses "You speak with us, and we will listen, but let God not speak with us, lest we die" (Exod. 20:19). Moses' personal experience of Yahweh thus becomes just that; it is Moses' experience, while for the people it means the arrival of a stage of mediated divine communication. Yahweh himself carves the Decalogue, but Moses carries it to the people. The community of descendants of Adam, Noah, Abraham, Isaac, and Jacob are never to experience direct divine speech again. Rather, the divine message is always thereafter to be mediated through the voice, appearance, and personality of a human agent. In a word, prophecy. Indeed, this stage in the expression of divine presence among humans in biblical narrative itself leads immediately to another stage, as Aaron and Miriam, having joined with Moses in the experience of prophecy along with seventy elders, challenge Moses with the words, "Has not Yahweh also spoken through us?" (Num. 12:2). Yahweh responds:

> If there will be a prophet among you
> I Yahweh shall make myself known to him in a vision
> In a dream I shall speak through him
> Not so my servant Moses
> In all my house he is faithful
> Mouth to mouth I shall speak through him
> And by vision, and not by enigmas
> And he will see the form of Yahweh
>
> (Num. 12:6–8)

Thus, after Moses, prophets are to experience only dreams and visions, and the people are to receive only the prophets' reports thereof. In Moses' own time, meanwhile, the people's experience of the divine is mediated through Moses, or "masked" through the *kābôd* and the *'ānān,* or channeled through a series of layers, the courtyard, the *petaḥ,* the Holy, the *pārōket.* Finally, in Yahweh's last words to Moses before summoning him to Abarim, he says, "I shall hide my face from them; I shall see what their end will be."

Two narrative phenomena are at work here. Apparent control of human events shifts continually into human hands, and the apparent immanence of the deity diminishes. The relationship between the two is complex but essentially complementary, and they grow together in the subsequent narratives. Moses' power to alter a miracle is outdone when Joshua, on his own initiative, calls to the sun to stand still in the sky. The text specifically notes the extraordinary character of this act: "There was no day like that before it or after it that Yahweh hearkened to the voice of a man . . ." (Josh. 10:14). Joshua has selected his own miracle. Subsequent figures may not bring the sun to a halt, but their personal control of miracles in general expands. Power is deposited prenatally in Samson in such a way that his own personal interests, tastes, and weaknesses direct it—sometimes in the people's interest, sometimes in his own. The personal manipulation of miracle reaches a high point in Elijah and Elisha, who seemingly use power at their whim for anything from summoning bears to tearing apart some brats who mock a prophet's baldness to reviving the dead. In the final personal miracle of biblical narrative, Isaiah offers Hezekiah the choice of naming the direction in which the sun will move its shadow.

At the same time that prophets of the post-Mosaic age are portrayed as performing acts of power that are beyond those of Abraham and Moses, all of the standard signals of the divine presence in biblical narrative cease. The two standard terms for divine appearances are the Niphals *nglh* and *nr'h*. The last biblical person to whom Yahweh is said to be *nglh* is Samuel (1 Sam. 3:21). The last *wayyērā'* is to Solomon (1 Kings 3:5; 9:2; 11:9). The last appearances of the *kābôd* and the *'ānān* are on the occasion of the dedication of the Temple of Solomon (1 Kings 8:10–11). The last appearance of an angel witnessed by a human is to Elijah (2 Kings 1:3, 15). (The last depiction of an angel at all in biblical narrative—unseen—is in the portrayal of Sennacherib's siege of Jerusalem, 2 Kings 19:35; Isa. 37:36; 2 Chron. 32:21.) The last major public miracle, that is, one witnessed by a large segment of the nation and serving a critical purpose in the story of Yahweh's communication with them, is that of Elijah at Carmel (1 Kings 19). One by one the apparent signs of Yahweh's immanence in the world are disappearing. In a fascinating juxtaposition, the portrayal of the last of the disappearing signs, Elijah at Carmel, is followed by the portrayal of Elijah at Horeb. Again we see a lone prophet on Horeb/Sinai, but Elijah's experience there is a reversal of that of Moses. In the place of the supreme theophany come three phenomena that are sometimes associated with theophany (earthquake, wind, and fire), each followed by the specific qualification "Yahweh was not in (it)," and all are followed by *qwl dmmh dqh,* a sound of thin hush. Yahweh then repeats to Elijah his earlier question, *māh lᵉkā pōh?* At precisely the narrative juncture at which divine appearances, cloud and glory, angels, and public miracles cease, comes this account of the deity's blatant refusal to appear as before. Yahweh never again speaks to a king or to the people. The manner of his communication with prophets is never specifically portrayed. The only remaining channel to him in biblical narrative is that which is pictured in the Deuteronomistic Name Theology, that is, the

Temple, in which he causes his name to dwell. With the destruction of the Temple at the conclusion of the Book of Kings, the last channel is removed. The prediction that Yahweh's face will be hidden is fulfilled as both Judah and Israel are said to be "cast from before my face" (2 Kings 23:27). Yahweh plays no apparent role whatever in the Books of Ezra and Nehemiah, and he is not mentioned in Esther. The narrative from Genesis to Esther has come the full cycle from a stage on which God is alone to one on which humans are on their own. Though no longer in control of miraculous powers, humans have arrived at complete responsibility for their fortunes.

This developing *hastārāt pānîm,* tied to covenant, forms a traceable plot development through biblical narrative, and one that is remarkably unified given the multiplicity of books, sources, and authors. Not every pericope of biblical narrative relates to covenant or *hastārāt pānîm,* but enough portions do relate so as to provide the stuff and structure that hold the work together.

I submit, therefore, that literary study which addresses "the book" as a book is not only legitimate but fruitful. Again, this does not mean ignoring the composite character of the text and speaking about it as if it were by one author. This, perhaps, is the flaw in Auerbach's treatment of the sacrifice of Isaac, for he compares "the Homeric" to "the Israelite" perspective, deriving the latter from Genesis 22 alone. Genesis 22, after all, is part of the fragmentary E source and was quite probably reworked by a later editor. Indeed, the *hastārāt pānîm* phenomenon itself is in part the result of the combination of the sources. For example, the combination of JE and P in the plagues and wilderness accounts resulted in an increased density of accounts of miracles in the Mosaic age. Both sources contained accounts of plagues of blood and frogs,[11] and so these were editorially merged, but most of the other plagues were different in the two sources,[12] and so the combination of the sources produced a larger total for plagues than either source apparently contained originally. Likewise, with the wilderness traditions, the E and P versions of the incident at Meribah were not editorially compatible, having opposite denouements. The editorial decision to retain both versions increased the number of miracles that a reader would understand to have occurred in the wilderness. And so on. The nature of the specific sources, and the specific redactional decisions, produced an impression that miracles were more numerous in Moses' time.

The nature of the sources of the Deuteronomistic History was different. These sources were not alternative versions of stories to the degree that the Pentateuchal sources were. The Deuteronomist rather combined a history of the kings of Israel with a history of the kings of Judah, rarely having to turn two versions of essentially the same story into two separate accounts. Therefore the stories of miracles in Kings were not doubled in the way that the stories in Exodus and Numbers were. When the Torah and the Deuteronomistic History were joined to form a continuous work, this matter of sources and editing resulted in an enhanced impression that there were more miracles in the Mosaic age than in later ages. In studying the Hebrew Bible in its final form, therefore, we must attend to the process of composition in all its stages if we are to understand how it came out as it did. In fact the most interesting question of all may be how the diminishing-presence phenomenon worked out so well, given the sizable number of authors and editors involved, and given that they were spread over centuries. The phenomenon does not fit the chronology of the authors themselves. That is, it cannot simply be explained as the result of early authors portraying theophanies and miracles more than later authors. On the contrary, the developing hiddenness of the deity follows the internal chronology of the narrative. Apparently, no matter when an author lived he or she would picture the most distant times as ages of miracle, and more recent times as less so. Perhaps the reason for this is a common human inclination to picture ages of power as lying in the distant past (or the distant future, namely, apocalyptic), but not in our own day. Like the Chinese curse "May you live in interesting times," Western thinking, too, may have reflected a fundamental mixture of fear and fascination with the nearness of divinity. And the production of a composite book over generations and centuries not only could not submerge this feeling, it reflected it.

What is the significance of interpreting the full Bible as a book? Why do it? I would answer, first, because the reader does it anyway, consciously or not, in a haphazard way, and second, because it opens up new channels of interpretation, channels of major importance. First among these is the phenomenon of the diminishing presence of God, which I have summarized here. If it is accurate to say that Yahweh's presence gradually diminishes from the beginning of the Hebrew Bible's story to the end, then this is a most crucial fact of plot in the Bible—from either a literary or a theological perspective. The Hebrew Bible thus tells the story of humankind's movement from a supernaturally charged world of a cracking cosmos, splitting seas, divine voices, and talking animals to the world that we know, a world in which the immanence of God is an enigma, a matter of faith.

One can derive a range of interpretations from this total book perspective. Consider the case of Esther, a sometimes admired, often maligned book, sexy, concerned with dirty politics, with no mention of God, for whatever reason the only book of the Hebrew Bible not represented at Qumran, and a book that some wish were not in the canon at all. Seen in the light of the diminishing apparent presence of Yahweh through the course of biblical narrative, though, it is an appropriate and striking concluding book for the narrative, portraying the people of Israel in a hostile world in which one can no longer count on miraculous divine intervention for rescue. Seen in the light of the increasing responsibility ascribed to humans through the course of the narrative, Esther is no less interesting, especially given current sensitivity to the place of woman in the Bible. Woman, Eve, has been blamed for millennia for entering upon the course of action that brought humans out of their initial state of harmonious relations with Yahweh (Genesis 3). It seems only fair, ironic, and appropriate that the narrative concludes with a story in which the humans, now in a world in which the presence of God is hidden, turn to a woman as their chief hope of rescue. One may interpret the Eve-to-Esther connection differently, but one can hardly ignore it. Each of the Bible's bookends has a woman's face carved on it.

Besides *Yahweh hammastîr pānâw* and "From Eve to Esther," literary study of the unified biblical text offers another interpretive channel of considerable significance, namely, the book's focus upon itself. We have observed that divine revelations, miracles, angels, and so on, are absent by the conclusion of the Book of Kings. What does remain, however, in the Books of Ezra and Nehemiah is the Torah itself. In the absence of the apparent acts of God, there is the Word of God. The Hebrew Bible becomes a book about itself. One portion of the Bible, the first five books, figures as an entity in later portions. It acquires a particular internal literary status in the conclusion of its own narrative. By fastening upon this unusual literary datum, one opens the door to rich layers of interpretation. This is best illustrated in Nahum Glatzer's splendid essay titled "Franz Kafka and the Tree of Knowledge,"[13] in which Glatzer confronts (with Kafka) the biblical story of the humans' initial estrangement from God and exile from the realm of the Tree of Life. The price of the acquisition of knowledge is the loss of the Tree of Life. But it is precisely through the channel of knowledge, Glatzer observes, that God provides compensation for the loss. He reveals the Torah, and what is the Torah, *'ēs hayyîm hî'*—it is a Tree of Life (Prov. 3:18). I would add the observation that in Genesis 3 the purpose of the cherubs is to guard the Tree of Life, and later in the narrative, two golden cherubs watch over the ark in the Tabernacle, and Solomon sets two golden cherubs in the Holy of Holies, spreading their wings over the ark in the Temple. The Torah offers the choice of life and death and declares "Choose life." Ezra arrives without a staff of power, but he carries the book which offers more than restoration of sovereignty in the promised land. It offers restoration of, or at least compensation for, that which has been lost since the third chapter of the Bible's story.

Thus the study of the Bible as a unified book leads ultimately to a recognition of the status of the book on its own terms—a book that declares its worth from its own story.

As I stated above, this story's continuity did not happen by chance. The editors showed enormous skill in assembling it out of sources. They had the concept of a continuing story that flowed through generations and centuries, they were able to collect and to connect the component sources into such a story, and they constructed inclusions that made key events into denouements rather than just further events in an uninterpreted sequence. For instance, the Israelites eject the Canaanites from the land, and then they are ejected themselves; they start as a people in Egypt, and they return to Egypt when their nation is defeated (Deut. 28:68; 2 Kings 25:26); their story begins in the Chaldees, and they end in flight from the Chaldeans (Gen. 15:7; 2 Kings 25:26); the story begins with God on his own and ends with humans on their own.

The study of the Bible in its united final form reveals an exegetically rich story. The analytical study of the composition, redaction, and transmission of the Bible reveals how it arrived there, and it exposes a wealth of information about history and art in the process. It is not necessary to debate the relative merits of diachronic versus synchronic readings of the text. They are complementary, not competitive, and there is time and reward enough for both.

NOTES

1. Erich Auerbach, *Mimesis*, trans. W. R. Trask (Princeton: Princeton Univ. Press, 1953).
2. Dan Jacobson, *The Story of Stories* (New York: Harper & Row, 1982).
3. Robert Alter, *The Art of Biblical Narrative* (New York: Basic Books, 1981).
4. Northrop Frye, *The Great Code* (New York: Harcourt Brace Jovanovich, 1982).
5. Richard Elliott Friedman, *The Exile and Biblical Narrative*, HSM 22 (Chico, Calif.: Scholars Press, 1981), 1–26.
6. Gerhard von Rad, "The Deuteronomic Theology of History in I and II Kings," in *The Problem of the Hexateuch* (New York: McGraw-Hill, 1966), 208–11.
7. Frank Moore Cross, *Canaanite Myth and Hebrew Epic* (Cambridge: Harvard Univ. Press, 1973), 308–17.
8. Richard Elliott Friedman, "Sacred History and Theology: The Redaction of Torah," in *The Creation of Sacred Literature*, ed. R. E. Friedman, Near Eastern Studies 22 (Berkeley and Los Angeles: Univ. of California Press, 1981), 31–34.
9. See, for example, Baruch Halpern, "Sacred History and Ideology: Chronicles' Thematic Structure," in *Creation of Sacred Literature*, ed. Friedman, 35–54.
10. Friedman, *Exile and Biblical Narrative*, 36–42, 124–36. On the term "the hiding of the face," see my "The Biblical Expression *mastîr pānîm*," *Hebrew Annual Review* 1 (1977): 139–47, and Samuel E. Balentine, *The Hidden God: The Hiding of the Face of God in the Old Testament* (New York: Oxford Univ. Press, 1983).
11. JE: Exod. 7:14–18, 20b–21a, 23–29; 8:3b–11a. P: 7:19–20a, 21b–22; 8:1–3a.
12. JE: Exod. 8:16–28; 9:1–7, 13–34; 10:1–19, 21–26, 28–29; 11:1–8. P: 8:12–15; 9:8–12.
13. Nahum N. Glatzer, "Franz Kafka and the Tree of Knowledge," in *Essays in Jewish Thought* (University: Univ. of Alabama Press, 1978), 184–91.

Part Four

TRADITIONS OF SCHOLARSHIP

10 EDWARD L. GREENSTEIN

A JEWISH READING OF ESTHER

Many factors influence our responses to a story. High among these rank our expectations of what it is supposed to be and what it is supposed to do. Is the story, for example, a comedy at which we should laugh, or is it a tragedy at which we should cry? What we understand to be the literary genre of a particular work will color our reading by setting up the initial and perhaps even the ensuing expectations against which we will measure our reactions. We will assess a "true" story differently from a fictitious one, even if the two appear virtually identical. We bring to our reading a varied array of presuppositions and interpretive strategies, and these affect the way we make sense of a text before so much as a letter of print meets the eye.[1]

The Book of Esther occupies a different position in the Jewish and Christian Bibles, and its significance differs in Jewish and Christian life. Thus, we are hardly surprised that, as many have observed, Jews have tended to love Esther while Christians, particularly since Martin Luther harshly rejected it, have tended either to dismiss it or merely to tolerate it.[2]

In the part of the Christian Bible denigrated as the Old Testament—the antiquated, superseded covenant—Esther takes its place in the chronological "history" of Israel. It immediately tails Ezra and Nehemiah, for were Esther a historical narrative, its events would be contemporaneous with theirs. Yet taken as a historical narrative, Esther, in Hermann Gunkel's words, "cannot be read by a Christian or a non-Jew without great distaste," for it fires up intense Jewish nationalism, celebrates anti-Gentile Jewish vengeance, and promulgates Purim, a festival that means nothing to the church.[3] Many Christian theologians and even certain Reform Jewish biblicists would drop the book from the scriptural canon.[4] Whatever else may lie behind such attitudes, there exists a patent assumption that the narrative of Esther constitutes serious history or is at least a secular tale. The ear that hears the story with such offense belongs to a deadpan face; no tongue in cheek there.

In the Jewish Scriptures, on the other hand, Esther's position is determined by its function in Jewish liturgy. The "scroll" of Esther was gathered with the other four scrolls that were ordained to be chanted in the synagogue in the course of the liturgical calendar. Arranged in their liturgical sequence, the five scrolls comprise a unit in the *Ketuvim,* the "Writings." Esther comprises the text read aloud in the synagogue at the Feast of Purim. In the Jewish canon, then, Esther counts not so much for its real or imagined place in history, as for its function as the proof text and publicity for Purim. Esther belongs to Purim. It is in the context of Purim that Jews hear the book, and it is the atmosphere of Purim that pervades its Jewish reception. Even more importantly, Jews have read in the story of Esther and Mordecai a paradigm of their people's vulnerability to racist hatred.[5] No Jew can fail to be affected on hearing the Esther Scroll's catalogue of the people's catastrophes and close calls. When, in a recent article in the *New York Times,* Isaac Bashevis Singer nonchalantly referred to the threat of Haman in the scroll as a near "Holocaust," he displayed such a paradigmatic reading.[6] So in Esther's Jewish triumph, Jews celebrate their own survival.

Scholars have long debated whether the Book of Esther might have existed in some form prior to its adoption as the Purim text, or whether it was connected "from the outset" with the festival whose observance it prescribes as Otto Eissfeldt and others have held.[7] But even if that question remains unresolved, this much is clear: the scroll was not canonized and read in the synagogue except as the Purim text. Whatever its inception, the biblical story of Esther was never heard except in the context of Jewish communal festivity. Accordingly, there was virtually no circumstance wherein a Jew might hear the scroll's words without simultaneously experiencing the strong influence of the surrounding carnival-like Purim scene.

The constant *Sitz im Leben* of the Esther Scroll, that of a festive celebration, has always determined the seriousness—or rather lack of seriousness—with which it has been taken. In fact, such a Jewish reading of Esther makes perfectly good sense of the scroll and its alleged anomalies. Therefore, with tongue nestled in cheek, let us review the nature and themes of the Esther narrative. We shall find a specific homology between text and context—between that which takes place on stage, so to speak, and that which, in act and in fantasy, takes place in the audience.

In recent centuries, Jews have customarily observed Purim by spinning satirical playlets out of the Esther tale or another tradition.[8] Indeed, some historians have imagined that the biblical story itself originated in this way.[9] According to this view, various components of the narrative reflect ritual dramas of a pagan spring/new year festival.[10] The conflicts and movements of the story would then mirror the ritual combats and processions of the celebrants. This reconstruction of the Purim text's, Esther's, historical background is certainly plausible. But whether the Esther narrative began in ritual drama or not, historical Jewish celebration of Purim would readily find in Esther a reflex of its own activities.

Before penetrating further this match of text and context, we may mention some of the literary reasons behind the supposition that the Esther story grew not from history but from invention. Of course, there are historical reasons for questioning the narrative's authenticity.[11] Assuming that *'Aḥashverosh* refers to Xerxes I, who reigned in the fifth century B.C.E., Herodotus was his contemporary. Thus, Herodotus records that Amestris was queen, and that Persian kings could only marry with the seven noble families of Persia. This alone rules out the historicity of the tale. The lengths to which certain scholars will go to try to defend the narrative as historical proves the weakness of their claim.[12]

But the scroll even gives itself away in 2:6. There it says that Mordecai was exiled by Nebuchadnezzar with the Judean king Jeconiah (Jehoiachin). This implies the date 598 B.C.E.—more than a century before Xerxes I began to rule. I emphasize the peculiarly literary cues to the story's nonhistoricity because it is these to which an ordinary Jewish audience would respond. One need not have read Herodotus to pick up on them—even the Talmud shows its alertness in this regard (*b. Megilla* 7a). In the midst of a passage which challenges the sanctity of Esther, various tannaitic views are adduced to support its inclusion in the Bible. The arguments are: (1) Esther is inspired (*beruaḥ haqqodesh ne'emra*) because it knows the private thoughts of its characters (6:6: "Haman said in his heart"); (2) Esther is inspired because it is uncanny (2:15: "Esther bore grace in the eyes of all who saw her"); (3) Esther is inspired because God revealed crucial information to Mordecai (2:22: "The matter become known to Mordecai"—somehow!); (4) Esther is inspired because it is incredible otherwise (9:16: although Mordecai permitted the Jews to loot their victims' property, they did not!). All these observations a literary critic, such as Robert Alter, would regard as signs of fiction.[13]

More obvious signs of fiction lie in the comedic hyperbole that permeates the text.[14] For instance, the king rules 127 provinces (while Herodotus attributes to Xerxes only 20 satrapies); he throws a banquet for 180 days; the beauty contestants spend 12 months preparing (the ancient Syriac translation incredulously read "days" for "months" here); Haman offers Ahasueras 100,000 talents of silver to exterminate the Jews; to impale Mordecai, he erects a pole 50 cubits tall.

The scroll also parodies Persian authority. (This, we shall later see, is highly pertinent to its theme.)[15] The king decrees first that the rule of his banquet is no restrictions on drinking (1:8)![16] And when his queen refuses to show off her beauty before his guests, the king exploits the full protocol of Persia to circulate an edict "to every province in its own script, and to every nationality in its own language, that every man is prince in his house and may speak in the language of his own nationality" (1:22).[17] While the decree's logic may be small-minded, it nonetheless characterizes the story. Here, one wife disobeys one order from the king, so the king commands all wives to obey all husbands. Later, one Jew, Mordecai, will similarly trespass one law—to bow to Haman—and Haman will seek to execute all Jews. It is not very different when Esther fears for her one life at the expense of all Jewish lives (4:11). She overcomes her reluctance only when Mordecai points out that if all Jews are threatened, so is she (4:13).

The story as a whole gives a marked appearance of being contrived. As S. R. Driver noted, "the incidents at each stage seem laid so as to prepare for the next, which duly follows without hitch or interruption."[18] Furthermore, irony abounds, usually at Haman's expense. Haman seeks to harm (3:6: *shalaḥ yad,* to "extend a hand" against) the man who has saved the king from those who wished to harm him (2:21: *shalaḥ yad*).[19] He cast lots to fix the date for killing the Jews on the eve of the Jewish holiday of redemption, *Pesaḥ* (3:7).[20] When the king asks to see him in order to consult on the best way to honor Mordecai, Haman is already waiting at the court, seeking permission to hang that same Mordecai! Haman is thus doubly confounded when the man the king desires to honor turns out to be his nemesis and when he himself must parade the Jew through the capital. Then, when the queen invites Haman to her banquet as a first step in bringing his downfall, he believes he is to be feted. And when, in the scroll's most ludicrous scene, an exposed Haman falls on the queen to beg her compassion, the king interprets his conduct as an advance on his wife! The end of the irony is that the king's famous counselor Harbona proposes to impale Haman on the pole he built for Mordecai (7:9). Indeed, this reversal is rather gleefully underscored as follows: "They impaled Haman on the pole that he had set up for Mordecai" (7:10).

Humor and plot contrivances lend the story an air of fiction. Indeed, an audience could hardly fail to associate the Esther tale with many other familiar fictions and legends. For instance, resemblances between Esther and the court intrigues of the *Arabian Nights* have been widely noted.[21] Comparable too are the ancient tale of Ahiqar, of which the Jews in Elephantine possessed an Aramaic copy in the fifth century B.C.E.,[22] the story of Candaules and his queen narrated in Herodotus's *Histories,*[23] the miracle tales of Daniel 1—6 and 3 Esdras 3—4,[24] and the episode of Holofernes' killing in Judith 12, to mention but a few. Esther shares with folk tales these common features: the heroine, poor Esther, is an orphan; she is elevated to royalty, like Cinderella; the king offers this beloved queen up to half his kingdom; the display of his wealth is calculated to impress.[25]

This last item contrasts sharply with the norm in other biblical narratives. There, extensive visual description is highly unusual. Even the *mishkan,* the tabernacle in the wilderness, which absorbs most of Exodus 25—40, is never described. Its building instructions are related and the actual construction is narrated, but once it is erected it is not visualized. In the Esther Scroll, however, description can become lavish. Esther not only dilates on the palace's elegance, it mimes its luxury by employing uncharacteristically expansive language.

> In those days, as the king Ahasueras sat on his throne of kingship, which is in Shushan, the citadel, in the year three of his kingship he made a drink-fest for all his ministers and servants, the elite of Persia and Media, the nobles and administrators of the provinces before him; displaying the wealth of glory of his kingship and the prestige of the grandeur of his greatness, many days, eighty and one hundred days; and at the completion of these days the king made for all the people found in Shushan the citadel, from great to small, a drink-fest of seven days, in the court of the garden of the domicile of the king (1:2–5).[26]

And so it continues.

A careful listener who is well versed in Scripture might also perceive that the Esther text draws upon themes, motifs, and phrases from earlier Hebrew literature. Full studies have been devoted to the many parallels in topoi and language between Esther and the Joseph story, another tale of a Hebrew rising to high position in a foreign court.[27] Scholars have also attempted to read parallels between Esther and the primary myth of Hebrew redemption, the exodus.[28] But even if these comparisons fail to convince, similarities such as the following do exist:

> It was, when they said to him each day and he did not hearken to them. (Esth. 3:4)
> It was, when she spoke to Joseph each day and he did not hearken to her. (Gen. 39:10)

Or:

> The king removed his signet-ring from his hand, and he gave it to Haman. (Esth. 3:10)
> Pharaoh removed his signet-ring from his hand, and he gave it to the hand of Joseph. (Gen. 41:42)

Indeed, there exist many such apparent parallels. The report in Esth. 2:6 that Mordecai was exiled with Jeconiah by Nebuchadnezzar seems lifted from Jer. 29:1, the prophet's letter to the Babylonian Diaspora. Ahasueras's edict to all husbands (Esth. 1:22), in which each is ordered to speak in the language of his own nationality, appears to adapt Neh. 13:23–24. Sending food parcels to neighbors (Esth. 9:22) probably derives from Nehemiah also (Neh. 8:10–12), and the "words of well-being and faithfulness" embodied in Esther's epistle (Esth. 9:30) recall Zech. 8:19, where the prophet admonishes the Judeans to "love well-being and faithfulness" while they fast.[29]

Even the protagonists depend on biblical prototypes. King Ahasueras, whose name is transcribed in the scroll as *'aḥashverosh,* is certainly the Artaxerxes whose name is spelled identically in Dan. 9:1 and Ezra 4:6. Indeed, the character of the royal buffoon in Esther seems to constitute the antithesis of Israel's wise king, Solomon. Like Solomon, the king enjoys an extensive domain, reigning "from India to Nubia" (Esth. 1:1), while Solomon governed "in all the kingdoms from . . . the west-bank of the (Euphrates) River . . . to Gaza . . ." (1 Kings 5:1, 4). But whereas Solomon sought wisdom (*ḥokhma*) rather than glory (*kavod*) and wealth (*'osher;* 1 Kings 3:13), Ahasueras notably lacks the former but boasts of his glorious wealth (*'osher kevod* . . . ; Esth. 1:4).[30]

As for Mordecai, the court Jew, surely he is modeled on Nehemiah, whose career—not coincidentally—began "in Shushan the citadel," at the Persian palace (Neh. 1:1). Just as Nehemiah knew his Bible when more or less quoting Deuteronomy in his prayer (Deut. 30:4 in Neh. 1:9), so the narrator in Esther makes good use of the Hebrew classics.

But more important than such parallels between individuals is that, as nearly everyone has noted, the scroll construes the contest between Haman and Mordecai as the paradigmatic war between Israel and Amalek (cf. Exod. 17:8–16; Deut. 25:17–19). This war is represented more personally in 1 Samuel 15 as that between Israel's king, Saul son of Kish the Benjaminite, and the Amalekite king, Agag. In Esther, Mordecai son of Ya'ir son of Shim'i son of Kish a Benjaminite, plays the role of Saul (Esth. 2:5; Ya'ir and Shim'i are both common biblical names),[31] while Haman "the Agagite" (Esth. 3:1) stands in for his eponymous ancestor. In a more subtle variation, David slays the Amalekite who abetted the death of Saul (2 Sam. 4:10). What worked subtly will certainly play out in this showcased clash. Clearly, the Jewish audience knows who the biblical pattern implies will win.

The mythic lines along which the contest is drawn are underscored by the text's regular reference to the antagonists by epithets.[32] Mordecai is "the Jew"; Haman, "the evil" (7:6), is "the adversary of the Jews" (*ṣorer hayyehudim*). This latter epithet the narrative puts to comical and ironic effect by incorporating it into the following matter-of-fact description: "The king removed his signet-ring from his hand, and he gave it to Haman son of Hammedatha, the Agagite, the adversary of the Jews" (3:10). The king, of course, has not yet learned the identity of Haman's enemies.

Similarly, Ahasueras, Vashti and Esther, and even Shushan are represented by epithets ("king," "queen," and "city/citadel," respectively). In fact, not only are the protagonists' identities generalized, as several readers have observed, these characters stand for virtually universal types.[33] For instance, there is the stupid king who must always seek advice from his ordinary servants (2:4) as well as from his professional counselors. The first move this king makes on his own, following the story's opening feast, is to love Esther (2:17). Such a plot line was surely to please the Jewish audience. Beyond this single act, the king is used as a lever for obtaining their goals by the major antagonists, Haman and Mordecai-Esther. Of course, he is an easy mark, for he cannot even remember from 1:21 to 2:1 that he has banished Queen Vashti. Esther comprises not just the stupid king. The stubborn queen, the lovely and modest queen, the wise and loyal courtier, the cruel, hapless villain—all these personae find their places in the Esther narrative. Indeed, there is not much to the plot at all beyond the fulfilling of predictable functions by these typological characters.

So with its uncomplicated plot, black-and-white portrayal of conflict between the evil Haman and the fair Esther and upright Mordecai, and flat, cardboard caricatures of the actors, the story of Esther is a skit, not a drama.[34] It is a cartoon, and thus precisely the sort of show one would expect to see on Purim.

As already indicated, the Purim play, the story of the scroll, is the very image of the Jewish celebration. "A man is obligated to drink on Purim until he does not know 'Cursed is Haman' from 'Blessed is Mordecai'"—thus the tradition in the Babylonian Talmud (*Megilla* 7b). To this, the Palestinian Talmud adds: "Cursed is Zeresh, Blessed is Esther, Cursed are all the Wicked, Blessed are all the Jews."[35] Indeed, the model or mirror for the Purim drinking is provided by the Purim text itself.[36] There, the king and queen each host a drink-fest to honor the king's reign (*mishte,* lit., "place of drinking," chap. 1), the king celebrates Esther's crowning with a drink-fest (chap. 2), Ahasueras and Haman sit down to drink when the word of doom for the Jews goes out (chap. 3), Esther throws two drink-fests to expose Haman and his plot (chap. 5), the two banquets take place (chap. 7), and the Jews rejoice in their triumph with "a drink-fest and holiday" (8:17) and "a day of drinking and merry-making" (9:17, 18). Mordecai institutionalized the drinking by making it an integral part of Purim's annual observance (9:22).

From a historical perspective, the practice of dressing in costume on Purim is best documented from the later Middle Ages onward. It is very possible, however, that this custom of masquerading also "belonged to Purim from the very start," or constituted part of the Jewish festival's probably pagan precursor.[37] One certainly sees the form of the masquerade in the scroll, where both Esther (5:1) and Mordecai (6:8) don regal apparel, dressing up as Gentile royalty. Indeed, the Jew Mordecai is paraded around in his borrowed outfit (6:9).

Yet another longstanding custom of Purim, which is already documented in antiquity, hearkens back to the Esther text. This is the burning or hanging of Haman in effigy.[38] If scholars who trace Purim back to a pagan mock combat are right, again, the practice and the story are but reflexes of one another.

Finally, on Purim, as Jewish tradition has it, anything goes. Consequently, it has been customary for Purim celebrants to flaunt and parody Jewish practice and teaching.[39] In Esther, both Esther and the Jews similarly transgress or ignore Jewish law. For instance, like Joseph in Egypt but significantly unlike

Daniel and his friends in the court of Nebuchadnezzar (Dan. 1:8–16), Esther does not keep the dietary laws. Realizing this, the Talmud makes her vegetarian (*Megilla* 13a). Again like Joseph, Esther marries a Gentile. Moreover, in apparent oblivion of the Festival of Pesaḥ, she seems to have her people forego the matzah, bitter herbs, and lamb of the holiday, in order to fast on her behalf (4:16; cf. 3:12).[40] The *Targum Sheni* to 9:4 picked up this additional violation of the Torah: the hanged bodies of Haman and his sons were left out overnight, in neglect of Deut. 21:22–23. Now these trespasses of Jewish law may reflect a certain laxness in Jewish Diaspora observance, or they may evince the same playfulness that has characterized Purim from as far back as we can trace it. Such a reading corresponds to the lighthearted tone of the story, the carnival milieu of the Purim text, and the most frequently noted peculiarity of the scroll, the omission of God's name.

The hoary prohibition against vocalizing the divine tetragrammaton and the fact that many Dead Sea Scrolls write YHWH in a distinctly archaic script (old Hebrew/Phoenician rather than square Aramaic) demonstrate the ancient Jews' sensitivity to the use of the holy name of God. They would not pronounce it in an inappropriate context. Now no one denies that God's role in the Esther narrative is assumed to lie behind the series of remarkable coincidences that enable Esther to rescue her people. It is generally understood to be implied in 4:14, where Mordecai prods a diffident Esther thus: "For if you keep-silent, silent, at this time, succor and saving will rise for the Jews from *another place,* and you and your father's house will perish. And who knows if for a time like this you have reached the kingship."[41] Still, the utter omission of the divine name calls for explanation—and it has been variously explained. Drawing on the facts that not only is God not named, but the pervasive biblical historiographic theme that God punishes covenant infractions and then forgives and saves is absent, Shemaryahu Talmon has proposed that Esther belongs to the genre of ancient Near Eastern wisdom literature.[42] That literature typically avoids theologizing in a specific way and tends toward the pragmatic. M. Z. Segal and Robert Gordis have even gone so far as to suggest that the author of Esther eliminated Jewish religious references as part of a plan to disguise the text as a non-Jewish Persian chronicle.[43] Both these explanations fail to convince me. First, in Talmon's interpretation, the scroll's ethnocentrism and its farcical fun remain problematic. Considering these, it is hardly a vehicle for serious wisdom instruction as he implies. As for the interpretation proposed by Segal and Gordis, it suffers from our lack of an actual Persian chronicle to compare with Esther and from the implicit thorough Jewishness of the book.

Others, who find the absence of the divine name to point to the story's secular origins are, I believe, nearer the mark.[44] As certain scholars have seen, the best explanation is that Purim was, and has always been a frivolous festival, a time for jesting and revelry.[45] As the Esther scroll would be read only at such a celebration, it was no time to pronounce the sacred divine name. The omission of God's name was, then, a necessary precaution, consonant with the text's presumed *Sitz im Leben.*

It is significant that it is only the Jewish canonical version of Esther (the Masoretic) that lacks the divine name. Ancient Greek and Aramaic versions, some of which it has been argued may derive from precanonical prototypes, all employ God's name and develop God's explicit role in the narrative to greater and lesser—mostly greater—extents.[46] It would seem likely that in omitting God's name, the singular canonical version was singularly appropriate for use at Purim. Indeed, how but in jest could a Jewish story name its two heroes after the Babylonian god and goddess, Marduk and Ishtar? This is clearly no place for the tetragrammaton. In other words, the scroll was custom-made for the feast.

Given the basic assumption that the Esther story is mock serious, and thus homologous with Purim observance, we may then address the question of what the scroll says, beyond its obvious promulgation of the holiday. To my way of understanding, to ask what a text says is the same as asking what that text does, or even what we do with that text.[47]

If we attend to Esther's recurrent motifs and its patterns of arrangement and style, we see that they conduce to this one theme: to mitigate the real anxieties of Jews living as a minority in a largely non-Jewish society, Jews fantasize that it is they who dominate, not they who are victimized. As we have seen, it is all done in good fun, and temporarily each year it relieves some of the burden of being Jewish in a hostile or potentially hostile environment.[48]

In order to justify his official request, which he is prepared to back up with an extraordinary fund of money, Haman says this about the Jews: "There is one people spread and scattered among the peoples in all provinces of your kingdom; and their laws are different from every people, and the laws of the king they do not do" (3:8). The first half of Haman's statement is uncontroversial and morally neutral, but the second half is threatening to the king and, if it were believed, to the Jews. Haman's evidence for the second claim, so far as we know, is slight; the Jew Mordecai has stubbornly refused to bow down to Haman, which he is obliged to do by order of the king (3:2). Haman may have been wrong to hate all Jews on account of only one, but he was not wrong about Mordecai. Mordecai did transgress the royal law. This the text underscores by its elaborate wording:

> And all the king's servants who were in the king's gate would go-down-on-knees and prostrate-themselves to Haman, for so had the king commanded for him; but Mordecai would not go-down-on-knees and would not prostrate-himself. (3:2)

The exact repetition of both verbs and the unnecessary use of the second negative ("would *not* prostrate-himself") highlight Mordecai's disobedience.

Esther, too, deliberately breaks the royal law when she visits the king uninvited: "And so, I shall enter before the king which is not according to the law, and if I perish, I perish" (4:16).

Jews living in a Gentile society do have a problem of dual loyalty. There are the laws of the covenant on the one hand and the laws of the king on the other. At times the Jew may be torn between the two. This conflict exercised the first half of the Book of Daniel (especially chaps. 1, 3, and 6), and it would seem to trouble Esther. This inner Jewish tension is outwardly signified by the mark of dual identity. To the Jews, the scroll's heroine is Hadassah, but in Persian society she is Esther (2:7).[49] Daniel, Hananiah, Mishael, and Azariah must appear in the court of Nebuchadnezzar as Belshazzar, Shadrach, Meshach, and Abed Nego, that is, as Babylonians (Dan. 1:7). Esther's true allegiances are exposed in 2:20, where it is made clear that "what Mordecai says Esther does."

The command-and-obedience motif surfaces at a number of points in the narrative.[50] For example, it forms the hub of the episode involving the rebellious queen Vashti in chapter 1. It ends with the king's proclamation that all wives must obey their husbands. Mordecai's instruction to Esther in chapter 2 to conceal her Jewish identity (for it will be necessary for the development of the tale) similarly turns on command-obedience. Esther's complicity constitutes the obedience segment of the motif. This she repeats when she implicitly listens to Mordecai and reveals the plot against the king. As we have already noted, the issue of obedience continues through chapter 3. There, Haman, incensed at Mordecai's disrespect, seeks to destroy all Jews. To his mind, they do not obey the king's law. In chapter 4, Esther again hearkens to Mordecai and approaches the king. Note that here Esther specifically chooses Mordecai's instruction over Ahasueras's law, and in turn, Mordecai listens to Esther and proclaims a Jewish fast (thus anticipating his proclamation of a Jewish feast later on). Haman also follows advice, however. In chapter 5, he listens to his wife and friends and builds a pole for hanging Mordecai. Yet in the next chapter, to his terrible chagrin, Haman must obey the king's order to honor Mordecai. On the other hand, in chapter 8 the king cannot obey Esther and rescind the decree to exterminate the Jews, but this is because such complicity would ruin the story's reversal. This is clear since, in chapter 9, he will accede to Esther's request to hang Haman's ten sons. Finally, Jews all over obey the edict of Mordecai to observe the Feast of Purim (9:23). But while the prominent theme of obedience does serve to reinforce the ostensible function of the scroll, to promote the widespread observance of Purim, on a deeper level, it manifests the problem of the Diaspora Jew, who, like Esther, must choose between Jewish tradition and the temporal authority.

In one way, the scroll laughs off the conflict by lampooning the Persian king and his silly, irreversible laws.[51] But while laughter may bring temporary relief, it does not remove the problem. Thus, no sooner does the issue of dual loyalty emerge in the scroll—when Esther is said to do what she is told by

Mordecai (2:20)—than the exemplary citizenship of Mordecai finds a sharp illustration. The Jew brings to the king's attention a plot to assassinate him—and the criminals are the most trusted of Persians, the king's guards. The importance of Jewish aid to the throne is appreciated when the king flamboyantly rewards good citizen Mordecai.

The Jews, so the scroll would have it, are not a threat to the king. *Au contraire,* they benefit him. Moreover, since the king unwittingly favored a Jewish girl to be his queen, there is nothing intrinsically inimical about the Jew. Indeed, it was the palace that wanted Esther, she "was taken," *vattillaqaḥ* (2:9, 16), there. Like Esther, then, the Jews are okay, and like her, they should not have to perform any extraordinary acts to win public acceptance and approval. Aware of the reasons Jews might be perceived as noxious, the scroll insists they have intrinsic worth.

The scroll's representation of Jewish life in the Diaspora is fraught with anxiety. At any moment and for no apparent cause, the king might bring to power an anti-Semite—and the king would likely not take pains to challenge an arbitrary request from his powerful second-in-command. This world allows powerful men to buy rights by which they may carry out personal vendettas, operating under the pretense of serving the public.

Living in such a precarious position, vulnerable to the suspicion and enmity of the majority population, a people would need at some time to give vent to its repressed tensions. Purim fills this need, as does the Esther Scroll. Together they imagine a complete reversal of positions:

> On the day on which the enemies of the Jews hoped to overpower them, *it became reversed* when it was the Jews who overpowered those who hated them. (9:1).

(As Loader has noted, even the terms in this verse are reversed: "enemies" . . . "Jews" becomes "Jews" . . . "those who hated them.")[52] Purim would be celebrated in commemoration of the Jewish triumph, of "the month in which [the Jews'] anxiety was *reversed* to gladness, and their grieving-period to a holiday" (9:22).

The theme of reversal in the Esther Scroll has been widely treated. Following Gunkel's lead, Hans Streidl called the entire narrative "a big *nahafokh*" (reversal).[53] Without rehearsing all the oft-noted particulars, we ought to observe that reversals take place in two major relationships. On the individual level, they occur between Haman and Mordecai, and on the collective level, between the Jew-hating Persians and the Jews. In anticipation of the collective Jewish victory, Mordecai supplants Haman. Haman is actually impaled on the edifice he had built for Mordecai (7:10), and the king takes the royal signet-ring he had given to Haman and presents it to the Jew (8:2). Esther then places Haman's household under Mordecai's charge (8:2), and the story ends by telling us that Mordecai the Jew was made the king's second-in-command in Haman's place (10:3).

The tight link between the contest of Haman and Mordecai on the one hand, and that of the Jew-haters and the Jews on the other, comes into sharp focus in the parallel decrees promulgated by Haman and Mordecai. In 3:12–15, Haman has his proclamation "to destroy, to kill, and to annihilate all the Jews, from young to old, infants and women . . . and to loot their spoil" circulated around the empire "to all the provinces of the king." After Haman's downfall and his own rise to power, Mordecai reverses Haman's proclamation by substituting Jews for Persians (8:9–14). The Jews will play the part of the persecutors. Mordecai's version of the edict, however, diverges from the language of Haman's by stressing that the Jewish action will be defensive in purpose. The Jews "in every city" are "to assemble and stand for their life" in order "to destroy, to kill, and to annihilate all (armed) *forces* of any people or province *who were adverse to them*" so that they can "take vengeance on their enemies."

Up to this point, Mordecai still controls the reversal of Jews and Jew-haters. He can tell the Jews what they ought to do. But once the edict has issued from Mordecai, the contest passes from his control to that of the Jews. As a people, the Jews now decide the nature of their reversal. A true reversal will place the Jews precisely where their enemies wanted to be, and had their enemies followed Haman's decree, they would have exterminated the defenseless Jews. The revenge the Jews finally exact repels many commentators. As Bernhard W. Anderson has put it, the Jews' "unblushing vindictiveness stand[s] in glaring contradiction to the Sermon on the Mount."[54] While theoretically the Jews might have contented themselves with self-defense, as Gunkel and others have recognized, a proper reversal would require that the Jews do to their enemies what those Jew-haters would have done to them.[55] And the text repeatedly describes the Jews' victims as "the enemies of the Jews" (9:1), "[Jew-]haters" (9:1), "those seeking [the Jews'] calamity" (9:2), and the like. From the summary in 9:16 it must be assumed that even the unidentified "people" (*'ish*) that the Jews killed on the second day of their action in Shushan (9:15) were "their enemies" and "those who hated them" (9:16).

Other evidence suggests that the Jews' killing of their enemies forms the appropriate reversal. The so-called Greek A-Text of Esther relates the following dialogue between Esther and Ahasueras:

> Moreover Esther said to the king, "Grant me permission to punish my enemies with slaughter." And Esther the queen took counsel with the king also against the sons of Haman, that they also should die together with their father. And the king said, "So be it." And she smote the enemies in great numbers . . . [56]

As (most recently) David J. A. Clines has noted, the Jewish revenge amounts to poetic justice—and in the Hebrew Bible that serves as a well-known code for the workings of God.[57] But the revenge is more; it is the necessary reversal that can satisfy the Jewish fantasy of being on top.

The transposition of the Jews and the dominant Persians in the narrative is consummated when many Gentiles within the Persian Empire "become Jews" or "act Jewish" (*mityahadim;* 8:17) owing to their "fear of the Jews."[58] This unexpected and perhaps even preposterous turn of events inverts the historically much more common situation in which Jews, being in the minority in the Diaspora, assimilated to the majority. Our heroine Esther, in fact, had once to hide her Jewishness (2:20). While on one level, this deception was a crucial preparation for sabotaging Haman, on another it represents the smoothest course for Jewish survival in the Diaspora, as perceived by the scroll. Jews must mix in with society and not make waves. What "justified" the anti-Jewish program of Haman was the Jews' strange law and their insistence on being different. Thus, the easy way to avert anti-Jewish hostility would be to act Persian. On Purim, however, the Jew imagines a circumstance in which a Persian would want to act Jewish.

This motif of reversal reaches its apogee and completes the circle of the story's plot when the Jews imitate the Persian manner of celebration. They too enjoy days of merriment and drinking.

There are, then, two main themes conveyed through Esther. First, Diaspora Jews suffer a problem of dual loyalty, torn between being good Jews and good citizens of the empire; second, the scroll imagines a reversal of Jewish and Persian positions at least on Purim, the occasion on which the scroll is given its annual reading. Both these themes revolve around the concept of duality, and it is part of the narrative's art that twoness characterizes the style in which the story is related. In Esther, theme and style interpenetrate. The recurrent "doubleness" in the narrative reinforces both the theme of dual loyalty and that of reversal. This twoness manifests itself primarily in the following two ways: scenes and language are both "doubled."

Typically, doubled scenes have been explained by scholars as the result of the author's composing the text from two or more precursors, one about Mordecai and one about Esther.[59] Although reconstructions do vary somewhat, in general one plot has Mordecai best Haman, his rival at the royal court, while the other has the queen (Esther) accomplish a prestigious courtier's downfall. This way of dealing with Esther's doubled scenes has some merit, enabling us to interpret certain perplexing details of the narrative. For instance, the story suggests jealousy as Mordecai's motive for not bowing to Haman. Also, the two stories taken together explain the two Jewish edicts (one by Mordecai and one by Esther), the two days of Purim (one from one story, one from the other), and the anomalous appearance of Mordecai's name in 9:29.[60] There, the text introduces Esther's epistle with the feminine singular verb *vattikhtov,* "she wrote," mentions Esther as the subject of the verb, and then adds as a second subject "and Mordecai the Jew." It appears that Mordecai was interpolated into the verse. Nevertheless, according to Cazelles, who elaborately divides the scroll into two sources, the most peculiar doubling does not arise from two sources. Cazelles believes that the two parties Esther holds for Haman and the king, and at the first of which she merely asks her guests to attend the second, belong to the same source.[61] But while the question of whether the doubled scenes were all present from the outset may remain open, the fact of numerous twice-seen scenes in the canonical Esther is not at issue. Let us list these scenes. In the opening chapter, both Ahasueras and Vashti host feasts (the one for men, the other for women). Vashti's disobedience in chapter 1 is doubled by that of Mordecai in chapter 3, and in each case, as we have said above, the group to which the intransigent individual belongs must pay the price. Then, Ahasueras's royal decree to destroy the Jews in chapter 3 is revised and reversed in chapter 8, when Mordecai issues his own proclamation. In chapter 4, by informing Esther of Haman's plan, Mordecai echoes his own behavior in chapter 2 where through Esther he communicated the assassination plot to the king. Twice in chapter 5 Ahasueras asks Esther what bothers her, and twice Esther invites him and Haman to banquets. When, in chapter 6, Haman stands in the outer court waiting to see the king, we recall the preceding chapter in which Esther awaits the king in the inner court. And when in chapter 6 Haman shares with family and friends his bad news that Mordecai is to be honored, the scene parallels his earlier complaint of how Mordecai has upset him. Moving on to chapter 7, Esther's drink-fest follows upon the preparatory one in chapter 5. Then, when in chapter 8 Esther approaches the king and receives the nod of the royal scepter, we remember her more tremulous visit in chapter 5. Still in chapter 8, where doublings seem to concentrate, Mordecai replaces Haman as vizier and again dresses up in noble garb, thus doubling the parade of chapter 6 and contrasting with his appearance in sackcloth from chapter 4. If repetition seems prevalent in chapter 8, chapter 9 is nearly all twice-told. Here, the two heroes send two edicts to the Jews after the Jews have perpetrated two days of massacre on their enemies; they call for two days' holiday for two populations (urban and rural); the language even doubles the doubled acts in what seems an exaggerated and consequently parodic—perhaps even self-mocking—form:

> The Jews upheld and accepted, for themselves and for their descendants, and for all those joining them, irreversibly [i.e., for now and forever], to observe these two days, as they are written and at their time, each and every year (*bekhol shana veshana*); and these days are commemorated and observed in each and every generation (*bekhol dor vador*), (by) each and every clan (*mishpaḥa umishpaḥa*), (by) each and every province (*medina umedina*), and by each and every city (*ve'ir va'ir*). And these days of Purim will not pass from the Jews, and their commemoration shall not end among their descendants. (9:27–28)

Even within this brief passage the following terms appear twice: "the Jews," "their descendants," "not to be reversed/pass" (*velo' ya'avor*), "to observe," "to commemorate," "these days (of Purim)."

Indeed, as we noted above, the entire text of Esther abounds in verbal doublets or dyads. These lend a profound effect of duality to the tale. Streidl and others have noted this stylistic feature already, so we shall content ourselves by citing examples from chapter 1 only.[62] There, these doublets appear: "Ahasueras, he is the Ahasueras" (v. 1); "from India to Nubia" (v. 1); "his ministers and his servants" (v. 3); "Persia and Media" (v. 3 and passim); "the nobles and administrators" (v. 3); "the wealth of the glory of his kingship and the prestige of the grandeur of his greatness" (v. 4); "many days, eighty and one hundred days" (v. 4); "from great to small" (v. 5); "each and every man" (v. 8); "eunuchs, serving the king . . ." (v. 10); "to show the peoples and the ministers" (v. 11); "the king grew very angry, and his wrath burned" (v. 12); "the sages, the astrologers" (v. 13); "law and ruling" (v. 13); "ministers . . . , attendants of the king (*ro'ei penei hammelekh;* v. 14); "the king and the ministers" (v. 16); "against all the ministers and against all the peoples" (v. 16); "derision and insult" (v. 18); "her fellow-woman, her better" (v. 19); "the king and the ministers" (v. 21); "to each and every province in its own script, and to each and every nationality in its own language; that every man should dominate in his house and speak in the language of his own nationality" (v. 22).

Ultimately, the number of words conjoined in a string takes on symbolic significance in the Esther Scroll. While the problem of dual loyalty and the relief of imagining a reversal both align themselves across one axis, in a text where two thus constitutes the pervasive number, emphasis can be achieved through using a limited number of dramatic strings comprising three or four terms.[63] For instance, in Esther, violence or its threat is betokened by triads (three terms). Thus, Haman plans "to destroy, to kill, and to annihilate" the Jews (3:13; 7:4), and the Jews responded in kind by destroying, killing, and annihilating their enemies (8:11) with a strike of "sword, killing, and annihilation" (9:5). On the other hand, Jewish relief from this threat, which is what Purim is about, is expressed in fours. On the day when they return attack for attack, the Jews enjoy "light, and merriment, and jubilation, and prestige" (8:16). And the Jews in the countryside celebrate "merriment, and drink-fest, and a holiday, and sending parcels every man to his neighbor" (9:19; see also 9:22). As four surpasses three, merriment overcomes conflict. Consequently, by observing Purim and hearing the comedy of the scroll, Jews may drown their routine anxieties in imagination and joy.

NOTES

1. See, for example, Stanley Fish, *Is There a Text in This Class?* (Cambridge: Harvard Univ. Press, 1980).

2. Luther's various comments are referred to and discussed in Heinrich Bornkamm, *Luther and the Old Testament,* trans. Eric W. Gritsch and Ruth C. Gritsch (Philadelphia: Fortress Press, 1969), 188–89. Luther's remark that the Jews "love the Book of Esther which so befits their bloodthirsty, vengeful, murderous greed and hope" clearly betrays the anti-Semitism behind his attitude.

3. Hermann Gunkel, *What Remains of the Old Testament, and Other Essays,* trans. A. K. Dallas (New York: Macmillan Co., 1928), 16.

4. Among the Christian responses, see Robert H. Pfeiffer, *Introduction to the Old Testament* (New York: Harper & Brothers, 1941), 747; Otto Eissfeldt, *The Old Testament: An Introduction,* trans. Peter R. Ackroyd (New York: Harper & Row, 1965), 511–12. Many of the first millennium church fathers also rejected Esther. Bernhard W. Anderson deals with this subject in "The Place of the Book of Esther in the Christian Bible," *JR* 30 (1950): 33 (reprinted in *Studies in the Book of Esther,* ed. Carey A. Moore [New York: Ktav, 1982], 131). Moore's "Prolegomenon" to the volume is also worth attention.

Among the Reform Jewish biblicists, see Abraham Geiger, as cited in Elias Bickerman, *Four Strange Books of the Bible* (New York: Schocken Books, 1967), 217; Samuel Sandmel, *The Enjoyment of Scripture* (New York: Oxford Univ. Press, 1972), 44.

5. For example, Hayyim Schauss, *The Jewish Festivals: History and Observance,* trans. Samuel Jaffe (New York: Schocken Books, 1962), 254–55.

6. Isaac Bashevis Singer, "Yiddish Theater Lives, Despite the Past," *New York Times,* 20 Jan. 1985, sec. 2, 22.

7. See Eissfeldt, *Old Testament,* 508, and, for example, Brevard S. Childs, *Introduction to the Old Testament as Scripture* (Philadelphia: Fortress Press, 1979), 599: "There is general agreement that the major purpose of the book of Esther is to provide historical grounds for the celebration of the feast of Purim."

8. See N. S. Doniach, *Purim or the Feast of Esther* (Philadelphia: Jewish Publication Society of America, 1933), 138ff.

9. For example, Werner Dommerhausen, *Die Estherrolle* (Stuttgart: Katholisches Bibelwerk, 1968), 128–33; compare H. L. Ginsberg, "Introduction [to Esther]," in *The Five Megilloth and Jonah* (Philadelphia: Jewish Publication Society of America, 1969), 82–88.

10. See, for example, Bickerman, *Four Strange Books,* 199–202, and Theodor H. Gaster, *Myth, Legend, and Custom in the Old Testament* (New York: Harper & Row, 1969), 832–34.

11. For a summary, see Carey A. Moore, *Esther* (Garden City, N.Y.: Doubleday & Co., 1971), xlvff.

12. For example, Robert Gordis, "Religion, Wisdom and History in the Book of Esther—A New Solution to an Ancient Crux," *JBL* 100 (1981): 358–88. After a strenuous attempt to find some historical validity in the narrative, Gordis must admit "Clearly the Book of Esther is not a historical work in the modern sense of the term. It represents a traditional reworking of what may well have been a historical incident" (p. 386).

13. Robert Alter, *The Art of Biblical Narrative* (New York: Basic Books, 1981), 23–46. Alter perceives Esther as "a comic fantasy utilizing pseudo-historical materials" (p. 34).

14. See, e.g., W. Ernest Beet, "The Humorist Element in the Old Testament," *The Expositor* 22 (1921): 59–68. Cf. also, e.g., D. Harvey, "Esther, Book of," *IDB* 2:151a; Bruce William Jones, "Two Misconceptions about the Book of Esther," *CBQ* 39 (1977): 173 (in Moore, *Studies,* 437).

15. For example, Abraham D. Cohen, "'Hu Ha-goral': The Religious Significance of Esther," *Judaism* 23 (1974): esp. 93 (in Moore, *Studies,* 128); David J. A. Clines, *The Esther Scroll: The Story of the Story* (Sheffield: JSOT Press, 1984), 31–33.

16. Following the New Jewish Version (Jewish Publication Society of America). Contrast the 1917 JPS rendering "none did compel"; compare the RSV, etc.

17. See Gaster, *Myth, Legend, and Custom,* 836.

18. S. R. Driver, *An Introduction to the Literature of the Old Testament* (New York: Meridian Books, 1956), 482.

19. On the idiom *shalaḥ yad* in the sense of harming, see Paul Humbert, "Etendre la main," *VT* 12 (1962): 383–95. For the idiom bearing this sense in Phoenician, see my article, "Trans-Semitic Idiomatic Equivalency and the Derivation of Hebrew *ml'kh*," in *Ugarit-Forschungen* 11 (1979): 335, with n. 48.

20. For example, Moore, *Esther*, 43, and Sandra Beth Berg, *The Book of Esther* (Missoula, Mont.: Scholars Press, 1979), 182.

21. By, for instance, Duncan Black Macdonald, in *The Hebrew Literary Genius* (Princeton: Princeton Univ. Press, 1933), 139–40; Bickerman, *Four Strange Books*, 177-78; Gaster, *Myths, Legend, and Custom*, 830; Moore, *Esther*, 1.

22. For bibliography and translation, see H. L. Ginsberg in *ANET*, 427–30. On the comparison, see Shemaryahu Talmon, "'Wisdom' in the Book of Esther," *VT* 13 (1963): esp. 426–27, 438–43.

23. Herodotus, *Histories* Book I, 8–13; see Hermann Gunkel, *Esther* (Tübingen: J. C. B. Mohr [Paul Siebeck], 1916), 5, and idem, *Das Märchen im Alten Testament* (Tübingen: J. C. B. Mohr [Paul Siebeck], 1921), 143.

24. Eissfeldt, *Old Testament*, 508.

25. Gunkel, *Das Märchen*, 141–43.

26. For a detailed stylistic discussion of this passage, see Dommerhausen, *Die Estherrolle*, 17–21. For further illustration of the text's expansive style, see M. Z. Segal, *Mevo' hammiqra'* (Jerusalem: Kiriath Sepher, 1967), 726–27.

27. For example, L. A. Rosenthal, "Die Josephgeschichte mit den Büchern Esther und Daniel verglichen," *ZAW* 15 (1895): 278–84; M. Gan, "The Book of Esther in the Light of the Story of Joseph in Egypt," *Tarbiz* 31 (1962): 144–49 (in Hebrew); Berg, *Book of Esther*, 123–65. On the relationship between Esther and Daniel and Judith see, too, Ruth Stiehl, "Das Buch Esther," *WZKM* 53 (1956): 4-22 (in Moore, *Studies*, 249–67).

28. Especially Gillis Gerleman, *Studien zu Esther: Stoff, Struktur, Stil, Sinn* (Neukirchen-Vluyn: Neukirchener Verlag, 1966); idem, *Esther* (Neukirchen-Vluyn: Neukirchener Verlag, 1970–73).

29. Ginsberg, "Introduction," 88.

30. Talmon relates Ahasueras to Solomon differently. See "'Wisdom' in the Book of Esther," 433–34.

31. For *Ya'ir*, see Num. 32:41; Judges 10:3–5; 2 Sam. 20:26. For *Shim'i*, see Exod. 6:17; Num. 3:13; 2 Sam. 16:5; 21:21. It is noteworthy that both names are associated with David.

32. Hans Streidl, "Untersuchung zur Syntax und Stilistik des hebräischen Buches Esther," *ZAW* 55 (1937): 94–95.

33. For example, Gunkel, *Esther*, 77–78; Talmon, "'Wisdom' in the Book of Esther"; Segal, *Mevo' hammiqra'*, 2:720–21.

34. For example, Charles C. Torrey, "The Older Book of Esther," *HTR* 37 (1944): 21–22 (in Moore, *Studies*, 468–69); Moore, *Esther*, liii–liv.

35. See *Tosafot* to *b. Megilla* 7b.

36. See Isaac Klein, *A Guide to Jewish Religious Practice* (New York: Jewish Theological Seminary of America, 1979), 238. For the banquet motif in Esther see Berg, *Book of Esther*, 31–57.

37. Schauss, in *Jewish Festivals*, 268, inclines to the former view, while Theodor H. Gaster (*Festivals of the Jewish Year* [New York: William Sloane Associates, 1953], 221–29) prefers the latter.

38. Doniach, *Purim*, 72–75, 172.

39. Ibid., 138ff.

40. See Clines, *Esther Scroll,* 36–37.

41. For example, Dommerhausen, *Die Estherrolle,* 73–74, and Clines, *Esther Scroll,* 153–55.

42. Talmon, "'Wisdom' in the Book of Esther."

43. Segal, *Mevo' hammiqra',* 2:721; Gordis, "Religion, Wisdom, and History in the Book of Esther."

44. For example, Driver, *Introduction,* 486; Eissfeldt, *Old Testament,* 511. Clines (*Esther Scroll,* 154) maintains that the narrator omitted God's name in order to convey the theological message that although divine providence will protect the Jews, they, too, must take some initiative in resolving their difficulties. Such an earnest interpretation strikes me as dissonant with the burlesque tone of the scroll.

45. For instance, Torrey, "Older Book of Esther," 11 (in Moore, ed., *Studies,* 458); Anderson, "Place of the Book of Esther," 35b (in Moore, *Studies,* 133b).

46. Torrey, "Older Book of Esther," and Clines, *Esther Scroll.* See also Moore, "Prolegomenon," xxiv.

47. Fish, *Is There a Text in This Class?*

48. Gaster, *Festivals,* 230; Jones, "Two Misconceptions," 171 (in Moore, *Studies,* 437); W. Lee Humphreys, "A Life-Style for Diaspora: A Study of the Tales of Esther and Daniel," *JBL* 92 (1973): 211–23; Berg, *Book of Esther,* 34–35; John Craghan, *Esther, Judith, Tobit, Jonah, Ruth* (Wilmington, Del.: Michael Glazier, 1982), 9. Contrast Bickerman, who fails in *Four Strange Books* to see a "Jewish problem" in Esther (p. 188).

49. This should resolve the difficulty Berg finds in trying to explain why Esther is first introduced in the scroll as Hadassah (*Book of Esther,* 168).

50. See, for example, ibid., 72–93.

51. Cohen, "'Hu Ha-goral'," esp. 93 (in Moore, *Studies,* 128); Clines, *Esther Scroll,* 16ff., esp. 31–33.

52. J. A. Loader, "Esther as a Novel with Different Levels of Meaning," *ZAW* 90 (1978): 417–21, esp. 419.

53. Streidl, "Untersuchung," 105; Gunkel, *Esther,* 76–77. See, more recently, Berg, *Book of Esther,* 103–21; Clines, *Esther Scroll,* 155ff.

54. Anderson, "Place of the Book of Esther," 32b (in Moore, *Studies,* 130b).

55. In *Esther,* 76, Gunkel observes that the "strongest opposition" the narrator contrives is that "on the very same day on which the Jews were to be murdered, they themselves murder their enemies." See also Streidl, "Untersuchung," 105; Loader, "Esther as a Novel," esp. 419; Clines, *Esther Scroll,* 159.

56. Trans. in Clines, *Esther Scroll,* 241.

57. Ibid., 153.

58. In order to support his own thesis about the various literary strata in the scroll, Clines interprets the *paḥad* of the Jews felt by the Persians who became Jewish as "awe" rather than "fear" or "dread" (*Esther Scroll,* 65, 97). Such an interpretation lacks any foundation. The phrase *nafal paḥad hayyehudim 'aleihem* in Esth. 8:17, like the nearly identical phrases in 9:2 (which refers to "dread of the Jews") and 9:3 (which refers to "dread of Mordecai"), means only "the dread of the Jews fell upon them." It is a reference to sheer fear of the avenging Jews. The sense of "awe" attaches itself to *paḥad* only when it is used of God. The phrase in Esther has the sense of *śamaḥ miṣrayim beṣeitam ki nafal paḥdam 'aleihem* in Ps. 105:38: "Egypt was glad when they [viz., the Israelites] went out, for their [i.e., the Israelites'] dread had fallen upon them." See, further, Moore, *Esther,* 82.

59. Cazelles, Bickerman, Dommerhausen, Lebram, Humphreys, and Clines all give

such an explanation: Henri Cazelles, "Note sur la composition du rouleau d'Esther," in H. Gross and F. Mussner, ed., *Lex tua veritas: Festschrift für Hubert Junker* (Trier: Paulinus Verlag, 1961), 17–29 (in Moore, *Studies,* 424–36); Bickerman, *Four Strange Books,* 171–88; Dommerhausen, *Die Estherrolle,* 26; J. C. H. Lebram, "Purimfest und Estherbuch," *VT* 22 (1972): 208–22 (in Moore, *Studies,* 205–19); Humphreys, "A Life-Style for Diaspora," 214; Clines, *Esther Scroll,* esp. 115–74.

60. See Moore, *Esther,* 95; Clines, *Esther Scroll,* 56.

61. See the critique in Clines, *Esther Scroll,* 116, 120–21.

62. Streidl, "Untersuchung," esp. 74, 84–85. See also Segal, *Mevo' hammiqra',* 2:726; Dommerhausen, *Die Estherrolle,* 144; Moore, *Esther,* l–li; Berg, *Book of Esther,* 79–80.

63. See Streidl, "Untersuchung," 85.

11 FREDERICK E. GREENSPAHN

BIBLICAL SCHOLARS, MEDIEVAL AND MODERN

Although the Bible has been studied for millennia, biblical scholarship (characterized by a lack of dogmatic constraint and a commitment to determining the text's original meaning) is often considered a modern invention. Whether traced to the rise of classical studies during the Renaissance or such Reformation principles as *sola scriptura,* biblical scholarship is considered part of the scientific way of thinking, correlated with if not actually caused by such revolutions as those associated with the names of Lyell and Darwin. It is thus no accident that while histories of biblical interpretation may go back to antiquity, those of biblical scholarship generally begin within the last few centuries and note earlier figures only as having anticipated the modern approach or having made its development possible.[1]

It is my contention that this view is inaccurate, more likely reflecting modern biblical scholars' self-perception than historical fact.[2] Specifically, I will attempt to show that many of the methods and concerns most typical of contemporary scholarship can be found already among medieval Jews. With a growing body of evidence suggesting that the so-called founders of what was to become modern biblical scholarship derived many of their insights and methods from Jewish teachers, it would appear that these correlations are not accidental. The modern approach is not a *creatio ex nihilo* or even *de novo,* but rather a new chapter in a much older and richer tale.

One example of this modern misconception is the frequent assertion that Spinoza's observation about the Pentateuch—that it could not be entirely from the hand of Moses[3]—was a key moment in the development of critical consciousness. Less familiar, however, is his admission to having derived this insight from the twelfth-century scholar Abraham ibn Ezra.[4] Ibn Ezra also alluded to the possibility that the last chapters of Isaiah are by a different author than the book's earlier sections.[5] Recognition that these chapters' thematic concerns are different from those which precede had already come from the eleventh-century Spaniard Moses ben Samuel Ha-Kohen Gikatilla, who suggested that Psalms 42, 47, and 106 were written during the exile, at which time the last two verses of Psalm 51 were also added.[6] Isaac ibn Yashush (eleventh century) expresses a similar view in his assertion that the list of Edomite kings in Genesis 36 was interpolated during the monarchic period.[7]

Such statements are too often regarded as isolated, even accidental cases in which an individual medieval exegete happens to have anticipated what is now accepted. Assuming that these were Dark Ages simply begs the question, as do presumptions about what the orthodoxy of the time would have tolerated, particularly when such inferences are made on the basis of modern dogma. It has been shown, for example, that the Mosaic authorship of the Pentateuch, espoused already in the talmudic sources, was based more on historical speculation than theological dogma. Judaism may require that the Torah had been revealed by God, but it did not, at least initially, demand that it came through Moses.[8] We must, therefore, examine the medieval scholars' own statements in order to determine what they believed. The results will clearly show that Jewish biblical scholars, and particularly those who lived and worked in Muslim countries, were part of a dynamic enterprise whose traces can be seen already in the debates which range across the pages of the Rabbinic Bible, providing vivid testimony to the freedom felt in the search to determine Scripture's meaning.

The existence of similarities between premodern and contemporary biblical scholarship is already well known in some areas. Maimonides' suggestion that boiling a kid in its mother's milk was an ancient pagan ritual[9] is still widely cited and even accepted, notwithstanding recent demonstrations that the Ugaritic text often thought to confirm this theory does not, in fact, support it.[10] Another such case is the development of the comparative method. Generally attributed to Judah ibn Quraish (ninth century), this approach seeks to explain difficult biblical forms by recourse to similar words in related languages. Ibn Quraish went well beyond Saadia Gaon's use of tannaitic texts[11] when he included Aramaic, Arabic, Greek, Latin, and even Berber as potential sources of cognates for biblical words.[12] Isaac ibn Barun (eleventh century) applied this method not only to lexicographical difficulties, but to problems in grammar and syntax as well.[13] There can be no doubt but that had Ugaritic and Akkadian been available, their relevance would also have been considered. It is of some interest to observe that, within the limits of available information, there existed no precedent for this approach—neither in the work of contemporary Arab linguists nor among the earlier schools of Greek, Latin, and Sanskrit philology.[14]

A more specific and less familiar instance when medieval scholarship anticipated the modern pertains to the Hebrew verbal system. There are four fundamental Semitic conjugations. These are the base stem (*qal*), another in which the middle root letter is lengthened (*pi'el*), and two prefix stems, one characterized by a *n* (*nif'al*) and the other by *h* (*hif'il*). Each can be modified to produce subsidiary conjugations; for example, when *t* is prefixed to the *pi'el* yielding the reflexive *hitpa'el*. Evidence from several Semitic languages suggests that such modifications could be made in other conjugations, and indeed the Bible contains traces of words which may have been formed in just this way.[15] Vowel changes can function similarly. The passive *pu'al* and *hof'al* are formed in this way from the *pi'el* and *hif'il* respectively. In theory, one would expect a similar conjugation derived from the *qal*. Jakob Barth has argued that traces of this can be found in biblical Hebrew.[16] Noting that passive forms of several verbs otherwise known only in the *qal* are vocalized as *pu'al* or *hof'al*, he suggested that these are actually *qal* passives which the Masoretes, by whose time the form had died out, did not recognize and therefore vocalized in accordance with whichever conjugation could support the attested consonantal sequence. What Barth did not mention was that this insight had been achieved nine hundred years earlier by Samuel ibn Nagrela regarding such forms as *yuttan* (Lev. 11:38) and *yuqqaḥ* (Isa. 49:25).[17]

Another example pertains to the dynamics which govern the generation of roots. Taking his cue from several Arab philologists, Joseph Greenberg sought to identify the patterns underlying Semitic root formation. Focusing primarily on Arabic, he concluded that two consonants articulated in the same part of the oral cavity (dentals, labials, etc.) are not likely to be found within the same root or, if they do so occur, are usually the first and last letters. In other words, they are placed as far away from one another as possible.[18] As Greenberg notes, this observation had been anticipated by early Arabic philologists, who used it to identify loan words within the Arabic corpus.[19] (He includes also one Jew, Abraham ben Meir de Balmes; as we shall see, there are many others.) Greenberg further points out that this principle is not found in "the standard Semitic grammars."[20] When mentioned now, it is usually credited to him. Kalevi Koskinen has confirmed the principle's applicability to biblical Hebrew[21] without recognizing that it had already been described and utilized by medieval Jewish scholars from the time of Saadia, a full millennium before.[22]

The Jews are generally held to have borrowed these insights from Arab philology, a view supported by such explicit citations as Ibn Janaḥ's reference to Sibawaihi[23] and Ibn Ezra's to Al-Khalil's *Kitāb al-'Ain*.[24] As Salo Baron notes, however, Arab philologists were often of Jewish extraction,[25] and furthermore, similar if more primitive conceptions can often be found in earlier Jewish sources.[26] In any event, the relation between Arab and Jewish philology is likely more complex than is generally stated.

Restricting our view to the Jewish side, we find that the medievals accepted the notion stated already in the mystical *Sefer Yeṣirah* according to which the letters of the alphabet can be divided into five groups depending on where in the oral cavity each sound is made.[27] These are the gutturals (א, ה, ח, ע), labials (ב, ו, מ, פ), palatals (ג, י, כ, ק), sibilants (ז, ס, צ, ר, ש), and, finally, dentals (ד, ט, ל, נ, ת).[28] The conclusion that individual roots cannot contain more than one letter from any of these groups would appear to have been inductively derived in a way not radically different from Greenberg's empirical test.[29] Rather than resting on a priori theory, such views evolved from observation and description of the language itself.

Discussion and refinement of this principle were also empirically based. Mebasser Halevi, a tenth-century rabbi who lived in Baghdad, notes the existence of several roots containing combinations that Saadia has asserted do not exist, and drew some of his examples from Saadia's own dictionary.[30] Menaḥem ibn Saruk, citing cases where otherwise impossible juxtapositions can result from the addition of a prefix, recognized that this principle seems to apply only to radicals.[31] Although aware of the juxtaposition of *š* and *ṣ* in the root שצף and *ṭ* and *d* in אטד and פטדה, Ibn Janaḥ accepted the general principle and noted that the reverse sequences are not attested.[32] Ibn Ezra used this criterion, much as had the Arab philologists mentioned above, to argue that the name Yarḥa is Egyptian rather than Hebrew (1 Chron. 2:34).[33]

Alongside the historical method, few activities are considered more typical of modern biblical scholarship than text criticism and its efforts first to identify words or letters inaccurately preserved in existing biblical texts and then to reconstruct a more authentic and original reading. But there is no inherent reason why medieval scholars could not have accepted the possibility that their copies of the Bible were in error. Modern fundamentalists certainly are able to hold such views without difficulty.[34] While Judaism ascribes religious authority to the MT, it recognizes the presence of textual variants and, by implication, errors.[35] Moreover, modern text-critical research has amply documented the diversity of medieval biblical manuscripts.[36]

In light of these realities, it should not be surprising to note that the ninth-century Karaite Isma'il of 'Ukbara observed "some things in the Scripture were not (originally) as they are now written."[37] Both Rashi and Ibn Ezra note what they considered to be textual errors.[38] A more conservative if nonetheless daring approach to this problem is Ibn Janaḥ's famous theory of substitution, according to which the biblical authors "intended one thing, but wrote another."[39] The writings of these scholars are filled with references to ellipsis, pleonasm, and consonant transposition. While not stating that the MT is incorrect, such views seek grammatical or syntactic principles which might justify interpreting the text as if it contained something else.[40]

The most dramatic approach of this sort is the theory of permutation—under certain circumstances specific consonants can interchange.[41] Known in Hebrew as *ḥilluf* and in Arabic as *badāl,* this principle enabled interpreters to correlate seemingly distinct words. The descriptions offered suggest that the medievals developed this theory empirically, observing the semantic similarity of differently spelled but similarly pronounced words such as *parzel* (e.g., Dan. 2:33–45), which appears to be the same as *barzel,* and *ṭʿh* (Ezek. 13:10), which correlates with *tʿh.*[42] Saadia notes the phonological and semantic similarity of *kôvaʿ* (1 Sam. 17:5) and *qôvaʿ* (1 Sam. 17:38) as well as *krsm* (Ps. 80:14) and the Rabbinic *qrsm.*[43] From such observations, the medievals sought to understand the process involved, concluding that in biblical Hebrew individual consonants could be replaced by others with the same point of articulation.[44] Several of them add that this may be conditioned by the need for euphony within a particular word.[45]

Recognized correlations between Hebrew, Aramaic, and Arabic words provided additional pairs of equivalent consonants, such as *ṣ* and *ṭ* or *z* and *d.*[46] From such observations developed several studies, generally within the context of larger linguistic works, on the nature of permutation.[47] Most often, these list specific consonant pairs which can interchange, providing numerous examples. The phenomenon was not, however, believed to be only phonetically or dialectically conditioned. Other factors too might occasion such a shift, the most interesting and germane among which, for our purposes, is physical resemblance.

While the rabbis had cautioned that letters must be carefully drawn so as to avoid possible confusion,[48] the medievals were the first to assert that where one consonant is attested, a similarly shaped letter might be substituted.[49] As in other areas, here too such conclusions rested on concrete examples. Among the cited cases of ר־ד interchange is the fact that דדנים in Gen. 10:4 appears as רודנים in the parallel genealogy of 1 Chron. 1:7.[50] Other instances are the equivalence of וידא in Ps. 18:11 with וירא (2 Sam. 22:11),[51] מְצוֹדִים in Qoh. 9:14 with מָצוֹר (e.g., Deut. 20:20),[52] הֲדַד in 1 Chron. 1:50 with הֲדַר (Gen. 36:39),[53] חֶמְדָּן (Gen. 36:26) and חַמְרָן (1 Chron. 1:41),[54] דִּיפַת (1 Chron. 1:6) and רִיפַת (Gen. 10:3),[55] דְעוּאֵל (Num. 1:14) and רְעוּאֵל (Num. 2:14),[56] הַדָּאָה (Lev. 11:14) and הראה (Deut. 14:13),[57] גרד in Job 2:8 and גרר,[58] and כידוד (Job 41:11) and כידור (Job 15:24).[59] Ibn Gikatilla argued that נ and כ can interchange, noting that the form כַּנְּלֹתְךָ (Isa. 33:1) appears to be derived from the root כלה.[60] Others cited ב and כ, apparently because these seem to vacillate as prepositions.[61] It is of some interest that Ibn Janaḥ lists several cases in which נ and מ are interchangeable, including such pairs as מֹף (Hosea 9:6) and נֹף (Isa. 19:13), הָרָם (Josh. 13:29) and הָרָן (Num. 32:26), and כִּמְהָם (2 Sam. 19:38) and כִּמְהָן (2 Sam. 19:41).[62] Abraham Ha-Bavli adds their use as prefixes in מבוכה־נְבוֹכָה and מוֹרָא־נוֹרָא,[63] while others noted their inconsistency as suffixes in such forms as תַּנִּים and תַּנִּין,[64] or פדיום (Num. 3:49) and פדיון.[65] It is of some interest that although this last pair (מ־נ) of consonants are quite distinct in standard Hebrew script, their Phoenician ("paleo-Hebrew") counterparts are very similar.[66]

Not all the medievals accepted the possibility of permutation either in general or with regard to similarly shaped consonants. In the words of Joseph ibn Kaspi, "Heaven forbid that there be interchange of one letter for another anywhere in Hebrew!"[67] While not denying the correlations which led to this theory's formulation, those opposed rejected the inference that permutation was the reason for these similarities.[68] According to Abraham ibn Ezra, "Only the letters א, ה, ו, י interchange and ס and ש since they are close in articulation."[69] From his point of view, א, ה, ו, and י can interchange not because they are homorganic, but rather as weak letters—a quite different justification from that proposed by other scholars.[70] His allowance that ס and ש might interchange must be understood as a concession to numerous biblical examples.[71] And yet, despite these objections, Ibn Ezra himself uses permutation to explain several biblical forms. We have already noted this with regard to the pair מ־נ. He makes similar remarks regarding ה and ת.[72] More intriguing than his willingness to allow for such interchanges, which are after all limited to auxiliary letters, is the reasoning he gives. Having cited a case of ת־ה interchange, Ibn Ezra adds "I do not know the reason why, only that since the script is similar. See—a short line is added to the ה to show that it is in construct."[73] In a similar vein, he attempted to correlate letters' shapes with the anatomic organ which produces their sound,[74] an effort which flies in the face of the distinction known since classical antiquity between what Latin grammarians called a letter's *potestas* and its *figura*.[75] By asserting a link between a word and the object it designates, such views imply a connection between language and world whether physical or metaphysical,[76] representing thereby one pole in the ancient linguistic debate between nature (φύσις) and convention (νόμος).[77] Be that as it may, the notion that similar-looking letters can interchange is, of course, fundamentally the logic of scribal error. Under whatever guise and for whatever reasons, the medievals thus permitted themselves the possibility of effective emendation, even as they had allowed for the need to add or transpose words and letters.

It is worth pointing out that some medievals extended these possibilities still further, as in the claim that alphabetically adjacent letters can interchange.[78] Ibn Parhon called such techniques *gematria* and *'atbash*, under which headings were included all kinds of consonantal permutation besides the more familiar ת-for-א and ש-for-ב variety.[79] Our biblical manuscripts preserve evidence for the acceptance of such exegetical methods in Jer. 25:26 where ששך, it is argued, represents בבל.[80] They are reflected already in the LXX and Targum Jonathan[81] as well as the Tosepta[82] and Baraita of the Thirty-two Rules ascribed to the second-century teacher Eliezer ben Yossi, Ha-Galili.[83] Such practices, which the Talmud traces to the time of Daniel,[84] and are especially prominent in Jewish mysticism and superstition,[85] can be traced back to classical antiquity. Second-century school exercise-tablets confirm reports that the alphabet was learned in both directions at the same time,[86] while Suetonius reports that both Caesar and Augustus used letter-substitution codes in which a consonant was replaced by the one which follows.[87]

As David Yellin has pointed out, the theoretical premise for all these techniques is the medievals' commitment to identifying the *peshat,* Scripture's simple and straightforward meaning. A methodological norm since the Rabbinic period,[88] the effort to determine and explain Scripture's literal meaning —what Origen calls the *sensus Judaicus*[89]—is the underlying dynamic of medieval Jewish exegesis. What must be accorded particular attention is the fact that in this quest the medievals clearly chose to assign context primacy over text.[90] The most coherent possible meaning of a given passage is ascribed more weight than the attested words or letters. In this respect, their approach is the exact opposite of the classical (Akiban) Rabbinic mode which assigned a divine origin to the biblical text and on that basis set about finding the meaning of seeming textual idiosyncrasies, whether orthographic, morphological, or syntactic. By contrast, these medievals sought a "simpler" interpretation. Moreover, while the writings of religious skeptics and heretics such as Ḥivi ha-Balkhi (ninth century)[91] afford particularly vivid "parallels" to contemporary methods and theories, we have now seen that such views were by no means limited to those outside the mainstream of Jewish life. Whether methodology was a cause or effect of the views espoused by some medievals, the same basic techniques and conclusions are to be found in the writings of less radical scholars.

The medieval approach is surprisingly compatible with our own because its commitment to *peshat* and contextual coherence correspond largely to modern working assumptions. To be sure, the medievals were not modern. Their occasional need to cloak these theories in euphemism—what some have called modes of "esoteric communication"[92]—evidences their own uncertainty as to the reception such views would encounter. But their felt problem and, more fundamentally, the approach which made such modes of expression necessary, are at base surprisingly similar to that of contemporary scholarship. While there can be no denying the limitations on scholarship that resulted from the paucity of resources or the pressures of orthodoxy (operative factors in any epoch), the medievals nonetheless were often able to overcome these by means of industry, ingenuity, and mastery of available tools. On more than one occasion it is possible that their willingness to work within the confines imposed by history may actually have helped them avoid modern biblical scholarship's propensity for embracing imaginative positions which must be retracted in light of subsequent, more careful scrutiny of the evidence.

If the gulf between medieval and modern study of the Bible is neither so vast nor so fundamental as is often claimed, the possibility of some historical connection between the two would seem deserving of careful examination. In fact, such efforts are already under way. An impressive demonstration of the medieval scholars' role has been put forth by James Kugel in his history of the view that parallelism is a defining characteristic of biblical poetry. Generally attributed to Robert Lowth (eighteenth century), who himself cited the sixteenth-century Jew Azariah de Rossi, the recognition of parallelism can in fact be traced back to such medievals as Menaḥem ibn Saruk, Rashi, his grandson Samuel ben Meir, and Abraham ibn Ezra.[93] Without denying the reality of Lowth's insight or the importance of his impact on subsequent scholarship, we must also recognize the foundations upon which he built. And connections have been shown in other areas as well.[94]

The history of biblical scholarship is thus broader and less disjointed than is usually asserted. It would seem to follow that biblical scholars would do well to consult the research of earlier, sometimes more distant forebears than they are usually ready (or able) to acknowledge. That such a process has already begun is apparent from increased interest on the part of those engaged in literary analysis of biblical narrative, where commitment to the text's unity and coherence are advantageous.[95] We have tried here to demonstrate that similarly valuable material may be found in more technical fields as well. While many of the relevant texts must be made more accessible, and we must overcome the widespread misconception that medieval scholarship is limited to those works found in standard editions of the Rabbinic Bible, certain lingering prejudices about the Middle Ages need also to be confronted. Once that is accomplished, many new resources can be recovered for biblical scholarship and a more coherent picture of the discipline's history achieved.

NOTES

1. Thus H. F. Hahn: "Until the latter part of the nineteenth century, biblical studies had usually taken the form of theological exegesis" (*The Old Testament in Modern Research* [Philadelphia: Fortress Press, 1966], 1); see also E. Krentz, *The Historical-Critical Method* (Philadelphia: Fortress Press, 1975), 7–9, and H.-J. Kraus, *Geschichte der historisch-kritischen Enforschung des alten Testaments von der Reformation bis zur Gegenwart* (Neukirchen Kreis Moers: Erziehungsvereins, 1956), 1–2.

2. On a related subject, K. I. Semaan quotes a 1964 report on "Non-Western Studies in the Liberal Arts College" regarding "the illusion shared by nearly everybody of European descent, that the history of the world is the history of Europe and its cultural offshoots" (*Linguistics in the Middle Ages, Phonetic Studies in Early Islam* [Leiden: E. J. Brill, 1968], ix). In this regard, one might also note that the second edition of R. Grant's originally (and accurately) titled *The Bible in the Church* (New York: Macmillan Co., 1948) used only its earlier subtitle, *A Short History of the Interpretation of the Bible.*

3. Benedict de Spinoza, *A Theologico-Political Treatise,* chap. 8 ("On the Authorship of the Pentateuch") in *The Chief Works of Benedict de Spinoza,* trans. R. H. M. Elwes (New York: Dover Publications, 1951), 1.120–32.

4. Ibid. Thomas Hobbes had drawn a similar conclusion, generally from the same passages, in his *Leviathan,* 3.33 (New York: E. P. Dutton, 1950), 328–30.

5. At Isa. 40:1; M. Friedlander, *The Commentary of Ibn Ezra on Isaiah* (New York: Philip Feldheim, 1964), 64 (in Hebrew).

6. S. Poznanski, *Mose b. Samuel Hakkohen ibn Chiqitilla nebst den Fragmenten seiner Schriften* (Leipzig: Hinrichs, 1895), 100–101, 109, 113.

7. Cited by Ibn Ezra at Gen. 36:31. (Unless specified otherwise, all medieval commentaries can be found in standard editions of the Rabbinic Bible.) Examples of the medievals' attitude to historical and textual problems are drawn from Nahum M. Sarna, "*Hebēṭim Lō'-Mĕṣuyîm shel Parshanut Hatanak Biyemey-Habeynayim,* in *Hagut*

Uma'aseh, Sefer Zikkaron Leshimon Rawidowicz, ed. A. Ivry and B. Ravid (Haifa: Tcherikover, n. d.), 35–42, to which I am especially indebted.

8. J. Petuchowski, "The Supposed Dogma of the Mosaic Authorship of the Pentateuch," *HJ* 57 (1958–59): 356–60. For an alternative view on this question, see already 4 Ezra 14:45.

9. Maimonides, *The Guide of the Perplexed* 3.48, ed. S. Pines (Chicago: Univ. of Chicago Press, 1963), 599.

10. The text is *UT* 52:14; for details, see M. Haran, "Seething a Kid in Its Mother's Milk," *JJS* 30 (1979): 23–35.

11. N. Allony, "*Kitāb 'al-Sab'în Lafẓa Lĕrab Sa'adya Ga'ôn,*" in *Ignace Goldziher Memorial Volume,* ed. S. Löwinger (Jerusalem: Rubin Mass, 1958), 2.1–47 (in Hebrew).

12. Isaac ibn Barun, *Risāla,* ed. J. J. L. Barges and D. B. Goldberg (Paris: B. Duprat and D. Maisonneuve, 1857); citations here are from the Hebrew translation *Sefer 'Îggeret,* by M. Katz (Tel Aviv: Dvir, 1950).

13. P. Wechter, *Ibn Barun's Arabic Works on Hebrew Grammar and Lexicography* (Philadelphia: Dropsie College, 1964). Ibn Quraish did similarly, but only to a very limited extent. See also Judah Halevy's observation that "Aramaic, Arabic, and Hebrew are similar to each other in their vocabulary, grammatical rules, and formations" (*The Kuzari,* 2.68 [New York: Schocken Books, 1964], 125).

14. W. Bacher, *Die Hebräische Sprachwissenschaft vom 10. bis zum 16. Jahrhunderts* (Trier: Sigmund Mayer, 1892), 15, and N. M. Sarna, "Hebrew and Bible Studies in Medieval Spain" in *The Sephardi Heritage,* ed. R. D. Barnett (New York: Ktav, 1971), 342–43. For Rabbinic precedents, see *y. Ber.* 9:1 end; *b. Šabb.* 31b, 63a–b; *b. Roš. Haš.* 26a–b; *b. Sukk.* 5b; *b. Sanh.* 76b; *b. 'Abod. Zar.* 24b; *Gen. Rab.* 3:1, 42:4; *Lev. Rab.* 1:3, 25:5; *Cant. Rab.* 4:1; *Lam. Rab.* 1:15, 2:13; *Tanḥuma Teruma* 7; *Tazria'* 8.

15. H. Bauer and P. Leander, *Historische Grammatik der hebräischen Sprache des alten Testamentes* (Hildesheim: Georg Olms, 1965), § 38f, t–v.

16. Jakob Barth, "Das passive Qal und seine Participien" in *Jubelschrift zum siebzigsten Geburtstag des Dr. Israel Hildesheim* (Berlin: H. Engle, 1890), 145–53.

17. Cited by D. Qimḥi, *Sefer Miklol,* ed. I. Rittenberg (Jerusalem, 1966), 62b. See also A. ibn Ezra, *Mo'znê Lĕšôn Haqqodēš* (Ophibeck: Segalspitz, 1791), 33a, and *Sefer Ṣaḥot,* ed. G. H. Kippmann (Fürth: D. Zürndorffer, 1827), 68b, where this insight is also credited to Moses ibn Gikatilla, as well as Jonah ibn Janaḥ, *Sefer Hariqma,* ed. M. Wilensky (Berlin: Ha'aqademiya Lemad'ê Hayahadut, 1928), 92, and *Opuscules et Traites d'Abou'l-walid Merwan ibn Djanah de Cordove* (Paris: L'imprimerie Nationale, 1880), 33–34, 260, and Solomon ibn Gabirol in his poem, "*'Ānāq,*" in H. N. Bialik and H. Ravnitsky, *Shirey R. Shlomo ibn Gabirol,* 2d ed. (Tel Aviv: Dvir, 1927), 1.173.

18. Joseph Greenberg, "The Patterning of Root Morphemes in Semitic," *Word* 6 (1950): 162–81. Geminates only seem to violate this principle, since they apparently developed out of biliteral roots which were expanded to conform to what became a triliteral norm; see Bauer and Leander, *Historische Grammatik,* § 58a.

19. See L. Kopf, "The Treatment of Foreign Words in Mediaeval Arabic Lexicology," in *Studies in Islamic History and Civilization,* ed. U. Heyd, ScrHie 9 (Jerusalem: Magnes Press, 1961), 199. For examples of the genre, see N. Allony, *Ha'egron, Kitāb 'Uṣul al-Shi'r al-'Ibrānī by Rav Sĕ'adya Ga'on* (Jerusalem: Academy of the Hebrew Language, 1969), 35, 87.

20. Greenberg, "Patterning of Root Morphemes," 163.

21. Kalevi Koskinen, "Kompatibilität in den dreikonsonantigen hebräischen Wurzeln," *ZDMG* 114 (1964): 16–58; see also D. E. Y. Sarna and L. H. Schiffman, "A Computer Analysis of Biblical Roots" (unpublished, 1968).

22. The earliest reference is by Saadia Gaon in his *Commentaire* on *Sefer Yĕṣîrâ* (ed. M. Lambert, Bibliothèque de l'ecole Pratique des hautes études 85 [Paris: Emile Boullon, 1891], 75). It is subsequently mentioned by Menahem ibn Saruk (*Maḥberet Menaḥem,* ed. Z. Filipowski [London, 1854], 10b0), Ibn Janaḥ (*Sefer Hariqma,* 38), and Moses ben Hanesiah (*Sefer Hashoham,* ed. B. Klar [Jerusalem: Meqiṣe Hanirdamim, 1946], 6). Abraham de Balmes lists possible and impossible combinations without exploring the reasons for this phenomenon (*Miqneh Avram* [Venice: Daniel Bomberg, 1523], 6d).

23. Ibn Janaḥ, *Sefer Hariqma,* 277; regarding Saadia, see A. Harkavy, *Zikaron Larishonim* (St. Petersburg, 1891), 5:44–45.

24. Ibn Ezra, *Sefer Ṣaḥot,* 12a.

25. Salo Baron, *A Social and Religious History of the Jews,* 2d rev. ed., 7 vols. (New York: Columbia Univ. Press, 1952), 6.243, 275; 7.16, 19.

26. Ibid., 7.223 n. 11. H. Hirschfeld notes that the biblical etiologies are already a rudimentary form of linguistics (*Literary History of Hebrew Grammarians and Lexicographers* [London: Oxford Univ. Press, 1926], 5), while some similar ideas can be found among the Masoretes (see D. Yellin, *Toldot Hitpathut Hadiqduq Ha'ivri* [Jerusalem: Qohelet, 1941], 10–17).

27. *Sefer Yeṣirah,* 2:2, which is cited by Saadia (*Commentaire,* 74) and Ibn Ezra (*Sefer Ṣaḥot,* 11b–12a). See also Ibn Janaḥ, *Sefer Hariqma,* § 2, p. 36; Ibn Ezra, *Yesod Mara'* (Kushta, 1930), 17; David Qimḥi, *Miklol,* 70a; Moses ben Isaac ben Hanesiah, *Sefer Hashoham* (ed. B. Klar [Jerusalem: Meqiṣe Hanirdamim, 1946], 6); Profiat Duran, *Sefer Ma'aseh 'Efod* (ed. M. Friedlander [Vienna, 1865], 35–36); De Balmes, *Miqneh Avram,* 7b. Sibawaihi had classified the Arabic consonants according to sixteen points of articulation (Semaan, *Linguistics,* 41); an example of an Arabic treatise on this subject has been translated by K. I. Semaan, *Ibn Sina's Risala on the Points of Articulation of the Speech Sounds* (Lahore: Sh. Muhammed Ashraf, 1963). Indian phoneticians had performed a similar analysis of their own language some thousand years earlier, but appear to have concluded that Sanskrit tolerates the juxtaposition of such letters although their pronunciation is affected (W. S. Allen, *Phonetics in Ancient India* [London: Oxford Univ. Press, 1953], 21–230).

28. For example, Ibn Janaḥ, *Sefer Hariqma,* 36; Ibn Ezra, *Sefer Ṣaḥot,* 12a; David Qimḥi, *Miklol,* 70a; Duran, *Sefer Ma'aseh 'Efod,* 35–36, Moses ben Hanesiah, *Sefer Hashoham,* 6 (see also Ibn Saruk's *Maḥberet Menaḥem,* 6a). There is some variation in the components of the various categories.

29. Thus Ibn Saruk, *Maḥberet Menaḥem,* lists non-occurring pairs without citing an underlying reason (p. 10b).

30. Allony, *Ha'egron,* 91.

31. Ibn Saruk, *Maḥberet Menaḥem,* 10.

32. Ibn Ezra, *Sefer Hariqma,* 38.

33. M. Wilensky, "*Sefer Śafah Berurah Lerabbi Abraham ibn Ezra . . . ,*" *Dvir,* 2 (1923), 296–97; see also idem, *Śafah Berurah* (ed. G. H. Lippmann [Fürth: Zürndorffer, 1839] 18a) and Ibn Ezra, *Sefer Ṣaḥot,* 12a.

34. James Barr, *Fundamentalism* (London: SCM Press, 1977), 279–84.

35. Rabbinic references to corrected scrolls or those who correct them can be found in *j. Sanh.* 2, 20c; *j. Shek.* 4:3, 48a; *t. Sanh.* 4:7; *b. Ket.* 106a; *b. Pes.* 112a; *Sifre Deut.* § 160. Note also the tradition that there were three textually distinct Torah scrolls at the Temple in Jerusalem as stated in *Sifre Deut.,* 356, *j. Ta'an.* 4:2, 68a, and *'Abot R. Nat.* B 46, p. 65a, as well as the tradition of *tikkunê soferim* (e.g., *Midr. Tanḥuma,* ed. Vilna [reprinted Jerusalem: Lewin-Epstein, n.d.], 89–90), which, whatever its original pur-

pose, surely implies that existing manuscripts might be different from the original texts.

36. Note especially the collections of B. Kennicott and J. B. de Rossi in the eighteenth century and C. D. Ginsburg in the early twentieth. David Qimḥi mentions this problem in his comment to 2 Sam. 3:35.

37. Quoted by Jacob al-Qirqisani; cf. L. Nemoy, "Al-Qirqisānī's Account of the Jewish Sects and Christianity," *HUCA* 7 (1930): 488; also Judah Hadassi, *Sefer Eshkol Hakofer* (Eupatoria, 1836), 41b.

38. See Rashi's comments to Job 14:24 and 1 Chron. 20:33 and Ibn Ezra's comments to Exod. 25:29 and 1 Chron. 28:17.

39. Ibn Janaḥ, *Sefer Hariqma,* 307–33; see also Solomon ibn Parḥon, *Maḥberet He'aruk* (Posonii: Anton von Schmid, 1844), 71.

40. J. Barr refers to such methods in modern scholarship as "virtual emendations" (*Comparative Philology and the Text of the Old Testament* [Oxford: Clarendon Press, 1968], 191).

41. C. H. M. Versteegh cites Latin, Greek, and Arabic parallels (*Greek Elements in Arabic Linguistic Thinking* [Leiden: E. J. Brill, 1971], 24–27); see Varro, *On the Latin Language* 5.6 (trans. R. G. Kent, LCL [Cambridge: Harvard Univ. Press, 1938], 1.6), and Quintilian, *Institutio Oratoria* 1.v:6–10, trans. H. E. Butler, LCL (Cambridge: Harvard Univ. Press, 1969), 80–83.

42. For example, A. Neubauer, "Abraham Ha-Babli. Appendice a la notice sur la lexicographi hébraïque," *JA* 6th series 2 (1863): 195–210. A similar observation was made regarding phonologically induced shifts in the *t* for the *hitpa'el;* see Ibn Janaḥ, *Sefer Hariqma;* 109, David Qimḥi, *Sefer Hashorashim,* ed. J. H. R. Biesenthal and F. Lebrecht (Berlin: G. Bethge, 1847), 129. For a good example of the empirical approach, see Moses ben Nahman's comment to Exod. 15:10.

43. Allony, *Kitāb 'al-Sab'în Lafẓa,* 157.

44. Wechter, *Ibn Barun's Arabic Works,* 55.

45. See J. Qimḥi, *Sepher Hagaluy* (ed. H. J. Matthews [Berlin: Meqiṣê Hanirdamim, 1887], 8).

46. For example, Ibn Quraish, *Sefer 'Iggeret,* 116, and Ibn Parḥon, *Sefer Maḥberet He'aruk,* 18b.

47. See S. L. Skoss, "A Chapter on Permutation in Hebrew from David Ben Abraham Al-Fasi's Dictionary 'Jāmi' al-Alfaẓ'," *JQR* n.s. 23 (1932): 1–43, for a complete listing and effort to show how deeply seated within Jewish tradition is this recognition. Another such treatise by Abraham Ha-Bavli was edited by A. Neubauer in *JA* 6th series 2 (1863): 195–216. Ibn Quraish refers to a section of his *Risāla* dealing with this (in part I, s.v. ל), however, it is not extant. Other such works were by Solomon ben Yeroḥam and Saadia Gaon, according to S. Skoss, "Saadia Gaon, the Earliest Hebrew Grammarian," *PAAJR* 23 (1954): 63.

48. *b. Šabb.* 103b; *b. Pes.* 112a; and *Lev. Rab.* 19:2.

49. Ibn Janaḥ, *Sefer Hariqma,* 104; Rashi at Job 15:24; Ibn Ezra, *Sefer Ṣaḥot,* 3; Moses ben Hanesiah, *Sefer Hashoham,* 7; and Duran, *Ma'aseh 'Efod,* 81.

50. Ibn Janaḥ, *Sefer Hariqma,* 107; Rashi at Job 15:24; and Skoss, "Chapter on Permutation," 30; Ibn Ezra cites these examples (*Sefer Ṣaḥot,* 31a) in order to reject this view.

51. Moses ben Hanesiah, *Sefer Hashoham,* 7; see also Skoss, "Chapter on Permutation," 30, and Neubauer, "Abraham Ha-Babli," 211.

52. Neubauer, "Abraham Ha-Babli," 211; and Skoss, "Chapter on Permutation," 30.

53. Ibn Janaḥ, *Sefer Hariqma,* 107; Neubauer, "Abraham Ha-Babli," 211; Skoss, "Chapter on Permutation," 30.

54. Ibid.

55. Ibid. and Rashi at 1 Chron. 1:6.

56. Ibn Janaḥ, *Sefer Hariqma,* 107; Skoss, "Chapter on Permutation," 30; Rashi at Job 15:24; Ibn Ezra, *Sefer Ṣaḥot,* 31; De Balmes, *Miqneh Avram,* 5c.

57. Ibn Janaḥ, *Sefer Hariqma,* 107; De Balmes, *Miqneh Avram,* 5c.

58. Rashi at Job 2:8.

59. Rashi at Job 15:24. Moses ben Hanesiah adds (*Sefer Hashoham,* 7) that מדהבה (Isa. 14:4) is to be derived from the root *rhb* as in Ps. 40:5.

60. Poznanski, *Mose ibn Chiqitilla,* 100; cf. 1QIsa[a] and many modern exegetes.

61. Ibn Janaḥ, *Sefer Hariqma,* 110; see also Duran, *Maʿaseh ʾEfod,* 82, and Skoss, "Chapter on Permutation," 29.

62. Ibn Janaḥ, *Sefer Hariqma,* 111; he also cites a case of ח־ה interchange (*Sefer Hashorashim* [Amsterdam: Philo Press, 1969], 116). See also Duran, *Maʿaseh ʾEfod,* 82.

63. Neubauer, "Abraham Ha-Babli," 214.

64. Ibn Janaḥ, *Sefer Hariqma,* 110; Ibn Ezra at Ps. 54:20 and *Moʾzney* 16b; also M. Wilensky, "*Sefer Śafah Berurah,*" 302; Duran, *Maʿaseh ʾEfod,* 82; and De Balmes, *Miqneh Avram,* 5c.

65. Ibn Ezra, *Sefer Ṣaḥot,* 28b; for other examples, see J. Qimḥi, *Sefer Zikaron,* 71.

66. The medievals were aware that the Bible had originally been written in a different script from their own (see already *b. Sanh.* 21b–22a; medieval references in Sarna, "Hebrew and Bible Studies," 348), although I am not aware of any evidence they could have known the shapes of its letters.

67. חלילה שיהיה בכל העברית תמורת אות באות (J. ibn Kaspi, *ʾAdney Kesef,* ed. I Last [London: I. Narodiczky, 1911]) on Isa. 61:6; see also *Sharshoth Kesef* (Jerusalem: Makor, 1960) s.v. עבש. Ibn Saruk took a similar position (*Maḥberet Menaḥem,* s.v. אבח), but see his treatment of עתם (D. Kaufmann, "Das Wörterbuch Menahem ibn Saruks nach Codex Bern 200," *ZDMG* 40 [1836]: 380). See also W. Bacher, "Der 'Prüfstein' des Menachem b. Salomo," in *Jubelschrift zum siebzigsten Geburtstag des Prof. Dr. H. Graetz* (Breslau: S. Schottlaender, 1887), 113.

68. Cf. Ibn Janaḥ, Sefer Hariqma, 113. Usually such pairs are regarded by these scholars as synonyms (e.g., Ibn Ezra in Wilensky, "*Śafah Berurah,*" 302). Duran rejects the evidence of proper names spelled differently in parallel passages (*Maʿaseh ʾEfod,* 81).

69. On Ps. 5:1; see also comments to Gen. 7:2; Ps. 80:16; Qoh. 12:5; and Wilensky, "*Śafah Berurah,*" 301.

70. Comments to Gen. 37:25; Isa. 19:4; Qoh. 12:5; Ibn Ezra, *Moʾzney,* 3a; and *Sefer Ṣaḥot,* 4b; see also Judah Hayug, *Two Treatises on Verbs Containing Feeble and Double Letters,* ed. John W. Nutt (London: Asher & Co., 1870), xi, 10, 13, etc. For Masoretic anticipation of this kind of interchange see Aaron ben Asher's *Dikduke Haṭĕʿamim* § 8, cited by Yellin (*Toldot,* 17).

71. For example, at Gen. 7:2; Num. 11:20; Isa. 13:22; Pss. 5:1; 80:16; Cant. 1:10; Qoh. 12:5; and Wilensky, "*Śafah Berurah,*" 301.

72. Ibn Ezra, *Moʾzney,* 16a; *Sefer Ṣaḥot,* 14a and 19a; comment at Ps. 120:6; see also Ibn Janaḥ, *Sefer Hariqma,* 73; and Poznanski, *Mose ibn Gikatilla,* 96 on Exod. 2:4 and Ps. 8:2, and Moses Hanesiah (*Sefer Hashoham,* 7).

73. ולא אדע לו טעם למה, רק בעבור המכתב שידמה זה לזה, הנה הוסיפו על ההא קו קטן, להורות שהוא סמוך (Wilensky, "*Śafah Berurah,*" 302). The fact that a similar interchange exists in Arabic and Aramaic, where these letters do not resemble each other, is used to prove the antiquity of the Hebrew script. See also Moses ben Nahman at Deut. 33:3.

74. Ibn Ezra, *Sefer Ṣaḥot,* 28; for a similar statement regarding vowels, see p. 1a.

75. For example, Diogenes Laertius, *Lives of Eminent Philosophers* 7.57, trans. R. D. Hicks, LCL (Cambridge: Harvard Univ. Press, 1925), 1.165, and Priscian, *Institutionum Grammaticarum* 1.2.3, in H. Keil, *Grammatici Latini* (Leipzig: Teubner, 1855), 2.6. Ibn Ezra's monistic view of the world is exemplified in his assertion that "since the human soul was created in God's image, its creations are like his creations" (*Sefer Ṣaḥot,* 1a).

76. For problems which were perceived in such a view, see R. H. Robins, *Ancient and Medieval Grammatical Theory in Europe, With Particular Reference to Modern Linguistic Doctrine* (London: G. Bell & Sons, 1951), 26; the greatest difficulty pertained to grammatical gender, which does not always correspond to physical sex.

77. See Plato's *Cratylus,* 390–93 (*The Collected Dialogues of Plato, Including His Letters,* ed. E. Hamilton and H. Cairns [New York: Bollingen Foundation, 1961], 428–30).

78. Ibn Parḥon, *Maḥberet He'aruk,* 11a and 15a; Moses ben Hanesiah, *Sefer Hashoham,* 7, 101, 127; J. Gikatilla, *Sefer Ginnat 'Egoz* (1615; reprinted, Jerusalem, 1969), 25b–26a. J. F. Staal points out that the pre-Christian Indian grammarian Paṇini had arranged the letters of the Sanskrit alphabet according to the manner of their articulation ("A Method of Linguistic Description, The Order of the Consonants According to Paṇini," *Language* 38 [1962]: 1–10).

79. See S. A. Horodetzky, "Gematria," *Encyclopedia Judaica* (Berlin: Verlag Eschkol, 1931), 7:170–79.

80. For example, RSV and J. Bright, *Jeremiah,* AB 25 (Garden City, N.Y.: Doubleday & Co., 1965), 161. That such a view is considered seriously by modern biblical scholars demonstrates that traditional Jewish views have, in fact, exercised an effect on modern scholarship (see also RSV at Jer. 25:26 and 51:1).

81. *Tg. J.* Jer. 24:26 and 51:1, and LXX Jer. 28 (= MT 51):1, where קמי לב is understood as כשדים.

82. *T. Sukk.* 5:2; see also *b. Šabb.* 104a; *Num. Rab.* 13:15–16; 18:21.

83. These are summarized by H. L. Strack, *Introduction to the Talmud and Midrash* (Philadelphia: Jewish Publication Society, 1931), 95–98; for the date, see B. D. Klein, "Baraita of the 32 Rules," *EJ* (Jerusalem: Keter, 1972), 3:195.

84. *B. Sanh.* 22a.

85. J. Trachtenberg, *Jewish Magic and Superstition, A Study in Folk Religion* (New York: Behrman's Jewish Book House, 1939), 263–65.

86. J. Grafton Milne, "Relics of Graeco-Egyptian Schools," *JHS* 28 (1908): 121–22; Quintilian, *Institutio Oratoria* 1.1.25 (LCL 1.33); and F. Dornseiff, *Das Alphabet in Mystik und Magie* (Leipzig and Berlin: Teubner, 1922), 132–33.

87. Suetonius, *The Lives of the Caesars,* §§ 56, 88 (trans. J. C. Rolfe, LCL [Cambridge: Harvard Univ. Press, 1979], 1.78, 256.

88. אין מקרא יוצא מפשוטו (*b. Šabb.,* 63a), cited by Ibn Janaḥ (*Sefer Hariqma,* 19) and Ibn Ezra (*Śafah Berurah,* 4b–5a).

89. E. I. J. Rosenthal, "Medieval Jewish Exegesis: Its Character and Significance," *JSS* 9 (1964): 267.

90. Yellin, *Toldot,* 39.

91. See J. Rosenthal, "Ḥiwi al-Balkhi, A Comparative Study," *JQR* n.s. 38 (1947–48): 317–42, 419–30, and 39 (1948–49): 79–94, as well as I. Sonne, "Biblical Criticism in the Middle Ages" in *Freedom and Reason, Studies in Philosophy and Jewish Culture in Memory of Morris Raphael Cohen,* ed. S. W. Baron, E. Nagel, and K. S. Pinson (Glencoe, Ill.: Free Press, 1951), 438–56.

92. Sarna, "Hebrew and Bible Studies," 348, 365 n. 134.

93. J. L. Kugel, *The Idea of Biblical Poetry, Parallelism and Its History* (New Haven: Yale Univ. Press, 1981), 173–76, to which references should be added Ibn Saruk, *Maḥberet Menaḥem,* 11b. See also Bacher, "Der 'Prüfstein,'" 103.

94. See J. Friedman, *The Most Ancient Testimony, Sixteenth-Century Christian Hebraica in the Age of Renaissance Nostalgia* (Athens: Ohio Univ. Press, 1983), and E. I. J. Rosenthal, "Medieval Jewish Exegesis," 207–8.

95. For example, R. Alter, *The Art of Biblical Narrative* (New York: Basic Books, 1981), and M. Fishbane, *Text and Texture, Close Readings of Selected Biblical Texts* (New York: Schocken Books, 1979).

PART FIVE

THEOLOGY

12 LOU H. SILBERMAN

THE QUESTION OF JOB'S GENERATION. *SHE'ELAT DORO SHEL "IYOB"*: BUBER'S JOB

In the autumn of 1941, Martin Buber published a Hebrew essay bearing the title "*She'elat doro shel 'Iyob*'" (The Question of Job's Generation) with quotation marks around Job.[1] It reappeared the following year (1942) as a section in his *Torat ha-Nebi'im.*[2] An English translation, *The Prophetic Faith,* appeared in 1949 with the section under consideration reappearing in excerpted form, the opening and concluding sections being omitted—to the detriment of Buber's thought—in 1968 and 1969.[3] The German text that was, I think, the original, for part of the book appeared in Dutch translation in 1940, was published only in 1950.[4] Yet despite the interest in almost everything Buber wrote, this essay, for it is complete in itself, has passed almost unnoticed. Curt Kuhl's survey of the literature dealing with Job on every level does not, so far as I could determine, mention it.[5] Neither Marvin Pope's commentary[6] nor that of Robert Gordis[7] refers to it. William Moonan's bibliography of critical discussions of Buber's thought[8] has four entries. The earliest of these, by Barry Ulanov, "Job and his Comforters,"[9] is unaware of the essay even as it is found in *The Prophetic Faith* and reconstructed what he thought to be Buber's Job from references and comments in other, later writings. Thus he transposed the discussion to a post-Auschwitz situation. He concluded his comments by suggesting that Buber "has [not] seen the subtlety of the role of the devil in the drama." Yet it is, as we shall see, insight into this that is one of the most compelling aspects of Buber's discussion. Bernard Martin,[10] noted by Moonan, also dealt with Buber's Job from the same after-Auschwitz perspective. Although he was acquainted with *The Prophetic Faith,* his references are all from Buber's later writings in which Buber has fragmentarily quoted himself. L. D. Streicker's comment is so passing as to require no more than mention.[11] It is only N. N. Glatzer who directed his attention to Buber's analysis of the biblical text.[12] Yet even his presentation did not do full justice to the subject. Buber's essay is divided into three parts. The first sets the historico-theological stage for the drama, and it is this Glatzer slighted with but a comment in the form of a question: "How does he read the book, which, he believes, was written at the beginning of the Babylonian Exile . . . ?" The third part that deals with what Buber understood to be the afterlife of the book in Psalm 73 he completely ignored. As noted above, both are omitted by Glatzer in the excerpted republications he prepared. But it is just Buber's argument for the historical placement of the book that determined what he understood it to be saying. This same comment is applicable to Jon Levenson's essay that focuses briefly on Buber's exposition of what he argues are four views of God in the book, without attending to the circumstances in which these vews are offered.[13]

Buber's discussion of Job has a foreshortened title in both the English and German texts. It is merely "The Question," "Die Frage." The absence of the phrase "dorot shel 'Iyob'" does, I believe, alter one's perception of the dynamics of the discussion. Indeed, the quotation marks around "Iyob" in the original title may not be ignored, for what is intended by them is that the fate of the literary character Job is not an individual's fate but stands for the community, the generation. The argument of the essay begins with a discussion of the disaster of the Babylonian Exile as "a productive force from the religious point of view: it begins to suggest new questions and to stress old ones. Dogmatizing conceptions are pondered afresh in the light of the events, and the faith relationship that has to stand the test of an utterly changed situation is renewed in modified form." What were the "dogmatized conceptions"? What the "new questions"? What the "old"? His answers refer to a "sense of the solidarity of the community" that had arisen in Israel in early times. General suffering was seen to be "an act of heavenly retribution . . . for . . . guilt, corporate and individual." However, with the fall of Judah this idea was increasingly called into question. The response to the prophetic word on the part of the people had not averted disaster. The teeth of the righteous generation (that of Josiah) had been set on edge for the sins of the father (Manasseh's generation). It is Ezekiel who brings the situation into sharpest focus: "He denounces the whole religious tradition of collective responsibility, a tradition the negative[14] result of which is the bitter irony of the proverb," about the children's teeth. Yet for Buber, Ezekiel's individualizing of the prophetic alternative is "not meant as a general article of faith." In the future, the people, now a mere "sum of individuals . . . each one stand[ing] for himself over against God" will be resurrected. "The people no longer exists as a covenant partner, until God will make for it the 'eternal covenant.'" As for the moment, the personal responsibility of the individual is in the forefront. "There is opened to *every man* of Israel a covenant relationship with God, each one, as formerly the people, being set at the crossroads between life and death." This is Ezekiel's message and through it "he establishes the concept of God in whose justice it is possible to believe, a God whose recompense of the individual is objectively comprehensible. Those deserving salvation are saved."

It is this theologoumenon that has, Buber indicates, infected the "teachings of Judaism up to a later generation and against which Jewish religion repeatedly protested." It is this message and this concept of God that was not accepted by "the generation of the Babylonian Exile," for it was no answer to its question: "Why do we suffer what we suffer?" Buber writes: "The question did not deny the belief in individual recompense, it merely denied the objective comprehensibility of the recompense," for "over against the dogma stood their experience." In the catastrophe, righteous and wicked perished together and in its aftermath "the wicked left alive . . . 'lived, became old, and even thrived mightily' . . . whereas the upright is 'become a brother of jackals'." "This," Buber insists, "is the experience out of which the book of Job was born, a book opposed to the dogmatics of Ezekiel, a book of the question which was then new and has persisted ever since." It was "the question of a whole generation about its historic fate." This is crucial to an understanding of Buber's Job.

He makes his stance quite clear through his reference to J. Hempel's statement that behind the treatment of Job's fate lie "very bitter experiences of a supra-individual kind." "It is true," he writes, "it is a personal fate that is presented here, but the stimulus to speaking out, the incentive to complaint and accusation, bursting the bands of the presentation, are the fruits of supra-personal suffering." If this is kept in mind, the full implication of Buber's discussion is lost. That discussion, in keeping with the language of the book, is of an individual but, ". . . behind this 'I' made so personal here, there still stands the 'I' of Israel."

The "why" of the generation is not a query after the nature of things, "a philosophical interrogation"; it is rather "a religious concern with the acting of God." "That everything comes from God is beyond doubt and question; the question is, How are these sufferings compatible with his godhead?" There are, as Buber writes, not two but four answers in the book; "four views of God's relationship to man's suffering."

The first is found in the Prologue, "an ancient popular book about Job, but bears the stamp of poetic formation." The God of the Prologue—here is where Ulanov misses the point completely—allows "a creature, who wanders about the earth and is subject to him in some manner, the 'Satan,' that is the 'Hinderer' or 'Adversary', to entice Him." It is this enticement or temptation of God that is crucial to our understanding and while Buber points to it emphatically, he does not detail it as it deserves to be elucidated. He sums up the result: "This creature entices the deity to do all manner of evil to this man, only in order to find out if he will break faith, as Satan argues, or keep it according to God's word." He does not spell out the dialectic and, indeed, he himself missed the point when he wrote that "the deity did all manner of evil." It is that temptation God avoids, for when Satan urges him, "Stretch forth *your* hand and touch all he possesses," God is but partially tempted: "All that is his is in *your* hand . . ." Again, Satan tempts God to move against Job, for in both cases he knows that were God himself to act there would be no way out. "Stretch forth your hand and touch him, his very self," but again God is partially tempted: ". . . *your* hand . . . only spare his life." God is tempted because God believes, as Buber suggests, that Job serves him "disinterestedly" (*hinom*) and this belief leads him "gratuitously" (*hinom*) to give Satan all but free rein. If anything—Buber does not seem to recognize this—the portraitist of Job stands together with him who sketched the Abraham of the *Aqedah,* as an upholder of the possibility of the ultimate and absolute faithfulness of man. It is that man who will not, in Buber's words, "dismiss [*brk*] God" but ". . . bows down to God and 'blesses' [*brk*] Him." Buber concludes his discussion of the Prologue with these words: "This is a peculiarly dramatic face-to-face meeting, this God and this man. The dialogue poem that follows contradicts it totally. There the man is another man, and God another God."

But is this so? Is there a face-to-face meeting in the Prologue? It may be that the God of the Prologue is not the God of the whirlwind, but is the Prologue about God? Is it not about Job? About the man of unflinching faithfulness? Without the Job of the Prologue there is no book! Buber is mistaken in seeing four answers to the question; four views of God. The Prologue offers no answer; no "view of God." It serves but to set the play in motion. In structuralist analysis of narrative, it presents the actant with his task. One need pay but little attention, at this moment, to the source of the task.

The "second view of God" according to Buber, "is that of the friends. This is the dogmatic view of the cause and effect in the divine system of requital: sufferings point to sins." This dogmatic view is a misappropriation of Ezekiel's position. His was, Buber seems to say, true only in an interim situation, "The passage of time between covenant and covenant." The friends are speaking of "an all embracing empirical connection between sin and punishment." Ezekiel, Buber writes, held that "punishment followed unrepented sin, but it never occurred to him to see in all men's sufferings the avenging hand of God. . . ." Whether Buber is correct in this or not, it is certain that the friends held such a position. They are the representatives of religion, by which Buber means, as often but not always, conventional religion, and religion offers Job "a reasonable and rational God, a deity Whom he, Job, does not perceive either in his own existence or in the world, and who obviously is not to be found anywhere save only in the very domain of religion." Such a God is "a great idological idol." It is against this "false representation" that, however, makes Job aware of the hiddenness of God, "a God who withdraws Himself," that Job rebels; or, rather against both it and God in hiding. It is not the God of the Prologue against whom Job cries out. There he had remained silent and faithful, God's hiddenness unrecognized; but how can one remain faithful to the friends' God?

Thus Buber turns to his third view. "It is the view of a God Who contradicts His revelation by 'hiding' His face." It is, as noted, the friends' presence that has accentuated that hiddenness. Here we are at the heart of the matter. Buber writes: "Clearly the thought of both Job and the friends proceeds from the question about justice." For Job, justice is "a human activity, willed by God, but refuted[15] by His acts." Job's suffering no longer allows him to believe in God's justice but he still believes in God: " . . . he is no longer able to have a *single faith* in God and in justice." "He believes now in justice in spite of believing in God, and he believes in God in spite of believing in justice."[16] But God is hidden from him. "This hiding, the eclipse of the divine light, is the source of his abysmal despair. And the abyss is bridged the moment man 'sees', is permitted to see again, and this becomes a new foundation." Yet Job can only hope to see; he does not yet see. Here again Buber underscores his position that what we face is a supra-individual experience. "It is the dread of the faithful 'remnant' in the hour of the people's catastrophe that here finds its personal expression." At this point Buber calls attention to the echoing "how long" between Job and Deutero-Isaiah who "expresses the despairing complaint of the faithful remnant which thinks that because God hides himself, Israel's 'way' also 'is hid' from Him, and He pays no more attention to it, and the prophet promises that not only Israel but all flesh shall see him." There is no answer, only the expectation that an answer will be forthcoming; thus Job's God is indeed a God who will answer. This third view clearly requires the Job of the Prologue, for it is only the man of steadfast faithfulness, there shown, who can be the angry rebel against God's hiddenness made manifest by the friends' "false" God.

The fourth view is that of divine self-disclosure in God's own speech. Buber notes that this section like others "is apparently a late revision" and the original text is beyond restoration. But, he insists, " . . . the speech is intended for more than the mere demonstration of the mysterious character of God's rule in nature to a greater and more comprehensive extent than had been done by the friends and Job himself. . . . It is also intended to do more than teach by examples taken from the world of nature about the 'strange and wonderful' character of the acts of God." Justice is still at the center of the poet's concern. Thus the speech of God, as Buber interprets it, is a declaration to the "man struggling for justice" of "another justice than his own, a divine justice. Not *the* divine justice but *a* divine justice, namely that manifest in creation." This is the crucial and most difficult point in Buber's interpretation. God's justice in creation is a "giving justice." Each creature is given its divinely appointed limit through which it may fulfill itself. Man, however, is not mentioned in this presentation of heaven and earth "in which it is shown to Job that man whose justice wishes to give to everyone its due can give another its due only by giving it its self."[17] Before this teaching Job admits he "had erred in speaking of things inconceivable for him." Justice, he now recognizes, is arrived at in a way other than he had thought.

This, however, is not the end of the matter. Job had, indeed, struggled with the problem of justice but he, too, had struggled with the problem of God. Only one, the first, had ended with a voice "from the tempest." The second remained: the remoteness of God. It is resolved, Buber indicates, because the voice that speaks is not just "a voice from the tempest" but "the voice of Him Who answers." Job had sought God in his remoteness; "now God draws near to him." Job now "sees" him and God enters into a dialogue with him. It is in and through that dialogue that God discloses himself. "The absolute power is for the sake of human person become person.[18] God offers Himself to the sufferer who, in the depth of his despair, held to God by his rebellious complaint; He, as it were,[19] offers Himself as an answer." This is, it seems, parallel to the solution of justice wherein another is affirmed as thou. Here, it is the encounter of God as thou that returns to Job, in the reciprocal relation I-thou, his own thou. Earlier, in dealing with the view of the friends, Buber wrote: "By allowing religion to occupy the place of the living God, He strips off Job's honor." The word here referred to is *kebodi.* In the context it ought to be understood in its root meaning, *gravitas,* the reality of Job as person, for at the end Job is reaffirmed as person.

What this difficult section appears to be saying is: man's sufferings are not unjust, for justice is granting to man the right to be man and suffering is a part of man's creatureliness, his being man. But more than that, in the presence of God the incommensurability of man's justice, that is true justice, and God's justice, that is true justice although other, ceases to be the sticking point, for man has learned to add God's justice to his own.

Buber now turns to a summing up of his argument. The first view of God is, he recognizes, necessary for the "enticement." The second offers the God of punishment or, in the Elihu speeches that are, he holds, a later addition, one who uses suffering as a means "of purification and education." Job's God "works against every reason and purpose." The God of revelation at once abolishes and fulfills "every reason and purpose held by man." Picking up on his statement that the God of the Prologue cannot be in any way related either to the God of the friends or of Job, he argues that " . . . the poet, who frequently shows himself to be a master of irony, left the Prologue, which seems completely opposed to his intention, unchanged in content in order to establish the foundation for the multiplicity of views which follows." Yet, as suggested above, Buber, having posited four views, strains his argument by insisting on the theology rather than the anthropology of the Prologue and, because of that, underestimates the entire anthropological direction of the book. "God justifies Job," he writes, ignoring the evident truth that Job as well justifies

God, for it is not only Job's faithful trust in God that is put to the test—Satan could not be less interested in that for it is God whom he entices—it is God's trust in Job that is put to the test and justified. Perhaps Buber does express this but in an indirect fashion when he writes: "And as the poet often uses words of the Prologue as motive words in different senses, so here he makes God call Job as there by the name of His 'servant', and repeats it by way of emphasis four times. Here this epithet appears in its true light. Job, the faithful rebel, like Abraham, Moses, David and Isaiah, stands in the succession of men so designated by God, a succession that leads to Deutero-Isaiah's 'servant of YHWH', whose suffering especially link him to Job." The "perhaps" must be underscored, for even here Buber's insistence upon a discontinuity between "servant" in the Prologue and elsewhere suggests his failure to recognize the anthropology of the book.

In concluding this section, Buber subtly and exquisitely suggests that Job has indeed learned the divine lesson: Job intercedes for his friends. After what they had said to him, he reaffirms them as person. "The significance of Job's intercession is emphasized by the Epilogue . . . in that the turning point in Job's history, the 'restoration' (Job 42, 10) and his healing, begin the moment he prays 'for his friends'."[20]

In his view of the Epilogue " . . . which apart from the matter of the prayer, the poet apparently left as it was . . . ," Buber, as in his discussion of the Prologue, ignores the implication of his position that the poem, however composed, is a product of the experience of the community in the Babylonian Exile. Once the folk tale is set in that context its original meaning is radically transformed. The "enticement" of God, seen against the emergence of the enduring faithfulness of Job in the poem, is something other than a mere story of a duped deity. And the Epilogue, often so contemptuously dismissed as an empty charade, a sop to the groundlings, can and ought to be seen in the new context side by side with Ezekiel's vision of the valley of dry bones and Deutero-Isaiah's ecstatic proclamation of the return:

> Raise your eyes and look about:
> They have all gathered together and come to you.
> Your sons shall be brought from afar,
> Your daughters like babes on shoulders.
> As you behold, you will glow;
> Your heart will throb and thrill—
> For the wealth of the sea shall pass on to you,
> The riches of the nations shall flow to you.
> Dust clouds of camels shall cover you,
> Dromedaries of Midian and Ephah.
> They all shall come from Sheba;
> They shall bear gold and frankincense,
> And shall herald the glories of the Lord.
>
> (Isa. 60:4–6)

Does not the Epilogue, more matter-of-factly, say just this? "Furthermore, the Lord blessed the end of Job's life more than the beginning; and he had fourteen thousand head of small cattle and six thousand camels, a thousand yoke of oxen and as many she-asses. He had seven sons and three daughters" (Job 42:12–13). This is certainly the language of folk tale but its intention is none other than that of Deutero-Isaiah's, a promise of return and restoration.

The third section of the essay brings us back to the meaning of the poem: the restoration of Job as person, through a careful examination of Psalm 73. It is, he suggests, the prayer of one who like Job has acquired his vision of God through suffering.

> He who has been instructed in Job's school is barred from the paths leading back to the religion of the friends; but that part of the living truth of faith, which is hidden and wrapped up in the teaching of Ezekiel, namely, that sin is not the cause of death, but is death itself. This is revealed[21] here on a higher plane, after the hardest suffering through the way of the world, and has acquired value both for the life of the individual and for that of history. When he has come to the "sanctuaries", the man of prayer will no longer forget that God's justice is His mystery, but even so, in the mystery, he experiences it.

Buber's Job was written at a time when the destruction of European Jewry, the "final solution," was but a cloud the size of a man's hand on the horizon of history. As noted above, both Ulanov and Martin have dealt with those fragments of his thought Buber used later on the few occasions he grappled with that horror. A fuller understanding of what he was saying on those occasions may be arrived at, if and when they are read against the background of "The Question of Job's Generation."

NOTES

1. Martin Buber, "*She'elat doro shel 'Iyob',*" *Mosnayim* 13, 5/6 (Tishri/Heshvan, 5702): 322–331.

2. Martin Buber, *Torat ha-Nebi'im* (Tel Aviv: Mossad Bialik, 1942).

3. Martin Buber, *The Prophetic Faith,* trans. Carlyle Witton-Davies (New York: Macmillan Co., 1948). The section under consideration, pp. 183–202, has been excerpted in Martin Buber, *On the Bible,* ed. N. N. Glatzer (New York: Schocken Books, 1968), 188–98, and again in N. N. Glatzer, *The Dimensions of Job: A Study and Selected Readings* (New York: Schocken Books, 1969), 56–65. All the quotations below have been taken from the English translation with constant attention to the Hebrew and German. I have indicated the several places where I have provided my own translation, for there are occasions, here as elsewhere, where Buber has not been well served by his translator.

4. Martin Buber, *Der Glaube der Propheten* (Zurich: Manesse, 1950), republished in *Schriften zur Bibel,* Vol. 2 of *Werke.* The first two parts of the book appeared in a Dutch translation as early as 1940 but the bibliographic source does not indicate from what language. "Het Geloof van Israel," trans. L. Alons in Gehardus van der Leeuw, *De godsdiensten der wereld,* I (Amsterdam: H. Meulenhoff, 1940).

5. Curt Kuhl, "Neuere Literarkritik des Buches Hiob," *TRu* n.f. 21, nos. 3, 4 (May, July, 1954): 163–205, 257–317.

6. Marvin Pope, *Job: Introduction, Translation and Notes,* AB 15 (Garden City, N.Y.: Doubleday & Co., 1965).

7. Robert Gordis, *The Book of Job: Commentary, New Translation and Special Studies* (New York: Jewish Theological Seminary of America, 5738 [1978]).

8. William Moonan, *Martin Buber and His Critics. An Annotated Bibliography of Writings in English* (New York and London: Garland Publishing, 1981).

9. Barry Ulanov, "Job and His Comforters," *Bridge: A Yearbook of Judeo-Christian Studies* 3 (1958): 234–68.

10. Bernard Martin, "Martin Buber and Twentieth Century Judaism," *Central Conference of American Rabbis Yearbook* 67 (New York, 1967): 149–64.

11. L. D. Streicker, *The Promise of Buber* (Philadelphia: J. B. Lippincott, 1969).

12. Nahum N. Glatzer, *Baeck-Buber-Rosenzweig: Reading the Book of Job.* Leo Baeck Memorial Lecture 10 (New York: Leo Baeck Institute, 1960), 9–15.

13. Jon Levenson, *The Book of Job in Its Time and in the Twentieth Century* (Cambridge: Harvard Univ. Press, 1972), 19–25, 75. See particularly n. 18.

14. The English translation omits "negative" before result, found in both the Hebrew and German.

15. This in place of the English translation's "opposed."

16. I have left "believe" although I am uncomfortable with it. It seems in the light of Buber's distinction in *Two Types of Faith, he'emin* should be translated ambiguously as "he has faith in." "Believe" comes down on the wrong side of Buber's distinction.

17. This is my paraphrase of the Hebrew in place of the English translation that is unclear.

18. The English translation has "personality," hardly a Buberian concept.

19. The English translation omits "as it were."

20. The English translation has "The first of all his healings, begins . . ."

21. The English translation has "is covered," clearly a mistake for "uncovered."

13 H. YAVIN

MODERN "DOXOLOGIES" IN BIBLICAL RESEARCH

Doxologies or declarations of praise for God are common in ancient hymns and prayers and are often found in their concluding words. The most famous are probably those in the Book of Psalms (Pss. 41:14; 72:18–19; 89:53; 106:48; 150 [the entire psalm]) which declare with some minor variations "Blessed be the Lord, God of Israel, from everlasting to everlasting. Amen and Amen." Turning to Mesopotamia, we find in addition to hymnal doxologies an extensive doxology in the form of the fifty names (attributes) of Marduk which climaxes the Enuma Elish, the Babylonian creation story which served as a glorification of Babylon's chief god. Both the psalms and the Enuma Elish are liturgical poetry; they were probably written for cultic or religious occasions, and were certainly recited then. Their doxological endings serve a double purpose which is both religious and poetic; they express the religious credo of the community, and they serve a poetic function in the structure of their texts—they provide closure either for one composition or, as in Psalms, for an entire section or "book."

Hymns and liturgies, however, are not the only place where doxological endings are found. There is a long tradition in the ancient Near East of nonliturgical but rather "literary" doxologies, doxologies at the conclusion of literary compositions. Sometimes the name in the doxology is a main character or has played a major role in the composition, as in "Praise to holy Lugalbanda" (*kù-lugal-bàn-da zà-mí*) in the Sumerian Lugalbanda Epic.[1] In other cases the doxology appears to be more *pro forma*. Thus Sumerian compositions of diverse genres—epics, disputations, proverb collections—end with praise to a deity. The deity is often, but not always, Nisaba, the goddess of writing.

This phenomenon has a counterpart in medieval (and even in some modern) Jewish scholarly religious works such as Bible commentaries. These works often conclude with a variation on the formula "Finished and complete. Praise to God, the Creator of the world." Such doxologies provide an appropriate form of closure in these nonliturgical works, for the Mesopotamian scribes and the medieval scholars, living in societies which did not distinguish between the religious and the secular, naturally perceived their writings as religious endeavors in some sense. At the very least, a sense of humility would move the writer to render homage to the power that made the writing of texts possible, the goddess of writing or the Lord of the universe. On a grander level (and this is true for the Jewish works) the author considered his or her writing a religious act, undertaken for the greater glory of God.

Modern biblical scholars who do attempt to separate their scholarship from their religious beliefs, however, would not be expected to incorporate doxologies into their writings. Yet such "doxologies" do exist—especially as endings—more often than has been realized. I consider the mention at the end of a work of God or Jesus by name or indirectly, or reference to religious beliefs, to be a form of doxology not unlike those which occur in ancient compositions. Like his or her ancient counterpart, the modern biblical scholar finds in this a satisfying closure of his or her work. But a doxology is never free from credal overtones and therefore it undercuts the "objectiveness" or "scientificness" that the work purports to have. It is more than anything else an indicator of the scholar's stance to his or her material. To judge from their endings, many modern works of biblical criticism continue to be written for the greater glory of God or, even more obvious to sensitive Jewish eyes, for the greater glory of the church.

Before looking at doxological endings, a look at endings in general is in order. How does a scholarly book or article end? Many authors may not give this much conscious thought but I would guess that many aim, perhaps unconsciously, for a sense of closure. This closure (or lack of it) may take the following form, which I illustrate from both biblical and nonbiblical scholarship:

1. A work may simply stop when it has made its last point. For instance, a biblical commentary ends when the last verse has been explicated, a historical study ends with the last event discussed. This could be considered ending without closure.

2. The end sums up the main point or thesis of the book, sometimes returning to the point of departure or even forming an *inclusio.* James Kugel ends the body of his book on parallelism with the words "biblical parallelism"—words that occur in the title and form the book's main subject.[2] Michael Fishbane's *Text and Texture* has a more definite *inclusio* in "The mind of man has always been fascinated by mysteries of origins" and "to find in a world of words a disclosure of the mystery of creation."[3]

3. The ending projects toward the future. This is a common way to conclude

narratives because it forms a bridge between the time of the tale and the time of the telling. In fairy tales it is the "and they lived happily ever after" ending. But it is not limited to fairy tales; similar types of endings have been documented in contemporary storytelling.[4] In scholarly expositions the future projected toward may be either the future of scholarship or the future of the subject under discussion. Reference to future scholarship can be illustrated by these excerpts from G. Roux and J. Barr:

> So much has still to be done in the fields of Assyriology and Mesopotamian archeology, and so many chapters in the history of ancient Iraq require completion that this delicate but fascinating and very useful task must be reserved for scholars of future generations. (G. Roux)[5]
>
> But it can be expected with assurance that the moving currents of linguistic study will guide us towards new trends in the general interpretation of the Old Testament. (J. Barr)[6]

Following up the subject matter beyond the focus of the study and toward the present and future occurs in the next examples:

> Islamic Persia was launched on its wonderful course with its Hafiz, Sa'di, Omar Khayyam and a myriad of writers and artists down to the present day. But behind the poems, the rugs and the art which are known all over the world today there is the heritage of the past, a glorious heritage which has maintained a continuity and an influence down to the present, sometimes unseen but none the less present. May it long continue. (Richard N. Frye)[7]
>
> With the coming of Alexander, Egypt, like the rest of the Middle East, was at the end of the ancient period and on the threshold of a new era. (Jack Finegan)[8]

4. The language of closure tends to become elevated. This is the literary analogue of the ritard or crescendo at the end of many musical compositions, and it may be similar to the linguistic changes that have been demonstrated in poem endings.[9] The excerpt from Frye just cited also illustrates heightened rhetoric. Sometimes heightening is achieved through the use of quotation. This provides a shift in style, an endorsement from an accepted authoritative voice, or, at times, the introduction of actual poetic language.

Such endings, or combinations of them, are widespread in both biblical and nonbiblical works. The problem is, however, that in biblical studies the line between heightened language and projection toward the future on the one hand, and doxology on the other, begins to blur. And so what an author may have intended simply as a form of closure turns into a doxology. There are several types of doxological endings which I categorize as follows: 1. Christological endings; 2. Ethical-moral endings; 3. Use of God's name; 4. The best is last. Illustrations of these four types were culled randomly and do not constitute a statistically valid sampling. They are taken from prominent books and articles in the field of biblical studies which present themselves as objective, scholarly works; no theological, confessional, or overtly denominational works were included. In other words, these works address themselves to the scholarly world, not to a particular faith community.

CHRISTOLOGICAL ENDINGS

> And here occurs a last and interesting point of commentary. Matthew included three women in his genealogical composition, Rahab the harlot, Bathsheba the not unwilling adulteress, and Ruth the Moabitess. Not particularly happy company for valorous Ruth, but of such as these three, the Bible consistently says, is built up the line of King David, and of one whom a later segment of the people of God would call *the* Son of David. (E. F. Campbell)[10]

This is a projection into the future, not to the present but to a point in time of special significance to Christians. The doxology also contains God's name, again in christological form (see below). Now this commentary on Ruth is part of the Anchor Bible series, a series whose every volume bears the notice that "The project is not sponsored by any ecclesiastical organization and is not intended to reflect any particular theological doctrine." This doxology, however, and others in the series as well, certainly do reflect a religious doctrine.

> Thus the collapse of the state of Judah began the Edomite occupation of southern Palestine, Idumea of the Books of Maccabees, Josephus, and the New Testament, whence Herod the Great came eventually to the throne of Jerusalem. (J. Gray)[11]

This is another projection beyond the scope of the study, and again it is to a time and place meaningful to Christians. Compare the ending of this archeological discussion with that of Finegan's nondoxological one cited earlier.

> In this alone may we rejoice, that here God made himself known to his people, and here, in the fullness of time, Our Lord Jesus Christ came to dwell among men. "Would that even today we knew the things that make for peace!" (Luke 19:42). (Denis Baly)[12]

This ending, employing heightened rhetoric, quotation, and projection toward the future, all of which are patently christological, is the ending of a book on *geography!*

> Looking around, one can then boldly make an apparently foolish confession of faith: truly, this person is the Son of God. (Daniel Patte and Aline Patte)[13]

This heightened, christological language ends an otherwise tediously technical book on the application of structural exegesis to sections of the New Testament.

> The transcending vision was bequeathed by the pre-exilic festival to later centuries, a vision of God's ultimate perfecting action, the new reign of God and his

> Anointed, an action still to come yet never far away, its brightness already sending shafts into this needy world. (J. H. Eaton)[14]

Abundant use of heightened language and projection here; a discussion of psalms begins to turn into a psalm.

ETHICAL-MORAL ENDINGS

These endings are not specifically christological or Jewish, but have religious or at least ethical overtones. When such endings occur in the writings of Jews associated with the Reform movement, such as Samuel Sandmel and Harry Orlinsky, they come very close to a declaration of faith, and may thus be considered a Jewish equivalent of the doxologies illustrated in the previous section.

> It is to the prophetic tradition more than any other source that western civilization owes its noblest concept of the moral and social obligations of the individual human being. Even if the prophets preached only to their fellow Israelites . . . their ringing words have carried from age to age that . . . to love God was to love justice, and that the love of justice placed within the conscience of each human being the ultimate inescapable obligation to denounce evil . . . and to live in the law and the love of God no matter what the cost. (H. Orlinsky)[15]

> Yet it is this same prophetic literature which speaks to man of hope, and provides man with purpose and a sense of clear direction to a better world. (S. Sandmel)[16]

Similar kinds of endings can be found in Christian-authored works, and here they appear to be not so much an expression of personal belief as neutralized or sanitized views of the religious importance of the Bible—something akin to advocating the "Judeo-Christian tradition." They may be nonsectarian, but they are certainly religious.

> The tone of these endings is often faintly sermonic (elevated language): And it is through this communication in word that Israel's experience can become ours, and Israel's faith our faith; for it is through this revelation that we are enabled to see through to the reality and the truth of the human experience which transcends the historical forms in which this experience has been expressed. (Thomas L. Thompson)[17]

USE OF GOD'S NAME

There are many biblical studies in which the author has managed to work God's name or a substitute for it into the last sentence, sometimes making it the last word. Some of these are overtly christological—Son of God, Jesus—but many are not. I view them as a form of heightened language, although since God is prominent in many biblical discussions, this may also be related to a kind of summing up. They remind me of the Sumerian "Praise to Nisaba" endings. They are the most neutral kind of doxological ending.

> Concealed within the prayer, therefore, one discovers yet another answer to the question, "What is the strongest?" The masterful dialogue comes to rest in God. (James L. Crenshaw)[18]

> By stimulating that sense of being the people of God, and by deepening that faith . . . Deutero-Isaiah played a crucial role in ensuring that survival, and so fully deserves recognition as a true prophet who faithfully proclaimed the word of God. (R. N. Whybray)[19]

> We would translate then "The upright walk in the paths of Yahweh." (F. I. Andersen and D. N. Freedman)[20]

The last two citations incorporate God's name along with summation (Whybray) or quotation (Andersen and Freedman), thereby achieving double closure.

THE BEST IS LAST

Throughout this study I have proceeded on the assumption that endings are significant, that when closure is provided it represents the thought that the author wanted his or her reader to be left with. This last thought may grow organically out of the last topic discussed, it may serve as a summation, or it may be an appendage to the main discussion. But however it arises, it sounds a triumphant note, and for this reason is able to provide closure. "The best is last" type of doxology has to do with arranging for a particular religious view to end and therefore climax a work.

This type of doxology can occur in two ways. In the first, it is simply a continuation of the last point discussed turned doxological. For instance, the last chapter of G. B. Caird's *The Language and Imagery of the Bible* is concerned with the language of eschatology, but the tone slips from that of academic discourse to doxology at the conclusion.

> About an *eschaton* John has nothing to say. Instead he introduces us to a person who says, "I am the Alpha and the Omega, the first and the last, the beginning and the end." Wherever in the course of time men and women come face to face, whether for judgment or for salvation, with him who is the beginning and the end, that event can be adequately viewed only through the lenses of myth and eschatology.[21]

Now one cannot argue that Caird designed his book so that he could end with an eschatological doxology, for the subject of eschatology belongs chronologically and thematically at the end of his study. There are, however, examples where one can see more clearly that the best—that is, what is closest to the author's heart—is saved for last. My examples are taken from introductions to the Hebrew Bible and a history of Israel, and they constitute a projection toward the future. In works of this sort projection to the future has two strains, the Jewish and Christian. It may be coincidental, but I find it suggestive that the Christian authors speak first of Judaism and then of Christianity, while the Jewish author reverses the order.

> The Old Testament ends like an incomplete drama, an unfinished symphony. According to Pharisaic Judaism, Israel's pilgrimage leads through the Old Testament to the Talmud and to a continued life of messianic expectancy. According to the New Testament, Israel's pilgrimage leads to Jesus, the Christ, who came not to destroy, but to fulfill the Law and the Prophets. (B. W. Anderson)[22]

John Bright ends *A History of Israel* with an extended discussion in a section entitled "The Destination of Israel's History: The Answer of Judaism and the Christian Affirmation." He first explains the failure of the Sadducees, then presents the Pharisaic option which led to normative Judaism. The latter he calls "a legitimate answer and, from a historical point of view, a correct one." But then he gives another answer, equally historically legitimate: "the one the Christian gives, and must give."[23] There is no doubt about which of these legitimate answers the author would choose, for he repeats at length the Christian view, ending with the following:

> The Christian, of course, must reply: "Thou art the Christ [Messiah], the Son of the living God." After he has said that . . . Old Testament history assumes for him a new meaning as a part of a redemptive drama leading on to its conclusion in Christ. In Christ, and because of Christ, the Christian sees its history, which is "salvation history" (*Heilsgeschichte*), but yet also a history of disappointment and failure, made really and finally *Heilsgeschichte*.[24]

On the other hand, Sandmel gives Judaism the last word in his introduction:

> Although Christianity reflects a sporadic ambivalence towards the Tanak, in its main-streams it has accorded it and still accords it a rightful place within its Scripture. The contrast between the Jewish view of the Tanak can be oversimplified in the following way: Christianity regards the Tanak as superseded but sacred, while Judaism regards it as sacred and unsuperseded.[25]

The four types of doxological endings that I have discussed are not mutually exclusive. It is not unusual to find them in combinations; for instance, the use of God's name (which I consider doxological in itself) often occurs in christological or ethical-moral endings. But since I, too, have saved the best for last, I offer as a final example a doxological ending which incorporates three of the features discussed: it is christological, uses God's name, and is also a case of "the best is last." This prize-winning example of closure—and it does provide dramatic closure—is from Marvin Pope's *Song of Songs*. In his commentary on Song 8:14, Pope concludes with the interpretation of the Midrash, followed by various Christian interpretations, thus illustrating once again "the best is last." The commentary, and thence the book, ends with a citation from a nineteenth-century commentary.

> Littledale concludes his commentary with eloquent quotations from Augustine, Lyranus, and the Apocalypse. . . . *Make haste, then, my Beloved,* for "the Spirit and the Bride say, Come. And let him that heareth say Come." And Thou, O dear and worshiped Lord, art not deaf to the call, "He who testifieth these things saith, Surely I come quickly: Amen. Even so, come, Lord Jesus."[26]

Pope's discourse is complex: it consists of quotes within quotes, voices echoing voices. And his ending is ironic, for it comments on a verse which to many has seemed a puzzling or unsatisfying end for a book of the Bible; yet Pope's ending contains all the rhetoric of strong closure—elevated language, quotation, projection toward the future. Moreover, the ending is extremely doxological. Not only does it exemplify "the best is last" and the use of God's name as the final word—both of these features reinforcing its christological content—but the concluding quotation is, more than any other I have cited, *a real doxology.*

Doxologies take different forms but the same thing happens in all of them. The author ceases speaking about the Bible and begins to speak like the Bible. The distance that an objective scholar places between him- or herself and his or her subject vanishes; the scholar becomes one with the subject.

I want to reiterate that these doxological citations were taken from commentaries; books on history, archeology, and geography; and books on methodology or state-of-the-art knowledge. These are not books about God or religion per se, and there is no compelling reason to mention God or religious beliefs at their conclusion—indeed, most works of biblical scholarship of this kind do not; doxological endings appear to be in the minority. It is quite possible to achieve closure in a work on the Bible without resorting to a doxological conclusion.

The fact that a significant minority of scholarly works does close with a doxology is interesting, to say the least, for what it shows about individual authors and about an academic field which is either oblivious of or indulgent toward this phenomenon. It is additional proof that, as most biblicists know but few admit publicly, modern biblical scholarship is, to a significant degree, still motivated by a religious impetus.[27] Despite the adoption of methodologies sanctioned by the arts and sciences, it is still the quest for religious faith and affirmation that drives the machinery of much biblical scholarship.

How significant is a doxological ending? Does it invalidate the objectivity of the research which precedes it? This is a question for scholars of all (or no) faiths. For a Jew the problem is more acute, because Christians still dominate the field of biblical studies and Christian doxologies are more numerous and more obvious than Jewish ones. How is a Jew to react when, having read a work which seems methodologically sound, he or she is suddenly confronted with a Christian doxology? Is he or she to ignore it, discount it as nonintegral to the work (a kind of non sequitur), or will he or she inevitably perceive the entire work as tainted by its doxology?[28]

NOTES

1. C. Wilcke, *Das Lugalbandaepos* (Wiesbaden: Harrassowitz, 1968), 128.

2. James Kugel, *The Idea of Biblical Poetry. Parallelism and Its History* (New Haven: Yale Univ. Press, 1981), 304.

3. Michael Fishbane, *Text and Texture* (New York: Schocken Books, 1979), 3, 142.

4. Cf. Wm. Labov, *Language in the Inner City: Studies in the Black English Vernacular* (Philadelphia: Univ. of Pennsylvania Press, 1972), 365.

5. G. Roux, *Ancient Iraq* (Harmondsworth: Penguin Books, 1964), 390.

6. J. Barr, "Semitic Philology and the Interpretation of the Old Testament," in G. W. Anderson, *Tradition and Interpretation* (London: Oxford Univ. Press, 1979), 64.

7. Richard N. Frye, *The Heritage of Persia* (Cleveland and New York: World Publishing, 1963), 244.

8. Jack Finegan, *Archeological History of the Ancient Middle East* (Boulder, Colo.: Westview Press, 1979), 349.

9. Cf. Barbara Herrnstein Smith, *Poetic Closure. A Study of How Poems End* (Chicago: Univ. of Chicago Press, 1968).

10. E. F. Campbell, *Ruth,* AB 7 (Garden City, N.Y.: Doubleday & Co., 1975), 173.

11. J. Gray, "Recent Archeological Discoveries and Their Bearing on the Old Testament," in Anderson, *Tradition and Interpretation,* 94.

12. Denis Baly, *The Geography of the Bible* (New York: Harper & Brothers, 1957), 266.

13. Daniel Patte and Aline Patte, *Structural Exegesis: From Theory to Practice* (Philadelphia: Fortress Press, 1978), 112.

14. J. H. Eaton, "The Psalms and Israelite Worship," in Anderson, *Tradition and Interpretation,* 271–72.

15. Are "law" and "love" code words for "Jew" and "Christian"? Quotation from H. Orlinsky, *Ancient Israel* (Ithaca, N.Y.: Cornell Univ. Press, 1960), 144.

16. Samuel Sandmel, *The Enjoyment of Scripture* (London and New York: Oxford Univ. Press, 1972), 283.

17. Thomas L. Thompson, *The Historicity of the Patriarchal Narratives* (Berlin: Walter de Gruyter, 1974), 330.

18. James L. Crenshaw, "The Contest of Darius' Guards," in B. O. Long, *Images of Man and God* (Sheffield: Almond Press, 1981), 88.

19. R. N. Whybray, *The Second Isaiah* (Sheffield: JSOT Press, 1983), 81.

20. F. I. Andersen and D. N. Freedman, *Hosea,* AB 24 (New York: Doubleday & Co., 1980), 648.

21. G. B. Caird, *The Language and Imagery of the Bible* (Philadelphia: Westminster Press, 1980), 271.

22. B. W. Anderson, *Understanding the Old Testament* (Englewood Cliffs, N.J.: Prentice-Hall, 1975), 600.

23. John Bright, *A History of Israel* (Philadelphia: Westminster Press, 1959), 452.

24. Ibid., 453.

25. Samuel Sandmel, *The Hebrew Scriptures* (New York: Oxford Univ. Press, 1978), 546.

26. Marvin Pope, *Song of Songs,* AB 7C (New York: Doubleday & Co., 1977), 701. The commentary is R. F. Littledale, *A Commentary on the Song of Songs. From Ancient and Mediaeval Sources* (1869).

27. Cf. R. E. Clements, *One Hundred Years of Old Testament Interpretation* (Philadelphia: Westminster Press, 1976), 3–4, 143; Ernest W. Saunders, *Searching the Scrip-*

tures: A History of the Society of Biblical Literature (Chico, Calif.: Scholars Press, 1982); M. E. Marty, "Review of *Searching the Scriptures*," *JBL* 103 (1984): 86.

28. I do not go so far as to suggest that there is an anti-Jewish bias in such works, although in a few there may well be. On this issue see Charlotte Klein, *Anti-Judaism in Christian Theology* (Philadelphia: Fortress Press, 1978).

14 JON D. LEVENSON

WHY JEWS ARE NOT INTERESTED IN BIBLICAL THEOLOGY

I

Soon after I began teaching I received a revealing phone call from a colleague in another institution. The caller was teaching "Introduction to the Old Testament," a course for both divinity-school and liberal-arts students. Among the latter was a Jew upset at what he perceived to be the Christian bias of the bibliography. Eager to be evenhanded, the professor called me to find out what Jewish scholar had written the best "biblical theology." My hesitation in answering was surely sufficient to call into doubt my colleague's confidence in my competence. Finally, I stammered out the names of a few serviceable works concerned with biblical concepts and authored by committed Jews such as Yehezkel Kaufmann (*The Religion of Israel*) and Nahum Sarna (*Understanding Genesis*).[1] The caller thanked me, but I remember thinking as I hung up that he ought to feel disappointed, for what he was hoping to get from me was the name of the Jewish equivalent of Walther Eichrodt's *Theology of the Old Testament* or Gerhard von Rad's *Old Testament Theology*.[2] And for reasons that I shall explore in this essay, there is no Jewish equivalent.

I had occasion to recall this little incident a few months ago, as I sat in a Protestant seminary listening to a distinguished Continental biblicist lecture on Old Testament theology. At the end of his talk, he remarked that in a year of research in Israel, he had been unable to find anyone interested in the subject. Finally, he had asked a member of the Bible department at the Hebrew University of Jerusalem about this curious situation, and the latter, known for his keen theological interests, replied that he thought no one in Israel, presumably including himself, had any interest in the whole exercise. The lecturer was visibly perplexed as he told this story. Sophisticated Israeli biblicists uninterested in Old Testament theology? It made no sense. In the end, he shrugged his shoulders in a gesture of mingled disbelief and resignation.

The expectation of these Christian scholars was not unreasonable. Whereas for centuries the field of biblical studies was divided along religious and even denominational lines—with little respect and less communication between groups—today, the field, at least in North America, boasts a vibrant ecumenicity. Collaboration in biblical work among Jews, Catholics, Protestants, and secularists no longer elicits surprise except among the laity and the extreme right of each religious grouping. Among professional academics and well-informed clergy, the pluralism of the field is assumed. Indeed, it can be readily discerned from the diversity of backgrounds and institutional affiliations among contributors to the two most influential American commentary series, the Anchor Bible (Doubleday & Co.) and Hermeneia (Fortress Press). The old identities have faded and are now often vestigial. On this, my own situation speaks volumes, for, an observant Jew, I teach Hebrew Bible at a liberal Protestant divinity school in a university of Baptist origin, and I have frequently contributed to the *Catholic Biblical Quarterly.* If Jewish participation is plentiful in academic programs, professional societies and journals, excavations, and commentaries, one would expect it to be no less plentiful in studies of "biblical theology" or, at least, in research on its Old Testament side. Instead, we may question whether there is any identifiably Jewish participation in that aspect of biblical studies. To be sure, Jews have contributed studies of theological themes in various texts of the Hebrew Bible. In his *Preface to Old Testament Theology,* Robert C. Dentan devotes one sentence to these Jewish thinkers, citing Martin Buber, Abraham J. Heschel, and Will Herberg as examples.[3] But whereas Christians have written scores of books and articles with "Old Testament Theology" or the like as their titles, I know of no book with that title or anything similar ("Theology of the Hebrew Bible," "Biblical Theology") written by a Jew. The best approximation is *The Philosophy of the Bible,* by David Neumark, late professor of Jewish Philosophy at the Hebrew Union College in Cincinnati.[4] This book dates from 1918, and even it is more a history of the religion of Israel than a biblical theology. The distinction, as we shall see, is essential.

The meaning of the term "biblical theology" is itself an issue much discussed in the discipline which goes by that name.[5] Dentan notes that the term "might *mean* either a biblical kind of *theology,* or the theological parts of *biblical* studies." Opting for the latter, he insists that "the only definition of biblical theology which does justice to the history of the discipline is that it is *the study of the religious ideas of the Bible in their historical context.*"[6] John Bright sets forth essentially the same dichotomy, although he notes a "third sense . . . the attempt of certain theologians and preachers to expound the Bible in its unity as authoritative in the church." Bright's own preference is similar to Dentan's. For him, "biblical theology" is "the theology that is expressed in the Bible."[7] It is common in these discussions to date the birth of the discipline to its separation from dogmatics late in the eighteenth century. If biblical theology has a birthday, it is March 30, 1787, when Johann Philipp Gabler gave his inaugural address upon assuming the theology chair at the University of Altdorf. "Biblical theology," Gabler insisted, "is historical in character and sets forth what the sacred writers thought about divine matters; dogmatic theology, on the contrary, is didactic in character, and teaches what a particular theologian philosophically and rationally decides about divine matters, in accordance with his character, time, age, place, sect or school, and other similar influences."[8] For Gabler, as for any Protestant, one of the most important of those "influences" was the Bible. But the distinction he so lucidly drew between biblical and dogmatic theology ultimately opened the door for the present pluralism in scholarship. If "biblical theology is historical in character," the affiliation of the biblical theologian is of no account for his or her work. As we shall see, this implication is one from which biblical theologians often recoil, and is in turn a major reason why this branch of biblical studies is less pluralistic than the others.

If the distinction from dogmatics is rather easily made, if not easily accepted, the distinction between biblical theology and the history of the religion of Israel is more problematic. Dentan contrasts the two thus: "One treats of the story of Israel's developments in its chronological sequence; the other describes the persistent and distinctive principles of Old Testament religion in some kind of logical or 'theological' order."[9] In other words, those principles are not examined in a historical vacuum, but they are assumed to have a stable identity through history, and it is this stable identity, rather than their growth and minor permutations, which interests the Old Testament theologian. He focuses not on the "long-cut" but on the "cross-cut" (*Querschnitt* is W. Eichrodt's term).[10] Bright is of essentially the same opinion, insisting that "the fact of diversity does not eliminate the possibility of an overarching unity, either in the biblical faith or any other."[11] If, however, there are "persistent . . . principles" or "an overarching unity," then it would seem that the historian of Israelite religion ought to be able to see them as well as can the Old Testament theologian. Bright, I think, would agree. His historical work and his theological work present essentially the same picture, in which "covenant" and "promise" are the twin centerpieces. They "run through the whole of the Old Testament and inform all of its parts."[12] If this were true, it would surely simplify the biblical theologian's task. All he or she would need to do is to describe the religion of Israel as the Old Testament wants it to be, and the result would be both a history of the religion of Israel (with due note of Israel's backsliding) and an Old Testament theology. The fact is, however, that this cross-cut, indeed any cross-cut, is really a Procrustean bed which cannot accommodate major segments of the book or, to be more precise, cannot regard as major the segments of the book which it does not accommodate. Covenant and promise dominate the Pentateuch, but they are missing from Proverbs, Qohelet, and the Song of Songs. The latter books, especially Proverbs, make no attempt to situate themselves within Israel's foundational story; they are unconcerned with the exodus, the revelation at Sinai, and the promise and conquest of the land. Indeed, they demonstrate no awareness of these themes. Bright's claim that in Proverbs "the place of Israel as [YHWH's] people, bound to live under his law, is clearly taken for granted"[13] is specious and circular. One cannot even assume the Israelite origin of all the proverb collections.[14] In light of the themes that Bright regards as constitutive of the "overarching unity" of the Old Testament, one is hardly surprised to find that his book on *The Authority of the Old Testament* refers to Amos five times and to Proverbs only twice, and never to a specific verse, even though Amos is less than one-sixth the length of Proverbs. Some themes are more widespread than others, but a widespread theme does not make an "overarching unity." The truth is that Bright's Old Testament theologian—and Bright is typical here—differs from a historian of the religion of Israel in that he or she selects certain themes which appeal to him or her and then presents the entirety of the Old Testament as an expression of only those themes, whereas a historian of religion without theological commitment would frankly acknowledge the diversity and contradiction of biblical thought and feel no apologetic need to concoct a "unity."

Dentan insists that the theologian's "Concern Should Be the Normative Religion of the Old Testament,"[15] but, like Bright, he does not see that this criterion is at odds with his commitment to the "historical context." The specifically historical context of the authors of Proverbs may not have included the Pentateuchal traditions, and the historical context of the Pentateuchal sources may not have included Proverbs. The juxtaposition of these various sorts of literature in the same book is a matter of *literary* context; it becomes a fact of *history* per se only very late in the period of the Second Temple—long after the historical contexts of the Pentateuchal literature and perhaps also the proverb collections had vanished. The construction of a religion out of *all* the materials in the Hebrew Bible violates the historian's commitment to seeing the materials in their historical contexts. The result will correspond to the religion of no historical community, except perhaps some parties very late in the period of the Second Temple. In short, the argument that Old Testament theology can maintain both an uncompromisingly historical character and its distinction from the history of Israelite religion is not valid.

If the distinction between the long-cut and the cross-cut is insufficient to differentiate Old Testament theology from the history of Israelite religion, another differentiation must yet be considered. There is a tendency among Christians (recently paralleled by remarks from a Jew, Moshe Goshen-Gottstein) to insist that biblical theology requires a measure of faith in its practitioners. "We may assume," writes Dentan, "that the Old Testament theologian of today, at least, will be a man [*sic*] of faith. . . ." "Faith," to quote the title of one of his subsections, "Helps Make Such Insight Possible."[16] Gerhard Hasel is less restrained. "What needs to be emphatically stressed," he writes, "is that there is a transcendent or divine dimension in Biblical history which the historical-critical method is unable to deal with."[17] Goshen-Gottstein discusses the distance involved in the religio-historian's stance toward his or her material as against that in a theologian's stance of "faith, identification, acknowledgment of value and meaningfulness, of taking a personal stand in the present, which draws nourishment from the same spring from which the teachings (*tôrôt*) of the past flowed. . . ."[18] As a means to differentiate the two disciplines, this idea works far better than the long-cut/cross-cut distinction, which, as we saw, cannot do justice to the variety and changeability of history. Even if we do not subscribe to the naive positivism that claims the historian simply tells what really happened (*wie es eigentlich gewesen ist*), we can still differentiate a scholar who strives after a not fully realizable objectivity from one who openly acknowledges his or her transcendent commitments and approaches his or her work in the vivid hope of deepening and advancing them. On the other hand, biblical theology here purchases its distinction from the history of religion at the price of its distinction from dogmatics. For if we shift the focus from the biblical writings to the contemporary theological use of them, even in a nontraditional mode, then we have substantially reconnected the umbilical cord that Gabler sought to sever two centuries ago. Our biblical theologian, like his dogmatician, will discuss "divine matters, in accordance with his character, time, age, place, sect or school, and other similar influences."[19] Even if one seeks, as Goshen-Gottstein does,[20] to maintain the autonomy of tradition, in his case normative Rabbinic law (*halakhah*), one cannot gainsay that the "personal stand in the present" of any Jew or Christian includes postbiblical elements. Indeed, if it does not, then the theology in question will be neither Jewish nor Christian, but only historical, and we are back to the dilemma discussed in the previous paragraph and Goshen-Gottstein's plea for a specifically Jewish biblical theology will have failed. How can a self-consciously Jewish biblical theologian take a personal stand on behalf of a text which he or she interprets against its Rabbinic exegesis? The effect would be the neo-Karaism against which Goshen-Gottstein cautions.[21] This is not to say that serious theological study of the Hebrew Bible for a Jew must be restricted to an uncritical repetition of medieval Rabbinic interpretations. It is to say, however, that the "personal stance" of a faithful contemporary Jew does not allow for the isolation of the Jewish Bible (*Tanakh*) from the larger tradition. Such an isolation is possible on historical grounds, but not on personal, existential grounds. One can attempt constructive Jewish theology with special attention to the biblical sources—and I believe there is a great need for such studies. But this is closer to what Christian faculties call "dogmatics" or "systematics" than to "biblical theology."

If it be admitted that biblical theology presumes existential commitment and that the commitment will necessarily include other sources of truth (the Talmud, the New Testament, and so on), then it becomes clear that biblical theology is different in kind from the other branches of biblical studies and that, unlike them, it cannot lend itself to ecumenical, pluralistic collaboration. One pursues either Jewish biblical theology or Christian biblical theology, but not both, for the term "biblical" has a different reference for the Jew and the Christian. The first sentence of Dentan's book says it all: "'Old Testament theology' is one part of a greater discipline called 'biblical theology' and cannot be studied in isolation from the larger subject." This is because "Old Testament theology is *a Christian-theological discipline* and, as such, does not deal with the Old Testament in isolation, but always has some concern for its relation to the New." It is, in fact, "a preparatory exercise for the study of the New Testament."[22] Here, Dentan is typical of the discipline in wishing to have it both ways. Biblical theology must be both "*the study of the religious ideas of the Bible in their historical context*" and "*a Christian-theological discipline.*"[23] But Christianity is not the historical context for a single religious idea in the Hebrew Bible, the latest of whose writings predates the earliest Christian material by a full two centuries. The Christian interpretation of non-Christian literature or, for that matter, the Rabbinic interpretation of non-Rabbinic literature, may have great strength. It may be defensible, even persuasive. But it cannot be historical.[24]

If Old Testament theology is "a preparatory exercise for the study of the New Testament," then an Old Testament theology that did not demonstrate the compatibility of the theologies of the two testaments would have to be judged a failure. Norman Porteous, after an exhaustive survey of the discipline, concludes that "a theology of the Old Testament, however, will not seek to obscure the fact that Christ did not merely decode the Old Testament but fulfilled it."[25] If this is a criterion for success in the field, then by definition no Jew could ever succeed in it, and the absence of Jewish interest is hardly mysterious. One could, in the spirit of a somewhat obsolescent ecumenism, expect Jews to make the same sort of connection with Talmud and Midrash that the Christian makes with the New Testament. Neumark, in fact, tried to do something close to this,[26] and, as we shall see, it is still surely the case that the continuity of Rabbinic and older Israelite religion is not sufficiently known among scholars. Nonetheless, the Jew will feel far less compulsion to make such connections, not least because Talmud and Midrash do not present themselves as the teleological consummation of the *Tanakh* (Jewish Bible), but only as the rightful continuation and implementation of biblical teaching. Rabbinic Judaism lacks the apocalyptic urgency of apostolic Christianity. The rabbis were not disposed to proclaim that this (in the present) is the real meaning of that (from the past). Their attitude toward the Hebrew Bible and theology in general was more relaxed and more pluriform. As a consequence, the endless discussion among biblical theologians as to the relationship between the testaments has not found and is unlikely to find a parallel among Jewish scholars.[27]

II

One reason for the distance Jewish biblicists tend to keep from biblical theology is the intense anti-Semitism which is evident in many of the classic works in that field. Old Testament theology is, in fact, often really the modern continuation of the ancient *adversus Judaeos* tradition in which the New Testament writers and the church fathers excelled.[28] After the insistence on the compatibility of Old and New Testament theology, few points are more *de rigueur* in the Old Testament theologies than deprecatory remarks about Rabbinic Judaism. A small sample of this unhappy literature should suffice.[29] Eichrodt informed his readers early on that Judaism has only "a torso-like appearance in separation from Christianity,"[30] a point that does not speak well of the intelligence of the two millennia of Jews who have never noticed. "It was not," he told us, "until in later Judaism a religion of harsh observances had replaced the religion of the Old Testament that the Sabbath changed from a blessing to a burdensome duty."[31] What he did not tell us is why Jewish sources into our own time have continued to speak of it as a blessing and to feel that its duties were liberating and exhilarating rather than burdensome.[32] In the Mishnah, Eichrodt observed, the "real worship of God [was] stifled under the heaping up of detailed commands from which the spirit has fled."[33] He did not, however, discuss the tannaitic liturgy which those commands regulate, with its heavy dependence on the Tanakh in both idiom and theology. In Judaism, he remarked, "the living fellowship between God and man . . . shrivelled up into a mere correct observance of the legal regulations," so that "the affirmation of the law as the revelation of God's personal will was lost."[34] Here it is apparent that Eichrodt, like most Christian theologians of his generation (and many today), has been misled by the Christian tendency to regard "Torah" as synonymous with "law" (Greek *nomos*) so that the whole haggadic dimension of Judaism is ignored. He literally missed the theology which grounds the halakhah and is, in the last analysis, inextricable from it. He took the Pauline polemic against the commandments for historical fact, failing to see that it was only one perspective, and, at that, an external one, born in the heat of polemic and devised for the service of certain rhetorical needs. The truly remarkable aspect of Eichrodt's anti-Judaism is his apparent failure to feel a need to argue his case, to delve deeply into Talmud and Midrash in order to demonstrate that they are what Christianity always said they were. In a historical scholar—Eichrodt was far from a fundamentalist—

this is odd. Perhaps this is where, in fact though not in theory, faith found its role: it exempted the scholar from his or her obligation to empirical reality.

The other great exemplar of Old Testament theology in our century, Gerhard von Rad, was more gentle in spirit. Rather than flaying Judaism, he generally pretended that it did not exist. In fact, his theology was, to a degree, predicated on the disappearance of Old Testament tradition after the death of Jesus. "The way in which the Old Testament is absorbed in the New," he wrote, "is the logical end of a process initiated by the Old Testament itself," and the analysis that suggests this does not utilize any "mysterious hermeneutic device."[35] Israel's history of redemption (*Heilsgeschichte*) is fulfilled in Jesus, and the inconvenient facts that most Jews did not think so and that Jewish literature remained alive, vigorous, and growing, are simply ignored. Joseph Blenkinsopp is surely justified in rejecting "this curious idea of a *Heilsgeschichte* which comes to an end at a certain point or (even more curious) which stops and starts again."[36] It would, to be sure, be unfair to attack von Rad and Eichrodt for failing to exemplify the pluralistic attitude that now prevails in biblical studies in America (with the exception of biblical theology). For in their formative years, such an attitude was unknown and not in conformity with the intense anti-Semitism of German theology.[37] On the other hand, it is not unfair to hold a historian of literature to the standards of historical research, and by those standards, these two theologians were woefully inadequate. They were unable to make the elementary if disquieting distinction between faith and fact. In this, they are typical of Old Testament theologians. A Christian theologian like Bright, who openly and respectfully acknowledges that "Israel's history does continue in Judaism,"[38] is the exception. The exception is much more likely to be found in the Anglo-American world than in the Germanic world whence the seminal works in Old Testament theology have emanated. Even as I write, the current rage in many Christian theological circles, "liberation theology," is rife with ignorant stereotypical depictions of the Judaism of Jesus' time.[39] New life is being breathed into the old defamations.

The derogations of Judaism by biblical theologians in the twentieth century are essentially the same as those promulgated by the historians of Israel in the nineteenth, and both are merely thin secularizations of calumnies that derive from the New Testament. The ideas of Julius Wellhausen (1844–1918), the greatest student of the Old Testament in the last century, are a case in point. Wellhausen made a sharp distinction between the religion of Israel and Judaism. *In nuce,* the latter is the former after it has died:

> When it is recognized that the *canon* is what distinguishes Judaism from ancient Israel, it is recognized at the same time that what distinguishes Judaism from ancient Israel is *the written Torah.* The water which in old times rose from a spring, the Epigoni stored up in cisterns.[40]

From the correct observation that the religion of late Second Temple times and beyond was book-centered in a way in which the earlier stages were not, Wellhausen moves to the questionable judgment that "Judaism" is cut off from its spring of vitality. "Yet it is a thing which is likely to occur, that a body of traditional practice should only be written down when it is threatening to die out," he wrote, "and that a book should be, as it were, the ghost of a life which is closed."[41] The spiritual death of the Jews is symbolized and perhaps caused by their severance from the land: "With the Babylonian captivity, the Jews lost their fixed seats, and so became a trading people."[42] If the term "trading people" seems to reflect the Jews of Wellhausen's Europe more than those of the Near East in biblical and Rabbinic times, it must be remembered that he wrote the classic work in which these remarks appear, *Prolegomena to the History of Ancient Israel,* at a time of swelling Jew-hatred. As Blenkinsopp points out, in the year after it was published, "1879, . . . Adolf Stöcker, founder of the Christian Social Workers' Party, described Orthodox Judaism in one of his speeches as a 'form of religion which is dead at its very core' and in the same year Heinrich von Treitschke, professor of history at the University of Berlin, spoke of the Jews as Germany's misfortune ('*Die Juden sind unser Unglück*')."[43] We must not allow Wellhausen's theological liberalism and his anti-clericalism to distract us from the degree to which he participated in the anti-Semitic culture of his time and place. That his was not a racial anti-Semitism of the kind that flowered in Nazism should not blind us to the fact that his work "made its modest contribution," in Blenkinsopp's words, "to the 'final solution' of the Jewish problem under the Third Reich,"[44] a generation after his death.

If Jews needed a reason to suspect the study of the Hebrew Bible in universities, Wellhausen and others like him surely provided it. No healthy person willingly puts him- or herself into a situation in which he or she will hear him- or herself defamed, pronounced dead, or both. In 1903, the Jewish riposte came in its most pungent form in an address by Solomon Schechter, one of the greatest scholars of Judaica of the time and the guiding light of the Jewish Theological Seminary of America in its formative years. Schechter's address was entitled "Higher-Criticism—Higher Anti-Semitism." It is this "Higher Anti-semitism of the critical historians," he argued, "which burns the soul though it leaves the body unhurt":

> The Bible is our sole *raison-d'être,* and it is just this which the Higher Anti-semitism is seeking to destroy, denying all our claims for the past, and leaving us without hope for the future.[45]

For this affliction, Schechter did not prescribe a return to uncritical, ahistorical traditionalism or a severance from the larger academic world and a reentry into the ghetto. Instead, he urged that fire be fought with fire, only of a purer kind:

> But this intellectual persecution can only be fought by intellectual weapons and unless we make an effort to recover our Bible and to think out our theology for ourselves, we are irrevocably lost from both worlds.[46]

The sour taste left by the anti-Semitism, however, did not die out so fast. Indeed, it remains potent today, and the theology for which Schechter called, which would enable Jews to recover their Bible in an intellectually defensible way which does not shut out either world, has yet to emerge. One reason is that the critical study of the Hebrew Bible is itself often seen by Jews as inherently anti-Semitic. The method and the uses to which it is put are not always adequately distinguished, and the fact that historical criticism has undermined Christianity no less than Judaism, as any Christian fundamentalist knows, is too often ignored.[47] As a result, even non-Orthodox institutions often shy away from critical study or "tiptoe through the tulips," studying some aspects of Jewish literature and history critically, and others traditionally. Thus, "Pentateuch criticism was avoided for most of the history of [Schechter's own] Jewish Theological Seminary."[48] When this is the case, theological work will be limited to a learned elucidation of the theology of the classic sources. This is no mean accomplishment, as one of Schechter's own works, *Aspects of Rabbinic Theology: Major Concepts of the Talmud,* nicely demonstrates.[49] But this is not what comes of the tense and parlous collision of tradition and modernity that generates among Christians the genre of "biblical theology." It is worth noting that whereas Christian theological training usually involves work in both historical and constructive theology, training in Jewish philosophy ("theology" is a somewhat alien term) tends to be historical in focus and to lack a constructive dimension altogether. I have found that if students of Jewish philosophy are asked, for example, what Maimonides thought of revelation, they are comfortable in answering, but if asked what we ourselves are to think of revelation, they are often stopped short and regard the question as a bit insulting. The analogous situation does not, for the most part, obtain among students of Christian theology.

Another consequence of the anti-Semitic tendencies of biblical studies has been a certain defensive, even reactionary posture among Jewish biblical scholars. One thinks, for example, of the *History of Israelite Religion* by perhaps the greatest Jewish biblicist of modern times, Yehezkel Kaufmann (1889–1963).[50] This eight-volume Hebrew work, some of which has appeared in English, is surely one of the great syntheses of ancient Israelite experience, perhaps its last great synthesis.[51] It is a work replete with novel insights and one which every student of the Hebrew Bible should own and consult frequently. On the other hand, it is saddening to think of Kaufmann, whose *magnum opus* came out between 1937 and 1956, shadowboxing with Wellhausen, who died in 1918. It is true that Wellhausen's ideas survived him and, for that matter, remain alive today among both Jews and Gentiles. But his evolutionary approach, with its great emphasis on written documents and inner-Israelite experience, had been in elipse since the 1890s. In the index to Moshe Greenberg's English abridgment of Kaufmann,[52] one finds numerous references to Wellhausen but none to Eichrodt or von Rad or even Albrecht Alt, whose historical focus paralleled Kaufmann's own in many ways.[53] All three were his contemporaries, yet it is Wellhausen who was his sparring partner. Kaufmann's history is written in the spirit of "Know what answer you will give to the unbeliever," to quote the Mishnah (*Abot* 2:19). In this, Kaufmann found a goodly measure of success, although he had more in common with Wellhausen than he may have realized. The fact remains, however, that Kaufmann was keenly aware of being a latecomer to the scene of biblical studies in a critical mode and, consequently, of having to clear out space in which to work. The reverence in which Kaufmann continues to be held among most Jewish biblical scholars is owing not only to the magnitude of his intellectual achievement, but also to the endurance of that need to clear out a place for Jews in the field and to counter the anti-Jewish positions which had taken root early in its history and had never been completely dislodged. But as Henry Kissinger once said of the liberals and intellectual discourse, Christian theologians have "preempted the categories" of biblical theology, and the Jew, like the conservative intellectual, can only sustain a holding action and occasionally get in a shot of his or her own. In other branches of biblical studies, the anti-Jewish impulse is much weaker and much less common. There, the legacy of the nineteenth century and of Christendom in general is more easily transcended; religious identities mean less, and the Jewish presence is correspondingly larger.

III

Historically, biblical theology has been not only non-Jewish, it has been Protestant. A full Roman Catholic embrace of the historico-critical method came about only in 1943 with the promulgation of the papal encyclical, *Divino afflante spiritu.* In spite of their rapid ascent to the top ranks of most branches of biblical studies in the last four decades, Catholic scholars have not changed the overwhelmingly Protestant complexion of biblical theology. This is as one would expect, given the greater weight the Christian Bible bears in Protestantism than in Catholicism. Although the Bible has become more important in Catholicism in the two decades since the Second Vatican Council, the Reformation doctrine of *sola Scriptura* ("by Scripture alone"), if it lives at all, lives only in Protestantism. It is important to remember that Protestantism tends to think of its Bible as a source of renewal, as the agent which enables the *ecclesia semper reformanda* ("the church forever in need of reform") to slough off its accumulated distortions and to recover its pristine gospel, which is its exclusive authority. "How often must I scream at you thick, ignorant papists to come with Scripture?" asked Martin Luther, with characteristic self-restraint. "Scripture. Scripture. Scripture. Do you not hear, you deaf goat and dumb ass?" "Paul wrote, 'scrutinize all teaching, and retain that which is good'." "If we would prove, as Paul says, what shall we take as a touchstone [*Probierstein*], other than the Scriptures?" "I will and must be subdued with Scripture," he wrote, "not with the uncertain life and doctrine of men, however holy they may be."[54] John Calvin laid down a comparable principle:

> Let this, therefore, be a firm axiom [*axioma*]: nothing should be permitted in the church as the Word of God except what is, first, in the Law and Prophets, and, secondly, in the writings of the apostles; and that there is no correct mode of teaching except within the prescribed limits [*praescriptio*] and under the rule of this Word.[55]

In light of this polarization of Scripture and tradition (which is a reflex of the polarization of God and man), the motivation to state the Scriptural doctrines precisely and purely becomes paramount. It is this inner-Protestant dynamic that is the mother of biblical theology in both of Dentan's senses, "a biblical kind of theology [and] the theological part of *biblical* studies."[56] In fact, the Protestant dynamic helps obscure that essential distinction, since it does not allow for much of a differentiation between a Protestant's own theology and that of his or her Bible. It is only in recent decades that some elite Protestant institutions have allowed students to pursue advanced work in theology without training in either Hebrew or Greek.

The unending Protestant quest for repristinization which spawns this great involvement in the Christian Bible finds scant parallel among the Jews. The motto of Anan ben David, founder of the Karaites, a Jewish sect that dates to the eighth century (C.E.) in Babylon, adumbrates the Reformation theology. "*Ḥappěśû šappîr bě 'ôraytā*," he admonished his followers in Aramaic, "search out the Torah thoroughly." For the Karaites, there is only one Torah, the Pentateuch, whereas for the rabbis, against whom they rebelled, Torah was twofold, written and oral, and it is this oral Torah which eventually finds graphic expression in the Mishnah, the Talmuds, the midrashic collections, and their medieval and modern descendants. Karaism was not without its effects. It spurred among Rabbanites the emergence of a mode of Jewish exegesis which pursued the "plain sense" of the Bible (*pěšāṭ*). Karaite commentators influenced the content of much Rabbanite exegesis. Nonetheless, Karaism itself has survived as only a tiny minority of that larger minority, the Jews. "Searching the scriptures" remains, at least in theory, a high priority of religious Jews, but not for the purpose of overthrowing Rabbinic enactments. No rabbi has ever cited the biblical principle of "an eye for an eye," for example, in order to clear away the Rabbinic law that corporal damages must be compensated monetarily and not in kind, as the *pěšāṭ* of Scripture might be thought to suggest.[57] Instead, biblical study in Judaism falls under the category of *talmûd tôrâ*, "the study of Torah," a sacred and central obligation (*miṣwâ*) in the Rabbinic universe, but a *miṣwâ* that applies to Mishnah, Gemara, medieval Rabbinic exegesis, and so on, as well. The traditional Jewish dynamic is quite the opposite of the Protestant and, unlike the latter, it does not foster an effort to isolate a peculiarly biblical theology.

The nineteenth-century Jewish Reform movement and its rebellious offspring, Conservative Judaism, made it possible for Jews to think of themselves as actively religious without having to fulfill many of the traditional commandments. The term "reform" can be misleading to Christians in that it might suggest a denomination that adheres to a high doctrine of Scripture such as that of the Reformed or Calvinist churches. To be sure, the Reform movement and its seminary, the Hebrew Union College—Jewish Institute of Religion, have historically tended to place more emphasis on *Tanakh* than on Talmud (unlike the Conservative movement and its Jewish Theological Seminary). Nonetheless, unlike the Reformed churches, Reform Judaism is not the offspring of the Renaissance with its slogan of *ad fontes* ("back to the sources!"), but of the Enlightenment with its rationalistic critique of all religion, including biblical religion. One sees this in the second and third planks of the famous "Pittsburgh Platform" (1885):

> 2. We recognize in the Bible the record of the consecration of the Jewish people to its mission as the priest of the one God, and value it as the most potent instrument of religious and moral instruction. We hold that the modern discoveries of scientific researches in the domain of nature and history are not antagonistic to the doctrines of Judaism, the Bible reflecting the primitive ideas of its own age, and at times clothing its conception of Divine Providence and Justice dealing with man in miraculous narratives.
> 3. We recognize in the Mosaic legislation a system of training the Jewish people for its mission during its national life in Palestine, and today we accept as binding only its moral laws, and maintain only such ceremonies as elevate and sanctify our lives, but reject all such as are not adapted to the views and habits of modern civilization.[58]

Here, it is clear that the *norma normans et non normata*, the ultimate, unconditioned norm, is not the Bible, but only its "moral laws" and "the views and habits of modern civilization," before which even Moses must bow the head and bend the knee. The Jewish Reformers did not, by and large, appeal to the Bible to purge Judaism of Talmudicisms; they did not seek to change the liturgy back to one principally of animal sacrifice or to substitute the talion for monetary compensation. Instead, they appealed to reason in order to purge the tradition of anything, whether biblical or Rabbinic, which they found incompatible with "modern civilization." The willingness of Reform Judaism to recognize historical development and to accept the principle of historical criticism made it more likely to become involved in modern biblical study, with less anachronistic infusion of Rabbinic ideas. Neumark's *Philosophy of the Bible* is testimony to this.[59] But the great impulse to develop a distinctly biblical theology which the quest for repristinization gives Protestants found no parallel in classic Reform Judaism and, a fortiori, none in the very different and rather more traditional Reform of today.

One finds a better parallel to the Protestant dynamic in some forms of secular Zionism. Here, the urge to repristinize the Jewish people is intense. Two millennia of rootlessness, persecution, passivity, dependency, spiritualistic escapism, and over-intellectualization were to be undone by a return to the land, the language, and, to a certain extent, the mores of the *Tanakh*. The rhetoric of reenactment was in plentiful evidence in early Zionism, and indeed, it can be heard to this day across most of the spectrum of Israeli politics—especially at the extreme right, with its demand for biblical borders and its occasional but alarming tendency to equate Palestinian Arabs with the seven Canaanite nations of the Torah. But whereas nowadays the extreme political right includes within it a very substantial Orthodox component, in the late nineteenth century there was a stronger although not universal tendency among Zionists to equate Orthodoxy with those negative attributes that supposedly had defined two millennia of Diaspora. Thus, it was possible to invoke the *Tanakh* in anti-clerical polemics. One thinks of a figure like Yehudah Leib Gordon (1830–1892), the greatest Hebrew poet of the Russian *Haskalah* ("Enlightenment"). Like most Hebrew poetry in every period, Gordon's was highly biblical in idiom. He chose biblical episodes for some of his most successful pieces. Yet he was also bitterly anti-clerical, and his long poem *Bĕqôṣô Šel Yûd* ("For a Mere Detail," literally, "For the Hook on the Letter *Yud*") remains the finest satire on Orthodox Judaism ever written. Gordon's involvement in biblical themes and language and his polemical attitude toward the Rabbinical establishment and the course of postbiblical Jewish history show some similarities to the tendencies of the Protestant Reformation. But it is inconceivable that Gordon would have written a biblical theology, if only because his biblicism was an expression not of theological commitment but of his recovered ethnicity, his militant sense of nationhood. This profound involvement in the *Tanakh* on the part of secular, even militantly secular people is a fixture of Israeli culture. One thinks of David ben Gurion, the first prime minister of the state, a confirmed secular socialist for whom bibical study was an avocation pursued with missionary passion, or of Moshe Dayan, the famous general and politician who was an amateur archaeologist, or of Yigael Yadin, also a famous general and politician, who was a foremost archaeologist as well as a scholar of the Second Temple period and its aftermath. I have had occasion to observe that young nonreligious Israelis often have a better command of the language and contents of the Hebrew Bible than senior Christian Old Testament scholars. But it is important to remember that the motivation is different. Most modern Jews are inclined to find their identity in Jewish history, not in Jewish theology. Even among observant Jews, as we shall see, the tendency is to focus on the sacred text, not on the theology that might be abstracted from it. To overgeneralize only a bit, those Christian Old Testament scholars may know biblical theology, but the Jews know the biblical text.

The replacement of Judaism by Jewish history is not unique to secular Zionism. Yosef Yerushalmi points out that whereas in the Middle Ages "the most profound intellectual synthesis" between Jewish and Gentile cultures "took place in the realm of philosophy," and not at all "in the sphere of historiography . . . in modern times we have, as it were, the reverse":

> There has been little genuine interpenetration between Jewish and general philosophy, but a deep and ubiquitous interaction with modern historicism. By this I mean simply that while there was a common realm of discourse and mutual influence among Jewish, Muslim, and Christian philosophy in the Middle Ages, this has not been true of Jewish and general philosophy in modern times. The primary intellectual encounter between Judaism and modern culture has lain precisely in a mutual preoccupation with the historicity of things.[60]

If we include the study of philology, its handmaiden, as a form of history, then we have in Yerushalmi's words a fine statement of the nature of the relationship between Jews and Christians in contemporary biblical scholarship. No common realm of discourse on theological topics exists. Indeed, as we noted earlier, it is doubtful that such commonality is even possible, for to the Christian, biblical theology is concerned with christological issues in a way that excludes the Jew and finds no parallel in Judaism. On the other hand, in the realm of philological and historical study, a comfortable commonality of discourse obtains, and Jews and Christians can work together without difficulty. In a sense, this is precisely the situation one would expect in light of the tendency of religion in the modern world to become a private, confessional matter confined to subcultures which, on religious issues, lack much ability to communicate. In the public realm, the realm of the macroculture, naturalistic, even scientific thinking ("technocratic rationalism") prevails, and public communication is possible for anyone who accepts this kind of thinking or pretends to. It is in this naturalistic realm that modern historiography and philology fall. And so, the anomaly is that what unites Jews and Christians in biblical studies is a common commitment to a nonsupernaturalistic approach to the text. Partnership is possible only on terms that cast the truth claims of both traditions into doubt. To the Jew, for whom the history of Israel confers some identity in the present, this historicization of biblical studies will usually seem less of a loss than to the committed Christian. For the Christian sees him- or herself grafted into the Israelite tree only by faith, and if he or she cannot elucidate the content of that faith, he or she cannot appropriate that history. For this reason, the Christian will be more committed to keeping alive the theological dimension, whereas the Jew is more inclined to rest content, at least publicly, with history and philology. In part, biblical theology results from the fact that Christians read the Hebrew Bible through a logic of displacement. It draws much of its energy from the anxieties of the younger sibling.

Apart from the exigencies of public discourse in a pluralistic world, there are compelling internal motivations for the replacement of Judaism by Jewish history. Yerushalmi makes the following observation:

> The modern effort to reconstruct the Jewish past begins at a time that witnesses a sharp break in the continuity of Jewish living and hence also an ever-growing decay of Jewish group memory. In this sense, if for no other, history becomes what it had never been before—the faith of fallen Jews. For the first time, history, not a sacred text, becomes the arbiter of Judaism.[61]

The Jews to whom this observation applied were driven to historical reconstruction not because of faith but because of the lack of it. They approached the past—even the biblical past—in hopes not of defining a theology but of finding a replacement for theology. The impulse to replace faith with history began to affect Christianity at about the same time. Wellhausen's historicism, in which biblical history replaces the (Christian) Bible and acquires its recently lost normativity, is an instance of the same process. But as we have seen, the nature of the Christian relationship to the Israelite materials serves as a check on the antitheological or antireligious impulse, a check that is not well paralleled among the Jews. This is one reason why historicism has survived longer in Jewry and why the antihistoricistic backlash of Protestant biblical theologians like Eichrodt and von Rad in the middle decades of the century found only small resonance in the Jewish community.

IV

The effort to construct a systematic, harmonious theological statement out of the unsystematic and polydox materials in the Hebrew Bible fits Christianity better than Judaism because systematic theology in general is more prominent and more at home in the church than in the yeshivah and the synagogue. The impulse to systematize among Christians tends to find its outlet in theology. Augustine, Aquinas, Calvin, Tillich, and Rahner, to name only a few, have no really close parallels in Jewry—figures such as Maimonides and Hermann Cohen notwithstanding. Among Jews, the impulse to systematize finds its outlet in law. The *Mishnah,* the *Mishneh Torah,* the *Shulchan Aruch,* and the *Aruch Ha-Shulchan* have no good counterparts in the church, despite traditions of canon law and moral theology. Christians often have the impression of Judaism that its belief system is too amorphous and ill-defined and that its legal system is excessively precise and overdetermined. Jews often have the impression of Christianity that its ethical and liturgical life is dangerously subjective, emotionalistic, and impressionistic and that its theology is too rigid and too abstract. Joseph Kitagawa, the eminent historian of religion, once put the contrast this way: if you ask an Asian to describe his religion, he will tell you about his practices; if you ask a Christian, he will tell you about his beliefs; Judaism, concluded Professor Kitagawa, is in this respect more like an Asian religion than like Christianity.[62]

Since the church early on concluded that the particular *practices* of the Hebrew Bible are not incumbent upon Christians, it again follows that the *beliefs* in that book will bear proportionally more weight among Christians than among Jews. Bright's discussion of the laws of the Sabbatical and Jubilee Years in Leviticus 25 is revealing:

> The chapter can scarcely be called one of the high points of the Old Testament. Indeed, the regulations described therein are obviously so little applicable to the modern situation that the preacher may be pardoned if he told himself that the passage contains no relevant message for his people whatever. . . . So let us say it: The Law, as law, is ancient, irrelevant, and without authority. But what of the theology of the law? . . . It seeks to tell us that the land is God's and that we live on this earth as aliens and sojourners, holding all that we have as it were on loan from him (vs. 23); that God narrowly superintends every business transaction and expects that we conduct our affairs in the fear of him (vss. 17, 36, 43), dealing graciously with the less fortunate brother in the recollection that we have all been recipients of grace (vv. 38, 42). And that is normative ethics! It speaks with an eternal relevance to the Christian. . . . The law we cannot obey; but we are enjoined in all our dealings ever to strive to make the *theology* of the law actual.[63]

In Bright's words one feels poignantly the precarious situation of the Old Testament theologian. A good Paulinist, Bright must steer clear of the heresy of judaizing. The implication that the laws must be obeyed, whenever possible, cannot be accepted. But across the straits from the Scylla of judaizing sits the Charybdis of Marcionism, with its bold proclamation that the Jewish Scriptures are irrelevant to the Christian. This, too, must be resisted. Only theology enables safe passage, for by converting law into theology, specific practice into general belief, Bright can grant Paul his doctrine of exemption from Torah without granting Marcion his idea that the Jewish God and Christ are antithetical. The specifics fade, the laws wither, but Old Testament theology endures forever.

The theology which Bright abstracts from Leviticus 25 is fully in accord with Rabbinic Judaism. The two religions part company, however, in that, traditionally, a Jewish thinker would not have presented the theology as a direct alternative to the specific legal institutions. Instead, he or she would have seen these two items as inextricable. Even when historical conditions had rendered a law unfulfillable, Rabbinic tradition regarded the law as still in effect and worthy of study in all its particularity. For example, in his *Mishneh Torah,* Maimonides codifies talmudic law about the Temple cultus which was destroyed in 70 C.E., early in the Rabbinic period and more than a millennium before Maimonides himself. The stubborn Rabbinic resistance to losing the particular in the general stands in stark contrast to the general drift of Christian exegesis. In a discussion concerning the adaptation of Judaism to a Gentile audience in Christian tradition, principally by Paul, Erich Auerbach presented the contrast this way:

> The total content of the sacred writings was placed in an exegetic context which often removed the thing told very far from its sensory base, in that the reader or listener was forced to turn his attention away from the sensory occurrence and toward its meaning. . . . [This is] the antagonism which permeates the early, and indeed the whole, Christian view of reality.[64]

Susan Handelman contrasts the Christian inclination toward spiritualization, allegorization, and other forms of abstraction with Rabbinic thought as follows:

> One of the most interesting aspects of Rabbinic thought is its development of a highly sophisticated system of interpretation based on uncovering and expanding the primary concrete meaning, and yet drawing a variety of logical inferences from the meaning without the abstracting, idealizing movement of Western thought.[65]

Although one hesitates to tar all of "Western thought" with one stroke of the brush, it must be granted that as regards Rabbinic and Christian interpretation of the Hebrew Bible, Handelman's generalization stands. As a result, the search for the one great idea that pervades and unifies the Hebrew Bible is unlikely to interest Jews. Instead, Jewish biblical theology is likely to be, as it always has been, a matter of piecemeal observations appended to the text and subordinate to its particularity. As Gershom Scholem put it, "not system but *commentary* is the legitimate form through which truth is approached."[66] I would only amend his remark so as to limit it to the haggadic dimension of Judaism. In the case of *halakhah,* Judaism does offer impressive architectonic structures in the form of lawcodes. But the haggadic and the halakhic dimensions of Judaism are complementary and not antithetical, and when *halakhah* is the basis for *'aggadah,* the former is not transmuted into the latter by theological alchemy. Rather, the particularities of the law remain alive and in force in and alongside the larger theological or ethical message.

The search for the one idea into which the Hebrew Bible is to be subsumed, for the "center (*Mitte*) of Old Testament theology," as the issue is known in the field, has produced a bewildering array of candidates, for example, covenant (Eichrodt), the holiness of God (Ernst Sellin), God as the Lord (Ludwig Köhler), Israel's election as the people of God (Hans Wildberger), the rulership of God (Horst Seebass), the kingdom of God (Gunther Klein), the rule of God together with his communion with humankind (Georg Fohrer),[67] God's acts in history (G. Ernest Wright),[68] communion alone (Th. C. Vriezen),[69] the Book of Deuteronomy (Siegfried Herrmann),[70] and the presence of God (Samuel Terrien).[71] It is interesting to note some rather obvious candidates which do not appear in this list and which have received little attention in the theologies. One is humankind's duties, a theme that occupies most of the biblical materials, legal, prophetic, and sapiential alike. "What does YHWH require of you?"[72] is a theme that cuts across a number of these aspiring centers and covers much of books like Proverbs, which covenant, holiness, rulership, acts of God, and presence, for instance, cannot. I do not say humankind's duties is the center of biblical theology. I am, for reasons that will become evident, skeptical of the entire pursuit of a center. My point, rather, is that with its devaluation of the deed ("works"), the Pauline theology of these Protestant Old Testament scholars has made it unlikely for them to propose a theme like this as the center of even Old Testament theology, lest it suggest the antithetical theology of Marcion. It is instructive to compare their approach with that of John L. McKenzie, a Roman Catholic scholar who set out to write "the theology of the Old Testament as if the New Testament did not exist."[73] McKenzie put the discussion of "cult" first in his book (whereas Eichrodt, for instance, put "covenant" first) and devoted only 25 pages out of 341 to "The Message of the Prophets" (whereas von Rad, for example, devoted well over a third of his second volume to the same theme). It is difficult to resist the suggestion that the faith of the theologian is the greatest factor in his or her positing a center for the Old Testament. In fact, it is not unusual for the authors to claim that the New Testament, *mirabile dictu,* has the same center. It is doubtful that the nature of the Christian religion, especially in its Protestant nuance, allows for any other conclusion unless one is to abandon altogether the normative role which, as we have seen, these scholars often claim for the discipline.

The assumption of the theologians who quest after the center or overarching unity of the Hebrew Bible is that all the books and pericopes therein announce the same message. This has a parallel in Rabbinic thought. "Forty-eight male and seven female prophets prophesied to Israel," reports an anonymous source in the Gemara, "and they neither took away from nor added to that which is written in the Torah, with the exception of the reading of the Scroll [of Esther on Purim]."[74] Here, the assumption is that the first of the three sections of the *Tanakh,* the Torah (Pentateuch), is prior and normative; the prophets only applied it. It is hard to see how a biblical theology that did not respect the doctrine of the priority and normativity of the Pentateuch could be Jewish (i.e., Rabbinic). The assumption of these theologians that one might learn the biblical message better from a book in another section of the canon and then utilize that book to correct or counterbalance the Torah (e.g., Jeremiah against Leviticus) derives from the modern Christian idea that the unit to be interpreted is the testament, an idea foreign to Judaism. In Section I, we saw that this notion that all the literature of the Hebrew Bible, which was composed over a millennium, has one message presents grave historical problems. Needless to say, the idea of the antiquity of the entire Pentateuch does too. Neither the Jewish nor the Christian assumption is in accord with historical criticism. The message of the Hebrew Bible is a function of the tradition in which it is contextualized. In their historical contexts, the numerous passages in it presented a multitude of differing and conflicting messages. The continuing lack of consensus as to the center of Old Testament theology offers ironic evidence for the diversity of theologies in that book.

I suspect that Judaism is somewhat better situated to deal with the polydoxy of biblical theology than is Christianity. Whereas in the church the sacred text tends to be seen as a word (the singular is telling) demanding majestically to be proclaimed, in Judaism it tends to be seen as a problem with many facets, each of which deserves attention. The way midrash collections introduce a new midrash is revealing—*dābār 'aḥēr,* "another interpretation." The Rabbinic Bible (*Miqrā'ôt Gĕdôlôt*), too, surrounds the text with a plurality of commentaries that often take issue with each other. Most of the Talmud is, after all, a debate, with majority and minority positions both preserved and often unmarked. This is very different from the theological literature of Christianity. A tradition whose sacred texts are internally argumentative will have a far higher tolerance for theological polydoxy (within limits) and far less motivation to flatten the polyphony of the sources into a monotony. What Christians may perceive as a gain, Jews may perceive as a loss.

V

If the deconstructionists have accomplished nothing else, they have at least taught us that meaning is a function of context. It is never self-evident what the context is in terms of which a unit of literature is to be interpreted. In the case of the Hebrew Bible, the candidates are legion. They include the work of the author who composed the unit, the redacted pericope in which it is now embedded, the biblical book in which it appears, the subsection of the Jewish canon which contains this book (Pentateuch, Prophets, or Writings), the entire Hebrew Bible treated as a synchronic reality, the Christian Bible (Old Testament and New Testament), and the exegetical traditions of the church or the rabbis. Each of these locations—and there are more—defines a context; it is unfair and shortsighted to accuse proponents of any one of them of "taking the passage out of context." Rather, the success of an interpretation is relative to the declared objectives of the interpreter. The great flaw of the biblical theologians is their lack of self-awareness on the issue of context and their habit, in the main, of acting as though the change of context made no hermeneutical difference. In point of fact, it makes all the difference in the world.

I want to illustrate the difference that context makes by analyzing an elegant little study of Gen. 15:6 by von Rad, "Faith Reckoned as Righteousness" (1951). Von Rad prefixed the text as follows:

> He believed YHWH; and he reckoned it to him as righteousness.
> [Von Rad's question about it is]
> . . . how precisely ought we to understand what we have referred to as the "theological" element here? Is it conceivable that the statement that faith is reckoned as righteousness arose wholly and solely from the reflections of a theologian? What is the derivation of the terms employed in this notable statement?[75]

In answer, von Rad traces the use of the verb *ḥāšab* ("to reckon") back to the pronouncement of a priest as he passes "a kind of cultic judgment" on a worshiper, "If any of the flesh of his sacrifice of well-being [*zebaḥ haššělāmîm*] is eaten on the third day, it shall not be acceptable; it shall not be reckoned [*lō' yēḥāšēb*] to him. It is an abomination" (Lev. 7:18). Similarly, if one slaughters an animal "and does not bring it to the entrance of the Tent of Meeting to present it as an offering to YHWH before YHWH's Tabernacle, bloodguilt shall be reckoned [*yēḥāšēb*] to him" (Lev. 17:4).[76] Since elsewhere we read of the priest's pronouncing an oral judgment which announces the will of God in the matter (e.g., Lev. 13:8), it seems likely that in the case of these offerings, the priest announced whether YHWH "reckoned" the sacrifice to the worshiper or not, that is, whether it has been accepted or not.[77] Von Rad found a similar declaratory formula in passages like Ezek. 18:9, which tells us of a man who has done all the right things that "he is righteous; he shall live—(*ṣaddîq hû' ḥāyōh yiḥyeh*)—oracle of the Lord God." Von Rad saw this as "a relic of the liturgical usage" and connected it with the judgment on the fitness of worshipers that one finds in the "temple-gate liturgies," such as Pss. 15:5; 24:5; and Isa. 33:16.[78] In light of this cultic background, we see the remarkable transformation that the author of Gen. 15:6 has brought about. There we find:

> The process of "reckoning" is now transferred to the sphere of a free and wholly personal relationship between God and Abraham. There is no cultic intermediary, no priest to speak as the mouthpiece of YHWH. . . . In a solemn statement concerning the divine purpose, it is laid down that it is *faith* which sets men on a right footing with God. . . . He says that only faith, which is the wholehearted acceptance of YHWH's promise, brings man into a right relationship—that YHWH "reckons" it to him.[79]

Consequently, von Rad concluded "that our author lived at a time and place in which ideas and terminology which were formerly tied to the cultus had come to be used more or less unconsciously in such spiritualised contexts. . . ."[80]

It is remarkable that von Rad nowhere in this essay refers to the New Testament, for Gen. 15:6 was a crucial text in the early church. Paul, combating the insistence of the Jerusalem church that Mosaic law obliged also

Gentile Christians, pointed to Abraham in support of the idea that faith provides an exemption from the commandments:

> [5]I ask then: When God gives you the Spirit and works miracles among you, why is this? Is it because you keep the law, or is it because you have faith in the gospel message? [6]Look at Abraham: he put his faith in God, and that faith was counted to him as righteousness. (Gal. 3:5–6, NEB)

Later, he made essentially the same point in his letter to the Roman church:

> [1]What, then, are we to say about Abraham, our ancestor in the natural line? [2]If Abraham was justified by anything he had done, then he has a ground for pride. [3]But he has no such ground before God; for what does Scripture say? "Abraham put his faith in God, and that faith was counted to him as righteousness." [4]Now if a man does a piece of work, his wages are not "counted" as a favour; they are paid as debt. [5]But if without any work to his credit he simply puts his faith in him who acquits the guilty, then his faith is indeed "counted as righteousness." (Rom. 4:1–5, NEB)

For Paul, Abraham served as proof that faith (*pistis*) could be detached from deeds and treated as totally self-sufficient. If so, then those who had faith in Christ had nothing to gain by accepting the obligations of the Torah. Von Rad's exegesis of Gen. 15:6 supports this line of thought beautifully. Faith spiritualizes the cult, nullifying both it and the priesthood in the process. It is now "only faith" which "brings man into a right relationship with God."[81]

It is instructive to compare Paul's handling of Gen. 15:6 with that of a Jew of the previous generation, Philo of Alexandria. Philo, too, makes much of Abraham's faith, specifically cites Gen. 15:6, and introduces in this connection many ideas unattested in Genesis.[82] But soon thereafter he notes, "This man carried out the divine law and all the divine commandments,"[83] evidently an allusion to Gen. 26:5, which grounds the promise to Isaac in the fact that "Abraham observed my charge, my commandments, my laws, and my instructions." Needless to say, this verse, with its implication that Abraham already knew the total body of revelation and scrupulously observed it, is not one cited by Paul. And so, we have two types of interpretations of Gen. 15:6, a Pauline type which takes the verse in isolation and insists on the autonomy of faith, and a Philonic type, in which faith and the observance of commandments are each predicated of Abraham on the basis of texts in Genesis. It is worthy of note that another New Testament document, the Epistle of James, takes, in essence, the Philonic position, citing Gen. 15:6 but warning as well that "a man is justified by deeds and not by faith in itself" (James 2:21–24, NEB).[84]

One of the great rallying cries of the Protestant Reformers was *sola fide*. Humanity is justified (or saved) by faith alone, and not through the church or the sacraments administered by its priests. It was this doctrine which turned Luther against the Epistle of James, which was one of four books he printed "separately at the back of his German translation of the New Testament."[85]

Paul, on the other hand, he admired, and it is Paul's reading of Gen. 15:6 that he explicitly endorsed in his own commentary.

> Accordingly, lest my discussions obscure what the best interpreter says, I shall speak rather briefly here. Read Paul, and read him attentively. Then you will see that from this passage he constructs the foremost article of our faith—the article that is intolerable to the world and to Satan—namely, that faith alone justifies . . .[86]

Luther goes on to attack "the rabbis of the Jews [who at the instigation of Satan] reveal their folly and the wrath which they harbor against Christ" by interpreting the verse to mean "that Abraham believed the Lord and thought that God was just."[87] Here, Luther surely overgeneralizes. Most of the Rabbinic commentators interpret the subject of *wayyaḥšĕbehā* ("and he reckoned it") as YHWH. But Nachmanides (1195–1270) had argued that it was in fact Abraham who reckoned God as righteous. "A man who had enough faith to slaughter his only beloved son and [to endure] all the other trials—why shouldn't he have faith in good news?" asked Nachmanides. Instead, he argued, the verse shows that Abraham's faith followed from his conviction that God is a God of righteousness. He cited as proof Isa. 45:23, "By myself have I sworn—oracle of the Lord—righteousness has gone out of my mouth, and the word will not turn back."[88] Luther's contempt for this interpretation originates in his Pauline theology, for, on purely grammatical considerations, either specification of the implied subject is defensible.

This sketch of the premodern exegesis of Gen. 15:6 shows that von Rad follows the Pauline-Lutheran way of interpretation. His assumption that "only faith . . . brings man into a right relationship" implies an exclusion which is not to be found in the Hebrew Bible and certainly not in the J document, the Pentateuchal source responsible for this verse as well as for Gen. 26:5, which notes the reservoir of merit established by Abraham's observance of law. The fact that the cult was not spiritualized away and that righteousness could be imputed not only for faith, but also for observance is ignored.[89] Von Rad also ignored completely the possibility that it is Abraham who is doing the reckoning and God who is being reckoned righteous. In part, this is owing to the mistaken assumption that he shared with most Christian Old Testament scholars that one can be well equipped for exegesis without knowledge of the medieval Jewish commentaries. In this, Luther, for all his anti-Judaism, was more advanced. Given von Rad's penchant for finding liturgical and cultic origins for things, he should have been attracted to Nachmanides' reasoning. After all, the affirmation of God's righteousness was a common liturgical act in ancient Israel.[90] What prevented von Rad from even considering the possibility seems to have been an eagerness to endorse the Pauline-Lutheran reading.

The context in which von Rad's interpretation situates Gen. 15:6 is one defined first by the verse itself, in isolation from the rest of the Abraham material in the Hebrew Bible and indeed from the Hebrew Bible itself. The understanding of righteousness as derivable from faith alone is a second aspect of context—one which derives from Pauline materials in the New Testament, especially as these materials have been understood in Lutheran tradition without regard for the Jacobean-Catholic trajectory in Christian tradition. Ultimately, the only context in which von Rad's essay can be considered successful is Reformation theology. He has ignored the historical context of ancient Israel and defied the various literary contexts defined by the J source, by the Book of Genesis, by the Pentateuch, by the Hebrew Bible in its entirety, by the Philonic-Rabbinic traditions, and by the Jacobean-Catholic dimension of Christian theology. Shall we deem his essay a failure? No. Within a limited context of human experience—and a different one (Reformation Christianity) from the one he intended (biblical criticism)—it is an impressive success. But it is precisely the failure of the biblical theologians to recognize the limitation of the context of their enterprise which makes some of them surprised that Jews are not interested in it.

NOTES

1. Y. Kaufmann, *The Religion of Israel* (Chicago: Univ. of Chicago Press, 1960); N. M. Sarna, *Understanding Genesis* (New York: Jewish Theological Seminary of America and McGraw-Hill, 1966).

2. W. Eichrodt, *Theology of the Old Testament,* 2 vols., OTL (Philadelphia: Westminster Press, 1961); G. von Rad, *Old Testament Theology,* 2 vols. (New York: Harper & Row, 1962).

3. R. C. Dentan, *Preface to Old Testament Theology,* rev. ed. (New York: Seabury Press, 1963), 81. In his bibliography, Dentan lists the works as follows:

Buber, Martin: *The Prophetic Faith.* New York: Macmillan Co., 1949.

Herberg, Will.: "Faith as Heilsgeschichte: The Meaning of Redemptive History in Human Existence," *The Christian Scholar* 39 (1956): 25–31.

Heschel, Abraham J.: *The Prophets* (Chaps. 9–17 on prophetic theology). New York: Harper & Row, 1962.

———: *Theology of Ancient Judiasm.* London and New York: Soncino Press, 5722/1962 (in Hebrew).

4. D. Neumark, *The Philosophy of the Bible* (Cincinnati: Ark Publishing, 1918).

5. On the discipline in general, see N. W. Porteous, "Old Testament Theology," in *The Old Testament and Modern Study,* ed. H. H. Rowley (Oxford: Clarendon Press, 1951), 311–45; Dentan, *Preface;* H.-J. Kraus, *Die Biblische Theologie: Ihre Geschichte und Problematik* (Neukirchen-Vluyn: Neukirchener, 1970); G. Hasel, *Old Testament Theology: Basic Issues in the Current Debate,* rev. ed. (Grand Rapids: Wm. B. Eerdmans, 1982); G. W. Coates, "Theology of the Hebrew Bible," in *The Hebrew Bible and Its Modern Interpreters,* ed. D. A. Knight and G. M. Tucker (Philadelphia: Fortress Press; Chico, Calif.: Scholars Press, 1985), 239–62.

6. Dentan, *Preface,* 87, 90 (his italics).

7. J. Bright, *The Authority of the Old Testament* (Nashville: Abingdon Press, 1967), 113–14.

8. Dentan, *Preface,* 22–23.
9. Ibid., 92.
10. Ibid., 64, 93.
11. Bright, *Authority,* 122. See also 126.
12. Ibid., 136. Cf. J. Bright, *A History of Israel,* 3d ed. (Philadelphia: Westminster Press, 1981), 148–62.
13. Bright, *Authority,* 136.
14. See G. E. Bryce, *A Legacy of Wisdom* (Lewisburg, Pa.: Bucknell Univ. Press, 1979).
15. Dentan, *Preface,* 108 (the quote is the title of a section).
16. Ibid., 116 (the quote is the title of a section).
17. Hasel, *Old Testament Theology,* 173.
18. M. H. Goshen-Gottstein, "Jewish Biblical Theology and the Study of Biblical Religion," *Tarbiẓ* 50 (1980/81), 45 (in Hebrew; my translation). See also 48–49 n. 24. Also noteworthy is his essay on "Christianity, Judaism, and Modern Bible Study," VTSup 28 (1975): 69–88, esp. 81–88.
19. Dentan, *Preface,* 23.
20. Goshen-Gottstein, "Jewish Biblical Theology," 54.
21. Ibid., 47.
22. Dentan, *Preface,* 15, 94, 98 (his italics).
23. Ibid., 90, 94 (his italics).
24. Cf. F. Baumgärtel, "The Hermeneutical Problem of the Old Testament," in *Essays in Old Testament Hermeneutics,* ed. C. Westermann (Richmond: John Knox, 1963), 135, and A. H. J. Gunneweg, *Understanding the Old Testament,* OTL (Philadelphia: Westminster Press, 1978), 222.
25. Porteous, "Old Testament Theology," 344.
26. See Neumark, *Philosophy,* xiv.
27. See Hasel, *Old Testament Theology,* 145–67.
28. See R. Ruether, *Faith and Fratricide* (New York: Seabury Press, 1974). In general, the New Testament writings depict the Jews and Judaism as hypocritical, pedantic, carnal, literalistic, misanthropic, godless, Christocidal, diabolical, or some combination of these. See, for example, 1 Thess. 2:14–16; 2 Cor. 3:4–16; Rom. 2:25–29; Matt. 6:1–18; 27:25; John 5:23; 8:44.
29. For a fuller discussion see C. Klein, *Anti-Judaism in Christian Theology* (London: SPCK, 1978), esp. 15–66; R. Rendtorff, "Die Hebräische Bibel als Grundlage christlisch-theologischer Aussagen über das Judentum," in *Jüdische Existenz und die Erneuerung der christlichen Theologie,* ed. M. Stohr, ACJD 11 (Munich: Chr. Kaiser, 1981), 33–47; idem, "The Jewish Bible and Its Anti-Jewish Interpretation," *Christian Jewish Relations* 16:1 (March 1983): 3–20; and J. Blenkinsopp, "Old Testament Theology and the Jewish-Christian Connection," *JSOT* 28 (1984): 3–15.
30. Eichrodt, *Theology,* 1:26.
31. Ibid., 133.
32. E.g., A. J. Heschel, *The Sabbath* (New York: Farrar, Straus & Giroux, 1951).
33. Eichrodt, *Theology,* 2:348 n. 1.
34. Ibid., 1:168 and 2:218.
35. Von Rad, *Old Testament Theology,* 2:321.
36. Blenkinsopp, "Old Testament Theology," 6.
37. See the work of Klein and the two works of Rendtorff referred to in n. 29.
38. Bright, *History,* 464.
39. For an exposé, see J. Pawlikowski, *Christ in the Light of the Christian-Jewish Dialogue* (Ramsey, N.J.: Paulist Press, 1982), 59–73.

40. J. Wellhausen, *Prolegomena to the History of Ancient Israel* (Gloucester, Mass.: Peter Smith, 1973), 410 (his italics). The *Prolegomena* was originally published as *History of Israel* in 1878.

41. Ibid., 405 n. 1.

42. Ibid., 108.

43. J. Blenkinsopp, *Prophecy and Canon: A Contribution to the Study of Jewish Origins,* University of Notre Dame Center for the Study of Judaism and Christianity in Antiquity 3 (Notre Dame, Ind.: Univ. of Notre Dame Press, 1977), 20.

44. Ibid.

45. S. Schechter, "Higher Criticism—Higher Anti-Semitism," in *Seminary Addresses and Other Papers* (Cincinnati: Ark Publishing, 1915), 36–37.

46. Ibid., 38. On the background, see N. W. Cohen, "The Challenges of Darwinism and Biblical Criticism to American Judaism," *Modern Judaism* 4 (1984): 121–57, esp. 133–34.

47. See J. A. Miles, "Radical Editing: *Redaktionsgeschichte* and the Aesthetic of Willed Confusion," in *Traditions in Transformation: Turning Points in Biblical Faith,* ed. B. Halpern and J. D. Levenson (Winona Lake, Ind.: Eisenbrauns, 1981), 19–20, a discussion of Chaim Potok's novel, *In the Beginning* (New York: Alfred A. Knopf, 1975), 444.

48. S. D. Sperling, "Judaism and Modern Biblical Research," in *Biblical Studies: Meeting Ground of Jews and Christians,* ed. L. Boadt et al. (Ramsey, N.J.: Paulist Press, 1980), 39.

49. S. Schechter, *Aspects of Rabbinic Theology: Major Concepts of the Talmud* (New York: Schocken Books, 1961). The book first appeared in 1909.

50. Y. Kaufmann, *Tôlĕdôt Hāʾĕmûnâ Hayyiśrāʾēlît,* 8 books in 4 vols. (Jerusalem: Bialik, 1937–1956; Tel Aviv: Dvir, 1976 [tenth impression]).

51. Kaufmann, *Religion,* and idem, *The Religion of Israel, Volume IV: From the Babylonian Captivity to the End of Prophecy* (New York: Union of American Hebrew Congregations, 1970).

52. See n. 1 (the Hebrew has no author index).

53. See A. Alt, *Essays on Old Testament History and Religion* (Garden City, N.Y.: Doubleday & Co., 1967).

54. Quoted in R. C. Johnson, *Authority in Protestant Theology* (Philadelphia: Westminster Press, 1959), 26–27. The goat-language is from a polemic of 1520/21 against Hieronymus Emser, whose "treatise had borne his coat of arms, elaborately adorned with the head of a long-horned goat."

55. Ibid., 48.

56. Dentan, *Preface,* 87.

57. The *lex talionis* appears in Exod. 21:23–25, Lev. 24:19–20, and Deut. 19:21. Its meaning and implementation in biblical times are matters of dispute.

58. W. B. Silverman, *Basic Reform Judaism* (New York: Philosophical Library, 1970), 44.

59. See n. 4. The fact that Neumark taught at the Hebrew Union College is significant.

60. Y. H. Yerushalmi, *Zakhor: Jewish History and Jewish Memory* (Seattle: Univ. of Washington Press, 1982), 85–86.

61. Ibid., 86.

62. In private conversation, October 21, 1983.

63. Bright, *Authority,* 152–53 (his italics).

64. E. Auerbach, *Mimesis: The Representation of Reality in Western Literature* (Princeton: Princeton Univ. Press, 1953), 48–49.

65. S. A. Handelman, *The Slayers of Moses: The Emergence of Rabbinic Interpretation in Modern Literary Theory* (Albany: State Univ. of New York Press, 1982), 19.

66. G. Scholem, "Revelation and Tradition as Religious Categories in Judaism," in *The Messianic Idea in Judaism and Other Essays on Jewish Spirituality* (New York: Schocken Books, 1971), 289 (his italics).

67. See Hasel, *Old Testament Theology,* 117–47, esp. 119–21.

68. G. E. Wright, *God Who Acts: Biblical Theology as Recital,* SBT 8 (London: SCM Press, 1952).

69. Hasel, *Old Testament Theology,* 120–21.

70. Ibid., 135–36.

71. Ibid., 82–83.

72. Deut. 10:12. Cf. Micah 6:8.

73. J. L. McKenzie, *A Theology of the Old Testament* (Garden City, N.Y.: Doubleday & Co., 1974), 334.

74. *b. Meg.* 14a.

75. G. von Rad, "Faith Reckoned as Righteousness," in *The Problem of the Hexateuch and Other Essays* (New York: McGraw-Hill, 1966), 125. (The devocalization of the tetragram is mine—JDL.) The same ideas appear in G. von Rad, *Genesis: A Commentary,* OTL (Philadelphia: Westminster Press, 1972), 184–85.

76. Ibid., 126.

77. Ibid., 127.

78. Ibid., 128–29.

79. Ibid., 129.

80. Ibid., 130.

81. Ibid., 129.

82. Philo Judaeus, *De Abrahamo* (Les Oeuvres de Philon D'Alexandrie; ed. J. Gorez; Paris: Editions du Cerf, 1966), 129 (§ 262).

83. Ibid., 132 (§ 275).

84. On the ideas of Abraham in first-century Judaism and Christianity, see S. Sandmel, *Philo's Place in Judaism: A Study of Conceptions of Abraham in Jewish Literature,* augmented ed. (New York: Ktav, 1971); H. D. Betz, *Galatians,* Hermeneia (Philadelphia: Fortress Press, 1979), 139–40.

85. D. H. Kelsey, "Protestant Attitudes Regarding Methods of Biblical Interpretations," in *Scripture in the Jewish and Christian Traditions: Authority, Interpretation, Relevance,* ed. F. Greenspahn (Nashville: Abingdon Press, 1982), 138.

86. *Luther's Works: Volume 3, Lectures on Genesis, Chapters 15–20,* ed. J. Pelikan (St. Louis: Concordia, 1961), 19.

87. Ibid., 21.

88. RaMBaN to Gen. 15:6.

89. E.g., Deut. 6:25 and Ps. 106:31.

90. E.g., Pss. 119:137 and 145:17. Note also how the lament begins in Jer. 12:1.

GENERAL INDEX

SCRIPTURE INDEX